POWER TOOL KNOW HOW

saves you money

POWER ROUTER

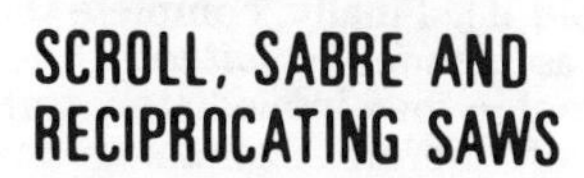

SCROLL, SABRE AND RECIPROCATING SAWS

ELECTRIC HAND DRILLS

CIRCULAR SAWS

POWER PLANER

PORTABLE ELECTRIC SANDERS

ROTARY GRINDERS AND CARVERS

PLUS

HOW TO ROUT 33 DIFFERENT JOINTS

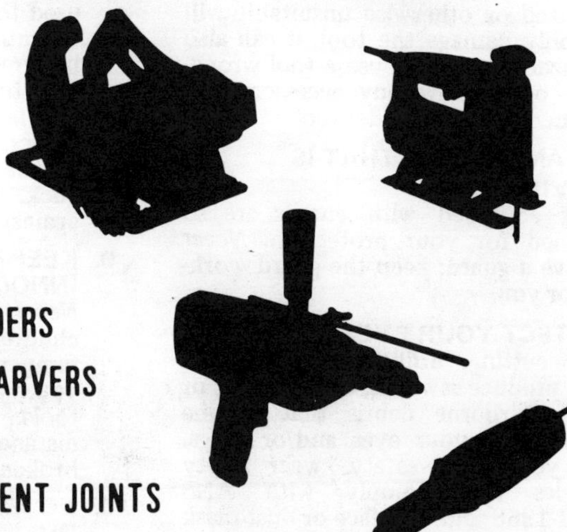

PREPARED FOR SEARS, ROEBUCK AND CO.

SEARS CRAFTSMAN

OVER 200 PROFESSIONAL OPERATIONS DESCRIBED AND ILLUSTRATED

CAT. NO. 9-2949 REVISED 1985 PRINTED IN U.S.A.

GENERAL SAFETY RULES FOR HAND POWER TOOLS

1. **KNOW YOUR TOOL**
   Read the Owner's Manual carefully. Learn your tool applications and limitations, also any specific potential hazards peculiar to this tool.

2. **GUARD AGAINST ELECTRICAL SHOCK**
   If your tool has a 3-prong, grounding type plug *always* plug it into *only* a properly grounded receptacle — and, if an extension cord is used, always use a 3-wire cord fitted with a 3-prong receptacle and a 3-prong plug so that grounding, as above, can be accomplished. If your tool is double insulated (a 2-prong plug), this type of grounding is not needed. *Never* use your tool when any part of your body is in water or in contact with a wet or damp object.

3. **USE YOUR TOOL *ONLY* IN APPROVED WAYS**
   Many tools can be forced to do jobs or to drive accessories for which they were not designed. Forcing a tool or using it to drive an accessory that is oversized or otherwise unsuitable will not only damage the tool, it can also be hazardous. *Never* use a tool wrongly — or to drive any accessory not designed for your model tool.

4. **USE ANY GUARD THAT IS PROVIDED**
   Tools equipped with guards are so designed for your protection. *Never* remove a guard; keep the guard working for you.

5. **PROTECT YOUR EYES AND LUNGS**
   Most cutting, drilling, grinding, etc. tools produce sawdust, chips, sparks or similar airborne debris that can be injurious to your eyes and/or lungs. For your own safety, wear safety goggles that comply with ANS 287.1-1968 and/or a face or dust mask whenever using such tools.

6. **WEAR SENSIBLE CLOTHING**
   Working with tools requires freedom of motion and freedom from possible entanglement. *Never* wear anything that could restrict your movements or become entangled in the tool or the workpiece (*no* tie, loose long sleeves, loose shirt-tail, long unbound hair, or the like). Rubber-soled footwear is recommended for surest footing.

7. **GUARD AGAINST ACCIDENTAL TOOL STARTING**
   Make certain tool switch is "off" *before* plugging the tool in for an operation. If you need to adjust the tool or to remove or install an accessory, *unplug* it first so there will be no danger of accidentally turning it on. *Never* attempt to make or correct a set-up involving a fixture or adjustment while the tool is running.

8. ***THINK* EACH OPERATION ALL THE WAY THROUGH**
   First, install the *correct* accessory for the job in the correct way — be sure it is tightly secured, properly adjusted, etc. — then remove any wrenches or keys used. Second, install and adjust, if necessary, any guard or guide, etc. required; and double check this set-up. Third, decide how and where to start, continue and finish the operation, planning your tool, hand and body positions as required. Fourth, make *certain* the workpiece cannot move out of position during the operation (check whatever method you have used to hold it). Finally, complete the operation as planned — *without* forcing your tool — then immediately turn the tool off before examining the results. *REMEMBER*: Some hand power tools develop considerable torque (twisting) power and/or kickback. Be prepared to hold the tool against these movements.

9. **KEEP YOUR TOOLS SAFE FROM INNOCENTS**
   Never leave your hand tools where children or unauthorized persons can tamper with or operate them. When you, yourself, are using your hand tools, keep all "visitors" at a safe distance should something (like a chip, broken bit, etc.) fly through the air.

10. **NEVER USE A DAMAGED OR DULL TOOL**
    Should a tool become damaged so as not to operate according to instructions, do *not* attempt to use it until it has been properly repaired. Keep your hand tools clean, properly lubricated (if necessary) and in good repair (especially, the switch and any accessory holding device, like a chuck). Do *not* attempt to use dull, rusted or damaged cutting or drilling accessories — these can be hazardous.

TABLE OF CONTENTS

INTRODUCTION

SECTION I – THE POWER ROUTER

CHAPTER V — TABLE-SHAPING, DECORATING, CARVING AND WOOD TURNING ACCESSORIES

SECTION II
SCROLL, SABRE & RECIPROCATING SAWS

SABRE AND SCROLL SAWS:

RECIPROCATING SAW:

SECTION III — ELECTRIC HAND DRILLS

SECTION IV – CIRCULAR SAWS

SECTION V – THE POWER PLANER

SECTION VI
PORTABLE ELECTRIC SANDERS

SECTION VII
THE ROTARY GRINDERS/CARVERS

SECTION VIII — WOOD JOINTS

TABLES

INTRODUCTION

IMPORTANCE OF OWNER'S MANUAL

The *Craftsman* hand power tool you have purchased is a quality tool with which you can easily and expertly accomplish the work for which it is intended, if you will use and maintain it in the ways that we recommend. Every job your tool is designed to do requires not only "muscle" but, also, some planning and follow-through thought. The tool provides the "muscle"; it is up to you to do the thinking.

Each different type and model number tool has its own specifications, and may require accessories and attachments and/or operating and maintenance procedures that are different from those for similar tools having different model numbers. Then, too, heavy-duty tools generally are designed for "bigger" and/or more continuous work jobs than can be done with lighter-duty models; and may even afford a wider range of applications (using accessories and attachments not intended for lighter-duty models).

We cannot cover all these differences here. *You must refer to your Owner's Manual*, furnished with your tool. It tells you the capacity and, if any, limitations of *your* model tool . . . which accessories and attachments you can use . . . the specific operating and maintenance requirements of *your* tool.

The instructions given in this book are general in content; they do *not* refer to any specific model tools. It is quite possible that your particular model tool is *not* adapted for some of the suggested operations. *You must be guided solely by the limitations and recommendations contained in your tool's Owner's Manual.*

BUYING THE RIGHT TOOL FOR A JOB

The "right" tool is:

1. The *kind* of tool which, with recommended accessories and attachments will accomplish the type of work to be done. For instance, it is obvious that a circular saw can't be used for drilling. Less obvious is the fact that an electric hand drill isn't designed for routing or carving. Still less apparent is the fact that a tool will generally do the work for which it is primarily designed better than a different kind of tool that is adapted for the work by use of an attachment (i.e.: a circular saw is faster, easier and better to use than an electric drill with a circular-saw attachment).

2. The *quality* of tool that is capable of doing the quality and quantity of work you expect of it. Generally speaking, the more expensive models are better built than the less expensive models. "Better built" may mean simply a more powerful motor and sturdier construction (such as ball or roller instead of sleeve bearings, precision machined instead of cast gears, etc.) with which to accomplish heavier-duty, more continuous type work. It may also mean better safety and operating features, more precise working adjustments, the availability of more and/or more professional-quality accessories and attachments, etc.

Less expensive models serve good purposes when used *only* for the limited operations intended; many users will never need the better models. On the other hand, it is a waste of money to burn out a "too-small" model, or to fail in a project because the tool hasn't sufficient stamina or the required features. *Before* you put your money on the line, try to anticipate the kinds of jobs you will do, and study the advertised tool features to determine what you will need. It is cheaper in the long run to buy the right tool to begin with.

PROPER USEAGE OF ANY POWER HAND TOOL

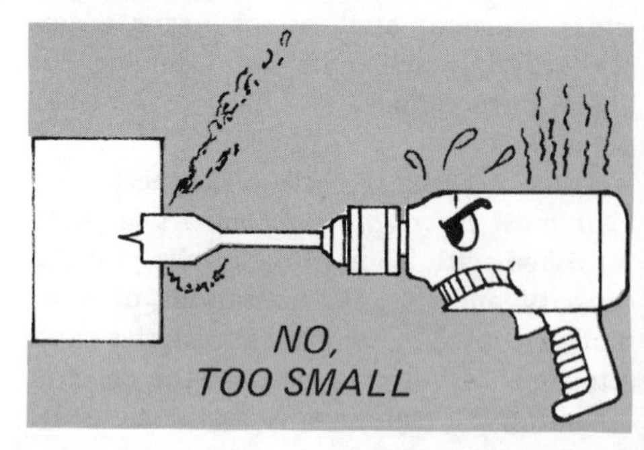

Use the Correct Accessories and Attachments

Power wood bits for an electric hand drill all have 1/4-in. shanks . . . therefore, even the 1-1/2-in. size bit can be fitted into the chuck of a 1/4-in. drill. However, a "bargain" priced 1/4-in. drill can*not* drive a 1-1/2-in. wood bit through hardwood in an acceptable manner . . . it simply does *not* have sufficient power. You might get the job done by drilling a little, waiting, drilling a little more, etc. (and burning the workpiece as you go); but only a drill with ample power (whether it has a 1/4-in. or larger capacity chuck) can do the job quickly and cleanly.

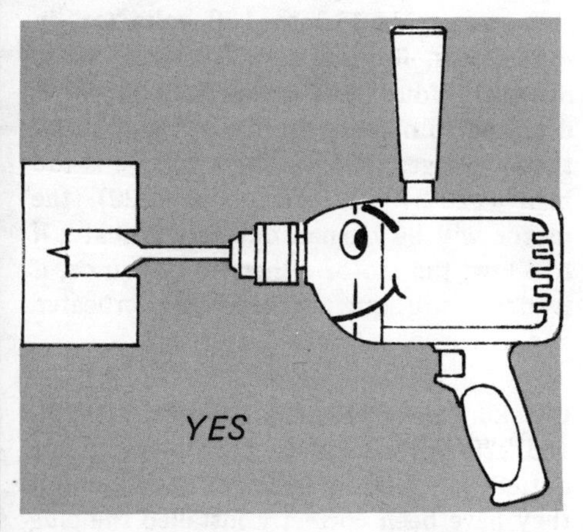

Similar limitations apply to some models of other kinds of hand power tools. Then, too, attachments are sometimes designed for use only with certain tool models, *not* with other models.

Your Owner's Manual will generally define the accessories and attachments suitable for your model tool. *Don't* damage your tool and/or your workpiece trying to use accessories or attachments for which it isn't designed.

Keep Your Tool Edges Sharp and Clean

There are three distinct disadvantages of a dull, rusted and/or gum and dirt ladened cutting edge (and, of course, a bent or broken one is of no value at all):

1. The cut being made will very likely be untrue (out-of-round, oversized, unstraight, out-of-position, etc., as the case may be), and the workpiece edges may be splintered, ragged or burned depending upon the type of workpiece.

2. The cutter (bit, blade, knife, etc.), being under excessive pressure to get the

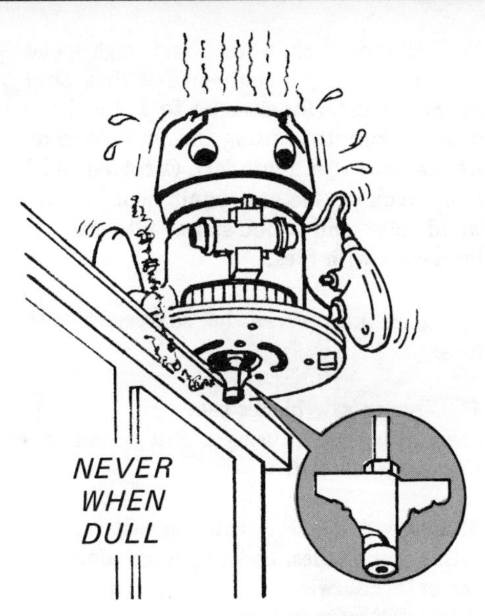

cut made, may overheat enough to lose its temper and become useless.

3. Because the additional force that you must use may overload and overheat your tool motor, the tool might be damaged.

In addition to the above, in some cases, forcing a tool can cause it to slip or to break in such a way as to be hazardous.

Most cutting edges can be resharpened time and time again; those that cannot should be replaced when dull. All cutting edges can be kept free of gum, dirt, etc. by cleaning with a gum and pitch solvent . . . or by wire brushing, if necessary. A light oil or rust inhibitor applied to cutting accessories each time you put them away will also help keep them in good condition.

As to resharpening:

1) Router bits can be resharpened on an attachment (the *Router Bit Sharpening Kit*) that can be purchased as a separate item. *Refer to Section I, "Sharpening Bits and Cutters".*

2) Ordinary carbon-steel and high-speed twist drills can be sharpened with a *Drill Bit Sharpener* (for sizes up to 1/4-inch) — or on a grindstone using the *Drill Grinding Attachment* (for a grinder). Carbide-tipped drills require factory equipment. Power wood bits and wood-screw bits can be sharpened with files.

3) Planer knives can be sharpened with files.

4) Circular saw blades can, also, be sharpened with files — using a *Saw Vise* and a *Circular Blade Setter.*

5) Sabre and scroll saw blades, reciprocating saw blades, and rotary grinders and carver accessories are cheaper to replace than to attempt to resharpen.

Refer to a current Sears Catalog for the sharpening accessories mentioned above — and to Sears Book, "Power Tool Know-How", No. 2918 for drill bits, planer knives and saw blades sharpening instructions.

Check Your Power-Supply Voltage

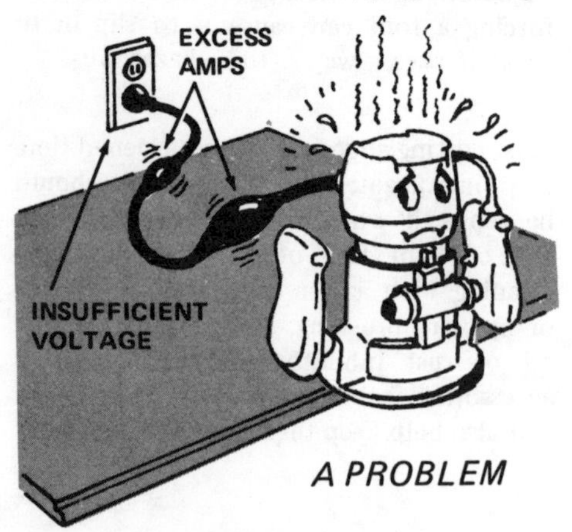

A PROBLEM

Just as you need a certain amount of food to keep going — and an extra amount when the going is toughest — so an electric motor needs a predetermined amount of electric power when running — and extra amounts when the load is increased. The electric power your motor receives is, by formula, amps (quantity of food) times volts (energy per unit of food) — and is primarily determined by the voltage of your source (i.e.; the outlet your tool is plugged into).

The "rated" voltage for most home use in this country is 110 to 120 volts (or, in some cases, it may be 220 to 240 volts, instead). Your hand power tool motor is designed to operate on one or the other of these voltages. If the outlet voltage is too high (220-240 instead of 110-120), the motor will be burned out very quickly; if too low, the motor either won't run or, if it does, will quickly become overheated and damaged.

Checking the difference between 110-120 and 220-240 voltages is no problem . . . the outlets are quite different in design, and if they have been correctly installed the plug on your tool cord won't fit the wrong one. However, faulty (undersized) wiring in the building and/or overloading of the utility supply lines or a circuit in the building can result in a voltage at the outlet that is *less* than rated (under 110 or under 220) volts. The only positive check for this is to use a voltmeter at the outlet (which you should do if you have one and know how to use it). A less positive indication of low voltage is a dimming of lights whenever the tool is turned on — or you can assume this is the case if your tool motor consistently seems sluggish or erratic in operation (in which case, have an electrician check the voltage).

A voltage that is more than 5% too low (less than approximately 104V or 209V, respectively) will require your tool to work with "food" that is low in energy so that more-than-normal amounts of "food" (amps) have to be consumed. Consuming extra "food" on occasion is no problem — this is what happens when your tool is temporarily overloaded; but any motor that must run continuously under such conditions quickly overheats and may be damaged (just as your internal organs might be damaged by a diet consisting of an over-abundance of low-energy food).

DON'T OVERTAX A MOTOR WITH LOW VOLTAGE

Guard Against Overloading

In the preceding we have tried to advise you regarding the damage that can be caused when your hand power tool motor is required to "eat" too many amperes. In the previous explanation, "low voltage" was the culprit; but, continuous overloading of your tool can also have the same result.

Whenever a tool is loaded (put to work instead of running free) it slows down a bit (just as you would if running uphill instead of on a level or downhill). If the load becomes very great (an excessively steep hill), the tool slows down by an excessive amount . . . and, in order to continue running at all, must consume considerably "more-than-normal" amounts of amperes.

As previously said, your tool is designed to accept such a condition on a *temporary* basis . . . it can, for instance, slow down and "bunch-its-muscles" to cut through a tough wood knot, or the like. But the heat rise in the motor during such a period is more than it is designed to accept on a lengthy basis. If the "temporary" overload is extended too long the total heat rise can become destructive to your tool motor.

Learn to listen to your tool. When running free it makes one type of noise; when working, the noise changes and the change becomes increasingly different as the work load is increased. Also, since you are holding the tool, learn to feel the amount

of heat it is generating . . . and, by all means, ease up on the load whenever the "distress" noise or excessive heat of a continuous overload endures for more than a temporary period.

Use Correct Fusing and a Correct-Size Extension Cord

The fuse in the line to your tool determines the maximum amount of amps (food) that can be "fed" to your tool, regardless of what the voltage at the outlet may be or what the overload condition may be. If more than a "safe" amount (of amps) is called for by tool running conditions (motor heavily overloaded, stalled or shorted), the fuse will "blow" to shut off the current and power at your tool.

Unless otherwise specifically stated in the Owner's Manual, the circuit to any hand-power tool should be protected with a 15-amp. (*no* larger) time-delay fuse. If it is at all practical to do so, provide a separate house circuit (from the building entrance switch) to your workshop for the exclusive use of your tools — and install a proper fuse (in the entrance switch) for this circuit. *Never* connect a tool to an unfused circuit.

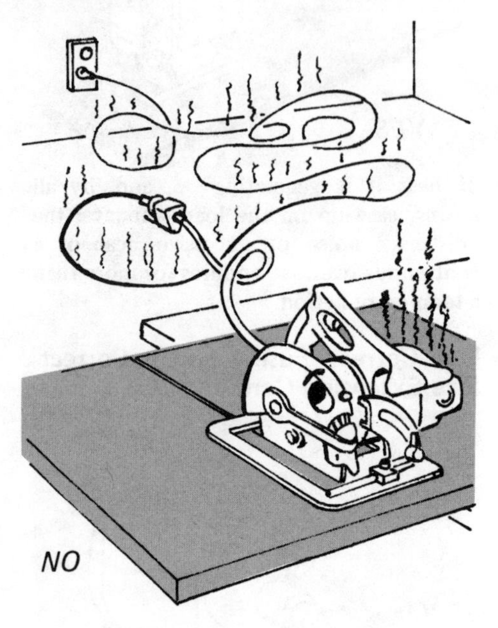

NO

WIRE TOO SMALL

The amount of voltage delivered to your tool is dependent, not only upon the voltage at the outlet used but, also, on the length and size of wire used in any extension between the outlet and the tool. Every wire (as in an extension) uses up a certain amount of the voltage (causes a voltage drop), which is determined by the wire size (#18, #16, etc.) and its length. Your Owner's Manual should tell you what size extension wire to use for different lengths of extension you may need . . . if not, be guided by the general requirements below (incidentally, No. 14 wire is larger than No. 18, etc.):

EXTENSION LENGTH	WIRE SIZE (AWG RATING)
Up to 10 Ft.	No. 18 or larger
Up to 20 Ft.	No. 16 or larger
Up to 50 Ft.	No. 14 or larger
Over 50 Ft.	No. 12 or larger

Care and Maintenance of Your Tools

TREAT ME RIGHT, I'LL DO MY BEST

Most power hand tools do not require lubrication . . . but your Owner's Manual will tell you about this and, if necessary, the when and how to lubricate. Every hand power tool should be kept as clean as possible — free from accumulated sawdust, dirt, etc. — and in good working condition (per instructions furnished in the Owner's Manual). Here are a few common-sense suggestions:

Keep your tools and accessories (especially, metal parts subject to rusting) in a *dry* place. If your workshop tends to be damp, install a de-humidifier — or, at least, wipe bare ferrous-metal parts with an oily rag prior to storage.

Do *not* allow sawdust to clog the air vents in a tool housing. Every electric motor needs free air circulation to keep it cool when running — and the air vents serve this purpose. Resinous sawdust and other chips, dirt, etc. can — if allowed to do so — fill these vents and cut off circulation. Preferably, blow them clean with air under pressure — or pick out the accumulation and wipe them clean.

Never use a tool with a worn-out or damaged cord or plug. If the grommet, where the cord enters the tool housing, has been pulled loose — if the cord insulation

TOO SMALL AN EXTENSION CHOKES OFF TOOL POWER

has been cut into or has aged so that it is cracking or peeling — or if the plug has been partially pulled loose, is cracked or broken, or the prongs are loose, replace the entire cord (with plug) or, at least, make appropriate repairs.

Never use a tool with a defective switch. Should the switch fail to turn the tool "ON" or "OFF" instantly (is sticking), or becomes loose or partly damaged, replace or repair it *before* using the tool.

Do *not* use a tool with a damaged housing. If the housing (in which the motor and gears are located) is broken or cracked, replace or repair it.

A tool that is losing its power — running too slowly at no load, bogging down too quickly under load, overheating, or has brushes that are arcing severely (sending out spark showers) — will be further damaged by continued use. Check for the trouble, which might simply be an accumulation of dirt or, more likely, worn-out brushes or a dirty commutator, or need of lubrication. Correct the trouble *before* using the tool.

Never "ask" a tool to drive a gummed, rusted, bent or broken accessory — such as: a router or drill bit with a chipped-off cutting edge or a bent or rusted shaft; a gummed, partly toothless, rusted or bent saw blade; etc.

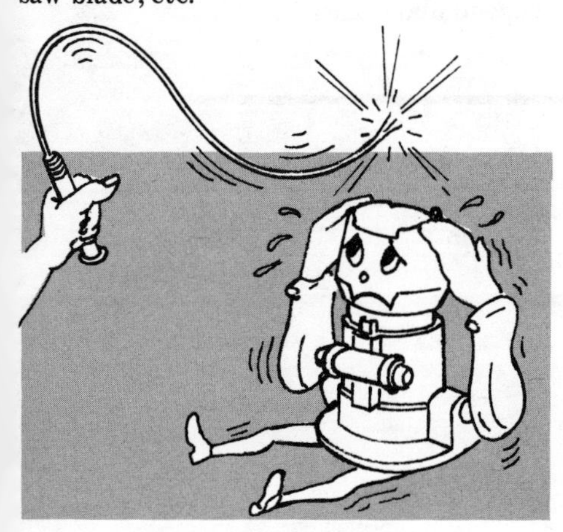

BEAT ME AND I'M LOST

Make certain that all screws, bolts, nuts, etc. used in the tool — especially those for installing an accessory — are securely tightened *each* time you start to use your tool . . . and be sure to remove any wrench or key used for tightening *before* turning the power on.

Study and understand the usages of your tool. *Don't* expect it to do things for which it has not been designed, such as doing too big or too continuous a job, or driving an accessory that is not recommended for it. Any tool — even the best — can be ruined by this kind of abuse.

IMPORTANCE OF DOUBLE INSULATION

I'LL SHOCK YOU IF I CAN!

In the past, the common method of grounding a power tool has been to provide a third (grounding) wire connected to the tool housing and to a third (round) prong in the tool plug. If the power-source receptacle is a modern type having a third hole for the round prong that is connected directly (in the building wiring) to ground, this grounding method will accomplish the purpose of preventing electrical shock to the tool user in case the tool becomes internally short-circuited.

However, most older buildings are wired *without* the modern-type (third hole) receptacles and without any special grounding provisions. In such case a

3-prong plug (with grounding wire) is of *no* use ... either (in order to use a 2-hole receptacle) the round grounding prong must be cut off, or an adapter must be used ... and the use of an adapter, unless special grounding provisions are made, does *not* accomplish anything.

Consequently, fitting a tool with a 3-wire, 3-prong-plug cord accomplishes absolutely nothing unless the tool user happens to have a modern (3-wire) wiring system in the building, or will go to the expense of providing extra grounding circuits (which is not easy to do in an old building). Under these circumstances, the user of any tool that is simply fitted with a 3-wire, 3-prong-plug cord is still subject to all the hazards of an ungrounded tool.

Therefore, instead of relying on such a dubious solution to the possibility of user shock, Sears has been foremost in developing shock-proof tools. *Double insulation* (now used for nearly all *Craftsman* hand power tools) provides safety against electrical shock *without* need of a grounding wire. These tools can be plugged into any new or *older*-type outlets — *no* adapters are needed. The secondary (*double*) insulation isolates the outer metal parts of the tool from the motor wiring (by insulating the armature shaft) — and, also, reenforces the primary insulation at all points of electrical stress.

Double insulation adds a bit to the cost of a tool — but it is your assurance that the tool is as electrically safe as modern science can make it, and is well worth the slight added cost. You don't have to worry about having a 3-wire building circuit or, instead, properly using an adapter (by connecting the adapter pigtail to a water pipe, or the like).

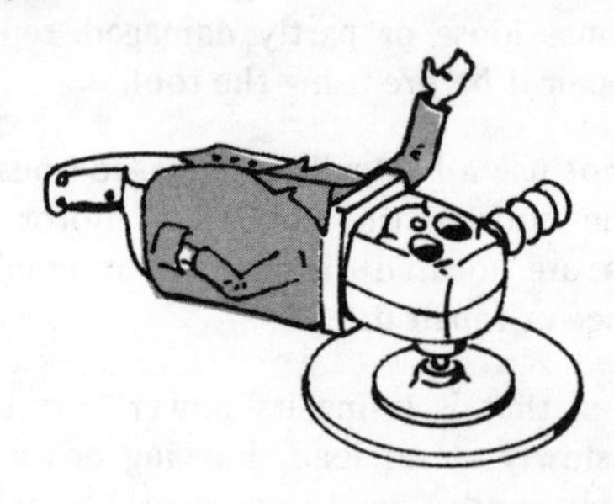

I'M COATED AGAINST SHOCK

VALUE OF A SEARS GUARANTEE

In this day of consumer protectionism every manufacturer and/or retailer is required to state absolute, clear-cut guarantee terms. Sears has *always* done so; it did *not* take a law-of-the-land to make a Sears guarantee valuable. Every Sears guarantee ever made has been honored exactly as intended — and Sears guarantees tell you *exactly* what you can expect. You *can* depend upon Sears.

SECTION I – THE POWER ROUTER

CHAPTER I
GETTING TO KNOW YOUR TOOL

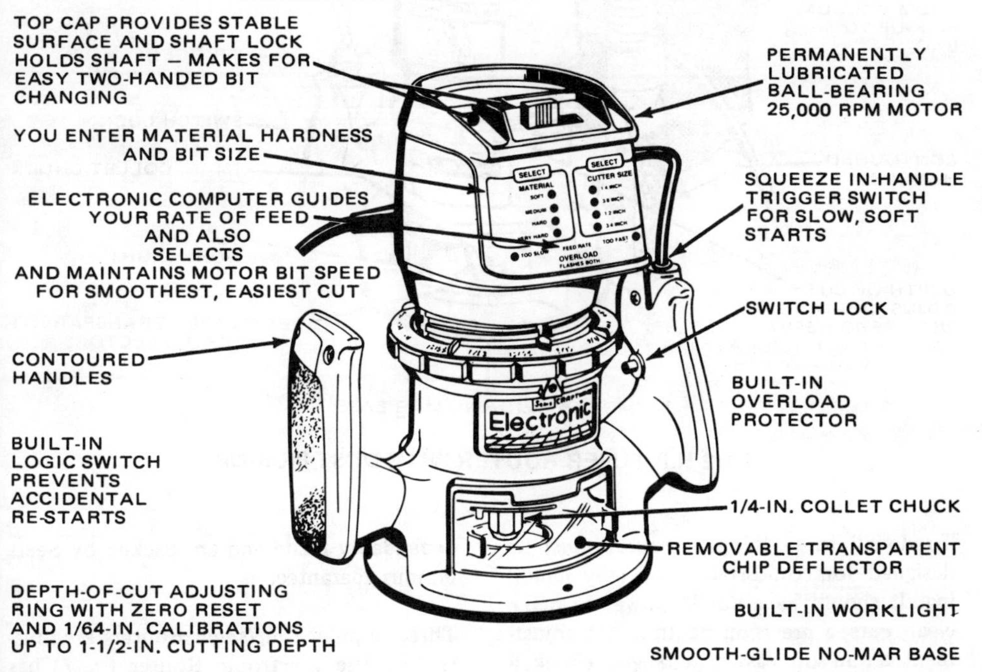

NEW ELECTRONIC ROUTER

TYPES AND FEATURES OF *CRAFTSMAN* ROUTERS

A power router serves the purpose of a wood chisel by providing an electrically powered means of chiseling out recessed areas to desired depth in a wooden-workpiece surface. It also serves as a carving tool with which designs can be either indented or raised on a workpiece surface. Indented grooves — straight or curved as desired — as small as 1/8-in. wide and from 1/64-in. to over 1-in. deep can be carved to form designs or to outline an area; or all the wood from a given area (to similar depths) can be removed, to leave a recess or create a raised panel of shape and size as desired.

In addition, a router can be used as a shaper for creating decorative edges — both external and internal edges — for making decoratively-shaped grooves (V, rounded, etc.), rosettes and carvings . . . and, with the proper attachments, for indent lettering, inlaying, design copying, dovetailing and other operations — and, *most important*, for carving tapered and/or highly decorative spindles of types which can*not* be duplicated with an ordinary wood lathe.

REFER TO A CURRENT SEARS CATALOG

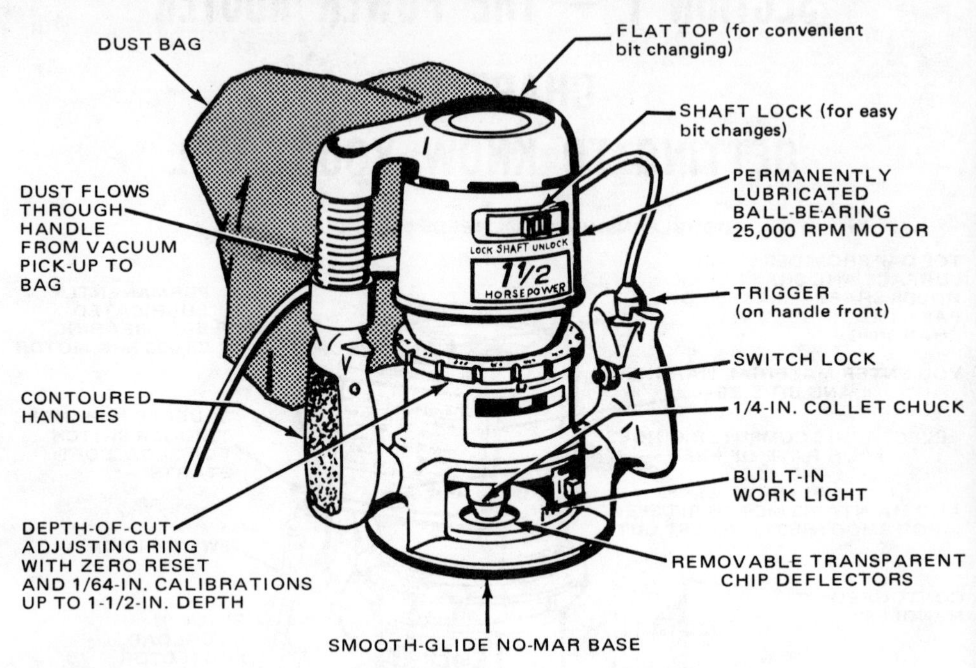

1-1/2 H.P. SUPER ROUTER WITH DUST PICK-UP

To do all these things a router *must* be designed for comfortable and easy handling. It should have ample power to make clean cuts; a precision depth-of-cut adjustment; a non-slip, easy bit-changing chuck; a smooth-gliding base, handles with which it can be firmly and positively guided, and a quick-to-use, convenient switch. In addition, there must be a *complete* assortment of bits (for all the different purposes), and all the different attachments needed for the various types of work.

Craftsman Power Routers are designed with *all* of these requirements in mind. They provide comfort and ease of handling together with the precision adjustments needed for professional-type work. The selection of *Craftsman* Router Bits (*pages 4-6*) and Accessories (*page* 7) will enable you to accomplish every type of work described in this book. Moreover, *Craftsman* Routers, Bits and Accessories are dependably made and are backed by Sears famous guarantee.

Three popular *Craftsman* Routers are illustrated. The Electronic Router (*p. 1*) has features that help even a beginner do excellent, professional-quality work . . . and the dust-collecting model (*above*) is especially desirable for in-home work. There also is a 1½ hp model without the dust pick-up, a

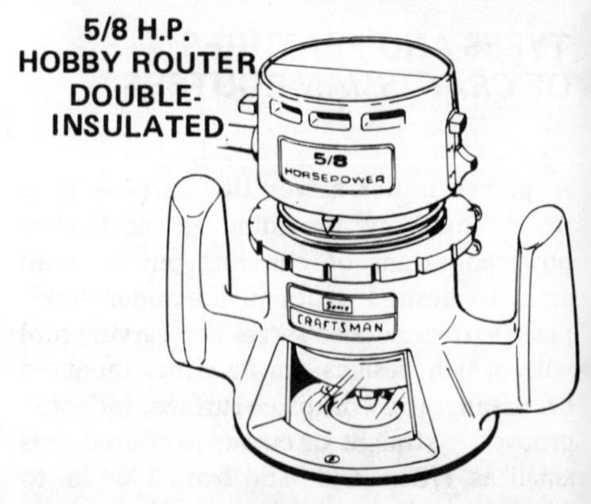

5/8 H.P. HOBBY ROUTER DOUBLE-INSULATED

1¼ hp model and a 1 hp medium-duty model. Select a router with sufficient capacity for the work you plan to do. Refer to a *current* Sears Catalog for buying information.

CRAFTSMAN-LIKE ROUTER OPERATION

Your power router is a relatively safe tool. Only a small portion of a bit is exposed after installation in the router, and this portion should always be down on, in or against a workpiece *before* the power is turned on. For your own safety, make a practice of disconnecting the router plug from its receptacle *whenever* you are changing bits, or are setting up an accessory or attachment of any kind. Wear an eye shield while operating your router.

To prevent spoiling a workpiece:

Securely tighten the chuck after installing a bit.

Do *not* attempt depth-of-cut, edge guide, or similar adjustments with the tool running.

Make certain that your workpiece can*not* move during an operation — clamp or otherwise securely hold it in position. Do *not* depend upon one hand to hold it.

Never use a dull, rusted, bent or gummed-up bit.

Keep a firm, *two*-handed hold on your tool throughout each operation — and *don't* let your attention stray for even one second.

Read the complete Safe Operating Instructions in the Owner's Manual packaged with your tool.

AN EYE SHIELD SHOULD BE WORN AT ALL TIMES ROUTER IS IN OPERATION

SOME ROUTER ACCESSORIES

MULTI-PURPOSE ROUTER GUIDE AND TRAMMEL POINT

It is *neither* practical to freehand guide a router on a straight course to cut a straight groove — *nor* to guide it freehand to parallel groove a curved or a contoured edge. However, with this basic attachment it is an easy job to cut straight grooves, grooves parallel to a workpiece edge (whether the edge is straight, curved or contoured) or to rabbet out any type of edge (straight, circular, elliptical or contoured within the minimum radius of the bit). Contour curves as tight as 1-in. radius can be accurately followed. *Refer to Chapter 2 for uses.*

When the trammel point is utilized this attachment guides the router around a *perfect* circle to cut a groove or shape an edge — or to make a cut-out, by routing through the workpiece, of any size from 2-1/4 to 24-in. There is *no* other way to do these jobs easily and professionally. *Refer to Chapter 2.*

ROUTER CASE

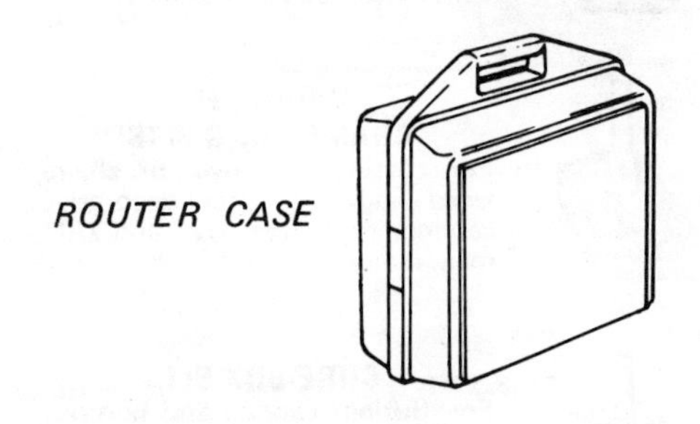

A sturdy Permanex polyethylene case that holds your router plus some bits and accessories.

SEARS HAS A CREDIT PLAN TO SUIT MOST NEEDS

ROUTER BITS AND THEIR USES

Following is a list of typical Sears Router Bit types and their uses — for latest buying information refer to a *current* Sears Catalog. All straight bits have either one or two flutes with cutting edges. Two flutes afford faster, smoother cutting. The one-piece bits have 1/4-in. diameter shanks; the stemless bits require use of their matching arbor with the appropriate guiding pilot.

KROMEDGE BITS

Precision-ground, high-speed steel bits fortified with chrome-impregnated steel surfaces that resist wear and gum build-up — stay sharp up to five times longer than ordinary bits.

STRAIGHT BITS
Flat on bottom for cutting square grooves, rabbets and dados and for leveling recessed areas, etc. Six sizes: 1/16", 1/8", 1/4", 3/8", 1/2" and 3/4" dia.

VEINING BITS
Round bottoms for decorative grooving, carving, lettering and making small coves, etc. Four sizes: 1/8", 3/16", 7/32" and 1/4" dia.

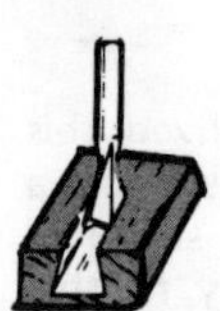

DOVETAIL BITS
Required for making dovetail drawer joints (with the *Dovetail Fixture, following pages*) and dovetail dados. Two sizes: 1/4" and 1/2" dia.

HINGE-MORTISING BIT
Special design 1/2" dia. bit for quick, clean cutting of hinge mortises (with the *Butt Hinge Templates, following pages*).

V-GROOVE CHAMFERING BITS
For cutting V-grooves or chamfered edges, and for decorative carving. Two sizes: 1/2" and 7/8" max. dia.

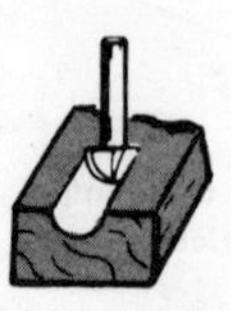

CORE-BOX BIT
For fluting, carving and contour turning on the *Router Crafter (following pages)*. Size: 1/2".

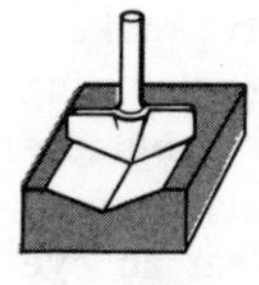

PANEL-RAISING BIT
A 7/8" dia. 150° bit for shaping raised- or indented-panel edges, or wide V-grooving.

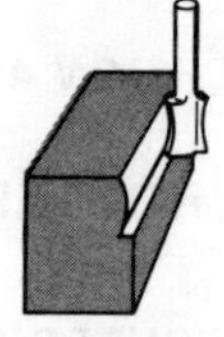

EDGE-ROUNDING BIT
A special-design edge-shaping bit. Can also be used for edges of panels previously raised or indented. Especially useful with The Edge Crafter *(page 10)*.

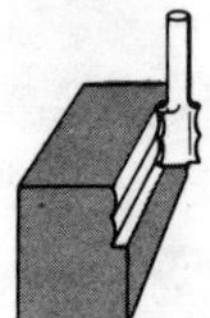

DOUBLE-BEAD EDGING BIT
Another special-design edging bit for same uses as the Edge-Rounding Bit. Especially useful with The Edge Crafter *(page 10)*.

SPECIAL CARVING BITS
Two different double-end bits. One (shown) has 45° and 60° vee ends; other (not illus.) has both 1/16" straight and 1/16" veining ends.

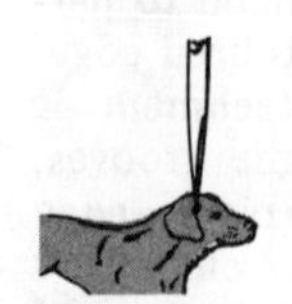

EXTRA-LONG CARVING BIT
Designed especially for detailed carving to depth.

COMB. PANEL CUTTER
A straight bit that is pointed for drilling. For making latticework or cut-outs, or edge trimming veneers. Size: 1/4" dia.

USE CRAFTSMAN BITS FOR PROFESSIONAL-TYPE WORK

COVE BITS
For edge decoration and making the concave side of a dropleaf table joint. Two sizes: 1/2" and 3/8" radius.

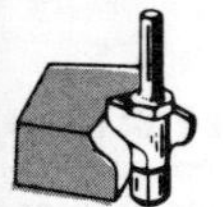

OGEE BIT
For making special-shaped Ogee edge decorations. Size: 3/16" radius.

ROMAN OGEE BITS
For making special-shaped Ogee edge decorations. Two sizes: 5/32" and 1/4" radius.

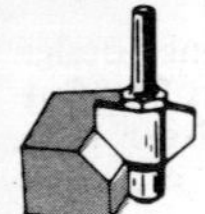

CHAMFERING BIT
For chamfering thick edges or bevel-edge panel raising when rabbeting bit is used for second cut. Size: 1/2" x 45° max. cut.

RABBET/SURFACE
Used with a pilot for rabbeting, without for surfacing or use with *Router Crafter.* Size: 15/16" dia. Cuts 1/4" 5/16" or 3/8" rabbet.

POINT-CUTTING QUARTER-RD. BIT
For decorative grooving, carving, beading and roping — with the *Router Crafter (following pages).* Size: 3/16" radius.

END-CUTTING OGEE BITS
Two bits for decorative carving, especially with the *Router Crafter (following pages).* Pointed bit is 9/32" dia.; other is 3/4" dia.

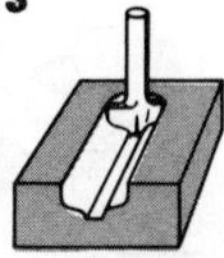

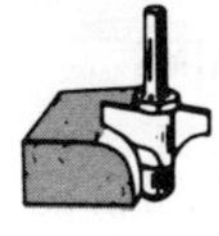

BEAD/QUARTER-RD.
For top-edge rounding or making convex side of dropleaf joint. Sizes: 1/4", 3/8" and 1/2" radius.

KEY-SLOT CUTTER
A 3/16" straight bit with a 3/8" cutting end to produce a keyhole shaped cut.

CARBIDE-TIPPED AND PROFESSIONAL BITS

Carbide-tipped bits have carbide cutting tips silver-alloy brazed onto steel bodies — last up to 15 times longer than the Krom-edge bits. The professional bits have thicker carbide tips designed for smoothest cuts on integral shanks of alloy steel with 1/2-in. ball-bearing pilots — for production quality work. Refer to a *current* Sears Catalog for professional type bits (*not* illustrated) that are available.

STRAIGHT BITS
Bottom and side-cutting bits for grooving, mortising, carving and indenting. Single-flute sizes 1/4" and 5/16" dia.; 2-flute sizes 3/8", 1/2" and 3/4" dia.

V-GROOVE CHAMFERING BIT
Designed for routing vee-bottom, 90-degree angle grooves up to 1/2-in. top width, depending upon depth-of-cut. Size 1/2-in.

COMBINATION FORMICA TRIMMER
For Formica (or similar laminate) trimming, either straight and flush with workpiece edge or flush at a 22° bevel angle. For use with the *Multi-Purpose Router Guide, following pages.*

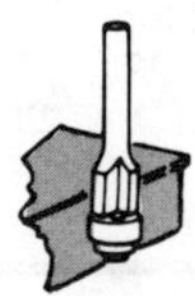

PILOTED STRAIGHT AND 22° FORMICA TRIMMERS
These ball-bearing piloted bits do *not* require a guiding accessory. One makes a straight cut-off flush with workpiece edge; the other, a 22° beveled cut-off.

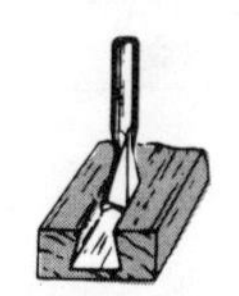

DOVETAIL BIT
This 1/2-in. bit is used with the *Dovetail Fixture (see page 9)* for making interlocking dovetail joints such as required for fine cabinetwork drawers.

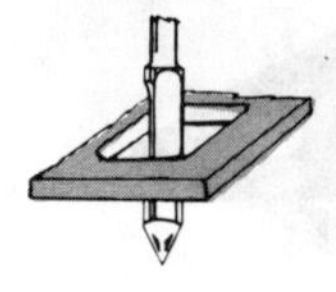

COMBINATION PANEL CUTTER
This 3/8-in. diameter bit is designed especially for drilling through a workpiece, then cutting a straight-sided slot.

REFER TO A CURRENT SEARS CATALOG FOR BUYING INFORMATION.

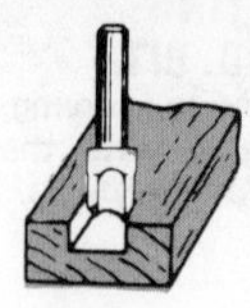

BUTT-HINGE MORTISING BIT

This is a fast-cutting, 1/2-in. diameter bit designed especially for mortising and operations like panel-raising or indenting that require much stock removal. Makes a clean, flat-bottom cut.

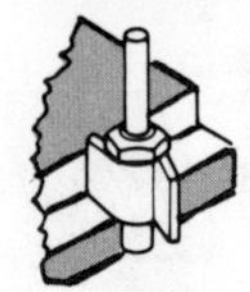

RABBETING/SURFACING BIT

Will cut a 3/8" rabbet using a 1/2" pilot, or a 5/16" rabbet using a 5/8" pilot. Refer to "Arbors etc.", below.

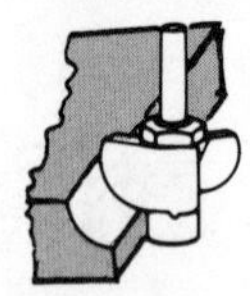

COVE/CHAMFERING BITS

For cove-cut edge shaping; must be used with an arbor and pilot. Sizes: 3/8" and 1/2" radius.

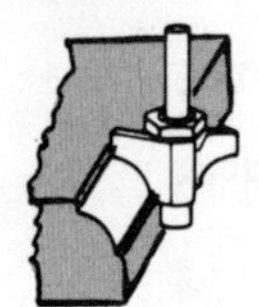

BEAD/QUARTER-RD. BITS

These are side-cutting bits for use with an arbor and pilot — for decorative edging. Sizes: 1/4", 3/8" and 1/2" radius.

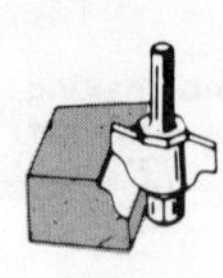

ROMAN OGEE BITS

For making shaped, decorative edges — must be used with arbor and pilot. Sizes: 5/32" and 1/4" radius.

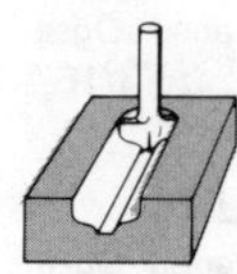

END-CUTTING OGEE BITS

Decorative grooving and carving bits can be used with the *Router Crafter (following pages).* Sizes: 1/2" and 3/4" dia.

CLASSIC BIT

A rounded-bottom fancy-design Ogee bit for use same as End-Cutting Ogee bits. Four sizes: 1/2", 3/4", 1-1/4" and 1-1/2" dia.

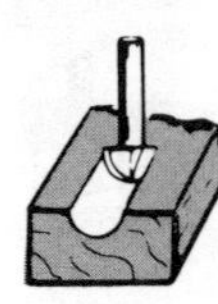

CORE-BOX BIT

For fluting, carving and for contour shaping with the *Router Crafter (following pages).* Three sizes: 3/8", 1/2" and 3/4" dia.

SLOTTING CUTTER SET

Includes two slotting cutters — for 1/16" and 5/64" kerfs . . . also, two spacer bushings.

ARBORS FOR STEMLESS BITS

The arbor at left, for Kromedge bits, includes a 5/16-in. and a 7/16-in. pilot. The one at right, for Carbide-Tipped bits, has 1/2-in. and 5/8-in. ball-bearing pilots.

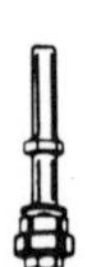

ROUTER-BIT CASE

Sturdy, polypropylene case has storage space for up to 44 of your router bits — provides a safe, convenient storage.

ROUTER BIT SHARPENING KIT

This accessory, which includes the grinding wheel, mounts on your router base and has micro adjustments that make it easy to *accurately* sharpen any Kromedge steel or carbide-tipped router bit mounted in the accessory. *Refer to Chapter 4.*

OTHER ROUTER ACCESSORIES

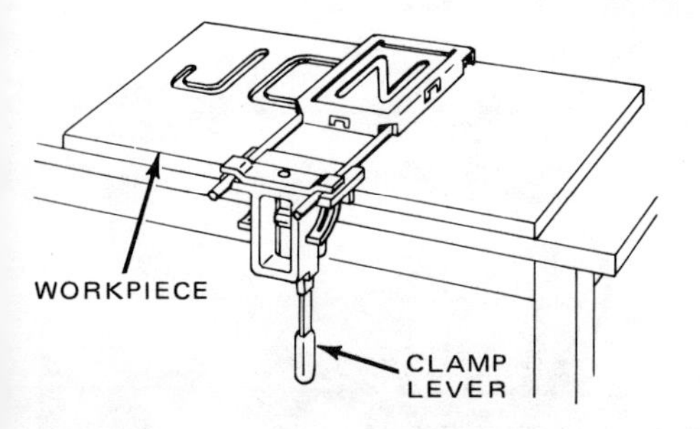

LETTERING TEMPLATE

This accessory provides a holding device and 72 guides (including 26 upper-case letters and 10 numerals in both 1-1/2-in. and 2-1/2-in. heights) and two (7/16-in. and 5/8-in.) guide bushings. Simple, easy-to-cut and read block characters are excellent for signs, etc. *Refer to Chapter 4 for instructions.*

ROUT-A-SIGNER

A more versatile lettering device for precise carving, by pantograph method, of block letters and numerals in sizes from 3/4-in. to 4-1/2-in. high, slanted 22° to 35° to right with varied spacing. Storage provided for 7-piece bit set and 58 character templates — comes with instruction booklet. Solidly built. *Refer to Chapter 4 for instructions.*

DOOR HANGING TEMPLATES

Mortising a door and jamb for the hinges is a slow and painstaking job with hand tools — but can be done quickly and accurately with your router, either the Hinge Mortising or a Straight bit (*page 4-5*), Template Guide Bushings (*following*), and a template. The *Butt-Hinge Template* (*refer to a current Sears Catalog*) comes in a set of two — for 3-1/2- and 4-in. long hinges, respectively — and must be repositioned for each mortise. The *3-Section Template* (illustrated) can be set up for identical positioning of two or three hinge mortises on both the door and the jamb for doors 3/4- to 2-1/2-in. thick, up to 7-ft. tall. *Refer to Chapter 4 for uses of both template types.*

REFER TO YOUR OWNER'S MANUALS FOR DETAILED INSTRUCTIONS

OTHER ROUTER ACCESSORIES

THREE-DIMENSIONAL DELUXE ROUTER PANTOGRAPH

With this accessory you can produce two- or three-dimensional signs, nameplates, plaques and other decorative pieces using lettering templates and can reproduce in wood three-dimensional patterns of plaster, wood, etc. Easy-to-use stylus for tracing. Comes with five lettering styles (Old English, Oriental, Script, Modern and Computer — in upper and lower case plus numerals) — and complete instructions.

There is also a two-dimensional Pantograph for tracing lettering and line drawings.

Refer to Chapter 4 for instructions.

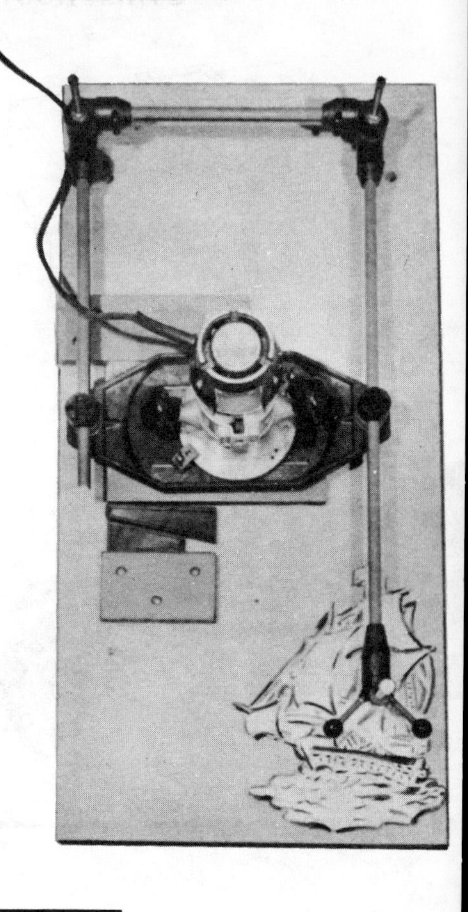

ROUTER-RECREATOR

A professional quality accessory for recreating statues, etc. up to 8-in. dia. by 8-in. tall, or lettered signs 10 x 24-in., decorative edging and plaques, designs on gunstocks or spindles to 24-in. long, etc. Operates on pantograph principle; very sturdy construction for accurate workmanship. Comes with two stylus rods and three tips (1/16", 1/8" and 1/4"), and instructions. An (extra charge) five-piece Recreator Bit Set is available; also, precut wood stock for signs, etc. *Refer to Chapter 5.*

TEMPLATE GUIDE BUSHINGS

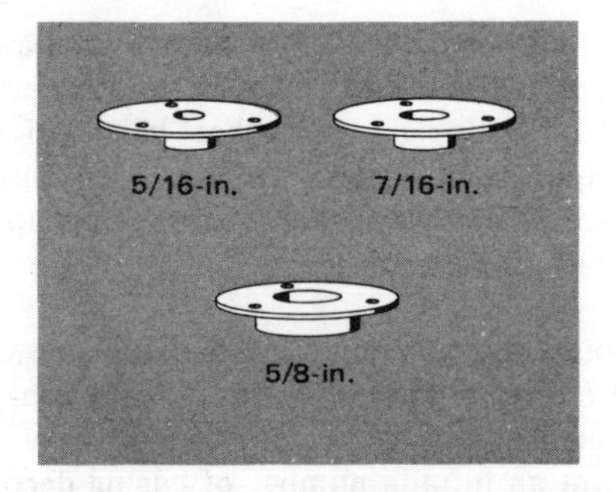

When installed in the router base one of these bushings serves like a pilot to provide a firm "footing" along which you can slide the router — against a template edge or workpiece shoulder — to guide your cut. The bushing — depending upon which of the three sizes you use — will always keep the bit a fixed distance from any template edge against which you are holding the bushing. For this reason, bushings are used whenever doing pattern or template routing — to copy a design or do inlay or similar work. *Refer to Chapter 3.*

DOVETAIL-JOINT FIXTURE

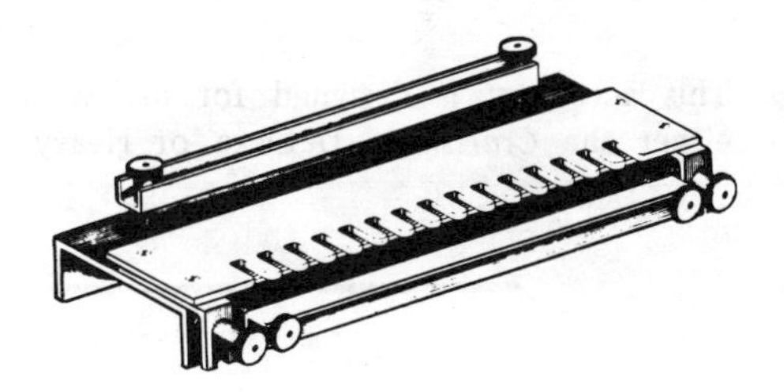

In all good cabinetwork the drawer sides are secured to their fronts with interlocking dovetail joints that hold the pieces securely together. With a dovetail router bit and dovetail-joint fixture you can easily make flush or rabbeted dovetail joints. Joint sizes depend upon the size of fixture comb and the size of dovetail bit (1/4 or 1/2-in.) used. Fixture size also determines maximum workpiece size. Refer to a *current* Sears Catalog for buying information — and to *Chapter 4.*

ROUTER "SHAPING" TABLE

Two different tables (*refer to a current Sears Catalog*) are available for converting your router into a stationary-type shaping tool.

A (hand) router is always fed *to the workpiece;* but when mounted under a table, workpieces are fed *to the router.* This makes it possible to accomplish many work projects which would be difficult to do with the router alone. Workpieces can be accurately guided to the bit along the adjustable fence, or by the sliding miter gauge. *Refer to Chapter 5.*

Also an inexpensive table without above features.

REFER TO A CURRENT SEARS CATALOG FOR BUYING INFORMATION

OTHER ROUTER ACCESSORIES

EDGE CRAFTER

This accessory is designed for use with either the *Craftsman* DeLuxe or Heavy-Duty Router Table. With it you can easily carve piecrust table tops or create round, oval, scalloped and other imaginatively shaped table tops, picture and mirror frames, and other similar workpieces up to 30-in. in diameter.

Four templates are furnished and you can also create your own. Templates can be used individually or in combinations to form an infinite number of edging decorations—especially if a variety of router bits is used. The Edge Crafter attaches to the router table and its roller-follower assembly traces the template on a line to guide the workpiece to the router. The router, bits and table are sold separately. Full instructions are included. *Refer to Chapter 5.*

DOOR AND PANEL DECORATING KIT

For use in routing a variety of surface designs on workpieces up to 36-in. by 36-in. in size, this accessory will prove invaluable for decorating doors, panels, drawer fronts and similar project pieces. Seven sets (four per set) of different design corner templates and one blank set (for a design of your own creation) are furnished—together with a radius arm, the guide rails and necessary clamps.

The corner templates are used when routing "squared" designs; the radius arm is for routing arcs and circles from 5-in. to 17-1/2-in. in radius (10-in. to 35-in. in diameter). A 1/2 hp or larger router and a 5/8-in. bushing—in addition to appropriate router bits—are required (sold separately). Instructions are furnished. *Refer to Chapter 5.*

DECOROUT-OR PLANER

With this versatile accessory you can easily raise or recess a great variety of decorative panels on a workpiece surface—or can level plane (ready for final sanding) any workpiece up to a maximum of 21-in. by 42-in. in size. You can also rout surface designs as with the Door and Panel Decorating Kit, preceding. Two or more separate workpieces, assembled up to the maximum size above, can be simultaneously planed for perfect thickness matching.

Four different-size templates in two different styles (Provincial and Reverse-Provincial), together with instructions are furnished. Additional templates (to create arcs and other designs) can be homemade. There is no limit to the variety of door, drawer-front, panel, etc. designs you can create. *Refer to Chapter 5.*

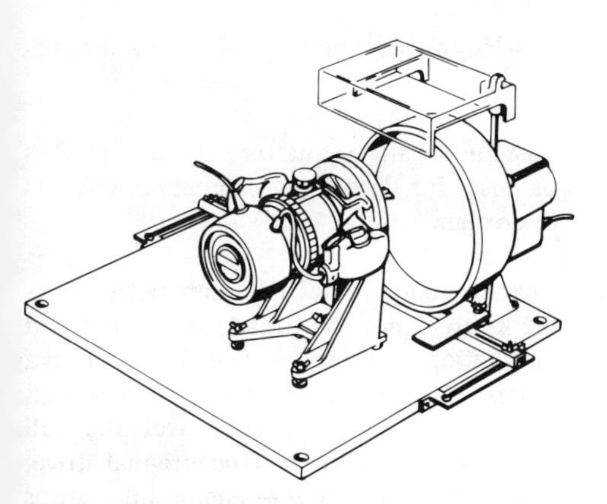

BOWL CUTTER

Sturdy, practical accessory makes it easy to rout a variety of bowl and glassware shapes simply by tracing paper template patterns (some furnished; some you can prepare). Accessory motor holds workpiece and rotates it at slow (4 rpm) speed while router bit is guided and fed to it for the cut by a sturdy aluminum carriage mounted on a 22 x 23-in. particleboard base. Complete instructions and a variety of templates furnished.

PIN ROUTER

Excellent for any project requiring repetitive straight or irregular cuts at least 3/16-in. deep. Has cast-aluminum carriage in which router is mounted for positioning above workpiece over a 20 x 27-in. table in which there is an adjustable guide pin. A template mounted to workpiece underside guides router over the pin for exact duplication of cuts. Complete instructions furnished.

ROUTER-BIT RECOMMENDATIONS

Special router-bit sets or individual bits are sold and recommended for use with many of the attachments and accessories described on these pages. Each provides the bits that you will find most useful with the attachment or accessory for which the bit (or bits) is recommended. *Refer to a current Sears Catalog for buying information.*

REFER TO OWNER'S MANUALS FOR SPECIFIC INSTRUCTIONS

OTHER ROUTER ACCESSORIES

THE ROUTER CRAFTER

This exclusive *Craftsman* accessory can be used with most routers designed for 1/4-in. diameter shank bits. With it you can shape an infinite variety of intricately carved wood spindles—for chair and table legs, lamps, pedestals, newel posts, etc.—from 1-in. to 3-in. square and up to 36-in. in length. Typical operations that can be performed with this accessory and the recommended router bits are:

- Fluting and reeding by making 2, 3, 4, 6, 8, 12 or 24 equally-spaced parallel cuts.
- Contour shaping—by following a pattern that you create, or by freehand guidance.
- Coving and beading to create designs around a workpiece, spaced apart as desired.
- Tapering of round or flat—(3, 4, 6, 8, 12 or 24) sided spindles—or of taper fluted or reeded ones.
- Right-hand or left-hand spaced roping.
- Right-hand, left-hand or crossed spiral grooving.
- Hollow-carving to produce see-through areas.
- Full-, half- or quarter-rounded spindles or posts for decorating cabinetwork fronts or corners.

The accessory comes complete with screws for router (not furnished) mounting and instructions for use. In addition, you can separately purchase a Drive Adapter that allows you to make cuts over the full length of a workpiece (the original drive, with which this is interchangeable, stops cuts short of the drive end of the spindle) and an eleven-piece Kromedge Router-Bit Set for making all the types of cuts desirable.

Your router does the carving while the accessory, which is hand rotated, guides it precisely in accordance with the set-up that you have pre-arranged. As many duplicates as desired can be made with one set-up. *No* woodworking experience is required because there are no wood chisels to hold and guide against a revolving workpiece (as when using a lathe). Opportunities for creating original and distinctive-looking workpieces are practically unlimited. The finished work requires very little sanding to produce professional results.

GENERAL ROUTING INSTRUCTIONS

THE SUB-BASE

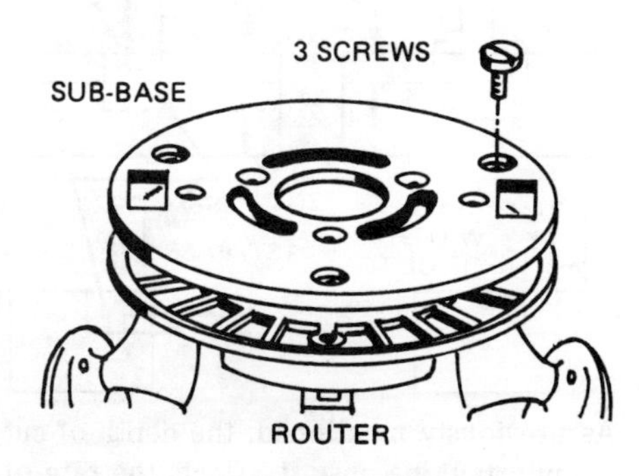

The polymer sub-base, attached to your router with three panhead screws, provides a glass-smooth surface that will *not* scratch or mar your workpieces. This sub-base should be removed (and safely stored) whenever conditions (such as a very hard or unfinished workpiece) or use of certain attachments (like the sharpening kit) make it advisable to protect the sub-base finish from damage.

RATE-OF-FEED

IMPORTANT: The whole "secret" of professional routing and edge shaping lies in selecting the proper rate-of-feed. The Electronic model automatically monitors your rate-of-feed.

Beware of Force Feeding

Clean, smooth routing and edge shaping can be done *only when* the bit is revolving at a relatively high speed and is taking very small bites to produce tiny, cleanly severed chips. If the router is forced to move forward at a fast pace, the rpm of the bit is slower than normal in relation to its forward movement — and the bit must necessarily take bigger bites as it revolves. "Bigger bites" mean bigger chips, and a rougher finish. Moreover, bigger chips require more power — and the router motor can become sufficiently overloaded to slow down and further aggravate the condition. In fact, under extreme force-feeding conditions the relative rpm of the bit can become so slow — and the bites it has to take so large — that chips will be partially knocked off (rather than fully cut off), with resulting splintering and gouging of the workpiece.

Your *Craftsman* router is an extremely high-speed tool (25,000 rpm no-load speed), and will make clean, smooth cuts if allowed to run freely without the overload of a forced (too fast) feed. What constitutes "force feeding" depends upon three things: Bit size, depth-of-cut, and workpiece characteristics. The larger the bit and/or the deeper the cut, the more slowly the router can be moved forward. And, if the wood is very hard, knotty, gummy or damp, the operation must be slowed still more.

You can always detect "force feeding" by the sound of the motor. Its high-pitched whine will sound lower and stronger as it loses speed. Also, the strain of holding the tool will be noticeably increased.

In addition to producing poor quality work, force feeding — if done too continuously — will overheat your router motor, and can damage it. It pays to use good operating judgment, even if a bit more patience is needed!

IMPROPER FEEDS

Avoid Too-Slow Feeding

It is also possible to spoil a cut by moving the router forward too slowly. When it is advanced into the work too slowly a

TOO MUCH PUSH MAY OVERLOAD TOOL MOTOR

revolving bit doesn't dig into new wood fast enough to take a bite; instead, it simply scrapes away sawdust-like particles. Scraping produces heat, which can glaze or burn and mar the cut — in extreme cases, can even overheat the bit so as to destroy its hardness.

In addition, it is more difficult to control a router when the bit is scraping instead of cutting. With practically no load on the motor the bit will be revolving at close to top rpm, and will have a much greater than normal tendency to bounce off the sides of the cut (especially, if the wood has a pronounced grain with hard and soft areas). As a result, the cut produced may have rippled, instead of straight, sides — and, unless very firmly held, the router might even take off in a wrong direction from the intended cut line.

You can detect "too-slow feeding" by the runaway, too-highly pitched sound of the motor; or, by feeling the "wiggle" of the bit in the cut.

Proper Feeding

The right feed is neither too fast nor too slow. It is the rate at which the bit is being advanced firmly and surely to produce a continuous spiral of uniform chips — without hogging into the wood to make large individual chips nor, on the other hand, to create only sawdust. If you are making a small-diameter, shallow groove in soft, dry wood, the proper feed may be about as fast as you can travel your router along your guide line. Contrarywise, if the bit is a large one, the cut is deep, and/or the wood is hard to cut, the proper feed may be a very slow one. Then, again, a cross-grain cut may require a slower pace than an identical with-grain cut in the same workpiece.

There is *no* fixed rule. You will learn by experience . . . by listening to the tool motor and by feeling the progress of each cut. If at all possible, always test a cut on a scrap of the workpiece wood, beforehand.

DEPTH OF CUT

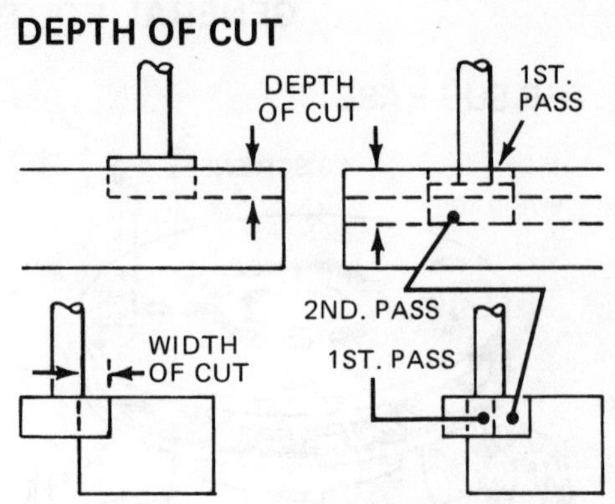

As previously mentioned, the depth-of-cut is important because it affects the rate of feed which, in turn, affects the quality of a cut (and, also, the possibility of damage to your router motor and bit). A deep cut requires a slower feed than a shallow one; and a too-deep cut will cause you to slow the feed so much that the bit is no longer cutting; is scraping, instead.

Sears Electronic model computes the proper feed rate for the workpiece hardness and bit size, and keeps you warned (flashing light) if you feed too slow or fast. It also maintains a constant bit speed for smoother work.

Making a deep cut is *never* advisable. The smaller bits — especially those only 1/16-in. in diameter — are easily broken off when subjected to too much side thrust. A large enough bit may not be broken off, but if the cut is too deep a rough cut will result — and it may be very difficult to guide the bit as desired. For these reasons, we recommend that you do *not* exceed 1/8-in. depth-of-cut in a single pass, regardless of the bit size or the softness or condition of the workpiece.

To make deeper cuts it is therefore necessary to make as many successive passes as required, lowering the bit 1/8- or 1/4-in., as the case may be, for each new pass. In order to save time, do *all* the cutting necessary at one depth setting, *before* lowering the bit for the next pass. This will also assure a uniform depth when the final pass is completed.

DIRECTION OF FEED AND THRUST

The router motor and bit revolve in a *clockwise* direction. This gives to the tool a slight tendency to twist (in your hands) in a *counter*clockwise direction, especially when the motor revs up (as at starting).

Because of the extremely high speed of bit rotation during a "proper feeding" operation, there is very little kickback to contend with under normal conditions. However, should the bit strike a knot, hard grain, etc. that would affect the normal progress of the cutting action, there *will* be a slight kickback . . . sufficient to spoil the trueness of your cut if you are not prepared. Such a kickback is always in the direction *opposite to the direction of bit rotation.*

To guard against such a kickback, plan your set-up and direction of feed so that you will always be thrusting the tool – to hold it against whatever you are using to guide the cut – in the *same direction* that the leading edge of the bit is moving. In short, the thrust should be in a direction that keeps the sharp edges of the bit continuously biting straight into new (uncut) wood.

Whenever you are routing a groove, your tool travel should be in a direction that places whatever guide you are using at the right-hand side. In short, when the guide is positioned as shown in the first part of the illustration, tool travel should be left to right and counterclockwise around curves. When the guide is positioned as shown in the second part of the illustration, tool travel should be right to left and clockwise around curves. If there is a choice, the first set-up is generally the easiest to use. In either case, the sideways thrust you use is *against* the guide.

Whenever you are shaping an edge, the feed should always be clockwise when working on an outside (convex) edge; but should be counterclockwise when working on an inside (concave) edge. The reason for this is that, when traveling the tool as instructed, the bit will have a "chopping action" – but will have a "gouging action" if you reverse

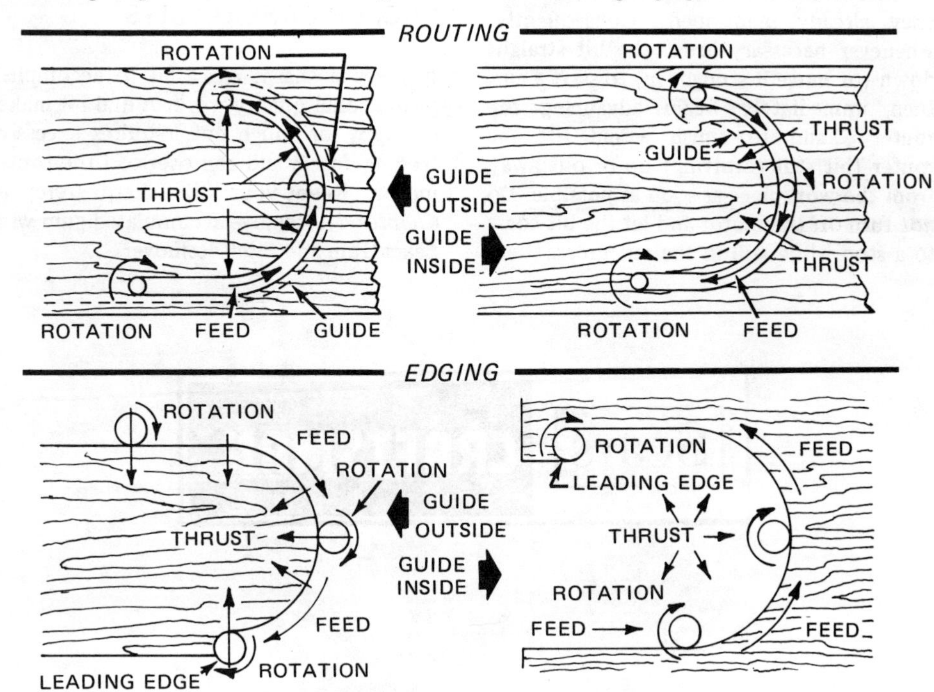

CORRECT FEED AND THRUST

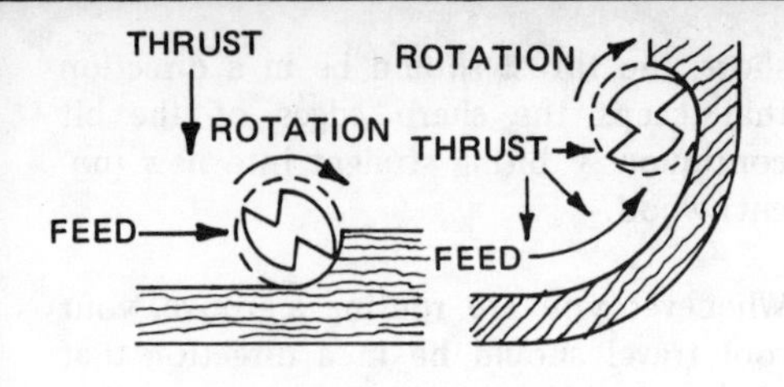

A "CHOPPING" ACTION

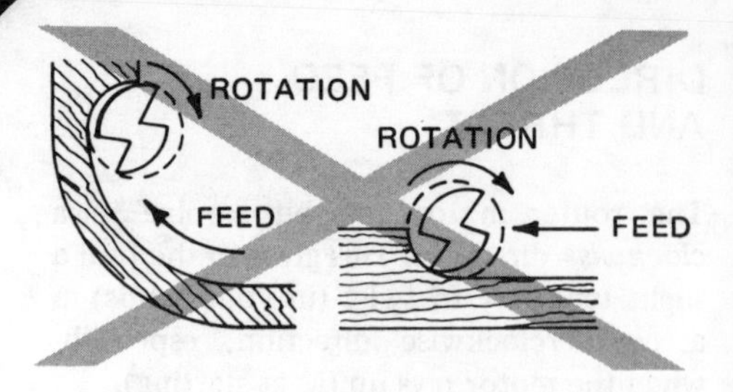

A "GOUGING" ACTION

the travel direction. "Chopping" is much preferable to "gouging" as there is less danger of ripping out chips by tearing the wood grain.

STARTING AND ENDING A CUT

As previously said, whenever a bit is revolving freely (*not* advancing into uncut wood) it may have a tendency to bounce around and enlarge the cut by chipping away at the cut sides. On the other hand, it is never advisable to start the motor with a bit already in contact with uncut wood (due to the initial rev-up kickback tendency already mentioned). Consequently, whenever necessary lower the bit straight down (or move it straight in) to start a cut, then immediately begin advancing the router . . . and to finish a cut lift the router (bit still revolving) up or out away from the workpiece as soon as possible. Do *not* turn off the motor and let the bit coast to a stop while still in the cut unless there is no other choice (refer to "Stopped Groove" *page 23*).

THE USE OF GUIDES

For all practical purposes it is impossible to freehand guide a router to follow a straight or curved marked line on the workpiece. The cutting action is so fast that even the slightest deviation from your line will result in a spoiled cut. Certain jobs — like most carving and routing out a large area — can best be done freehand; but all other types of work should be done with a mechanical guide of some kind.

PROPER CARE OF BITS

It takes a sharp, clean bit to accomplish professional quality work. A dull bit makes a sloppy or rough cut, requires excessive feeding force, and can overload the router motor. Keep your bits sharp (*refer to Chapter 4*). Remove accumulated gum with Sears Gum and Pitch Remover.

CHAPTER II – STRAIGHT, CURVED AND CONTOURED EDGING AND ROUTING

THE NEED FOR A GUIDE

As previously said, it is almost impossible to cut accurately along any desired line or workpiece edge without using some type of guide to keep the router traveling as you wish. Because it cuts so very fast, even the slightest "off-course" movement will result in a less-than-perfect cut; and your hands alone cannot be depended upon to prevent such movements when cutting along any line (or edge) more than a few inches long. Several types of guides and work-helpers are illustrated and explained here.

IMPORTANT: Many of the guides and work-helpers discussed in this chapter are not designed to hold the workpiece–*only* to guide the router. Therefore, when using such a device it is essential: 1) For the workpiece either to be large and heavy enough not to move during an operation; or 2) For the workpiece to be securely clamped to a flat, level surface such as a workbench top.

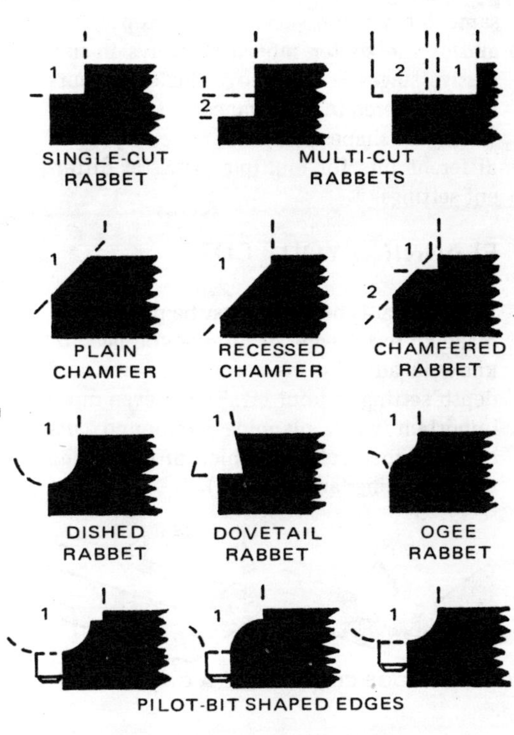

TYPICAL EDGE SHAPES

TYPES OF EDGES AND GROOVES AND THE BITS TO USE

Except where otherwise indicated, the cuts illustrated can be made in single passes. Straight rabbets and grooves are cut with *straight bits*—or, the *butt-hinge bit* can be used for shallow grooves. For dish-bottom rabbets and grooves use either a *veining bit* or the *core-box bit*. Chamfers and Vee-grooves, depending upon the angle desired, are cut with a *V-groove chamfering, carving* or *panel-raising bit*. The *ogee, classic and point-cutting quarter-round bits* are for decorative grooving; dovetail rabbets and grooves require a *dovetail bit*. Fancy workpiece edges are shaped by using either one of the *stemmed edging (rounding or double-bead) bits* or one of the many two-piece bits with a pilot (which bits cannot be used

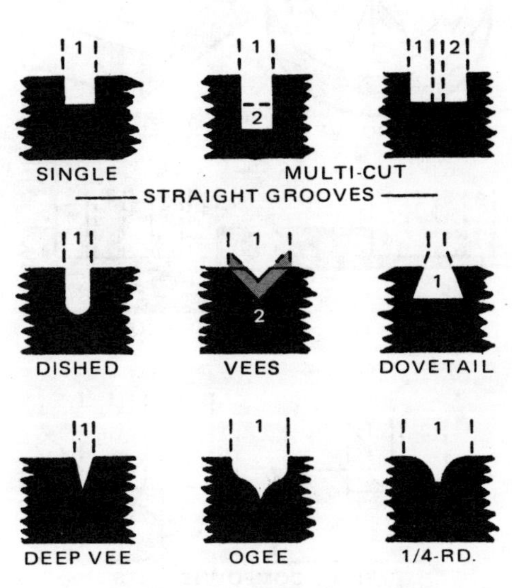

TYPICAL GROOVE SHAPES

for grooving). Carving is best accomplished with the *extra-long carving bit;* and the *combination panel cutter* is used for cutting through the workpiece.

By making two or more passes — with the same bit set for successively deeper cuts and/or the router moved sideways in successive stages — the above single-pass cuts can be altered in appearance. A still greater variety of shapes can be achieved by using different bits for multiple passes at different settings.

PLANNING YOUR CUTS

Professional-type work must be planned; to make an exact edge or groove you need to know in advance the exact placement and depth setting of your bit. This is even more important when planning compound cuts of any type (cuts for which different bits and/or settings are required).

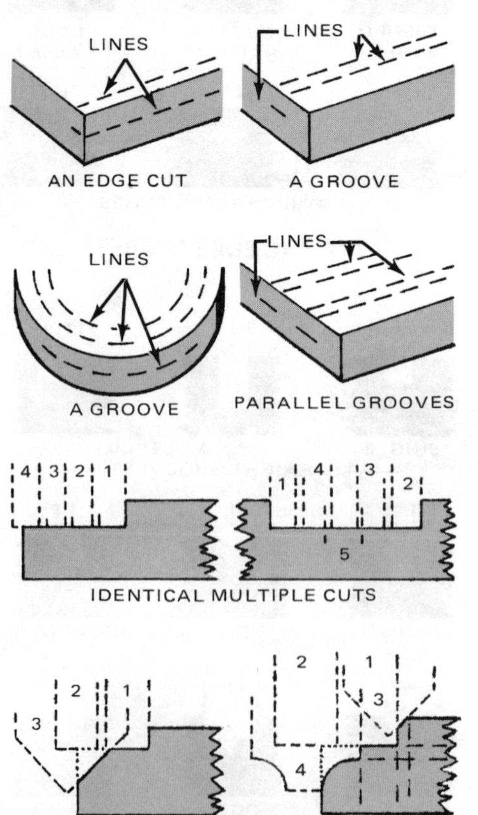

LINES FOR PLANNING

The best practice is to draw pencil lines on your workpiece to serve as guidelines when lowering the bit for cut depth and positioning the router for cut placement. In addition, make a plan view (typical ones illustrated) to show the positions of the various bits to be used and the sequence in which you will use these bits — then draw your guidelines on the plan view so that you can accurately transfer them to the workpiece.

When making multiple cuts it is best to make the most critical cuts *first.* For instance, for a rabbet the inside cut, No. 1 (which determines the rabbet width) is most critical; for a wide groove the two inside cuts, Nos. 1 and 2 (which determine the groove width) are the most critical. In both cases, all remaining cuts do not require exact placement so long as they overlap and serve to clean out the remaining wood.

When making compound cuts follow this same principle and, in addition, plan cuts so that each one will be called upon to remove as little wood as possible. For instance, in the two illustrations cut 3 could have been made first — but would then have had to remove more wood than when made third (as shown). Also, placement of cut 3 (and of cut 4 in the one illustration) would be more difficult if these cuts were made ahead of cuts 1 and 2.

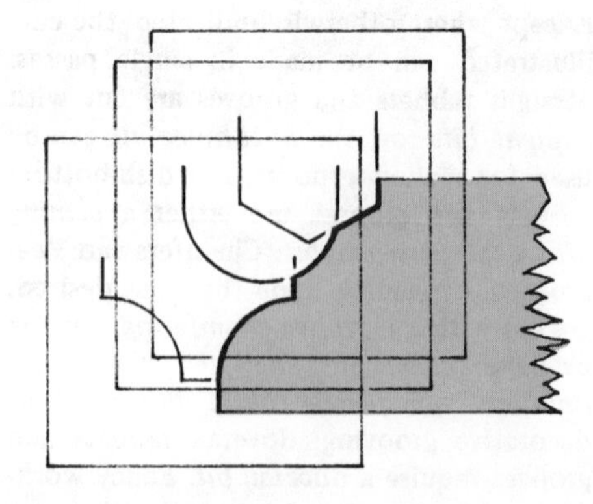

In order to create new and different edge shapes when making plan views for compound cuts (as above), it is helpful to have the outlines of your various bits drawn on tracing paper or vellum. These drawings can then be stacked (as illustrated) and moved around until an interesting edge shape is produced — and, afterwards, this shape can be traced for your plan view.

To draw the outline of a bit use it to make a full cut in a piece of scrap wood. For a one-piece bit, a "full" cut is a groove started at one workpiece edge with the bit lowered so the cutter top is flush with the workpiece top. For a two-piece bit, a "full" cut is one made with the pilot against the workpiece edge and the bit lowered as above. After making the cut stand the workpiece on end and trace the cut outline on paper — then, for a two-piece bit, add on the horizontal bottom line. Identify your drawings with bit numbers.

USING THE MULTIPURPOSE ROUTER GUIDE

Assembling the Guide on the Router

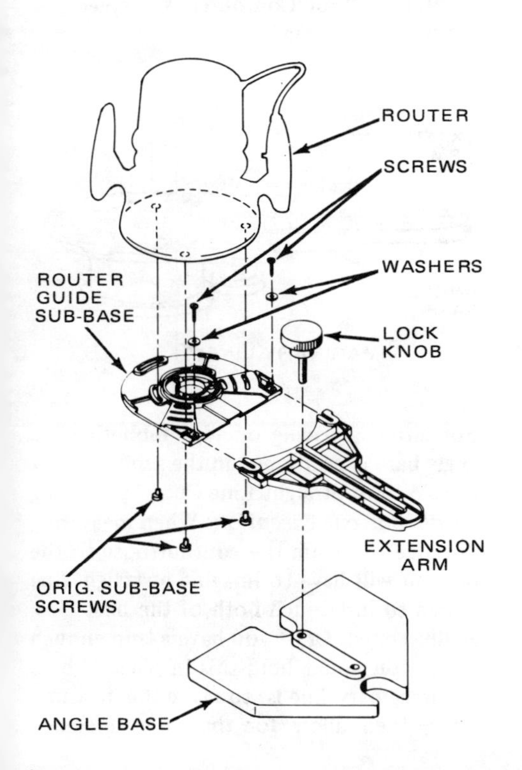

The router sub-base must be removed and the *router-guide sub-base* installed in its place, using the same three screws that held the router sub-base: Two screws and washers (furnished) attach the *extension arm* to the router-guide sub-base; the *angle base* can be attached to the extension arm with either the flat or the angle end facing the bit, and is held by the *lock knob*.

For Straight-Line Cuts

To use the guide for routing a straight groove parallel to a workpiece edge or for rabbeting the edge, the workpiece edge must be straight and smooth enough to slide the guide along. It is *not* advisable to try to shape the whole edge using this guide. Begin by drawing lines on your workpiece to locate the groove (or rabbet) and (on workpiece edge) to show the depth-of-cut.

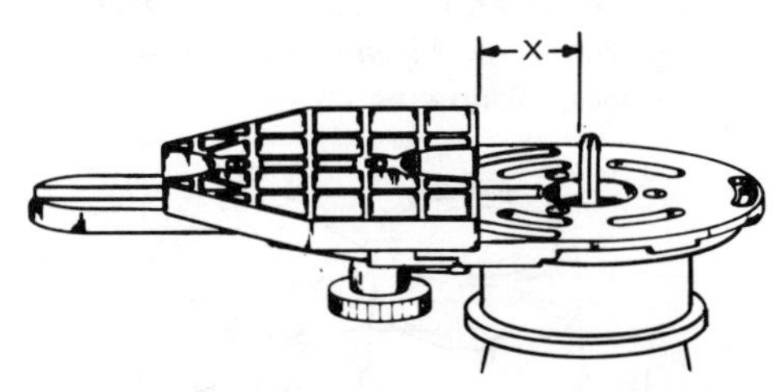

For grooving, measure the distance (on your workpiece) between the workpiece edge to be used for guiding and the *nearer* side of the marked groove. Install the bit to be used and adjust it to project down about 1/2-inch. Install the angle base on the extension arm with its flat side facing the router bit, then adjust it so that the flat side is exactly the same distance (X) from the *nearer* side of the bit as the distance measured above. Tighten the lock knob.

Adjust the bit for desired depth-of-cut by placing the router on the workpiece so the bit can be lowered alongside the edge where your depth-of-cut line is drawn. At

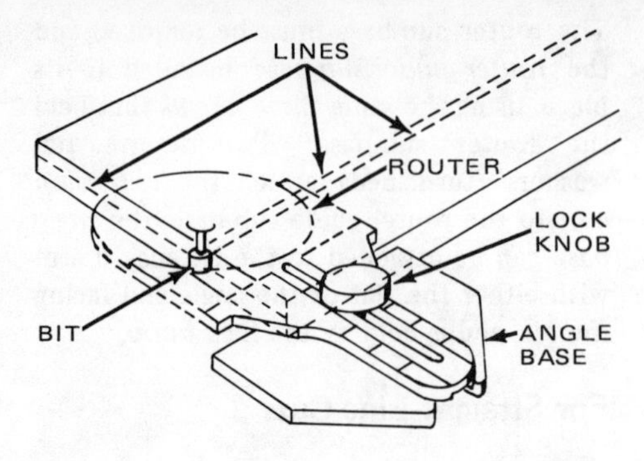

the same time, hold the guide against the workpiece guiding edge and check, by eye, to see that the bit aligns with your drawn groove lines—readjust, if necessary. Now, make the cut while holding the router firmly down on the workpiece and the guide squarely against the guiding workpiece edge.

NOTE: If the cut is to start somewhere in the workpiece surface, instead of at an edge as in the preceding, *refer to "Blind and Stopped Grooves,"* following.

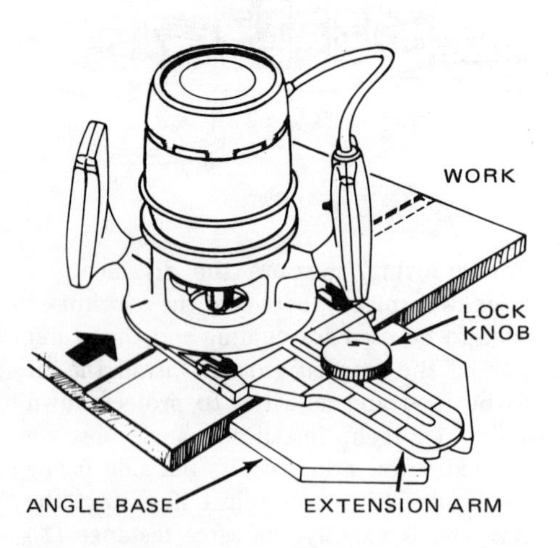

For rabbeting, instead of measuring the distance (X), as above, it is easier to adjust the angle base in the same way you adjust the depth-of-cut—that is, by eye. In either case, if more than one cut is needed (for a groove or rabbet too wide and/or deep for one cut), either measure or "eyeball" succeeding cuts, whichever is easier.

NOTE: Edge shaping, with one of the stemmed shaping bits (like the rounding or double bead) can be accomplished in the same way as rabbeting, by using the multipurpose router guide as described for any operation in this text.

For Large Circular or Elliptical Cuts

NOTE: For making perfectly circular cuts refer to "Perfect Circle, Grooving and Edging," following.

These cuts are made with the angle base positioned on the guide extension arm so that its contour nose, instead of its flat side, faces the router bit. The curvature of the workpiece edge to be used for guiding must have a large enough radius for *both* tips of the angle base's contour nose to make firm contact with the edge at all times during the operation. If curvature is too small, refer to "For Contoured Workpiece Cuts," following.

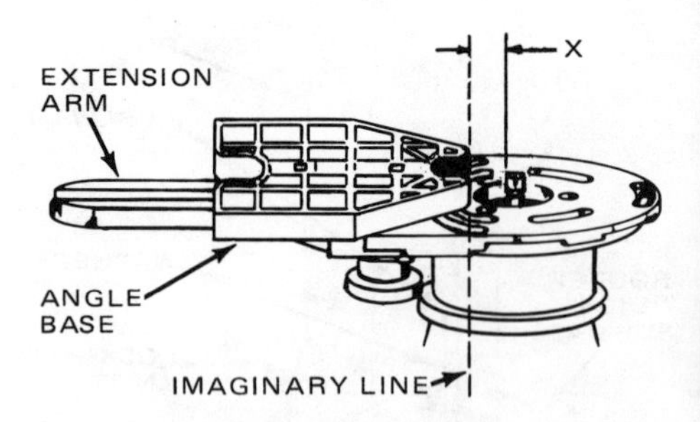

For either grooving or edge rabbeting the angle base is positioned in the same manner as told "For Straight Line Cuts," preceding —*with this one exception:* When measuring distance (X) from the contour nose to the bit you will have to imagine a straight line drawn to just touch both of the nose tips, as illustrated. Or, if you have a thin-enough ruler, you could hold this in place (where the imaginary line is) to make the measurement—then allow for the ruler thickness when setting the angle base position. In any case, if you doubt your setting, try your cut on a piece of scrap and readjust as necessary.

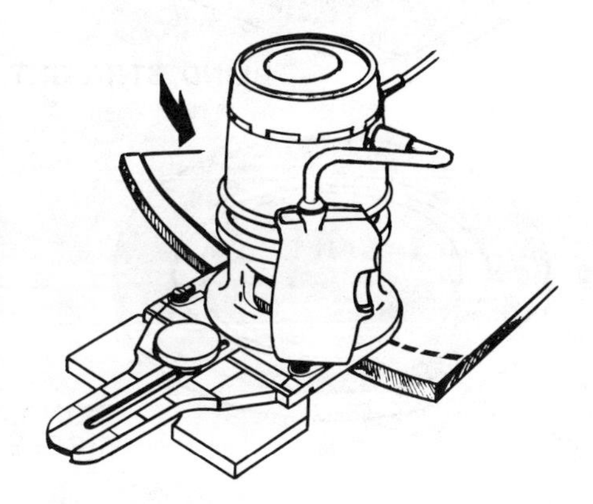

To start any rabbet cut you can push the bit straight into the workpiece edge until the two angle-base tips are in firm contact with the edge. To start a groove cut that does not begin at a workpiece end, hold the two angle-base tips against the edge so that you can slowly lower the router *straight down* until its bottom rests firmly on the workpiece surface. While making either type of cut swing the router as needed to be certain that *both* angle-base tips remain firmly in contact with the workpiece guiding edge.

> *NOTE:* The curvature of an ellipse is *not* uniform—is "broader" at the sides and "narrower" at the ends. A broader curve contacts the tips of the angle-base nose at points farther apart than the points contacted by a narrower curve—to create a smaller distance between the guide and the bit. For this reason, a groove cut around an ellipse may be noticeably closer to the edge at the sides than at the ends . . . the amount depending upon the difference in curvature at these positions. A rabbet cut is similarly affected.

For Contoured Workpiece Cuts

To either rabbet a contoured-workpiece-edge or to groove the surface to a like contour at some distance in from the edge,

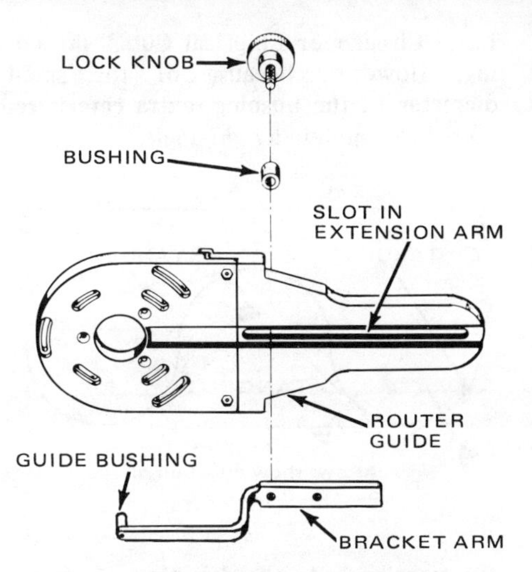

ASSEMBLING GUIDE BUSHING BRACKET ARM TO ROUTER GUIDE

the *Bracket Assembly Arm With Guide Bushing* (furnished with your Multipurpose Router Guide) is used to replace the angle base on the guide extension. The bracket assembly arm is installed as illustrated—and is adjusted to position the cut (for either a rabbet cut or a groove) in the same way as previously explained "For Large Circular or Elliptical Cuts"—except that your "imaginary line" is now tangent to the side of the *guide bushing* facing the router bit (i.e.: measure from closest point of guide bushing to bit).

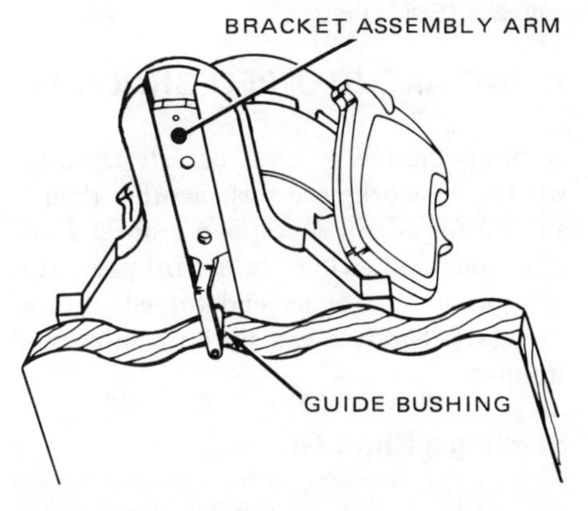

The guide bushing can follow any curvature small enough for the (small diameter) guide bushing to fit into—but it cannot turn a square or angled inside corner. Starting and cutting are the same as for "For

Large Circular or Elliptical Cuts," preceding. However, because of the small diameter of the bushing, extra care is required to maintain a *right-angle*.

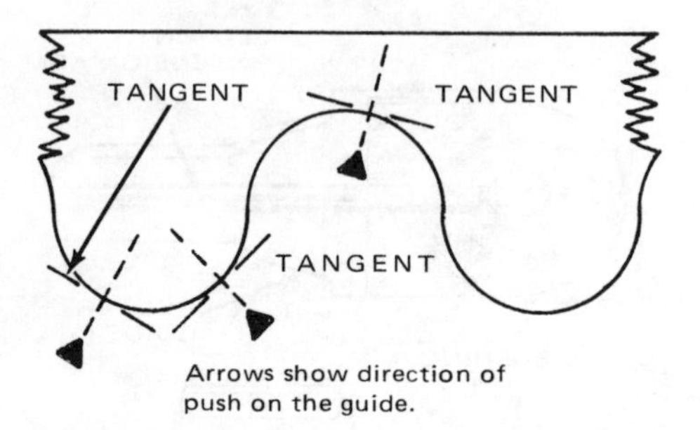

Arrows show direction of push on the guide.

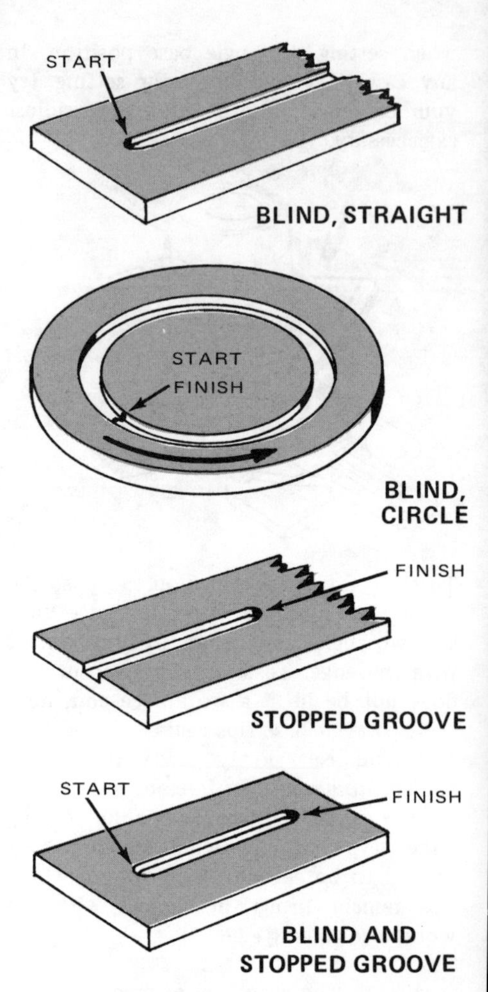

"A right-angle to the direction of travel" means at a 90° angle to the *tangent* of the curve (of the workpiece edge) at each point along the edge. If the router is allowed to get ahead of or behind the guide, the distance between the bit and the end of the bushing will be varied . . . the cut, instead of paralleling the edge, will waver in and out. The tighter a curve is the more difficult it becomes to correctly hold the guide. In fact, when rounding a very tight convex (outside) curve it is necessary to swing the guide around the curve while practically holding the router motionless; also, conversely, to swing the router around the curve while practically holding the guide motionless, when following a very tight concave (inside) curve.

BLIND AND STOPPED GROOVES

A blind groove is one that *starts* somewhere in a workpiece surface other than at an end (or edge). A stopped groove is one that *ends* somewhere in a workpiece surface other than at an end (or edge) or at the start. Grooves can be both blind and stopped.

Starting a Blind Groove

The problem with a blind groove is to start the cut accurately (on location lines and at proper depth) without spoiling the cut. Starting can be done "freehand" by rocking the router on its base—with the bit already set for the depth-of-cut—to lower the revolving bit into the workpiece at the starting point; but, unless your eye is very good and your hands very steady, chances are this will result in a sloppy cut at the start of the groove.

A more accurate method is to use both the multipurpose router guide and a stop block. The router guide position must be accurately established (*refer to "Straight Line Cuts," preceding*). In addition, measure the distance from one edge of the router base to the nearer side of the bit—then C-clamp (or otherwise secure) a wood block this same distance from the start of your groove. Now, adjust your bit for the desired depth-of-cut, then raise it until its bottom end is flush with (or above) the bottom of the multipurpose router guide base, while *counting the exact number of adjustment-ring turns* required to do this. Position the router on the workpiece against the stop block and with the guide firmly against the workpiece edge. Start the motor, then adjust the bit downward *the same number of turns* required preceding to raise it. When the bit is fully down, finish the cut in the usual manner.

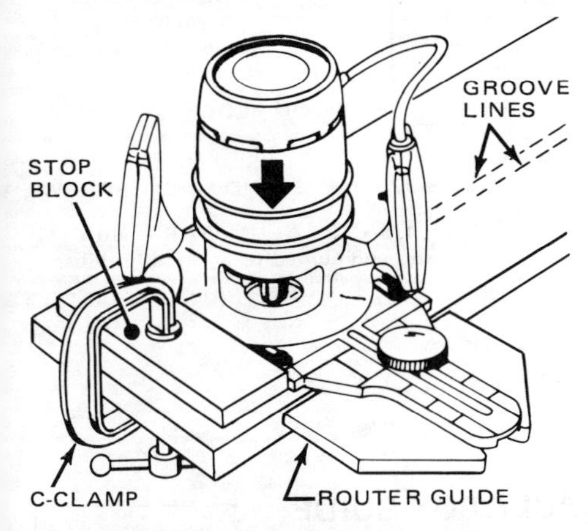

ROUTER POSITIONED FOR START OF A BLIND CUT

NOTE: If your router does not have an adjustment ring or any means of "counting" the distance bit is raised or lowered, you will have to set the bit for desired depth-of-cut, then lower the revolving bit *straight* down at the starting point, using the stop block and guide to start the cut correctly.

Finishing a Stopped Groove

The only problem with a stopped groove is being able to stop the cut at the exact location required. This is most easily accomplished by using a stop block, positioned by making the same measurement as for the stop block preceding. Continue your cut until the router base contacts the stop block . . . turn off the motor and wait for the bit to stop revolving . . . then lift the router up from the workpiece.

Tapered End-Depth Grooves

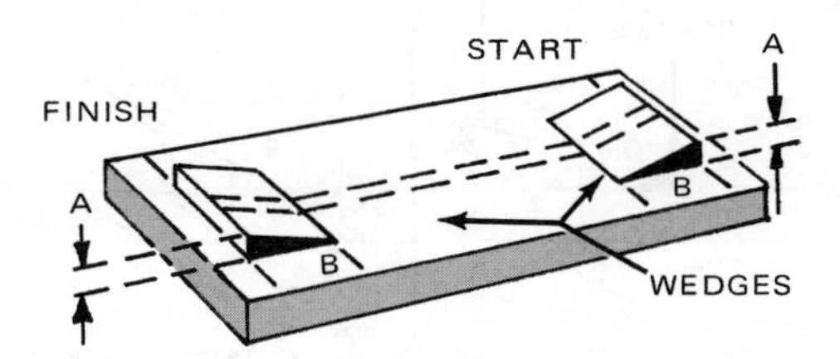

Either a blind and/or a stopped groove that surfaces at exactly the start (or finish) line can be cut with the aid of wedges, as illustrated. Height "A" of each wedge must be *exactly* the same as your depth-of-cut (or greater, see *NOTE*, following). Also, the top of each wedge must be large enough to support the router base without allowing the router to tip over. The length "B" of each wedge determines the abruptness of the taper.

Secure the two blocks (clamps or otherwise) at the start and finish lines, as shown. Draw your groove lines to continue up over the start-side wedge. Make your set-up exactly as for a straight-line groove and start your cut into the outer end of the start-side wedge (which will be grooved, accordingly). Finish the cut by traveling the router up into and over the far end of the finish-end wedge so that the bit grooves this wedge also.

NOTE: With "A" equal to depth-of-cut, both wedges will be cut in two by the operation. If "A" is greater than the depth-of-cut, they won't be entirely cut through (can be used again), but the start and finish points on your workpiece will be moved inward to the points where the wedges' heights do equal the depth-of-cut.

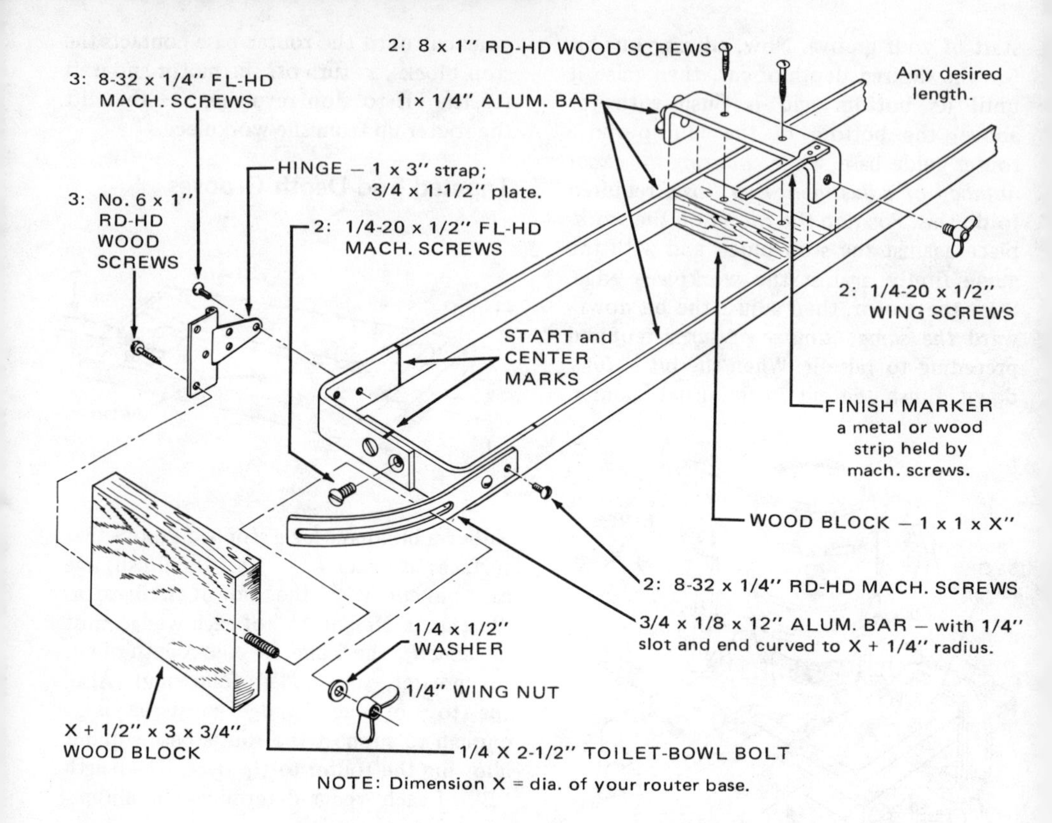

HOMEMADE ADJUSTABLE BOX GUIDE

The guide shown can be used for cutting blind and or stopped grooves of any desired length, either at right angles to one selected workpiece edge or at any desired angle. For a desired length groove, position the sliding (right hand) end and lock it with the two wing screws . . . or, it can be positioned out of the way if groove is not to be stopped. For any angle, swing the end wood block to desired angle and lock it with the wing nut. Clamp the guide to your workpiece with the wood block against the workpiece edge. As illustrated, guide swings only to the left; turn it upside-down for angles to the right. Also, if groove is to start closer to edge than "start" mark will normally be, use a straight piece of scrap wood between end block and workpiece edge to space back.

As shown, guide is made of solid wood pieces and 1/4- x 1-in. aluminum bar stock (available in 6 ft. and longer lengths). The end wood block is positioned to project 1-in. above and 1-in. below the bar. Spacing between the two bars must exactly equal router-base diameter. The "finish" marker should be positioned to slide directly over the side-rail top, with the end exactly at the groove end when router base touches the wood block.

USING A STRAIGHTEDGE GUIDE

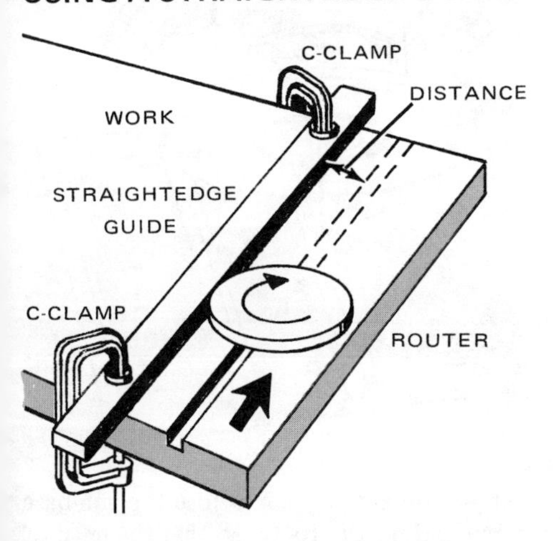

For grooves that are too far in from a workpiece edge to use the multipurpose router guide, a straightedge guide offers the best and easiest solution to the guide problem. Use any convenient piece of wood, metal or plastic that has a *truly straight*, reasonably hard and 1/8-in. or more thick edge, and is long enough to be clamped in place (at *both* ends) as shown. Preferably—because of the rotation torque explained in Chapter 1—position the guide to the left of the router as viewed from behind the direction of travel.

Positioning of the guide is accomplished by measuring the distance from one edge of the router base to the *nearer* side of the bit . . . then setting the guide *exactly* this distance from the *nearer* side of the groove to be cut. To make a number of parallel grooves equally spaced, move the guide over for each successive groove *exactly* the distance desired between the groove sides *nearer* to the guide.

USING AN ADJUSTABLE T-SQUARE

Instead of a simple straightedge guide you can easily construct an adjustable T-square, as shown. This has the added advantage of being able to be set at various angles to make grooves that are angled, instead of at

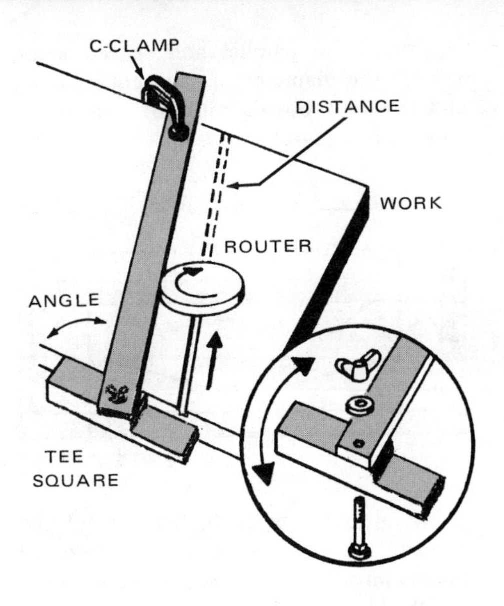

90°, to the starting workpiece edge. Use any available materials, as above, and construct the T-square as shown.

In use, the T-square must be securely positioned against one workpiece edge with its far end clamped in position to keep it stationary. Set-up and operation are the same as for a straightedge guide.

USING A BOX GUIDE

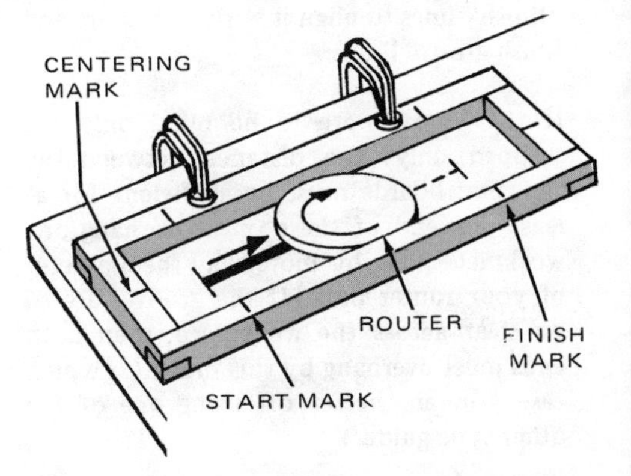

A homemade rectangular guide such as shown can be particularly helpful for cutting a number of parallel blind and/or stopped grooves—because it simplifies the set-ups. The inner edges of all four boards must be straight and smooth; the two side

rails must be parallel and spaced apart *exactly* the diameter of your router base; and the four boards must be nailed and glued firmly together.

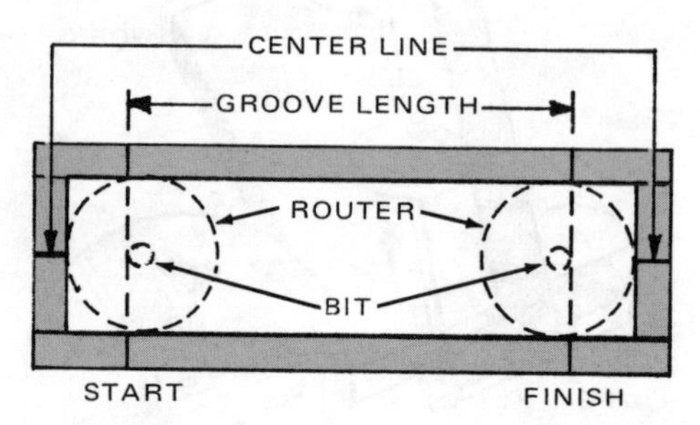

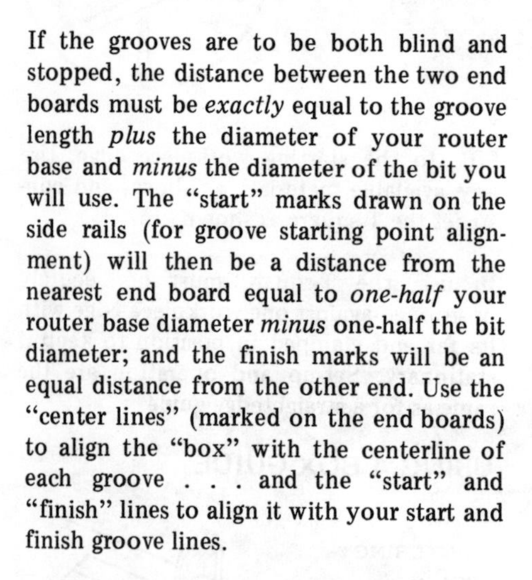

If the grooves are to be both blind and stopped, the distance between the two end boards must be *exactly* equal to the groove length *plus* the diameter of your router base and *minus* the diameter of the bit you will use. The "start" marks drawn on the side rails (for groove starting point alignment) will then be a distance from the nearest end board equal to *one-half* your router base diameter *minus* one-half the bit diameter; and the finish marks will be an equal distance from the other end. Use the "center lines" (marked on the end boards) to align the "box" with the centerline of each groove . . . and the "start" and "finish" lines to align it with your start and finish groove lines.

If the grooves are to be blind only (or stopped only) the distance between the two end boards must be sufficient for at least one end of the box to overhang one workpiece edge by more than the diameter of your router base. If the grooves are to go clear across the workpiece, then both ends must overhang by this much (in which case you are better off using one of the other type guides).

FIXED-SPACE PARALLEL STRAIGHT GROOVES

If the spacing this will provide is satisfactory, parallel grooves can be cut—*after* the first groove is finished—as illustrated. Substitute a hex-head machine screw for one of the three countersunk sub-base

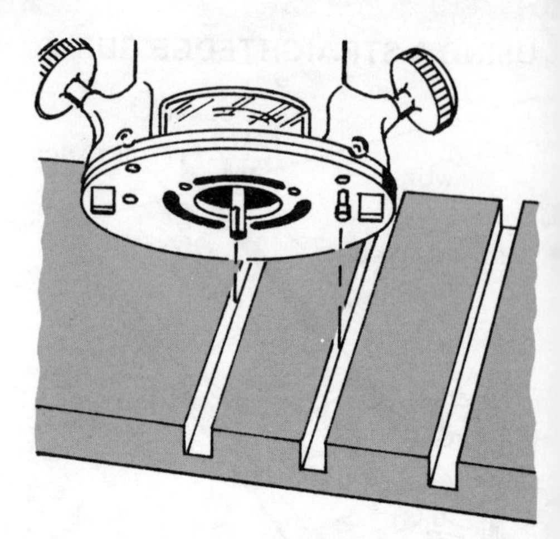

screws (be careful *not* to lose the sub-base screw). Hold the router so that the head of this screw will slide along the *nearest* side of the previous groove, while cutting each successive groove—and so that a line between this screw head and the bit center is always exactly at a right angle to the grooves. To make the first groove, either use a straightedge guide (preceding), *before* substituting the screw—or, cut this groove by sliding the screw head along the workpiece edge.

RABBETING OR GROOVING CORNERS

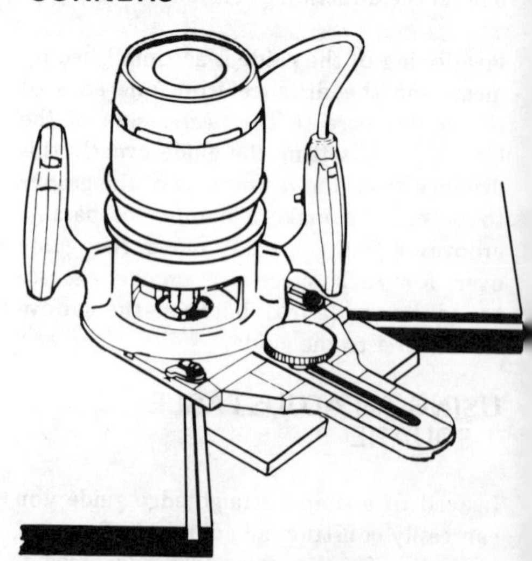

Installed as previously explained (*refer to "For Large Circular or Elliptical Cuts," preceding*), the angle-base contour nose of the multipurpose guide can be used to rabbet or to groove parallel to the edge any inside corner of 90° or greater. The resulting corner will have a radius like that of the bit used, but can be made perfectly straight-sided by chiseling out the slight curvature of the cut.

NOTE: These operations are especially useful for decorating picture frames, etc. by shaping both the inner and outer frame edges and parallel grooving the surface.

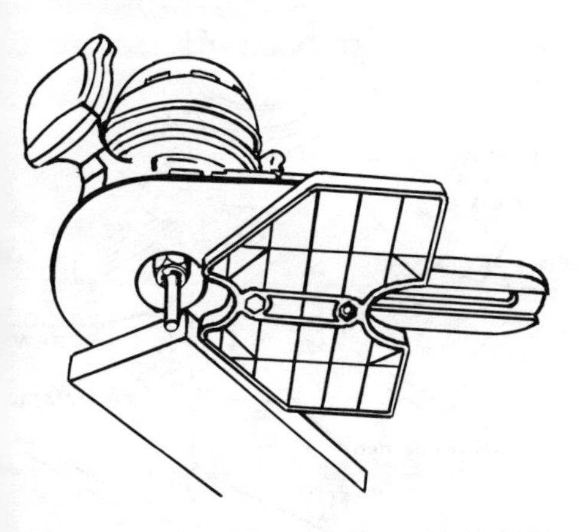

It is also preferable to use the contour nose of the guide for rabbeting or grooving (as above) any outside corner—of any angle (90° or more or less). One side of the nose will remain in contact with the workpiece edge until the cutter has passed the corner—afterwards, the other side of the nose can be used to make contact.

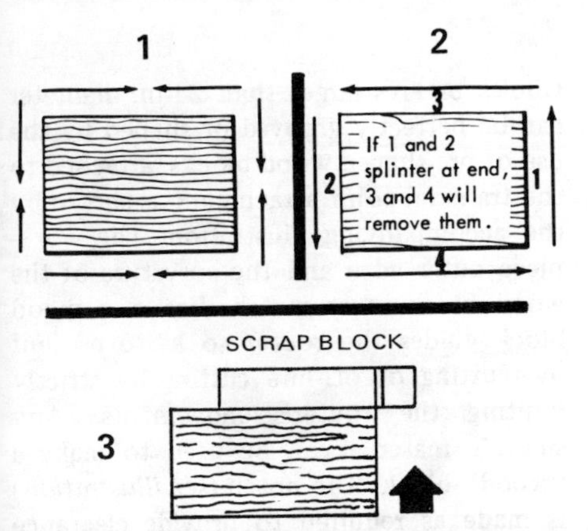

When edging a cross-grain workpiece edge there is always the possibility that the bit will tear off (instead of cut) the last few fibers, to leave a splintered edge. If you are edging completely around a workpiece with square or angled corners this problem can be overcome in one of the two (first above) methods shown. That is, either by always traveling the router *away from* the corner (No. 1), or by doing the two cross-grain ends first (No. 2)—in which case the with-grain cuts will remove any splinters that aren't too deep. When edging only a cross-grain end (No. 3) the only precaution you can take is to securely clamp a scrap block to the workpiece at the "out-end" of the cut, as shown.

PERFECT CIRCLE GROOVING AND EDGING

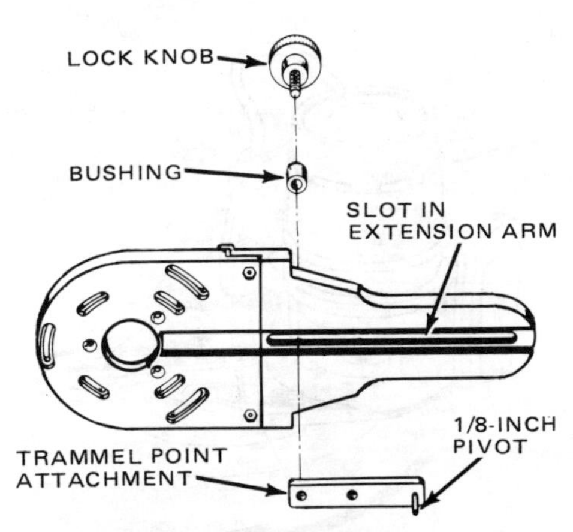

ASSEMBLING TRAMMEL POINT ATTACHMENT TO ROUTER GUIDE

Your router can be guided around a perfect circle by use of the *Trammel-Point Attachment* (furnished with the Multipurpose Router Guide). This attachment is assembled to the extension arm of the guide, in place of the angle base, as shown by the accompanying illustration. The attachment can be positioned with the 1/8-in. pivot either at the end closer or farther from the router bit, and the radius of the circle to be described is determined by its positioning and location (with the lock knob tightened)—from 1-1/8-in. min. to 12-in. max. A 1/8-in. dia. hole must be drilled (about 1/2-in. deep) in the workpiece at the circle center for insertion of the pivot. This can later be filled and finished over, as desired.

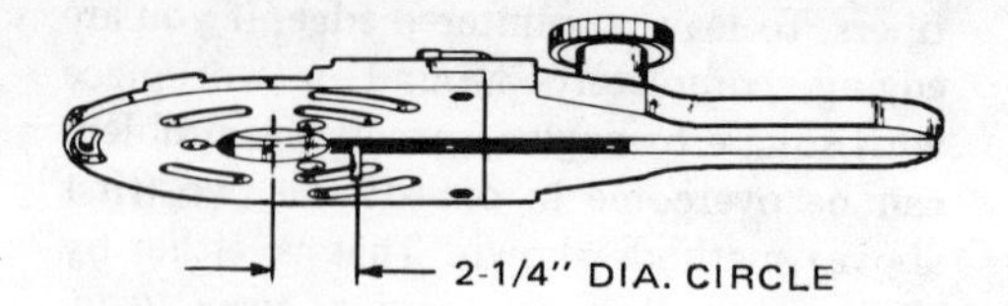

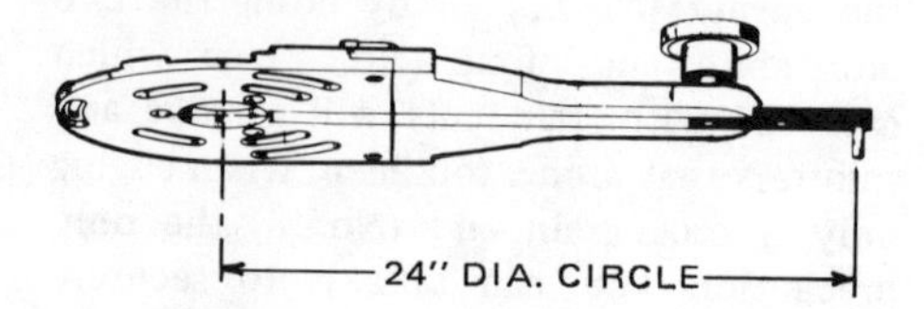

MINIMUM AND MAXIMUM CIRCLES PROVIDED BY TRAMMEL ATTACHMENT

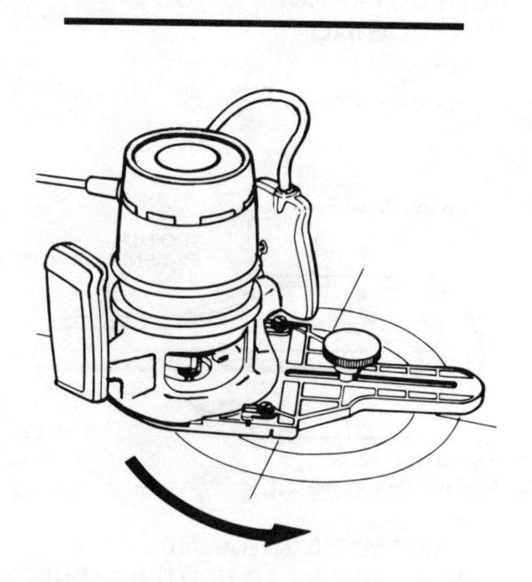

Either grooving in from the workpiece edge or edge rabbeting or edging (with a stemmed shaping bit) is accomplished by placing the pivot in the workpiece hole (above), adjusting the attachment location on the extension arm and the bit depth-of-cut (in the ways previously described)—and by then firmly holding the pivot in place while swinging the (running) router around in a circle. If desired, a perfectly circular piece can be cut out from any workpiece by using the Combination Panel Bit (*Chapter 1*). Use the bit to first cut a shallow groove, then readjust the depth-of-cut for successively deeper cuts until the workpiece is cut all the way through.

PERFECT-CIRCLE GROOVING OF CIRCLES OVER 24-IN. IN DIAMETER

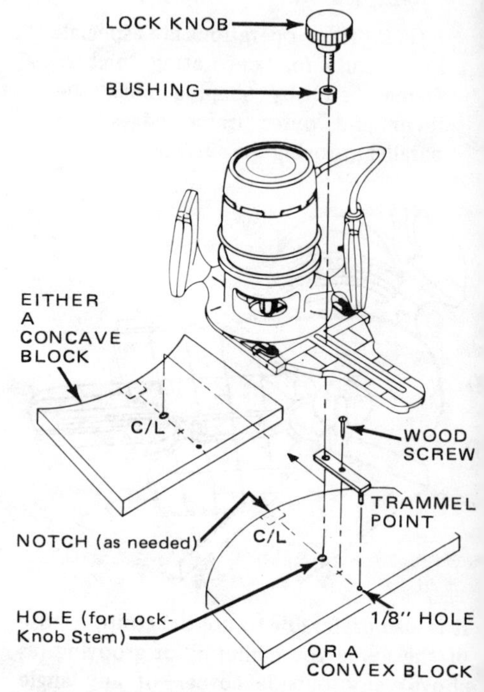

WOOD BLOCKS ATTACHED TO ROUTER WITH TRAMMEL POINT ATTACHMENT

Circles or arcs larger than 24-in. diameter can be perfectly grooved or shaped by the use of pre-shaped wood blocks, attached to the trammel-point attachment as shown by the accompanying illustration. The workpiece outer edge and the curvature of the wood block must match. Use of a wood block guides the router so as to prevent overcutting or off-line cutting by strictly limiting the router's movements. Any suitable material can be used to make a "wood" block. The notch (*see illustration*) is made as required to provide clearance for the router bit.

After the wood block is attached to the trammel point the adjustments and operation are the same as above described.

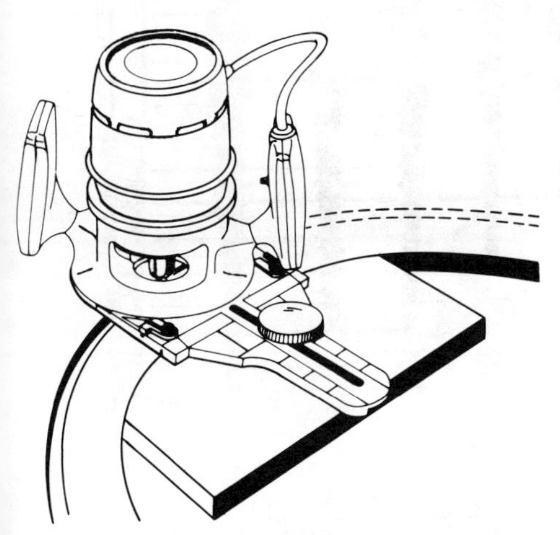

GROOVING WITH CONVEX BLOCK

EDGING WITH THE PILOT BITS

The arbor-type bits with pilots (*Chapter 1*) are excellent for quick, easy edge shaping of any workpiece edge that is either straight or curved at a curvature as great or greater than the radius of the bit to be used. The pilot prevents the bit from making too deep a cut; and holding the pilot firmly in contact with the workpiece edge throughout prevents the cut from becoming too shallow.

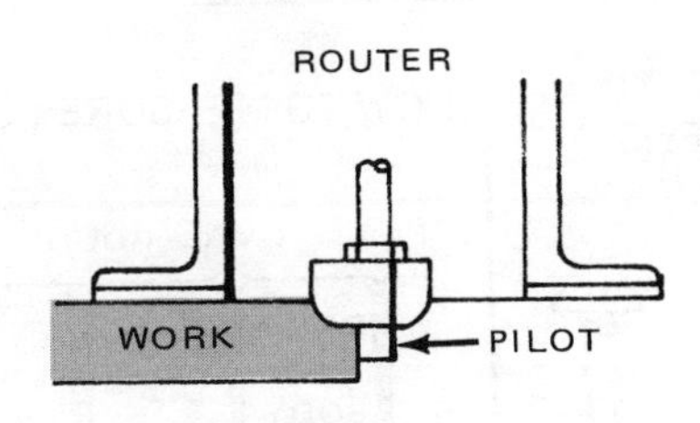

TOP EDGE SHAPING

Whenever the workpiece thickness together with the desired depth-of-cut (as adjusted by router depth setting) are such that only the top part of the edge is to be shaped (leaving at least a 1/16-in. thick uncut portion at bottom), the pilot can ride against the uncut portion, which will serve to guide it.

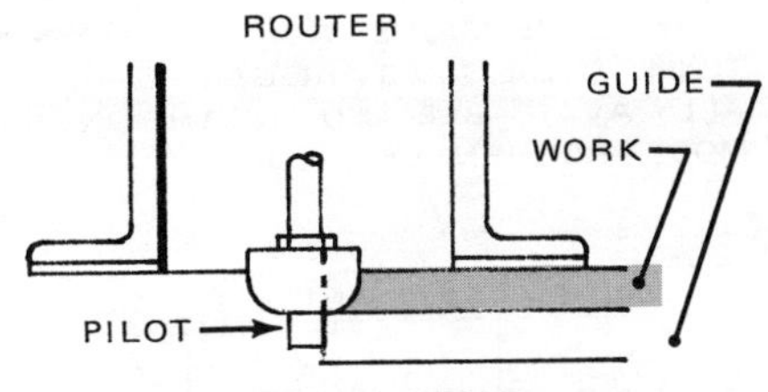

WHOLE EDGE SHAPING

However, if the workpiece is too thin and/or the bit set too low so that there will be no uncut edge to ride the pilot against, any extra board to act as a guide must be placed under the workpiece. This "guide" board must have exactly the same contour—straight or curved—as the workpiece edge. If it is positioned so that its edge is flush with the workpiece edge, the bit will make a full cut (in as far as the bit radius). On the other hand, if the guide is positioned as illustrated (out from the workpiece edge), the bit will make less than a full cut—which will alter the shape of the finished edge.

> *NOTE:* Any of the piloted bits can be used *without* a pilot for edge shaping with guides, as preceding. The size (diameter) of the pilot that is used determines the maximum cut width that can be made with the pilot against the workpiece edge (the small pilot exposes all of the bit; the large one reduces this amount by 1/16-in.).

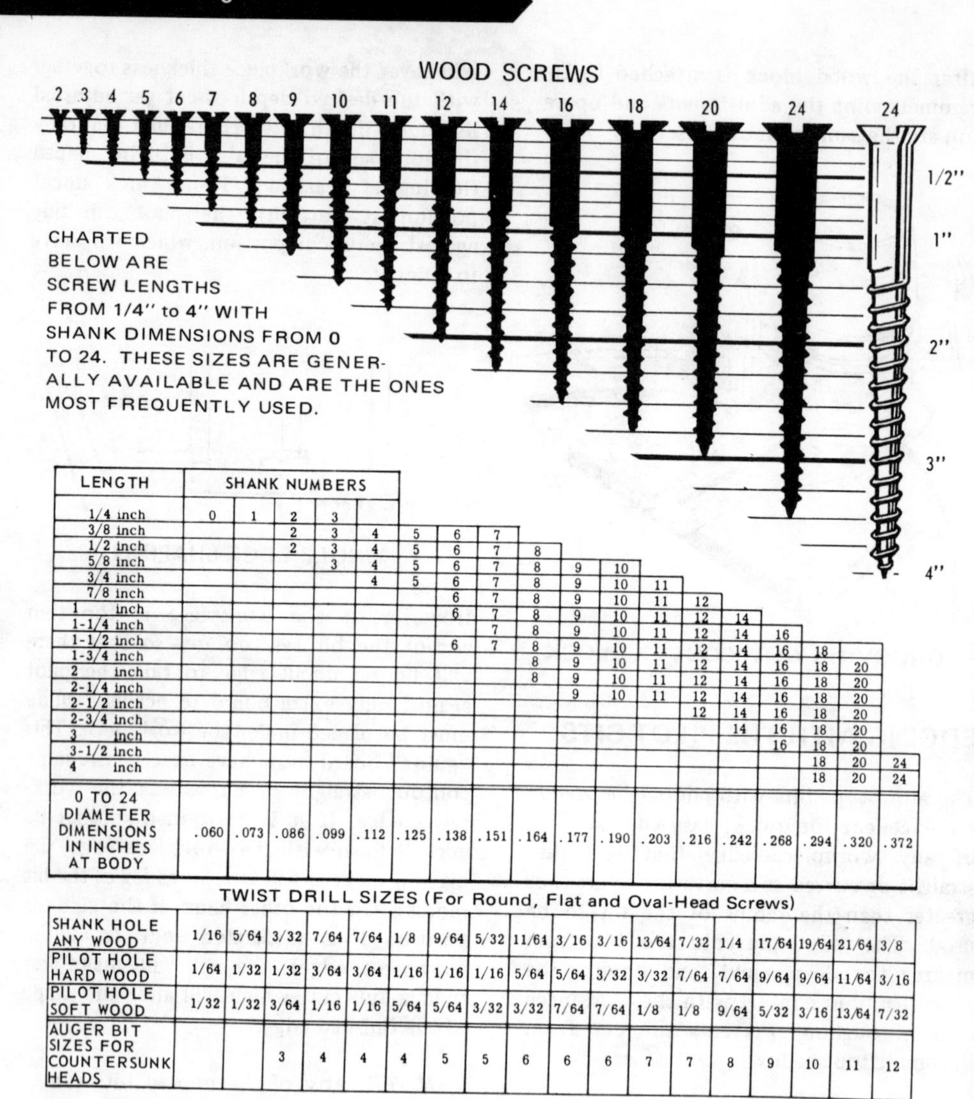

LENGTH	SHANK NUMBERS																	
1/4 inch	0	1	2	3														
3/8 inch			2	3	4	5	6	7										
1/2 inch			2	3	4	5	6	7	8									
5/8 inch				3	4	5	6	7	8	9	10							
3/4 inch					4	5	6	7	8	9	10	11						
7/8 inch							6	7	8	9	10	11	12					
1 inch							6	7	8	9	10	11	12	14				
1-1/4 inch								7	8	9	10	11	12	14	16			
1-1/2 inch							6	7	8	9	10	11	12	14	16	18		
1-3/4 inch									8	9	10	11	12	14	16	18	20	
2 inch									8	9	10	11	12	14	16	18	20	
2-1/4 inch										9	10	11	12	14	16	18	20	
2-1/2 inch													12	14	16	18	20	
2-3/4 inch														14	16	18	20	
3 inch															16	18	20	
3-1/2 inch																18	20	24
4 inch																18	20	24
0 TO 24 DIAMETER DIMENSIONS IN INCHES AT BODY	.060	.073	.086	.099	.112	.125	.138	.151	.164	.177	.190	.203	.216	.242	.268	.294	.320	.372
TWIST DRILL SIZES (For Round, Flat and Oval-Head Screws)																		
SHANK HOLE ANY WOOD	1/16	5/64	3/32	7/64	7/64	1/8	9/64	5/32	11/64	3/16	3/16	13/64	7/32	1/4	17/64	19/64	21/64	3/8
PILOT HOLE HARD WOOD	1/64	1/32	1/32	3/64	3/64	1/16	1/16	1/16	5/64	5/64	3/32	3/32	7/64	7/64	9/64	9/64	11/64	3/16
PILOT HOLE SOFT WOOD	1/32	1/32	3/64	1/16	1/16	5/64	5/64	3/32	3/32	7/64	7/64	1/8	1/8	9/64	5/32	3/16	13/64	7/32
AUGER BIT SIZES FOR COUNTERSUNK HEADS			3	4	4	4	5	5	6	6	6	7	7	8	9	10	11	12

SCREW HEAD STYLES

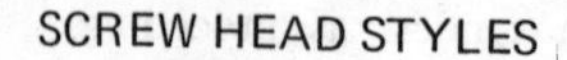

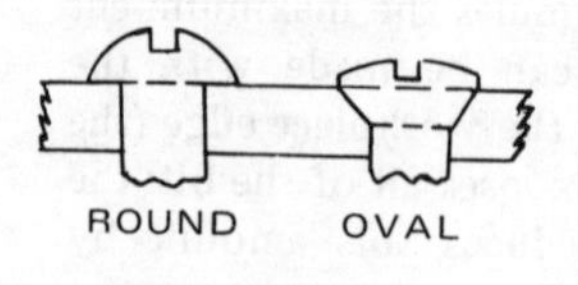

SHEETMETAL SCREWS

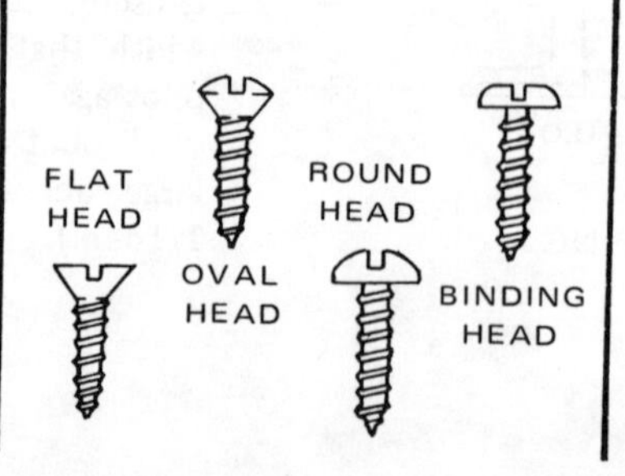

HOW TO MEASURE

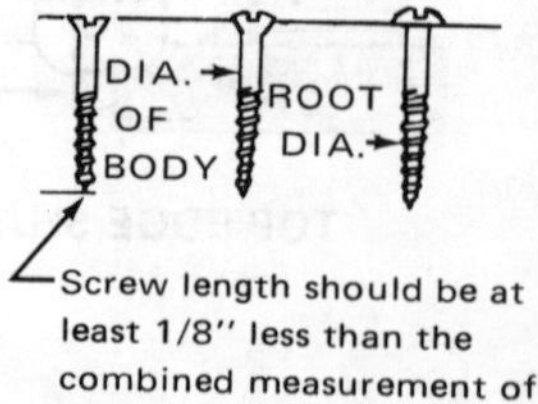

Screw length should be at least 1/8" less than the combined measurement of material being joined.

SCREWS – SIZES AND TYPES

CHAPTER III
FREQUENTLY USED ROUTER OPERATIONS

DESIGN GROOVING

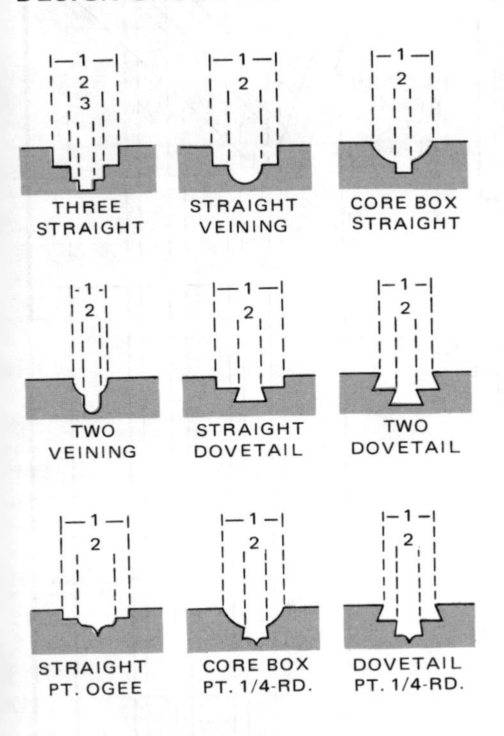

SOME INTERESTING 2- AND 3- BIT GROOVE CUTS

Aside from the various size and shape grooves to be cut with different bits, a little imagination in the planning of combination cuts and the placement of grooves will do much to help you create different and novel grooving patterns. Nine suggestions for groove patterns to be made by combining the cuts of two or more different-type bits, and six basic ways of using grooves to decorate a surface are illustrated. There are many more variations.

When using different-type bits to create a new groove shape it is generally best to start with the widest bit — then the smaller bit(s) may not have to cut deeper than can be cleanly done in a single pass. When doing a number of grooves make all of the first (largest) bit cuts consecutively so you won't have to change the depth setting; afterwards, change the depth setting and make all the next smaller-bit cuts; etc. Be sure to mark (or make note of) your guide settings so you can easily duplicate your set-up for each groove when making second, etc. cuts that must be exactly centered (unless, of course, you purposely desire to offset later cuts to achieve a different effect).

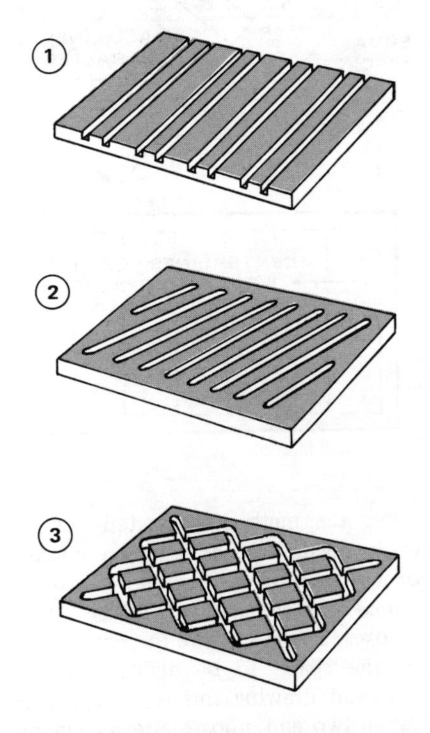

TYPICAL STRAIGHT-LINE GROOVING

No. 1 design for parallel grooves is best done with the multipurpose guide (unless the workpiece is too long to reach in for the

PLANNING GROOVE SPACINGS

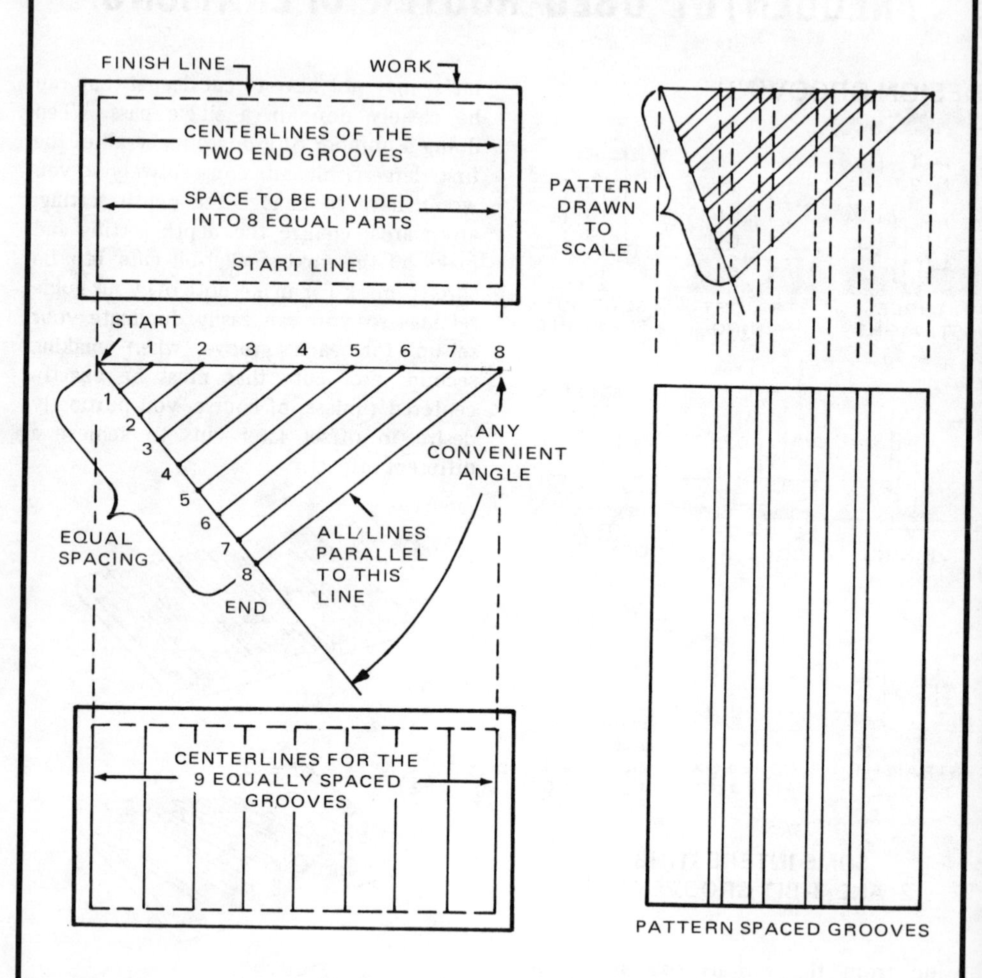

Using the method illustrated you can easily divide any shape or size board — or an area of the board — into any number of equally or oddly spaced grooves. 1. Draw a line the exact width of the space to be divided. (In the left-hand drawing this is the space between two end grooves already planned to be a certain distance from the board ends; in the right-hand one this is the whole width of the board.) 2. Draw a line of any convenient angle to the first. Along this line mark off dots spaced as desired (according to ruler measurements). At the left, these dots are equally spaced and numbered for the number of grooves desired; at the right the dots are proportionally spaced to achieve a desired pattern. 3. Draw a line from the last dot to the end of your first line — then draw lines from all the other dots *parallel* to this last-dot line. 4. Put dots where all these lines cross the first line — then use these dots to mark your groove spacings.

center cuts). One guide setting will serve for two cuts — each pair that are equidistant from the two sides. If workpiece is too long, do all cuts you can with the multipurpose guide, then finish using a straightedge or T-square (*Chapter 2*). Slanted grooves (Nos. 2 and 3) cannot be guided by the multipurpose guide. If the grooves are to run off at front and/or back of workpiece, best use an adjustable T-square guide; but since, as illustrated, they are both blind and stopped, your only practical choice is a box guide (preferably, the adjustable one, *Chapter 2*).

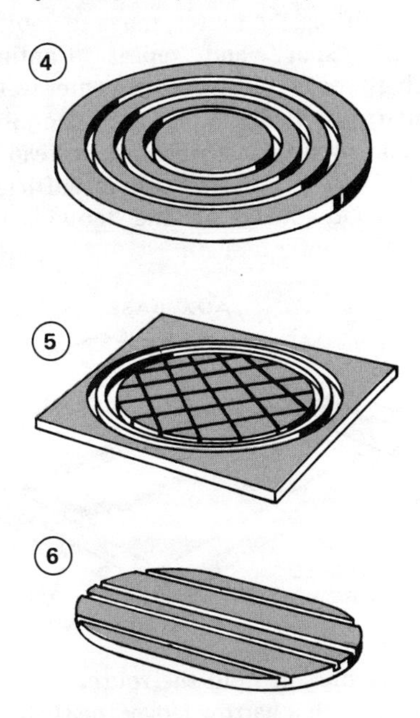

TYPICAL CURVED WORKPIECE GROOVING

The circular grooves for No. 4 can be made with the multipurpose guide or the trammel point (*Chapter 2*). Those for No. 5 must be made with the trammel point (since workpiece is square) . . . and the slanted, straight-line grooves require the box guide. For the elliptical workpiece, No. 6, the grooves can be done with a straightedge guide — or, as indicated by the illustration, you can secure the workpiece to another straight-sided board then use the multipurpose guide.

SURFACING AND INDENTING

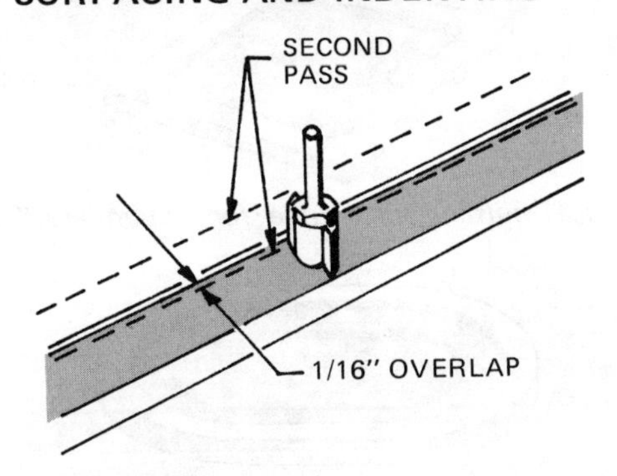

With the pilot removed the rabbet/surface bit (*Chapter 1*) is excellent for glass-smooth surfacing of an entire workpiece top, or of any large indented or raised area. In fact, when used at different depth settings it will quickly and easily produce indented panels of various depths. However, for smoothest results do *not* cut deeper than 1/16-in. per pass; make multiple passes to reach a greater depth. Also, when smoothing an area wider than the bit diameter, plan each new parallel cut to overlap the preceding one by about 1/16-in.

The larger straight bits and the hinge-mortising bit also can be used for these purposes — but, being smaller in diameter, take longer. Then, too, the straight bits do not leave as smooth a surface as the others. However, a small straight bit will make a more nearly square inside corner (for an indented panel), and may be desirable to use for this purpose. In any case, a perfectly square inside corner must be finished with a chisel.

Preferably begin — with whatever bit is chosen for this purpose — by outlining the recessed area. The illustrations show several ways in which area "boundaries" can be accurately outlined. If a small straight bit must be used for the first go-around of the outline, change to the largest possible bit and go around the "boundaries" one or two times more with slightly overlapped cuts — still using the same guides and set-ups — to widen the "boundary" groove

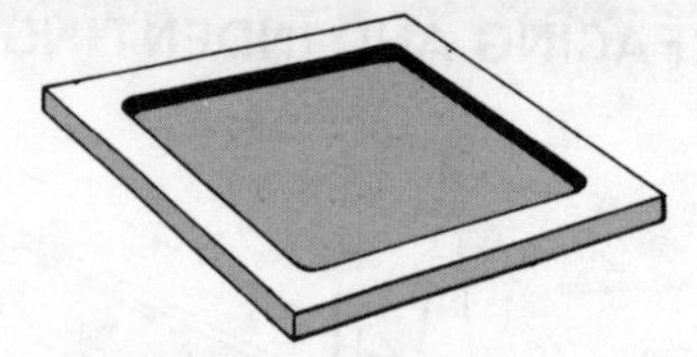

Use multipurpose guide for "boundary."

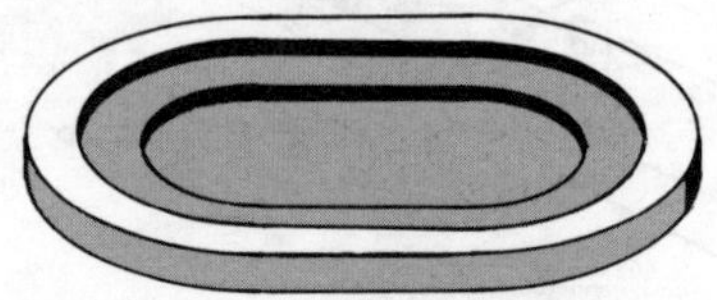

Use multipurpose guide for both "boundaries."

Use Trammel-point for the "boundary."

Do freehand – or with a pattern on top of work.

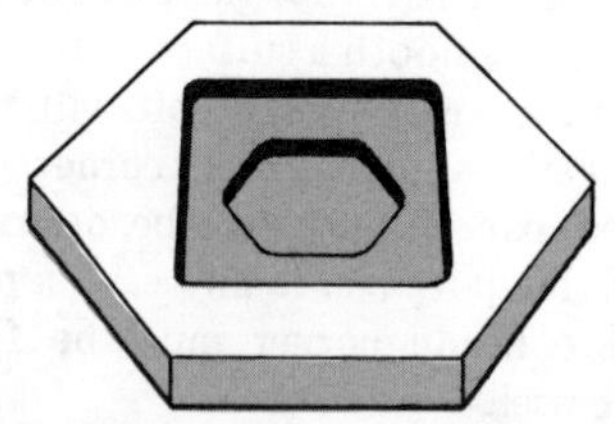

Use multipurpose guide and box guide as needed for "boundaries."

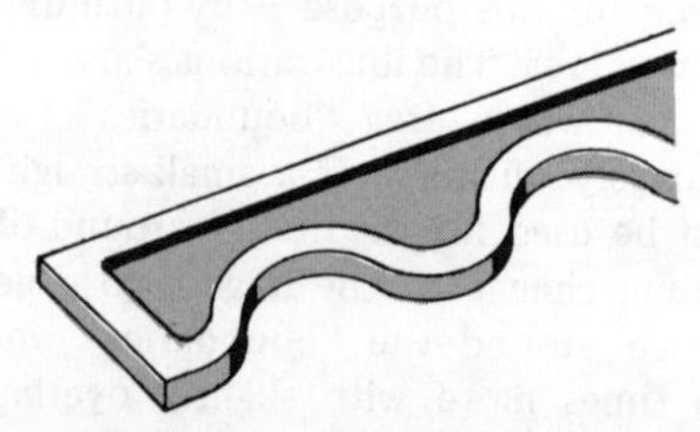

Use multipurpose guide with, then without bracket assembly arm for the "boundaries."

to at least 1-in. Be very careful to obtain the same depth setting for each bit used. (Trying depths on scrap wood is a good idea.)

After the "boundary" groove is completed all around to desired depth, you can finish the center to depth by freehand guiding the router. For this, use the largest possible bit, choose a "spot" at the area center about the size of your router base and circle this once with your bit – then work inward in narrowing circles until the whole "spot" is finished. Afterwards, preferably without lifting the router, move to another adjacent "spot" and repeat. Continue working "spots" out from the center to the boundary in all directions until the job is finished. By working outward, instead of inward, you may always have sufficient uncut wood (outside of the "boundary") to rest the router base on.

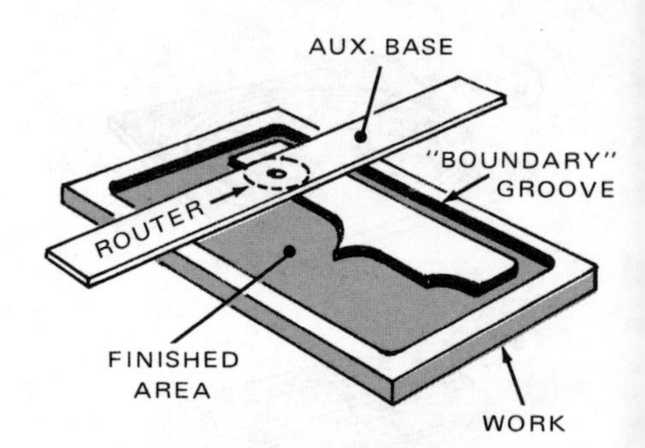

Never attempt to hold the router level by balancing it on a narrow ledge; the slightest dip will spoil your work. If, by chance, an indent area or shape leaves insufficient wood for a firm, level support, you will – *after* cutting the "boundary" groove – have to install an auxiliary router base, such as shown. Use something that won't spring – like 1/4-in. hardboard or heavier plywood. Make it just wide enough to cover the router base, but long enough so that when the router is all the way to either side of the indent this base will still rest on *both* workpiece edges. Remove the router sub-base and install the auxiliary base with the same screws (drilling counter-sunk screw holes as needed).

EDGING AND PANEL RAISING

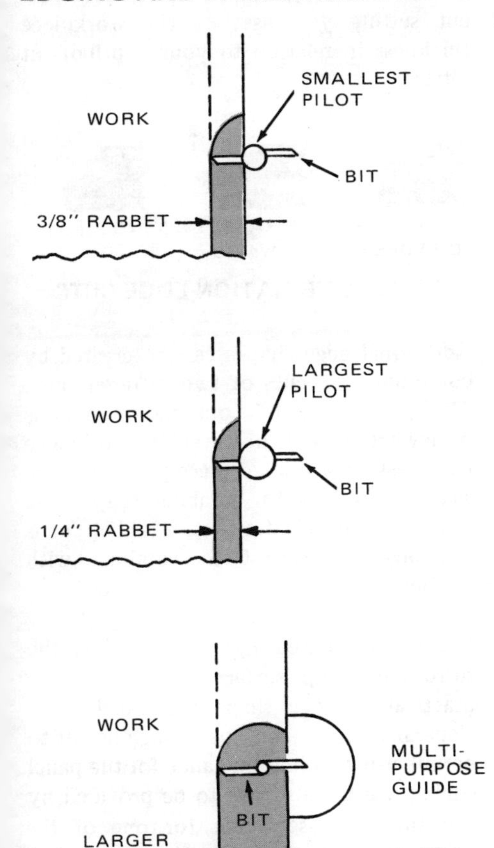

DIFFERENT GUIDES DIFFERENT CUT WIDTHS

NOTE: The following refers specifically to Kromedge bits; cut dimensions, etc. are different for Carbide-Tipped bits. Refer to catalog specifications.

The rabbet/surface bit (*Chapter 1*) is most commonly used for rabbeting a workpiece edge to leave a raised center panel. This bit is furnished with a small pilot and can be used with either of the two (larger) pilots furnished with the arbor set. These three pilots make 3/8-in., 5/16-in. and 1/4-in. wide rabbets, respectively. Wider rabbets can be made with the multipurpose guide (no pilot) . . . however, unless the edges are either straight or curved in a manner easy to follow with the guide and/or the bracket assembly arm, you can do faster, more precise work with one of the pilots.

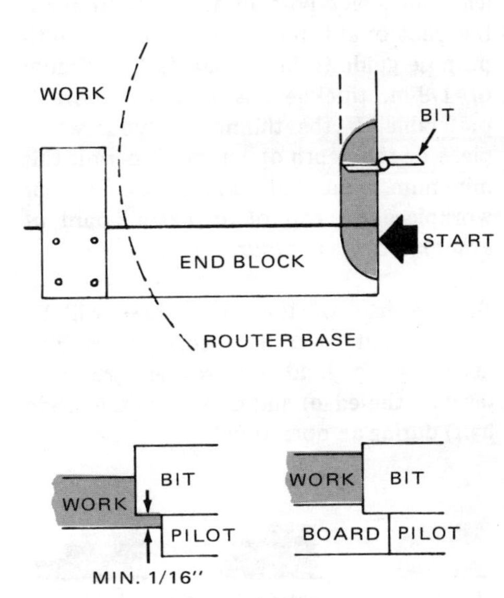

Whether using a pilot or the guide, there are three necessary operating rules:

1. *Never* attempt to start — or to finish — a cut at the end of a workpiece. If started at an end the bit's first bite will be too big — will make too wide a cut and/or splinter the edge (and probably kick the router back rather violently). If run out past an end, the end of the cut will be rounded to a greater width. *Always* start a minimum of the bit diameter in from an end; and stop the cut this same distance from the finish end. If your workpiece is longer than necessary these unfinished ends can later be sawed off. However, if sawing off isn't practical, make and use *end blocks* (as illustrated) in which to start and finish your edge cut. The piece labeled "END BLOCK" must be the same thickness as your workpiece and wide enough to support the pilot or guide; and the two pieces must be securely fastened together.

2. To start an edge cut always feed the bit *slowly*, straight into the edge, then start advancing it to complete the cut. At the finish, pull the bit straight away from the edge *before* turning off the motor.

3. Always plan the depth of your cut to leave an uncut portion at the bottom for the pilot or at top or bottom for the multipurpose guide to bear against. A minimum of 1/8-in. thickness is required; more is preferable. If the thinness of your workpiece or the depth of cut won't permit this minimum, you will have to clamp your workpiece on top of an extra board *of exact matching contour.*

Because half of the router base will be hanging out over the edge, it is also necessary to hold the router firmly in (against the edge) and down (on the inside half) during an operation.

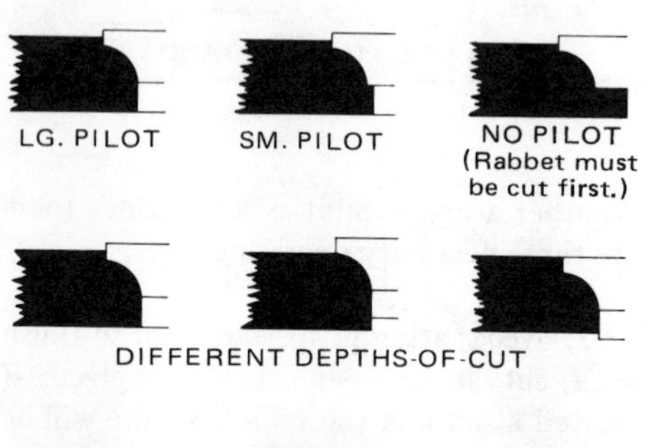

EDGE SHAPES VARIED BY USES

Designed specifically for edge shaping, all of the stemless bits (*Chapter 1*) that require use of the arbor set can be used in the same manner as above. Shafted bits of appropriate shapes also can be used. As shown by the illustration, there different factors can vary the appearance of the finished edge: 1) Whether you use one or another of the pilots or the multipurpose guide (no pilot); 2) The router depth-of-cut setting you use; 3) The workpiece thickness in relation to your depth-of-cut setting.

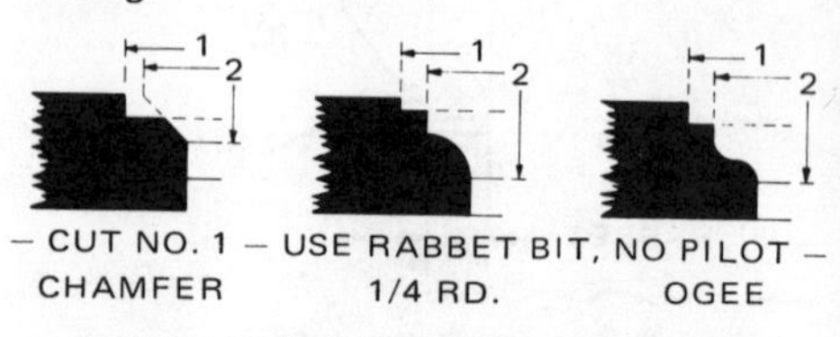

SOME COMBINATION EDGE CUTS

Additional edge shapes can be created by combining the cuts of two different bits. The practicality of combination cuts is somewhat limited, however, by workpiece thickness . . . a thicker piece provides more space in which to combine shapes. As shown by the illustrations, a rabbet cut is generally the easiest to combine with another.

If a panel is raised high enough above the surrounding top surface, it may also be practical to edge shape the panel sides. Generally, there won't be enough height to permit using a pilot; guidance for the panel edging will usually have to be provided by the multipurpose guide (or one of the other guides, *Chapter 2*). The chamfering, core box, point-cutting, cove and bead/1/4-bead/1/4-rd. bits are best suited for this purpose.

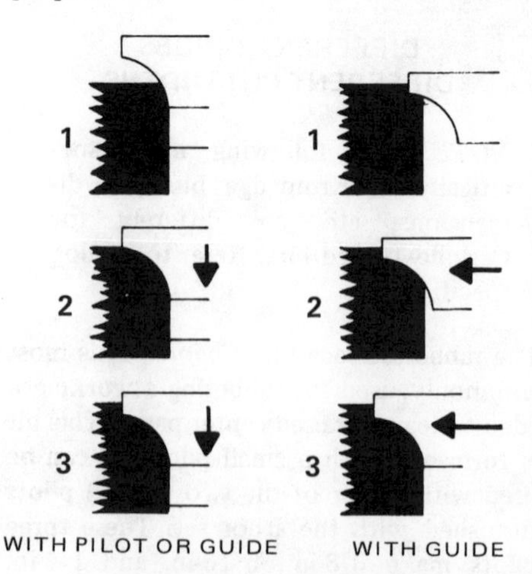

3 SUCCESSIVE PASSES

NEVER OVERLOAD YOUR ROUTER BY CUTTING TOO DEEP OR WIDE

Different woods cut differently — and the maximum amount of wood that can be removed in one pass by an edging cut must be determined by the cutting quality of each workpiece (whether it slows the router and burns, or splinters, etc.). Unless the wood is very hard you generally can make a full, pilot-guided cut in one pass. However, if there is any doubt, best test your planned cut first on a scrap of the workpiece wood. If two or more passes will be needed for a *pilot-guided* cut, always start with a shallow depth-of-cut setting, then deepen the cut as necessary. If two or more passes will be needed for a *no-pilot* cut, you can deepen the cut as above or can start with the full (final) depth-of-cut setting, then adjust your guide to make successively wider cuts as needed.

A DROP-LEAF TABLE

Use either a 3/8-in. bead / 1/4-rd. bit and a 3/8-in. cove bit, or use the two 1/2-in. sizes in combination. As illustrated, the table top edge is shaped with the bead / 1/4-rd. bit; the leaf edge, with the cove bit (*be sure to turn the leaf upside-down for shaping*). Use the large (7/16-in.) pilot with both bits.

NOTE: When setting the depths-of-cuts for the two bits allowances must be made to provide for the dimensions "X" (in table top) and "Y" (in table leaf). For best results, test each cut on scrap to make certain that the table top and leaf will fit together properly.

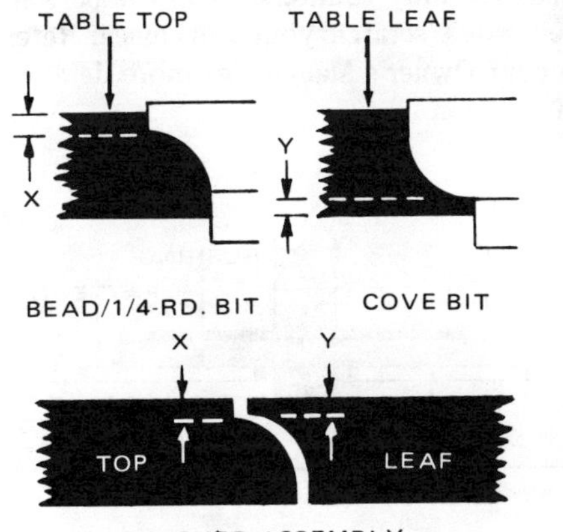

Generally, if the two workpieces are the same thickness, the leaf is cut first — then the top is cut using the same depth-of-cut setting. If the leaf is of thinner material, the second bit must be elevated when edging the top; but if the leaf is thicker, the second bit must be lowered for edging the top.

USING PATTERNS AND TEMPLATES

GUIDE BUSHINGS

The Guide Bushings

This accessory (*Chapter 1*) is required for most pattern and template routing, and for other operations described later. The three sizes refer to the *outside* diameters of the bottom projections, which are used to guide the router along the edge of a pattern. Consequently, the radius of the smallest concave curve of the pattern is the principal factor that determines which size bushing to use — and the smallest curve you can follow (with the smallest bushing) is one having a radius of 5/32" (half of 5/16).

A bushing is installed — with the three screws furnished with the set — at the inner side of the router sub-base. Tighten the screws securely, and make certain the

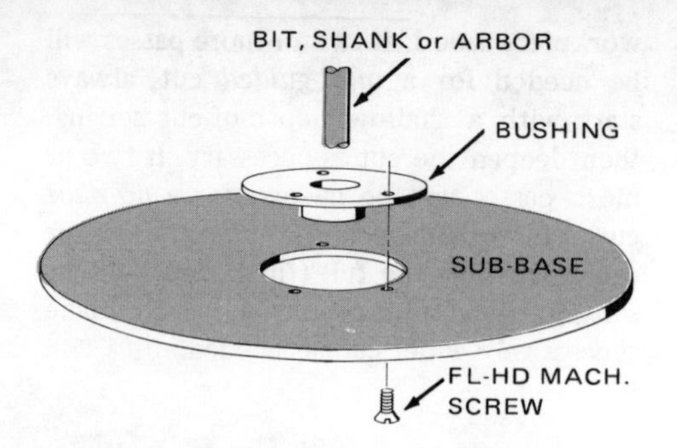

INSTALLING A BUSHING

heads are fully countersunk in the base so they won't scratch your workpiece. Refer to your Owner's Manual for more detailed information.

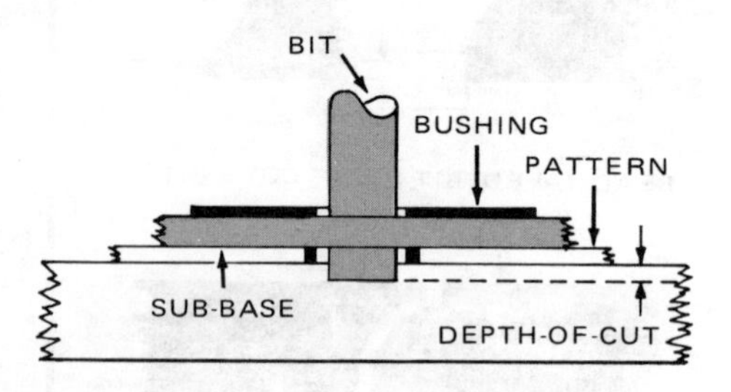

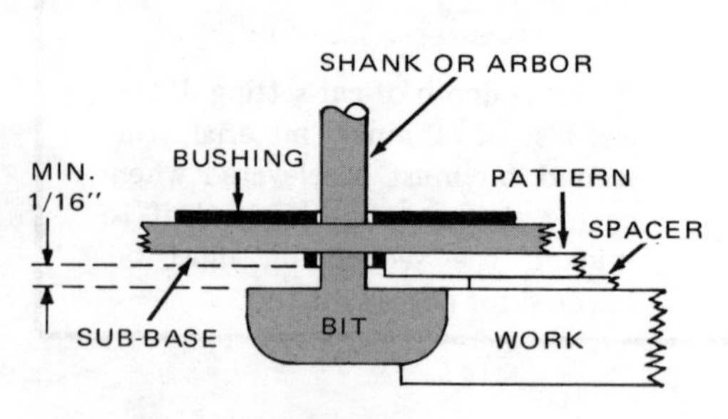

BUSHING SIZE

Other factors that may determine the bushing size are the size (diameter), shape and depth-of-cut setting of the bit to be used. Bits up to 1/4-in. maximum diameter can be positioned with the cutting portion positioned inside of the 7/16-in. bushing; if a larger bit is to be positioned in this manner, a larger bushing *must* be used, even if this means altering some too-small curves of the pattern. However, the 1/4-in. shank (or arbor) common to all bits will fit inside of the 5/16-in. bushing. Therefore, you can use any size bit with this smallest bushing if the top of the cutting portion is lowered to be at least 1/16-in. below the bushing. As illustrated, this may necessitate using a spacer between the pattern and workpiece; but it also might save you from altering a desirable pattern.

Uses of Patterns and Templates

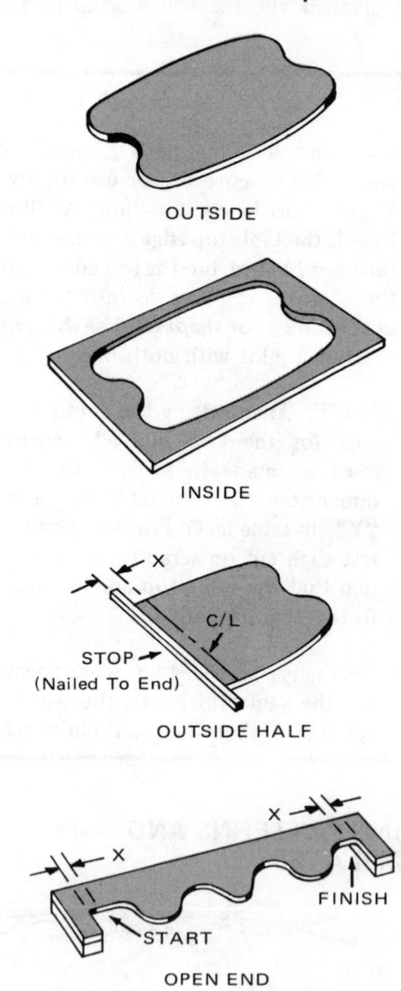

TYPICAL PATTERNS

For our purposes, a *pattern* is any shaped piece that will serve to guide the router for cutting a groove (or a through cut), or shaping an edge to produce a desired outline. Patterns generally are made of plywood or hardboard sawed to shape with a sabre, jig or band saw and, if necessary, filed or sanded to the required smoothness of contour. They are made so that either the multipurpose router guide or, preferably, the side of a guide bushing (or, in some cases the shank or arbor of the bit, or a pilot) will be used for sliding the router along the pattern edge to make the cut. If a bushing or the router guide does the guiding, the pattern edge does not need to withstand friction; 1/4- or 3/8-in. plywood with a *smooth* contact edge can be used. If the shank, arbor or a pilot is used, the pattern should have a harder edge; use 1/8- to 1/4-in. hardboard finished hard on both sides.

A pattern is very useful whenever a number of workpieces are to be identically routed or edge shaped. Also, if a very special shape is to be done to perfection, it may be worth your while to make a pattern even for one workpiece. If the contour of the design is symmetrical, only a half (or quarter) pattern need be made; this can be repositioned on a centerline (drawn on the pattern and the workpiece) for cutting the second half (or the other three quarters). As illustrated, a pattern can be "outside" (for working around) or "inside" (for working within) . . . or one might be made simply for an intricate contour with "open ends" that is to start and finish at precise points.

> *NOTE:* Contoured workpieces that are to be identically edge shaped must be identically sawed to shape if a pilot alone will be used as a guide. When a pattern is used they can be roughly sawed to shape.

A *template* is a pattern made for reproducing an intricate design — generally, to duplicate a carved design, to do inlaying, or to do intricate latticework (by making through cuts). Because the contours to be followed usually have small curves and short lines, either a guide bushing or the shank, arbor or pilot of the bit is used when guiding the router.

A TYPICAL TEMPLATE

In the latter case (due to friction), the pattern must be made of hard material. Moreover, a template takes some time to make and, therefore, should be stout enough for many reuses. We recommend using 1/4-in. hardwood or 1/4-in. hardboard that is hard surfaced on both sides. The same tools as above, plus your router, are generally needed for making a template. A whole template need not be made if a half-, or even a small-part-, template can be repositioned by guide lines on your workpiece to serve the purpose of the whole design.

Making a Pattern or Template for Grooving

Begin by making an exact-size drawing of your design, placing the lines where the

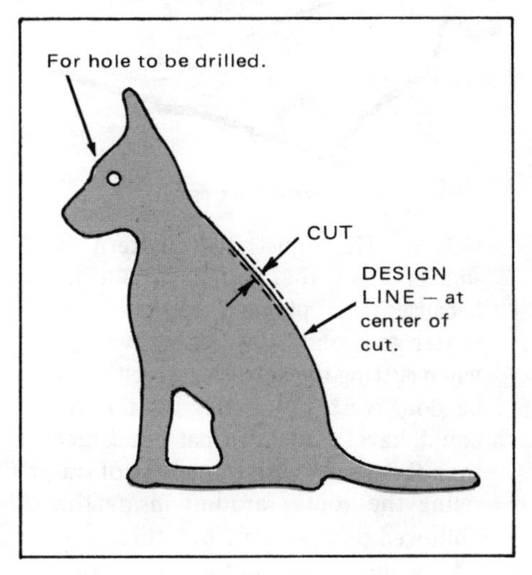

DESIGN FOR ROUTED OUTLINE

center of each cut is to be. Keep in mind that a router cannot cut an inside angle (any such must be chiseled out, later), and the minimum radius of the smallest bushing your set-up will allow you to use. Select your bushing, and note one-half of its diameter (5/32-, 7/32- or 5/16-in.). Add to your drawing the outline for the pattern, keeping the pattern outline *exactly* one-half of the bushing diameter away from the original outline at all points.

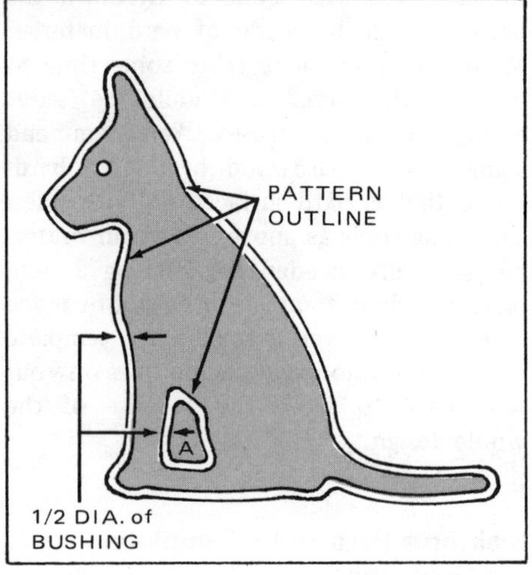

PATTERN DESIGN

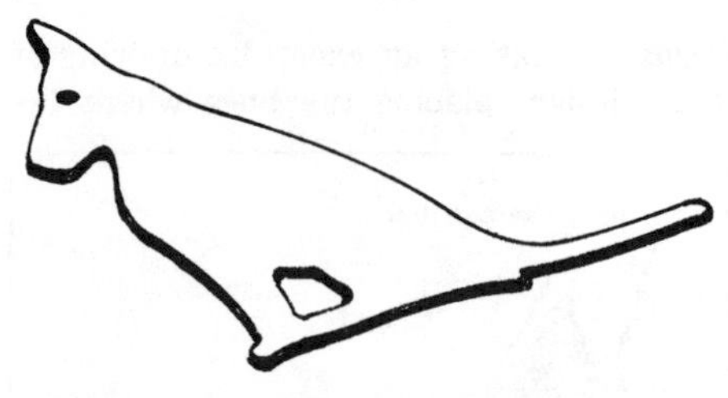

FINISHED PATTERN

NOTE: The illustrated pattern is *smaller* than the design in outline because it is planned to have the router go around the *outside* (except when cutting the area "A" which must be done with the router inside). We could have made the pattern *larger* than the design with the intent of traveling the router around *inside* the hollowed-out pattern, but then area "A" would have had to be a separate piece positioned on the workpiece for the router to travel around its outside. It's easier to use a one-piece pattern; also, when the pattern is smaller the concave curvatures become enlarged on the pattern, which increases the assurance that your bushing can follow them. Although hollowed-out patterns (for inside-edge router guidance) must sometimes be used — as for area "A" — it is better to avoid them if possible.

Transfer the pattern outline to the pattern material, then cut out the pattern.

Making a Pattern for Edge Shaping

Careful measurement of your bit's maximum diameter and some mathematical calculations are required to make an accurate pattern. Begin — as shown in the top views of the four illustrations — by making a drawing of your bit to size on transparent paper, and also show the guide you will use (arbor, bushing or pilot). Add the two lines: "Inside edge of cut" and "pattern edge" (which is always the contact edge of the guide). On a second piece of paper draw a cross-sectional view of the workpiece edge to be shaped, also to size — as shown in the bottom views. Now place the transparent-paper drawing on top of the second one and move it around until you have created the "shape desired" for the edge cut. Afterwards, draw the lines: "Pattern edge" and, if different, "work edge" as shown.

Dimension "X" — the distance between the pattern edge and the inside edge of the cut — will *always* be 1/2 the bit diameter minus 1/2 the guide (arbor, bushing or pilot) diameter. You can calculate the distance "Y" between the pattern and work edges (it is the distance from the work edge to the inside edge of the cut minus dimension "X"), or you can measure it on your drawing.

NOTE: The edge cuts made in views 1 and 2 are identical but, because the bushing (or pilot) diameter is 3/16-in. greater than the arbor diameter, the pattern edge for view 2 cut must be 3/32-in. inside of the workpiece edge (instead of coinciding with it as in view 1). Views 3 and 4 show other edge shapes produced using the bushing when the pattern edge is differently located. Still different shapes can be made if the pattern edge is *outside* of the workpiece edge and/or by raising or lowering the bit.

If the workpiece contour is not *exactly* sawed and sanded to shape, a bushing or pilot (*not* the arbor) must be used so as to contact the finished pattern edge . . . or, the arbor can be used if the pattern projects outside of the workpiece edge at all points.

On your pattern material, first draw a line (straight, contoured, circular, etc.) to represent the workpiece edge to be shaped. Now draw the pattern outline, if it is different, using dimension "Y" to position it correctly inside (or, if this is the case, outside) of the workpiece edge line *at all points.* Cut out your pattern to this shape.

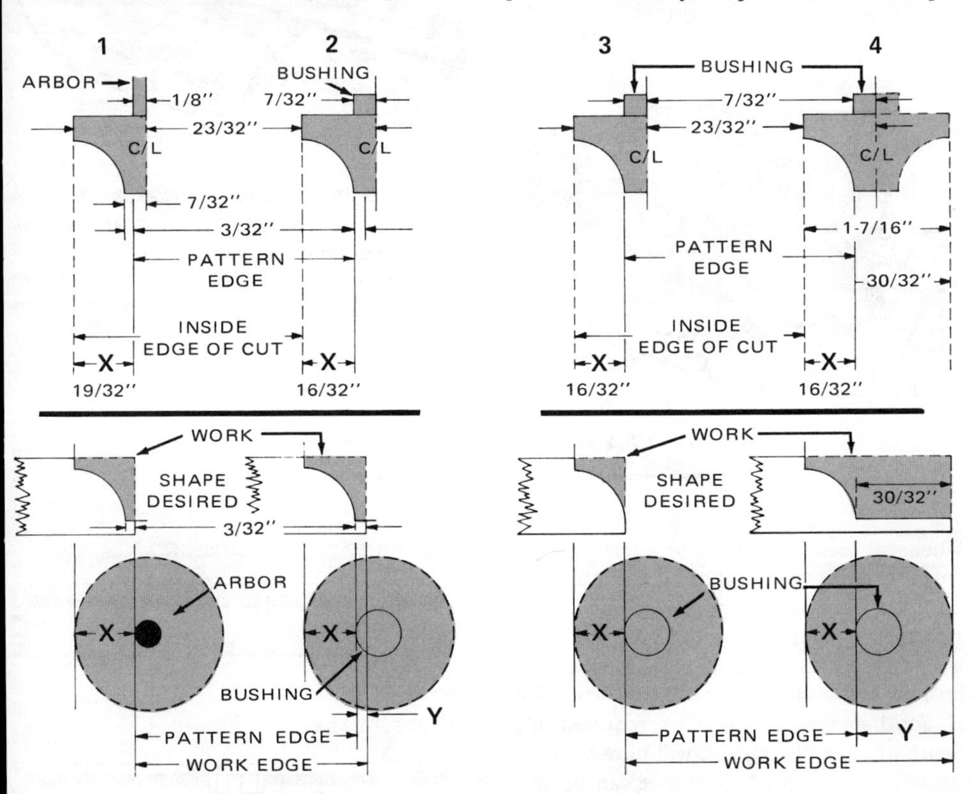

TYPICAL EDGE PATTERNS WITH 1/2" RAD. BEAD BIT AND THE ARBOR OR 7/16" BUSHING AS A GUIDE

NOTE: THE 7/16" PILOT CAN BE USED INSTEAD OF THIS BUSHING

Using a Pattern or Template

The pattern or template must be *firmly* positioned on the workpiece. Depending upon pattern shape you may be able to clamp it to the workpiece (top view) for one, uninterrupted grooving or edge shaping operation . . . or (center and bottom views) you may have to move the clamping device (C-clamps with or without a stiff board, as shown) during the operation. If moving is necessary, be very careful *not* to move the pattern when moving the clamps (or board). *(See next page.)*

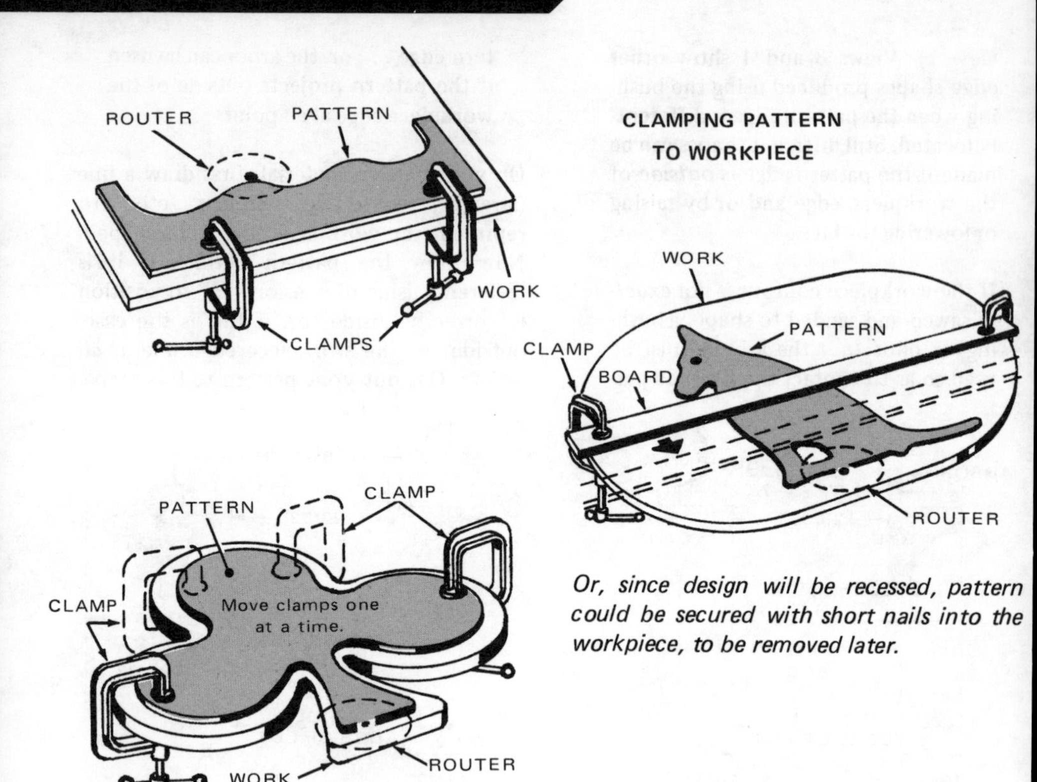

Or, since design will be recessed, pattern could be secured with short nails into the workpiece, to be removed later.

USING A PATTERN OR A TEMPLATE

Whenever using the arbor or a bushing as a guide the pattern should, if possible, be clamped directly onto the workpiece *top*. However, if your pattern material thickness is less than the depth-of-projection of the bushing below the router sub-base (or there is another reason, such as required bit depth-of-cut setting), you will have to use a spacer, as illustrated. A spacer can be any uniformly thick, flat scrap board(s) that is enough smaller than the pattern or its edge to be inside, out-of-the-way . . . and it should be permanently glued or nailed to the underside of the pattern.

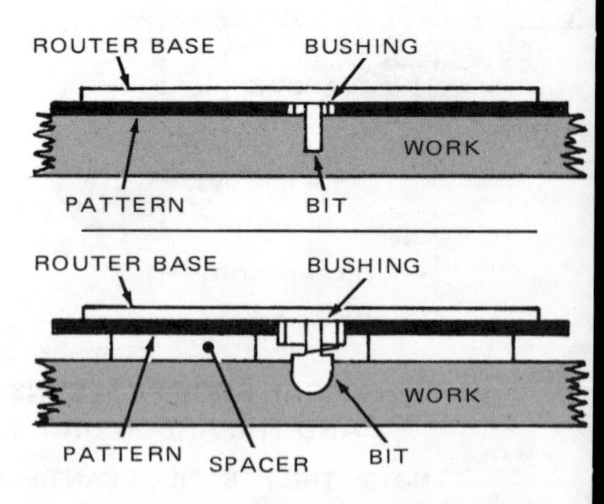

PATTERN ALONE OR WITH SPACER

Whenever using a pilot as a guide the pattern should be clamped (or nailed, if holes aren't objectionable) to the workpiece *bottom*. However, unless the depth-of-cut can be adjusted to allow a small "clearance" as illustrated, a spacer (as above) should be used.

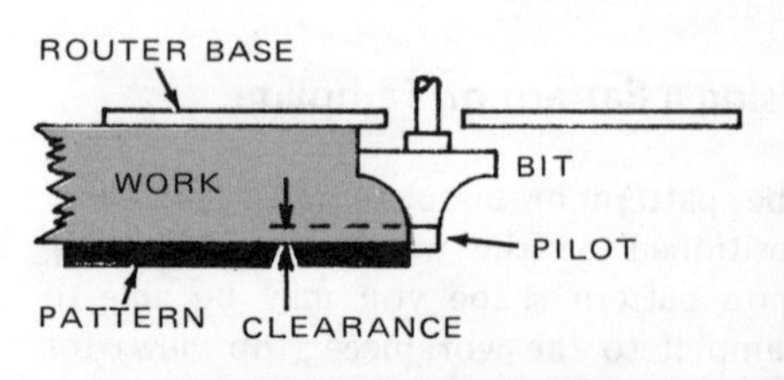

PATTERN WITH PILOT

With your pattern in place, start the router motor. For a groove, lower the bit at the start of the cut; for an edge, push it straight in at the starting point. Complete the cut, then lift the bit straight up (or straight out) at the finish. Throughout, keep the bushing (or arbor) in firm contact with the pattern edge.

CONTOURING AND EDGING WITH THE SAME PATTERN

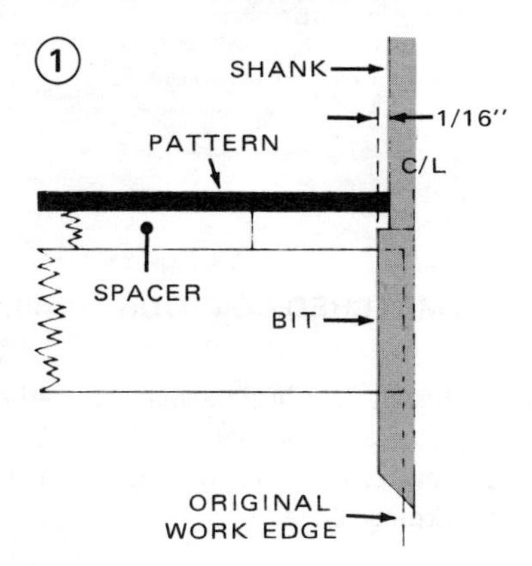

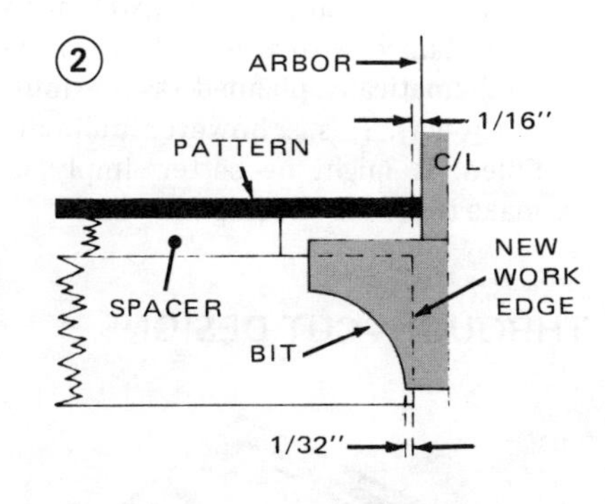

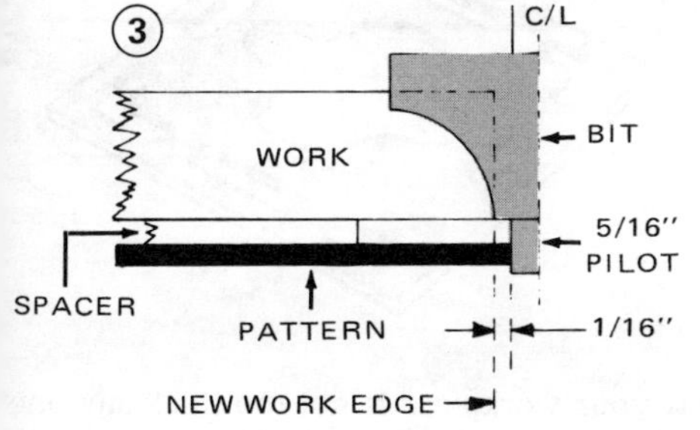

CONTOURING AND EDGING WITH ONE PATTERN

Often, it is very difficult to saw and sand a contoured workpiece to produce an edge smooth and regular enough for a pilot to follow perfectly (a pilot will follow every small imperfection). This is especially so if two or more identical workpieces are needed.

One solution is to make one perfect pattern, rough saw the workpiece slightly oversize (without sanding to smooth it), then perfect the workpiece edge by shaping the contour with a long-enough straight bit. View 1 of the illustration shows use of the *3/8-in. combination panel bit* for this purpose. In this view the workpiece is approximately 1/8-in. oversize and the pattern is 1/16-in. oversize . . . and the bit shank (1/4-in. diameter) is used as the guide. If a 1/4-in. straight bit is used the pattern would have to be exact finished size; or, if a larger (than 3/8-in.) diameter bit is used, the pattern oversize must be increased accordingly.

If a desirable edge shape can now be produced by the width-of-cut this arrangement will allow, the pattern can be reused for the edging operation (*without* moving it). View 2 shows the type cut that will be made by the *1/2-in. radius bead bit*, using the arbor as a guide; and View 3, the type cut if the 5/16-in. pilot is used as a guide. Use of the larger pilot or a bushing would produce other shapes . . . and still other shapes would result if different diameter straight bits had been used for the first operation.

ORNAMENTAL EDGING WITH A MIS-MATCHED PATTERN

After contouring a workpiece edge with a straight bit (*preceding*), the *same* pattern can be repositioned (farther inward or outward with respect to the workpiece edge) to obtain still different edge-shape effects. As illustrated, if the workpiece and pattern edges are straight, moving the pattern does *not* alter the relationship between their contours; the only difference to be gained in the type of edge shape is that which will be produced by a different width-of-cut of the bit. However, if the edges are anything else besides straight, moving the pattern will *mis-match* the contours.

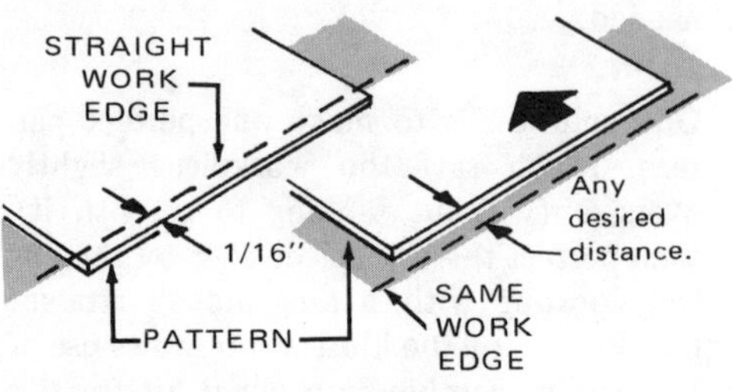

CONTOURS REMAIN MATCHED

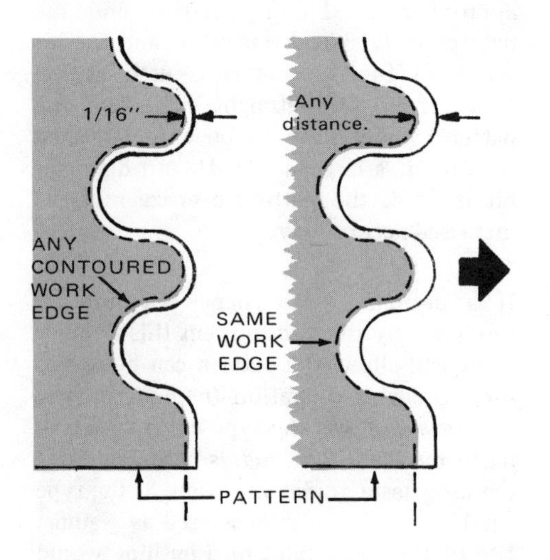

CONTOURS ARE MIS-MATCHED

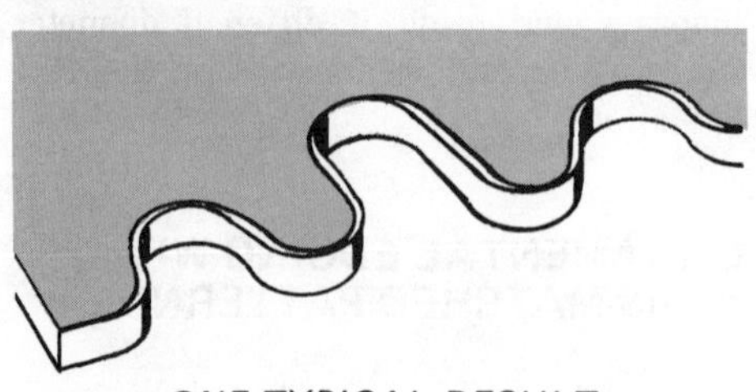

ONE TYPICAL RESULT

When pattern and workpiece edges are mis-matched, the bit's width-of-cut will vary at different points along the contour . . . may even (as illustrated) be reduced to zero at some points, if the mis-matching is sufficient. The edge cut will "feather in and out" to produce novel, ornamental effects. In the cases of circular and elliptical patterns (and workpiece edges) mis-matching like this can be used to create a deep-width cut at one side, feathered out at both ends to leave the opposite side uncut (or less deeply cut).

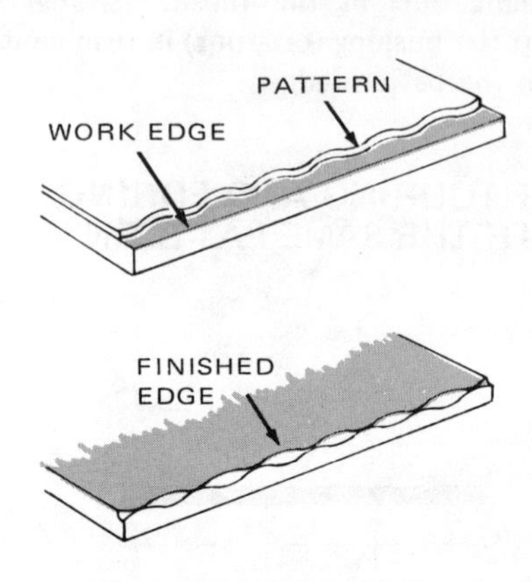

MIS-MATCHED CONTOUR SHAPES

Mis-matching to obtain special shaped-edge effects can also be accomplished by creating a pattern edge entirely different from the workpiece edge.

> *NOTE:* The results of mis-matching to be obtained with various bits can be mathematically planned (as previously shown). This is, however, quite detailed; it might be better simply to make trial runs on scrap material.

THROUGH—CUT DESIGNS

If your workpiece is not too thick any one of the straight or veining bits can be used to make a groove that will penetrate the workpiece thickness, even if several passes are required to complete the penetration.

By using a template to guide the router, through-cut grooving can be planned to "drop-out" areas of the workpiece to leave a design such as illustrated. If not too large in diameter for your design, the *3/8-in. combination panel bit* is best for this purpose (since it is pointed). Start each groove cut with the router positioned by your pattern, start the motor . . . then slowly adjust the depth-of-cut for the first pass. If necessary, after completing the first passes for all grooves, repeat the operation until the cut-throughs are finished.

The edges of cut-through areas can, afterwards, be edge shaped . . . by using a different bit with the same or a different pattern, as previously told.

MAKING INLAYS

Inlaying requires the use of *two matched templates* — a male, with which the inlaying material is cut to shape (by through-cutting), and a female, with which the workpiece is routed (indented) to the depth of the inlaying material. A *1/4-in. straight bit* is the easiest to use for both operations. If the design is small, you must use the bit shank as a guide; otherwise, one of the bushings can be used (but will require additional calculations). Keep in mind that the radius of your guide (shank or bushing) will determine the smallest concave curvature that your female template can have . . . any concave curvature smaller than this — or any inside angle — will have to be finished with a chisel. (Male template curvatures are less important because each mated concave curve of the male template will have a greater radius than the one in the female template.)

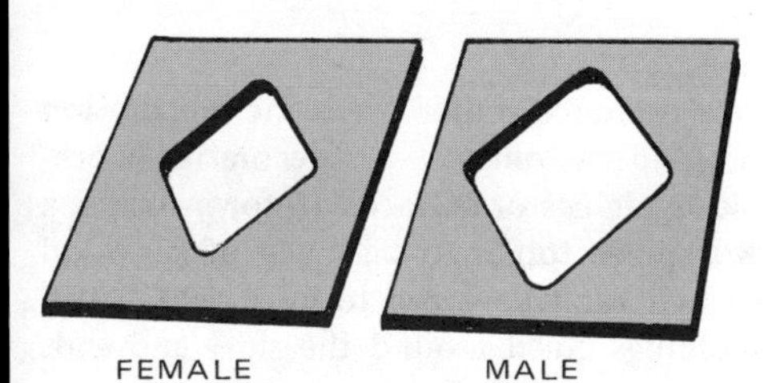

MATCHED INLAY TEMPLATES

NOTE: Inlaying material can be any desired thickness, but 1/16- to 1/8-in. is generally considered best.

After selecting the bit and bushing (if there will be one) to be used, plan your two templates, the outside dimensions of which should match your workpiece for easy positioning. First, make an exact (to size) drawing of your design.

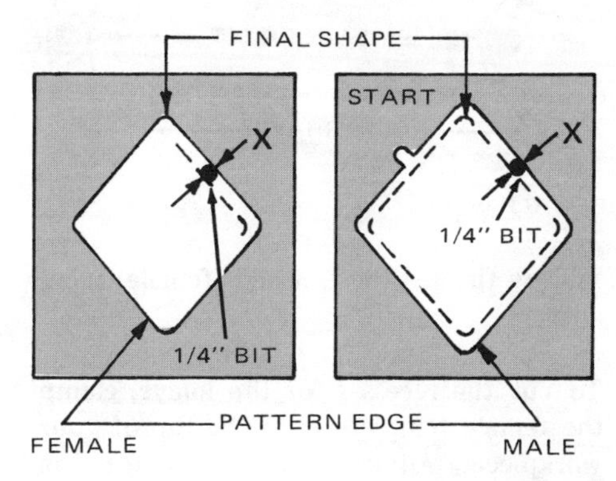

SIZING TEMPLATE OPENINGS

Transfer this to the female template. If the 1/4-in. straight bit is to be used, the female template openings will be *exactly the same* as the design openings; but if a larger diameter bit is to be used (or a bushing), the female design openings must be smaller by dimension "X" (bit radius *minus* guide — shank or bushing — radius).

Transfer your design to the male template. If the 1/4-in. straight bit is to be used, the male template openings will be larger by dimension "X" (exactly 1/4-in. all around). However, if a larger diameter bit or bushing will be used, dimension "X" becomes the bit radius *plus* the guide radius. To assure an easy fit of the inlay pieces, enlarge dimension "X" by up to 1/64-in. In order to provide a starting point for the cut, somewhere along the edge of each shape make an indent ("START") equal in radius to the radius of your bit.

After plotting the openings for the two templates, make the openings as accurately as possible. If completely accurate, the finished (male) inlay pieces will just

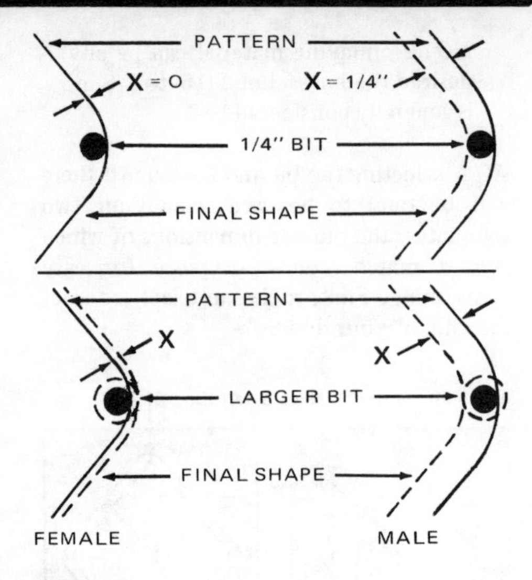

snuggly fit into the finished (female) inlay areas.

To cut the recesses for the inlays, clamp the female template onto the top of your workpiece. Adjust your router for the desired depth-of-cut. Start the motor and lower the bit into one of the cut-out template areas, then proceed to rout out this area (to a flat bottom) using the template for the boundaries. Do all cut-out areas in the same way.

NOTE: For flush-at-top inlays the depth-of-cut is the inlay material thickness plus a scant 1/64-in. for glue. The depth-of-cut can, however, be varied to produce inlays that are recessed or raised.

To cut the inlays, clamp the male template onto the top of your inlay material – with a same-size flat scrap board of at least 1/8-in. thickness underneath the inlay material. Adjust your router depth-of-cut to cut through the inlay material and about half-way down into the scrap. Start each inlay cut by lowering the bit into the pattern "START" recess, then rout the outline *without* cutting inside of the outline boundary. Any slight "bump" left where the "START" recess is can be sanded away, afterwards.

NOTE: Instead of an inside-cut male pattern, as described, outside-cut male patterns can be used. In this case, a separate pattern for each inlay design must be made – and each must be secured to the inlay material for routing-around (to cut out the inlay piece) – which, if designs are small, will present a problem. An outside-cut male pattern is the *same* size as the female for the same design, except it should be up to 1/64-in. *smaller* to allow for the inlay fitting. No "start" recess is needed since all the material around the pattern outline is waste.

To produce a simple design – such as an inlayed chessboard – it is often easier to saw-cut the inlay pieces. Afterwards, use these pieces to plan your female template (you can lay them in place and draw around them – and the pencil-line thickness will provide the clearance needed for fitting them in).

After glueing the inlay pieces into place, if a perfectly flush surface is desired it is best to sand the top as needed. By using differently colored and/or grained woods, as well as shapes, an infinite variety of novel inlays can be produced.

MAKING STRIP MOLDINGS

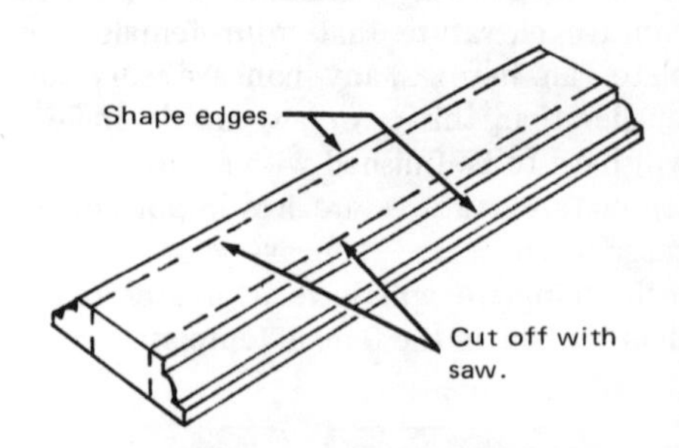

One desirable router use is the preparation of strip moldings – for decorating workpiece edgings or surfaces. If, for instance, a workpiece top is to be made of plywood (which can't be edged to look right), strip moldings glued around the sides and ends will make it look like solid (good quality) wood.

To make strip moldings simply use good, solid wood — any thickness and/or width suitable — and edge shape one or both edges as already told. Afterwards, saw-cut off the shaped edges — to any width desired — then, square-cut these strips to length (or miter the ends) to fit your workpiece. If the original board is wide enough, you can us it to produce a number of strips.

In addition, if a cut-off pre-edged strip is wide enough, it can be edged on the opposite side. This results in a two-sided formed strip that can then be cut to lengths and glued to a workpiece surface to form square, rectangular, or other-sided embossed-panel effects.

A MALE-TEMPLATE BOX

When very small inlay pieces are needed, one way to handle the cutting of them is shown. Make the box so that your male template is the hinged lid — and the inlay material plus the scrap needed underneath (to assure clean cut-outs) will be supported firmly under this "lid."

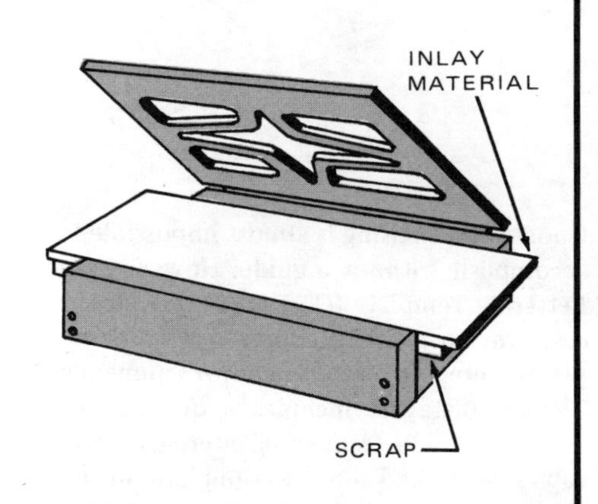

CHAPTER IV
SOME SPECIAL ROUTING OPERATIONS

SIGN MAKING WITH THE LETTERING TEMPLATE

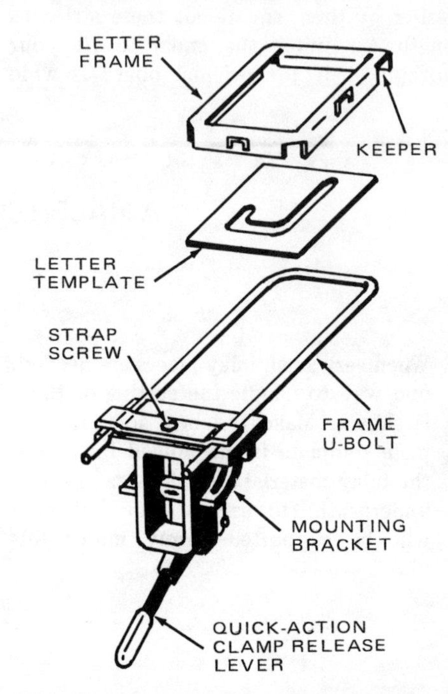

Good letter incising is almost impossible to accomplish without a guide. However, the Lettering Template (*Chapter 1*) provides an easy way to produce engraved signs, name-plates, etc. in letters and/or numerals. The template set includes a quick-action clamp-on guide frame and interchangeable capital-letter and numeral templates in two sizes (1-1/2-in. and 2-1/2-in. in height). It also includes two router guide bushings: a 5/8-in. bushing to be used with a 3/8-in. diameter or smaller router bit (a 5/16-in. size is recommended) for the 2-1/2-in. high templates — and a 7/16-in. diameter bushing to be used with a 1/4in. diameter or smaller router bit for the 1-1/2-in. high templates. Straight, veining or other router bits with cutting diameters mentioned can be used.

Install the proper bushing on your router (*refer to "Using Patterns and Templates"*, *Chapter 3* and to the Owner's Manual furnished with your template). To setup the guide, place your first letter template in the letter frame and place this frame on the frame U-bolt with the keeper engaged over the frame U-bolt end. Position your work-piece on the workbench parallel to its front edge, with the guide on top of the work-piece at the location of the first letter — then tighten the guide clamp. Loosen the strap screw, slide the frame U-bolt in or out to position the letter template on the desired horizontal line, then tighten the screw.

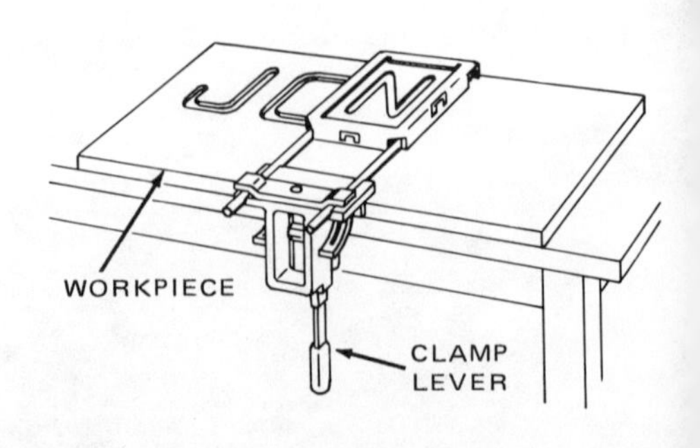

With the bit elevated above cutting level, position the router on the template with the guide bushing firmly against an *outside* edge of the letter template cut-out. Start the motor and adjust to the desired depth-of-cut. Rout around the letter cut-out to the starting point, keeping the guide bushing in contact with the *outside* edge of the letter cut-out. Lift the router straight up from the template.

For all succeeding letters, leave the depth-of-cut setting *exactly* as it is and do *not* alter the frame U-bolt setting. Remove the letter frame to insert the next needed letter template, and replace it as before. Loosen the guide clamp and move the guide horizontally to the next letter position, then retighten the clamp. For all letters and numerals, including "1" and "I", consistent letter spacing can be had by aligning the left edge of the letter frame with the right edge of the previously cut letter.

Vertical lettering can be done by rotating the square letter templates 90° in the letter frame, and by moving the guide down one side, instead of across the bottom, of the workpiece. Slant line or up-and-down lettering can be done by loosening the strap screw to reposition the frame U-bolt as desired for each succeeding letter. Other novel effects can be obtained by varying the depth-of-cuts and/or by coloring the incised letters. *Refer to your Owner's Manual.*

USING THE ROUT-A-SIGNER

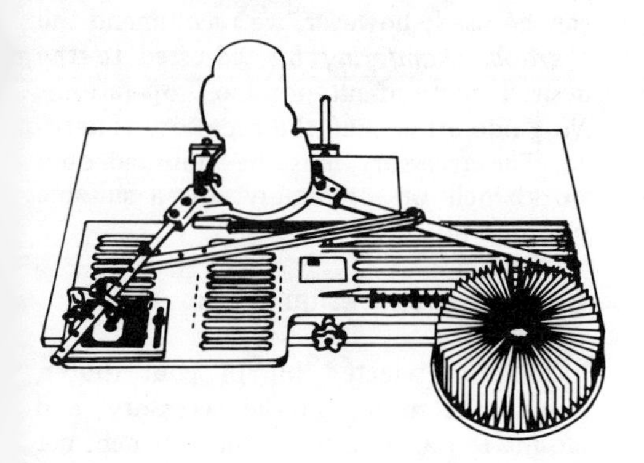

This is a lettering device that uses letter and numeral templates (similar to those of the lettering template, preceding) but, instead of directly guiding the router, each template is used to guide a stylus or an arm by which the router is guided. Hence, the two sets of block letters and numerals furnished (a 1-1/2-in. and a 2-1/2-in. high set) can be used to produce carved lettering from 3/4-in. to 4-1/2-in. in height, and these letters will be slanted to the right. They can be letter spaced by three different adjustable amounts and/or varied in sizes (such as having a larger letter to begin each word), and can be inscribed in one or up to four lines on a workpiece from 2-in. to 10-in. wide, from 1/2-in. to 2-in. thick, and of any length required. A convenient carousel for holding the 58 templates is furnished; also storage spaces for the seven router bits recommended for use with this accessory (the bit set is sold separately; *refer to a Current Sears Catalog*). The accessory comes partially assembled with an Owner's Manual (to cover assembly and basic operating instructions) and a how-to and idea booklet.

INSERTING TEMPLATE IN HOLDER

The seven-piece bit set recommended includes a 1/8-, 1/4- and 3/8-in. straight bit, a 1/2-in. V-groove chambering bit, a 3/16-in. veining bit, a double-end 45°/60° V-groove bit, and a 1/2-in. core box bit. The 1/8-in. bit is used to create 1- and 1-1/8-in. high letters that can be one-line centered on a 2-in. wide workpiece. A 1/4-in. bit is needed for 1-1/4- to 2-in. high letters one-line centered on a 4-in. wide workpiece; a 3/8-in. bit for 1-1/4- to 3-1/2-in. high letters on a 6-in. wide workpiece; and a 1/2-in. bit for 3- to 4-1/2-in. high letters on 8- and 10-in. wide workpieces. The smaller-size templates are for letters up to 3-in. high; the larger size templates for letters from 2- to 4-1/2-in. high. Bits other than the 1/8- to 3/8-in. straight sizes are needed for inscribing V-bottom letters. Bottom-cutting bits of like sizes having different shapes (such as a 1/2-in. straight, open or classic bit — *refer to Chapter 1)* also can be used for different effects.

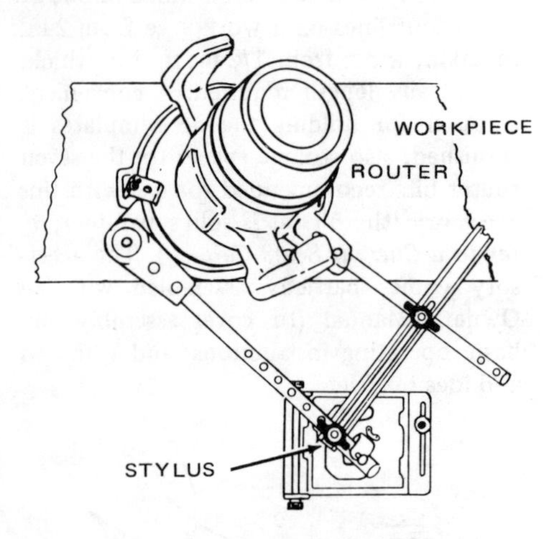

Your router — as it is without alteration — quickly mounts on the accessory router plate using bolts, etc. furnished. The workpiece is also quickly and easily mounted — on the accessory table — with a locking lever. Guide grooves on the accessory table are used for router positioning to locate the scribed letters with respect to a workpiece width. Templates can be quickly inserted or removed from the template holder. Other adjustments — for letter height, slant and spacing — are easily made. Two- to four-line signs are line spaced by using different ones of the table grooves for line centering. The actual engraving of each letter is accomplished by lowering the (revolving) bit, after adjusting the router for depth-of-cut, into the workpiece and then guiding the stylus through the template cut-out of the letter.

GUIDED DESIGN ROUTING

Uses of the 2-Dimensional Rout-A-Form

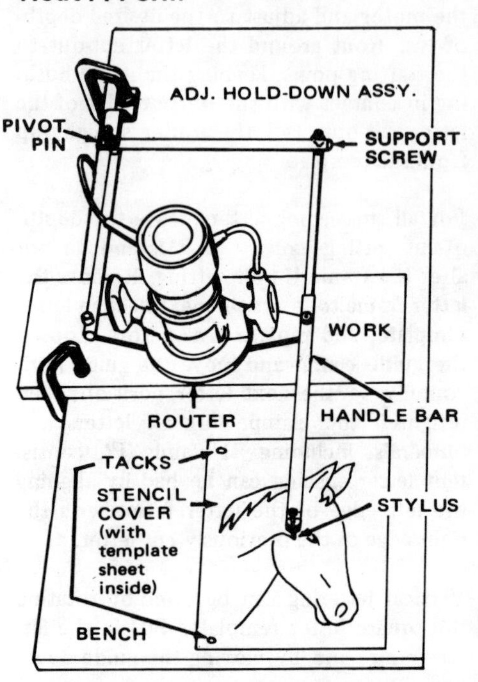

A great improvement over freehand routing, the *Craftsman* Rout-A-Form accessory (*Chapter 1*) enables even an amateur to produce intricately detailed, engraved designs, monograms and fancy lettering with ease and precision. The accessory guides the router movements as you use its stylus to trace any copied or original design that you wish to reproduce. Carved reproductions can be made at 42, 50 or 58 percent of the design size. Any suitable shanked bit can be used; however, we recommend the *V-groove/chamfering bit*, adjusted to the desired depth-of-cut, for most operations. *No* guide other than the accessory is needed. The accessory must be mounted on a workbench or, preferably, on a suitable plywood board.

Limited Area Design Work

Install the selected bit in your router, mount the router on the accessory, and mount the accessory on a workbench, per the Owner's Manual instructions. The position of the router on the fixture determines the amount of reduction (42, 50 or 58 percent) that will result when the design is copied.

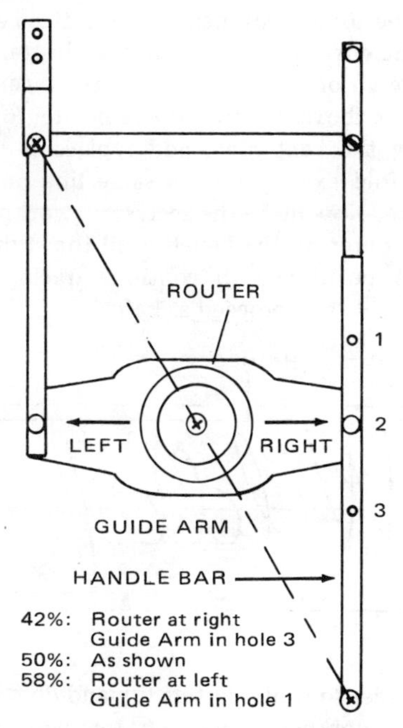

With the accessory handle bar approximately at 90° to the workpiece edge, as shown, position the stencil cover (furnished with the accessory) centered under the stylus — folded edge at the left — then thumbtack it in place. Your design drawing ("template sheet") can now be placed inside of the stencil cover.

Begin with the router bit adjusted up so that it won't touch the work when the router base is flat on the work. Use the handle bar and move the stylus to a starting point on your design. Holding it thus, start the router motor and adjust the depth-of-cut to your predetermined setting. *Without* further touching the router, firmly but gently guide the stylus accurately around your design lines as continuously as possible. Wherever a line breaks off and a new one starts, lift the handle bar up high enough to lift the bit out of the workpiece — then let it down again to reposition the stylus at the new line starting position. To follow a straight line use a ruler or straightedge to guide the stylus along. French curves, triangles and other suitable manufactured shapes can similarly be used where appropriate.

Extended Area Lettering and Design Work

The maximum workpiece area that a design can cover with one set-up is limited to approximately one-half the area of the stencil cover. If your template sheet is larger than the cover (higher and/or wider), or if your design calls for use of two or more template sheets (as when lettering), either the accessory or the workpiece must be moved to complete the design.

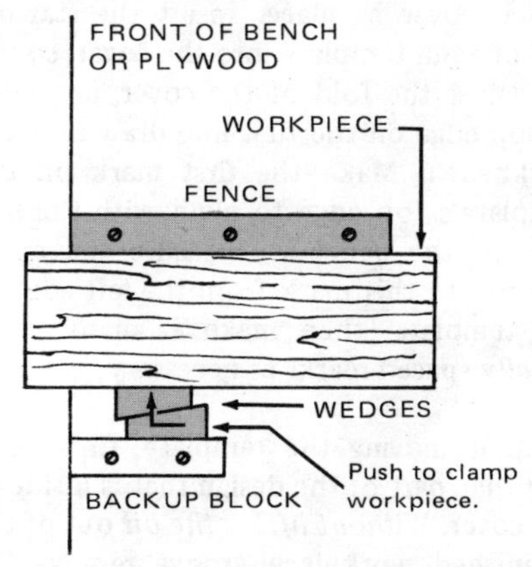

For easy and accurate work movement use suitable scrap wood to serve as a fence and a back-up block, as illustrated. Mount the fence and backup block, with screws, either on your workbench or on a large enough piece of 3/8- or 1/2-in. plywood (which can be set aside when not in use). Allow space between these parts for the width of your workpiece and the two wedges (which are furnished). The wedges are designed to securely hold the workpiece, or to quickly loosen and allow it to move in a straight line along the fence.

For carving a long, continuous design, the template on which your design is drawn must have a straight top edge, parallel to the design centerline. Locate the position of the stencil cover, as previously told, and

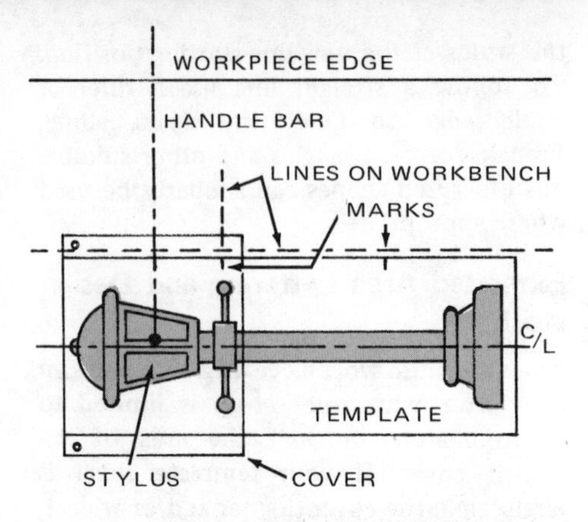

mark the workbench so you can relocate it – then draw two lines on the workbench as illustrated; one *parallel* to the workpiece edge, the other at 90° to the first. Tack the stencil cover in place. Insert the starting end of your template into the cover, squarly against the fold of the cover, and with its top edge on the first line drawn on the workbench. Make the first mark on the template's top edge to align with the 90° line on the bench . . . measure the exact distance to this mark from the left edge of the template, then make as many more *equally* spaced marks as necessary.

Without moving the template, finish cutting that part of the design that is inside of the cover. *Without lifting the bit* out of the unfinished workpiece groove remove the template from the cover, fold it *squarely, exactly* on the line of the first mark – then re-insert it in the cover with its top edge exactly on the same workbench line and its folded edge against the cover fold (so that mark number 2 will now be aligned with the 90° line on the bench). Loosen the wedges and slide the workpiece to the left – *with the bit still in the groove* – until the stylus is again correctly positioned on your design. Tighten the wedges and proceed with the operation.

Any length (left-to-right) design can be copied in this manner. However, if your design is also too high (top-to-bottom) to fit within the stencil cover, you have an additional problem that can be solved only by relocating the accessory, router and workpiece on the bench. The best way to accomplish this is to draw a centerline (as illustrated) on your template. When the template is inside the cover this centerline will be somewhere nearer the bottom edge of the cover than shown in the illustration. Carve all of the design down to the centerline, as above. Remove the template, fold it along the centerline, and replace it with this fold exactly on the same line on the bench. Now move the accessory, workpiece and router on the bench until the stylus is again positioned to continue tracing the design – then proceed as before.

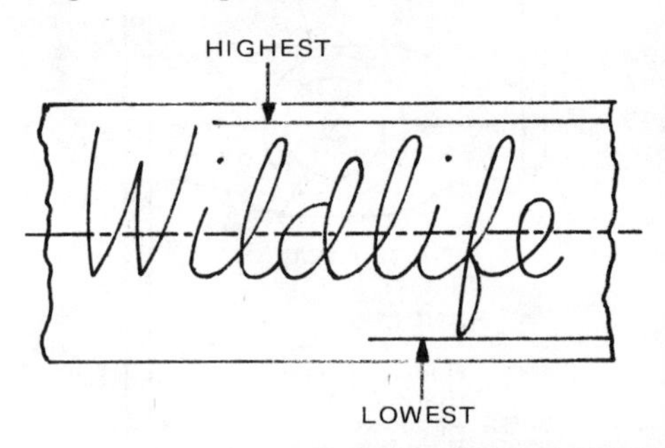

In order to center letters (up-and-down) on your workpiece, on your template mark the top of the highest letter and the bottom of the lowest one. Measure and accurately mark the centerline between the first two marks. Also mark your workpiece centerline (between its top and bottom edges). Now, when making your set-up, position your workpiece so that the router bit will rest exactly on the workpiece centerline. Position the stencil cover, with the template in it, so the stylus will rest exactly on the template centerline. Draw a line on the workbench where the top edge of the template is, and parallel to the workpiece (as in the preceding). All you need do now to keep your words centered on the workpiece is to keep the top edge of the template on this line.

Any design can be centered in this manner.

Capital letters – or any similar design to be made from a sequence of templates – require proper spacing to look right. The

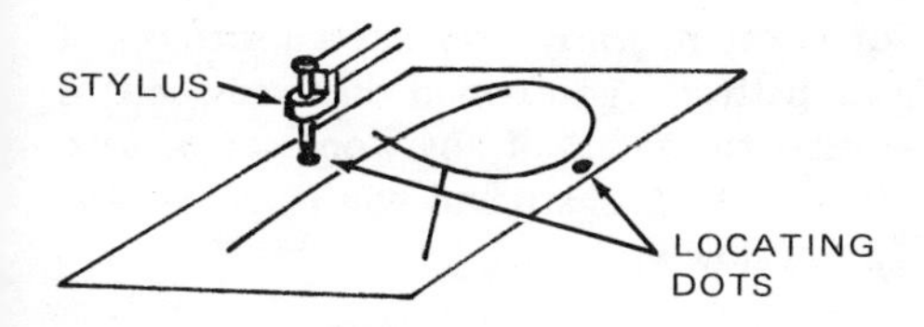

templates furnished with the accessory have "locating dots" — and similar dots can be made on any series of templates by laying them out as desired then marking them with matched marks.

To use the dots, after completing one template, lift the handle bar to lift the bit *out of* its groove, and place the stylus directly over the *right-hand* template dot. *Without* moving the handle bar, insert the next template in the cover, in the *same* position as the first (use the fold edge of the cover). Move the workpiece to the left until the stylus is directly above the *left-hand* dot of this new template. Lock the wedges, and proceed with the work.

The Owner's Manual, packaged with the fixture, contains useful suggestions for finishing your workpiece.

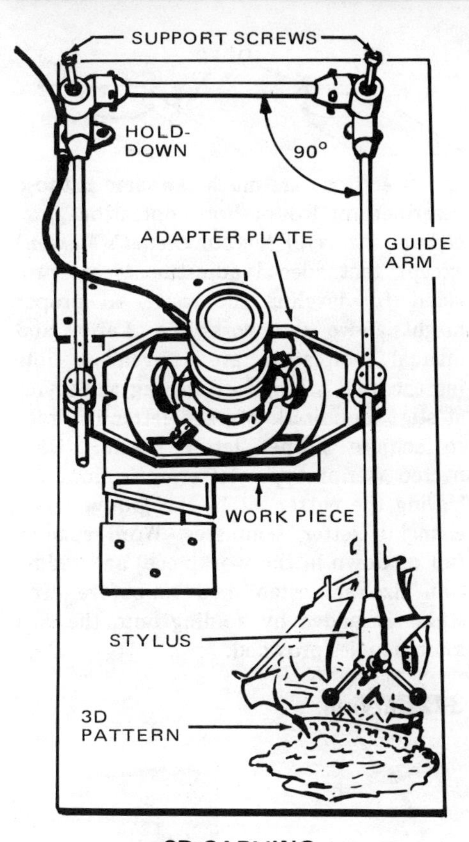

3D CARVING

Uses of the 3-Dimensional Router Pantograph

This deluxe accessory will enable you to create three-dimensional embossed or engraved plaques and similar low-relief ornamentations, as well as the two-dimensional lettering and design work described for the Rout-a-Form, preceding. Four different letter styles are furnished — Old English, Oriental, Script and Modern — with both upper and lower case letters (52 templates per style), plus one style — Computer — with upper case only, plus 10 numerals and 10 designs for line-drawing work. For three-dimensional work you can use any convenient pattern having a maximum size of 13-in. high by 24-in. long by 1-1/4-in. thick — made of plaster, metal, wood, etc. — that can be traced by the stylus. Carved (two- or three-dimensional) reproductions of the templates or patterns can be made at 40-, 50- or 60-percent of the original. No other guide is needed, but the accessory must be mounted on a workbench or suitable plywood board per Owner's Manual instructions for assembly.

Template Lettering, and Design Work

The V-groove chamfering bit (*Chapter 1*) is recommended for most lettering and design work, but either straight or veining bits in small diameter sizes can be used. Set-ups

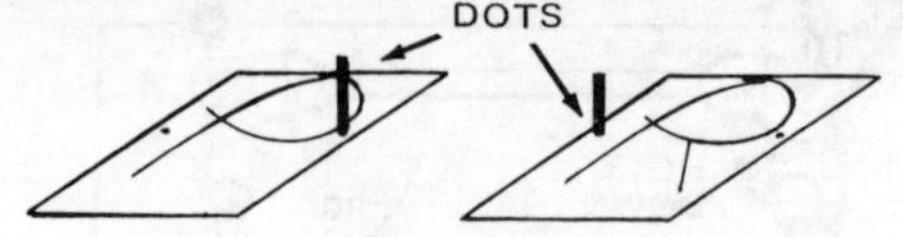

and operations are much the same as those described for Rout-a-Form operations, preceding (*also refer to your Owner's Manual*) except that special adjustments are provided for leveling the router at proper height above the workpiece. Letter and manual templates have convenient dots (at the two sides) for locating the stylus at start and finish of each letter in order to achieve proper letter spacing. Connected (script type) lettering is done by leaving the cutter bit in the groove while changing letter templates. Word spacing (up or down in the workpiece) and reduction size are established as before. The stylus is guided by holding onto the two knob handles provided.

3-D Carving

PATTERN

ENGRAVING

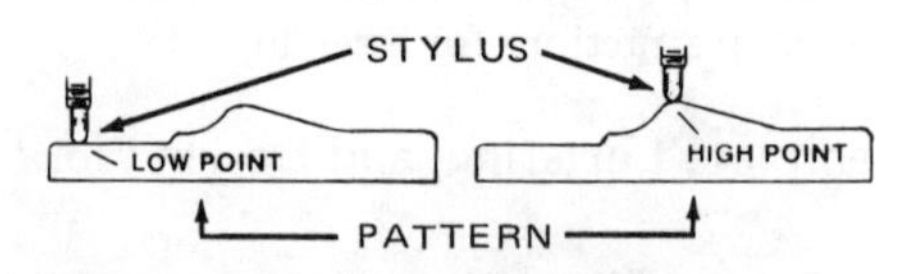

The set-up for three-dimensional carving is like that for two-dimensional work. Your workpiece should be 1/4- to 1/2-in. thicker than the maximum carving depth, and a 1/8-in. veining bit is recommended for nearly all carving work. Work is set up with the stylus adjusted to the lowest point of the pattern and the router height (above workpiece) also adjusted, accordingly. Carving is begun with the stylus at the highest point of the pattern so that you can progress downward (to lower points) while moving the stylus to touch every point on the pattern. An even, easy feed of the stylus is best, so that you can raise or lower it gently over uneven surfaces of the pattern. A softwood (like redwood) is easiest to carve, but any wood can be used if your bit is sharp and you maneuver the stylus slowly.

BUTT-HINGE MORTISING

The Accessories

One of the most important, standard professional uses of a router is the fitting of door hinges to the door and frame. Hinges must be flush mounted in the wood, which requires accurately-shaped mortises to proper depth that are painstaking to do with a hand chisel . . . but can be done quickly and easily with a router and the right accessory.

NOTE: Most inside doors are hung with two 3-1/2-in. butt hinges; most outside doors with two or three 4-in. butt hinges. Butt hinges may have round or square corners. The router bit produces round-corner mortises; for square-cornered ones the corners must be finished with a chisel.

Outside doors should *always* be hung — with the hinge pins inside — to swing inward. When there are two hinges the top hinge generally is positioned with its top about 7-in. below the door top; the bottom hinge, with its bottom 10- or 11-in. above the door bottom. If a third hinge is used it is positioned halfway between the other two.

Two different *Craftsman* accessories are available (*Chapter 1*): 1) Individual hinge templates, furnished as a set of two for 3-1/2- and 4-in. long butt hinges, which must be positioned and nailed in place for each hinge mortising job (on door or on jamb). 2) An adjustable template assembly that can be set up for any door 3/4- to 2-1/2-in. thick, up to 7-ft. high, with two or three hinges from 1-3/4- to 5-in. long — and, after the one set-up is made, can be used for quick, easy mortising of any number of like doors and the door jambs.

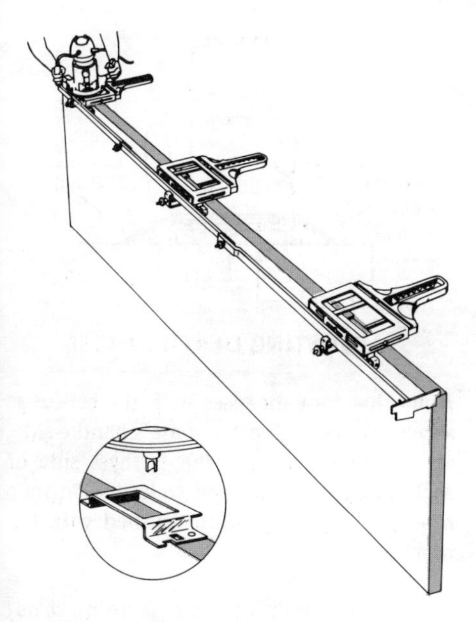

A 1/2-in. straight router bit (1-3/4-in. or longer) together with the 5/8-in. guide bushing (*Chapter 1*) are also required.

Using the Adjustable Template Assembly

Assemble the three slide bars using a sq.-hd. bolt, washer, spring and thumb nut for each of the two joints, as illustrated. Fasten one template at the approximate

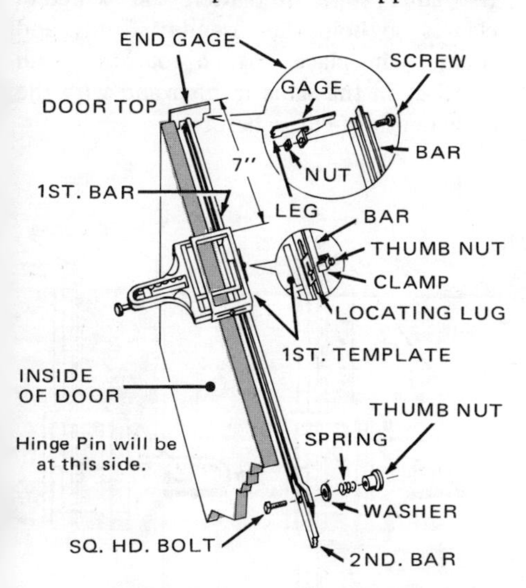

ASSEMBLING TEMPLATES TO SLIDE BARS ON DOOR

center of each bar by engaging the template locating lugs in the bar slot and securing the template with the slide-bar clamp and thumb nut. Determine whether the door will be a right-hand or left-hand door. If it is to be a *right*-hand door, stand it on edge so that when you are facing the *inside* of the door (side toward which door will swing), the door *top* will be at your *left*. For a *left*-hand door, when facing the *inside*, the door *bottom* will be at your *left*.

> *NOTE:* To determine whether a door will be right- or left-hand, stand on that side of the door jamb *toward* which the door will swing. If hinges will be at your right, it is a right-hand door . . . and vice-versa.

For a *right*-hand door, position the above assembly so that the slide bars are at the outside of the door and the template handles are at the inside (as illustrated). For a *left*-hand door, the slide bars will be at the inside, and the template handles at the outside of the door. With the assembly properly positioned, attach the end gage (as shown) to that end of the assembled slide bars which will be at the door *top*. Be sure that the gage is attached so that its leg is at the *same* side of the slide bars *as the handles* of the three templates. (This gage makes allowance for the spacing between door top and jamb.)

With the assembly on the door edge and the end gage touching the door top, loosen one of the template clamps (by lifting it), push it in against the door side, then tighten it. Repeat for the other two template clamps. These clamps hold the assembly in place.

Each of the three templates must now be adjusted for the hinge size, as follows. With the template handle facing you, loosen the two plate screws (so top plate is free to move), then place the gage in the *lower left* corner of the frame with the gage leg up against the door side. Tighten both screws. This establishes the mortise width.

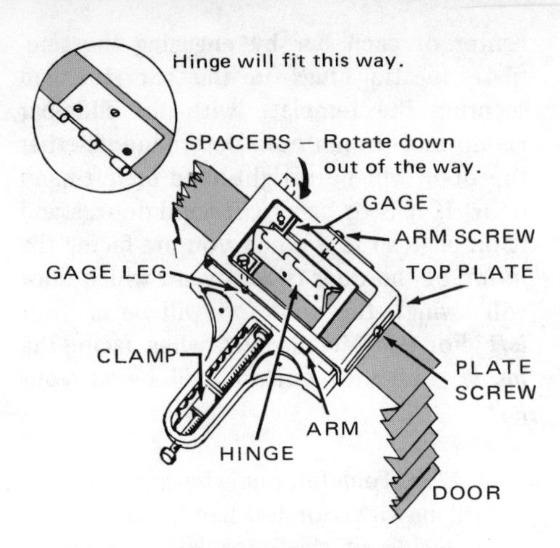

ADJUSTING A TEMPLATE

Loosen the arm screw so that arm is free to move. Place one of the hinges, as illustrated, down on the door edge between the gage and arm, move the arm to wedge the hinge between it and the gage – then tighten the screw and remove the hinge. This establishes the length of the mortise.

NOTE: If there will be only two hinges, *don't* adjust the center template.

The final step is to properly position the (two or three) templates on the slide bars. Do this one at a time, so as not to disturb the previously made slide-bar set-up. First, loosen the template clamp, then loosen the slide-bar clamp (*see first above illustration*). Position the template as required for hinge position. Retighten the slide-bar clamp – then retighten the template clamp making certain the template is squarely in position down on the door edge and up against the door side.

With the assembly fully adjusted, all that remains is adjustment of the router-bit depth-of-cut (which will vary according to hinge thickness). On one of the templates, place two hinges with the router on top of them, as illustrated. Adjust the router depth-of-cut until the bit end *exactly* touches the door edge (*without* lifting the router up).

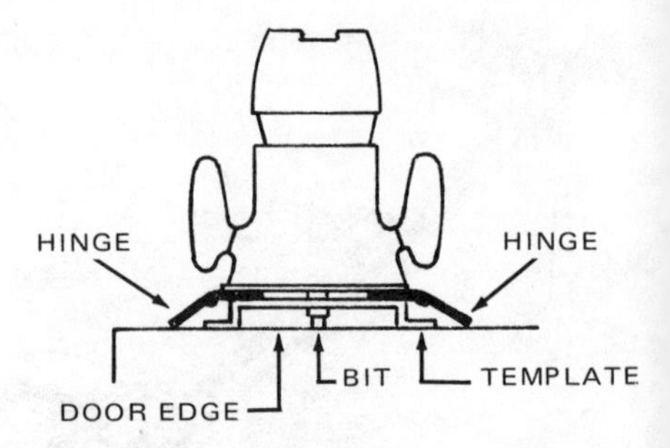

ADJUSTING DEPTH-OF-CUT

Rout the door mortises with the set-up as above. Stand at the template's handle side, and begin by routing the farthest side of each mortise from right-to-left. Continue routing right-to-left until finished with the mortise.

To rout the jamb mortises (jamb must *not* be rabbeted), remove the assembly from the door by loosening the three template clamps (do *not* loosen the slide-bar clamps). Rotate all six (two for each template) template spacers down at 90° to the template bottoms (this assures that door and jamb will be flush). Slide each template clamp out far enough, and position the assembly on the jamb, as illustrated (be certain the end gage is up against the jamb top). Retighten the template clamps to hold the assembly firmly and squarely in place – then rout the jamb mortises in the same manner and with the same depth-of-cut as before.

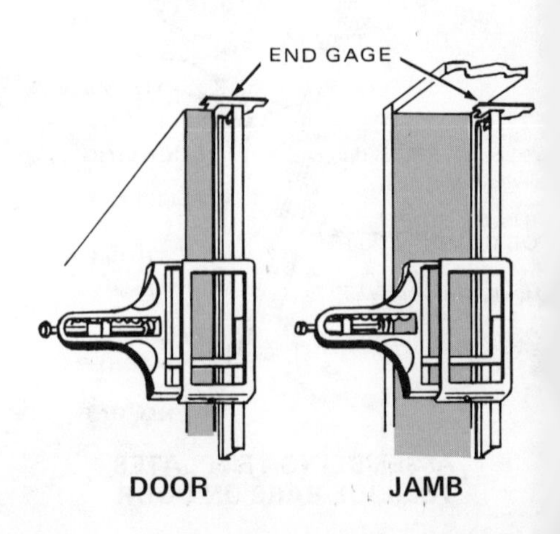

NOTE: Because they are adjustable for mortises of various widths and lengths, each of the three templates can be adapted for other mortising jobs — such as mortising for lock plates or any other rectangular pieces to be recessed flush (or deeper) in a wood surface. If the workpiece won't permit use of the template clamp, this can be removed — after which the template can be nailed in place (nail holes are provided).

Using the Individual Templates

These are furnished with the adjustable template assembly — as well as sold separately — because, although more difficult to use they are necessary for mortising any jamb that is already rabbeted (the adjustable template can*not* be used).

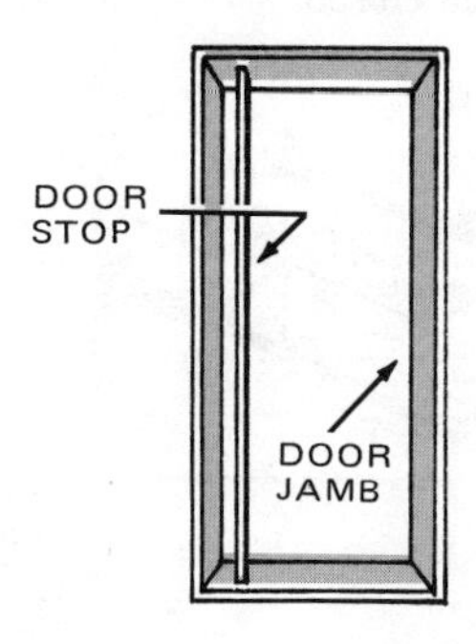

A gage for spacing of the hinges is required. This can be any piece of straight scrap wood — or, if the jamb has not been finished, you can use a piece of 3/8- x 2-in. wood that will later become the door stop. This gage must be cut to length to the *exact* height of the jamb (inside of the jamb).

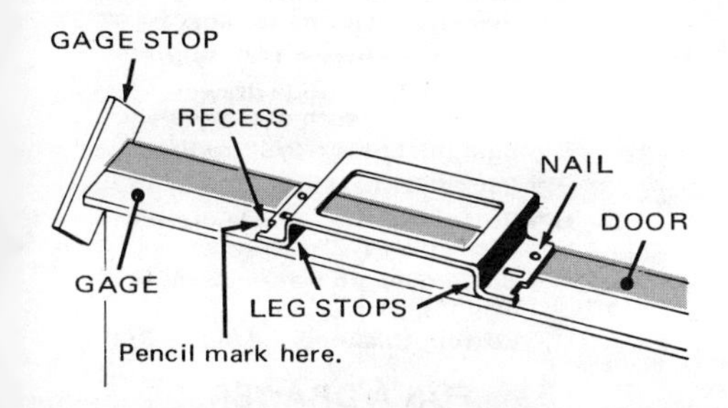

Choose the size template (3-1/2- or 4-in.) to be used. Using two 13x1-1/4-in. blued plasterboard nails (or equivalent), nail the template to the correct edge of the door (*read the preceding about determining right- or left-hand*). When nailing it, position it with the leg stops on the inside of the door (where the hinge pins will be) and the opposite template edge flush with the opposite side of the door. Also position it with the template top edge 5-1/2-in. from the door top (this allows 7-in. from top to hinge). Set the depth-of-cut as previously explained and rout the hinge mortise in the same manner as told preceding.

Before removing the template, nail a flat piece of wood to the door top to serve as a gage stop (*see illustration).* Hold your gage (preceding) against the door edge and against the template leg stops with its top end (mark it so) against the gage stop, then pencil-mark it using the recess in the top template leg as your guide.

To rout the bottom hinge mortise, renail the template to the door edge, as before but with its bottom edge 9-1/2-in. from the door bottom (for 11-in. hinge spacing), then rout the mortise. Next, position your gage as before (against the gage stop at door top), and pencil mark it using the recess in the top template leg.

If there is to be a third hinge, renail the template to the door edge as before, but center it between the first two positions. Rout the mortise, then again position the gage as before and pencil mark it using the template top leg recess as your guide. Now, remove the template and gage stop.

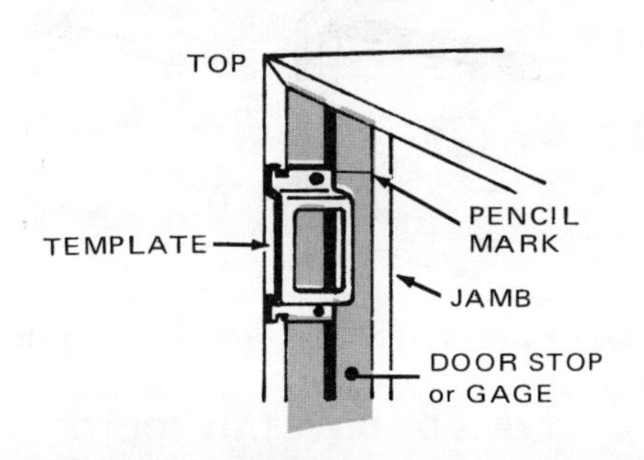

To rout the door jamb mortise nail your gage to the jamb, top end at top and with your pencil marks showing. If it is to be the door stop, nail it permanently, leaving the thickness of your door between it and the inner side of the jamb (side door will swing away from). Now position and nail the template in place on the jamb for each hinge, in turn, and rout the jamb mortises. When positioning the template, place the side *opposite* to the leg stops up against the gage, and the template top edge (*not* the recess) aligned with your pencil mark for this hinge.

DOVETAIL JOINTING

The Uses

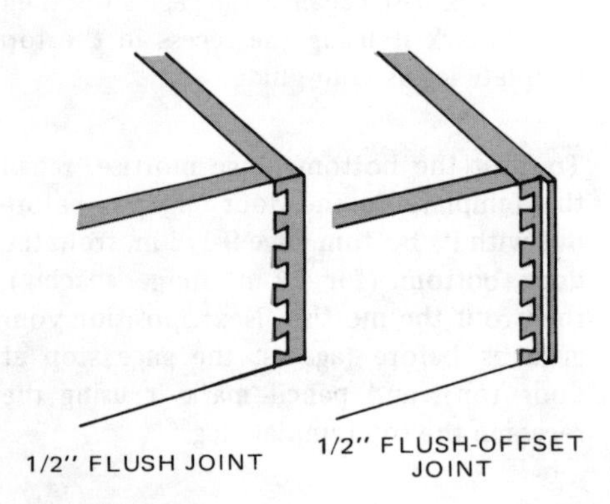

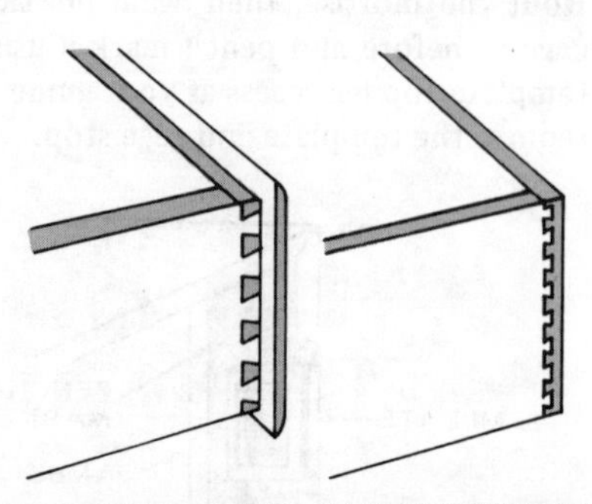

TYPES OF DOVETAIL JOINTS

For good cabinetmaking every drawer front should be joined to the sides with a dovetail joint, which holds solidly to prevent frequent drawer openings from loosening the front. Four types of dovetail joints are illustrated. Either a 1/2-in. or 1/4-in. flush joint is used when the drawer front is to be flush with the cabinet front when closed, and a stop (to keep the drawer from recessing too far) is placed behind the drawer. The flush-offset joint — for which each drawer side is recessed 1/16-in. from the edge of the front — is also for a flush-closing drawer, but one that has a close-fitting front with sides that fit less closely in the opening to allow freer operation. A rabbeted joint generally is used when the all-around 3/8-in. wide lip of the front is to serve as a stop and to hide the edges of the opening, and the drawer front will project out from the cabinet front when closed.

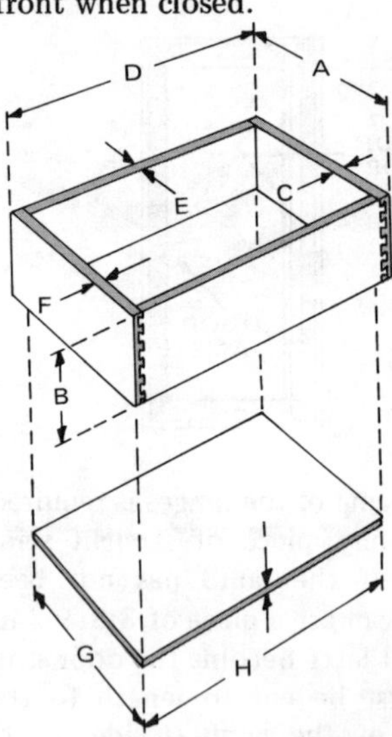

A = Length of front and back
= Opening length minus abt. 1/16"
B = Width of front and back
= Opening height minus abt. 1/16"
C = Front thickness = 1/2" to 3/4"
D = Side length = Inside drawer length plus depth of 2 dovetails
E = Side thickness = 3/8" to 3/4"
F = Back thickness = 1/2" to 3/4"
G = Bottom width = Inside drawer width plus 1/2"
H = Bottom length = Inside drawer length plus 1/2"
I = Bottom thickness = 1/4" to 3/8"

FOR A DRAWER

For additional drawer strength the back should also be joined to each side with a dovetail joint, in which case a flush joint is used. This joint is also excellent for joining the tops and bottoms of wall cabinets, boxes (and similar constructions) to the sides. It makes an accurately squared, solid framework on which to hang shelves and doors while letting the wall behind serve as the back.

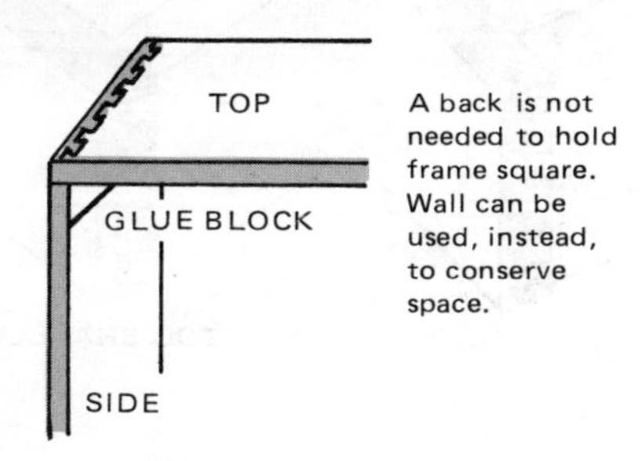

FOR A WALL CABINET

The Accessories

Dovetail-Joint Fixtures (*Chapter 1*) are available for handling wood (drawer fronts, backs and sides) of different widths and thicknesses, for cutting either 1/2-in. and/or 1/4-in. dovetails. All large drawers — such as for dressers — require 1/2-in. dovetails; the 1/4-in. size generally is used only for very small drawers — as for jewelry or silverware chests, etc.

To cut 1/2-in. dovetails you will also need the 1/2-in. dovetail bit . . . and you will use the 7/16-in. guide bushing, *Chapter 2* (which may or may not be furnished with the attachment). A 1/4-in. dovetail cut requires the 1/4-in. dovetail bit and the 5/16-in. guide bushing (which may or may not be furnished with the attachment).

Your dovetail fixture should be securely mounted on a firm workbench with the front edge of the base projecting slightly beyond the workbench front (to allow clearance for the workpiece that hangs down on the fixture). It can also be mounted, to be portable, on a 3/4-in. plywood base (refer to the attachment Owner's Manual). The two workpieces are mounted in the attachment as illustrated.

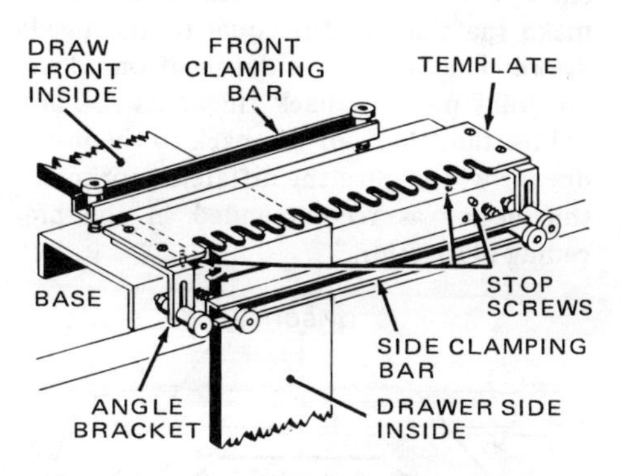

SET-UP FOR FLUSH DOVETAIL AT LEFT-FRONT OF A DRAWER

To Cut a 1/2-In. Flush Dovetailed Drawer Front and Sides

> *IMPORTANT:* The following pertains specifically to the Model 2571 Dovetail Attachment. For the variations due to use of other model-number attachments, refer to your attachment's Owner's Manual.

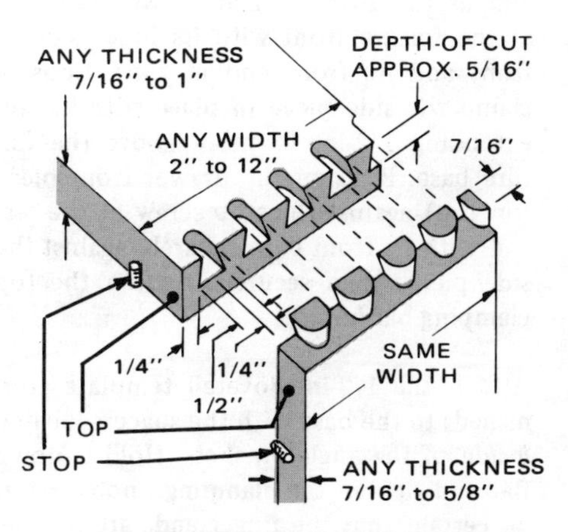

THE CUTS FOR A 1/2" FLUSH DOVETAILED DRAWER FRONT AND LEFT SIDE

The workpieces selected for the front, back and sides must be accurately sawed to size (refer to the accompanying illustration). If, instead of a dovetail-joined drawer back, the back is to be butt joined (ends of sides glued and/or nailed to edges of the back), make the side lengths equal to the inside drawer length plus the depth of one dovetail joint plus the back thickness . . . and reduce the length of the back to the inside drawer width. Size the different workpiece thicknesses as recommended in the preceding illustration.

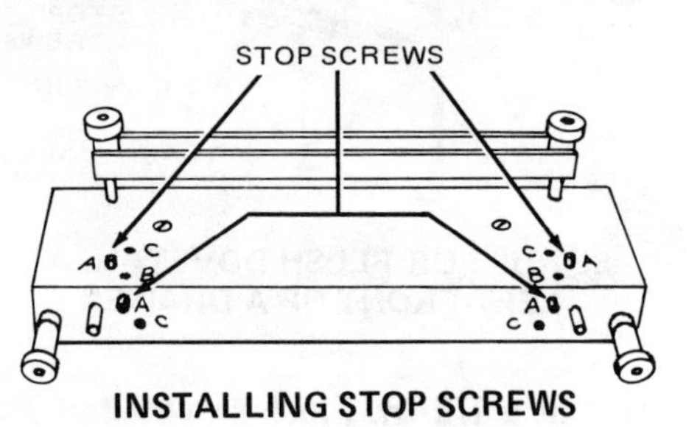

INSTALLING STOP SCREWS

Before installing the workpiece or template, insert four stop screws into the threaded holes "A" (*see accompanying illustration*) and tighten them securely. With the two clamping bars sufficiently loosened, install the two workpieces (drawer front on top, upside-down, left end at the front – and drawer left side at the fixture front with its inner side at front and its front end at top). Loosely clamp the side piece in place with its top extending 1/2-in. or more above the fixture base. Position the drawer front piece (on top) against the stop screw at the left and with its front edge squarely against the side piece, then securely tighten the top clamping bar knobs.

Attach the 1/2-in. dovetail template (furnished) to the base with the spacers located *inside* of the angle brackets. Hold it down flat and tighten the clamping knobs – but be certain that the finger ends are parallel to the outer edge of the top workpiece board. Now, relocate the drawer side board (at fixture front) to be flush at top with the top of the drawer front board and against the stop screw at its left side. Securely tighten the side clamping bar.

Install the correct bit and bushing and adjust your router to extend the bit 17/32-in. below the router base. In general, this is the most desirable setting for a snug 1/2-in. joint. However, an exact setting may prove to be difficult, so it is best to perfect it on scrap blocks.

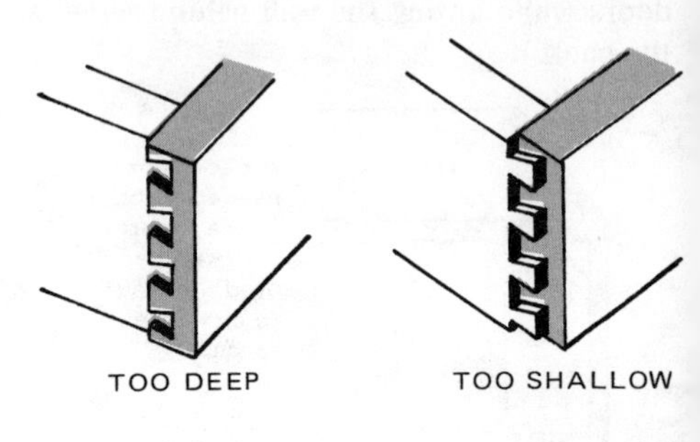

Read the following directions and cut a joint in the scrap pieces. The finished joint should fit just loosely enough to allow space for the glue. If it is too loose, increase the depth-of-cut slightly (by lowering the bit), if too tight, decrease the depth-of-cut slightly. If the cuts are too wide, turn the locknuts (behind the angle brackets) counterclockwise; if too narrow, turn the nuts clockwise – and, in either case, adjust them equally until desired width of a trial cut is obtained.

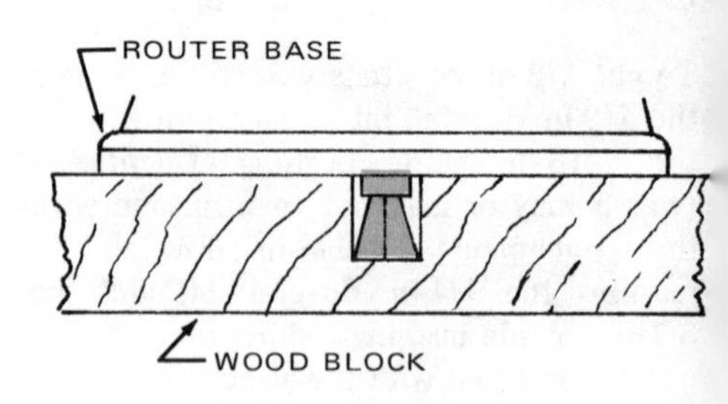

When satisfied with a trial dovetail use this exact bit setting to rout a groove in a wood block (*as illustrated*). This groove will then serve as your guide for all future 1/2-in dovetail cut settings. You can also mark the locknuts and base for resetting if later necessary.

To rout a joint hold the router flat and firmly down on the template with the guide bushing against the outer edge of the drawer side board. Begin by making a shallow straight cut, right-to-left across the front of the side board (this will prevent splintering its edge while cutting the dovetail joint). Now, make a dovetail cut, left-to-right, by guiding the router so that the bushing follows the template teeth — then repeat the cut, right-to-left to perfect it. Afterwards, *stop* the router, then remove it straight toward you; *never* attempt to lift it upward.

After finishing the left-front drawer corner as above, do the right-front corner by substituting the drawer *right-side* piece and turning the drawer front to place the uncut edge at front. Install both pieces in the fixture with their sides against the *right* side stop screws — otherwise, the procedure is as before.

To Cut a 1/2-In. Flush Dovetailed Drawer Back and Sides

The procedures are the same as the preceding with these exceptions:

1) To make the *left-* rear corner dovetail, place the back piece on top, upside-down and left end at front, and the left side piece in front, inner side out and rear end at top . . . and position both pieces against the stop screws at the *right* side of the fixture.

2) To make the *right*-rear corner dovetail, place the back piece on top, upside-down and right end at front, and the right side piece in front, inner side out and rear end at top . . . and position both pieces against the stop screws at the *left* side of the fixture.

To Cut 1/2-In. Rabbeted Joints

NOTE: For Model 2571 Attachment only; refer to attachment Owner's Manual for other model-number attachments.

This operation is like the preceding with the following exceptions:

The drawer front should be 3/4-in. longer and 3/4-in. wider than for flush joints and should be at least 3/4-in. thick, to allow for a 3/8-in. wide by 7/16-in. deep rabbet all around (preferably cut at the inside of the drawer front prior to the dovetail operation).

When installing the stop screws locate the two for the drawer side pieces as before (in holes "A") — but locate the two for the drawer front in holes "B".

To begin with install the template as before — the spacers at the *inside* of the angle brackets. Then, make the dovetail cut as previously told.

Next, remove the drawer side piece and reinstall the template (*without* moving the drawer front piece) with the spacers *outside* of the angle brackets and the template teeth parallel to the rabbeted edge of the drawer front. Make another dovetail cut (same procedure) in this drawer front board alone (to deepen the previous cut so the dovetail will be along the rabbeted edge).

To Cut 1/2-In. Flush-Offset Joints

These joints require only the two ends of the drawer front to be rabbeted. They can be cut exactly the same as the rabbeted joints, preceding — or you can use a thinner (5/8-in. thick) front board that is only 1/2-in. (or less) longer than for a flush joint (if you wish to have very shallow and narrow end lips.

To Cut 1/4-In. Joints

NOTE: For Model 2571 Attachment only; for all others refer to the attachment Owner's Manual. Also, refer to the Owner's Manual supplied with the 1/4-In. Finger Template.

These operations are the same as for 1/2-in. dovetails except that the 1/4-in. finger template, a 1/4-in. dovetail bit, and a 5/16-in.

guide bushing are required. Thinner workpieces (approximately half the thickness needed for 1/2-in. dovetails) can be used. Threaded holes "C" in the dovetail fixture base are used when installing the stop screws.

Another Method For Drawer-Front End Rabbeting

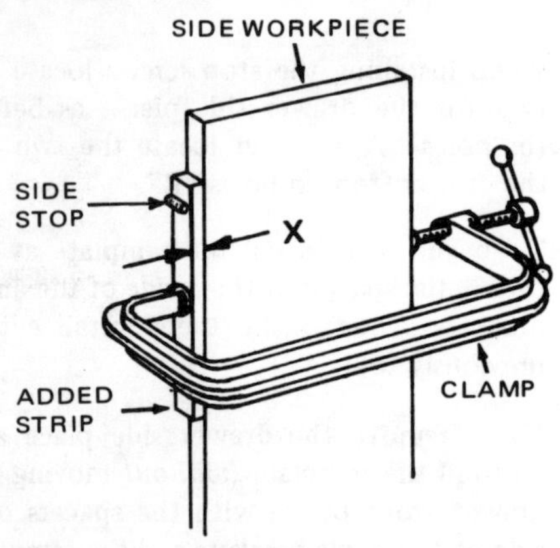

NOTE: The following applies when using any model-number attachment.

Using a 1/2-in. (or a 1/4-in.) flush-dovetailed drawer-front set-up you can substitute a drawer front having any desired width and depth of rabbeted lips on the top and bottom edges, and dovetail the two front corners by using an "added strip," as shown in the illustration. This strip must be a straight board of a thickness, "X," equal to the width of the drawer-front top lip. To cut the front-left drawer corner, clamp it to the left side of the drawer left-side piece so it will contact the fixture flush-cut positioned stop screw (on block); clamp it to the right side of the drawer right-side piece when cutting the right-front corner.

If the drawer front is to also have lips at each end, and you have a model 2571 attachment, a procedure like that described, "To Cut 1/2-In. Rabbeted Joints," preceding, can be used to deepen the cuts in the front board ends if the end rabbets are 3/8-in. wide. However, you can also use the strip (instead of repositioning the angle-bracket lockwashers) to mark the draw-front board for any width rabbets by laying the strip along the template back edge) to determine exactly how far to move the template to reset it for the second (deepening) cut(s) to be made with the drawer side piece(s) removed. This latter can be done with any model attachment. Don't forget that the drawer-front board must be increased in length and width to allow for the lips.

LAMINATING AND TRIMMING WORKPIECES

Laminate Applications

Laminated coverings are available in a wide variety of wood grains, flat and decorative design colors, etc., and can be applied over inexpensive solid woods or plywoods to give a workpiece (counter top or cabinet-work top, sides, doors, etc.) the appearance of having been constructed from better quality materials. Another considerable advantage of most such laminates is their exceptional durability (resistance to scratching, acids, heat, etc.), which makes them especially desirable as top coverings for such as coffee tables, serving trays, etc. (which may be subjected to staining or marring by liquids, foods, cigarette burns and hard knocks).

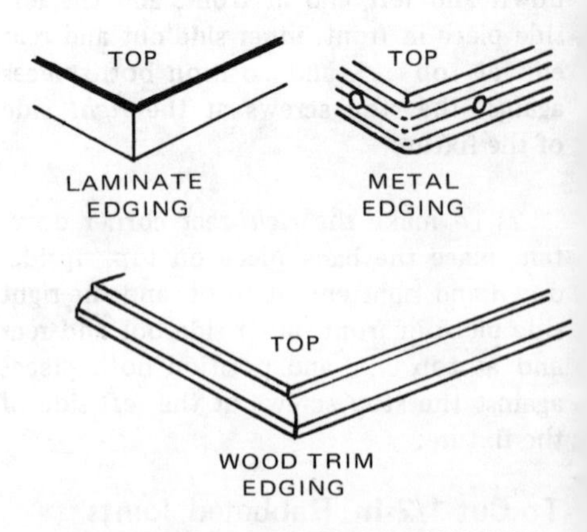

THREE TYPES OF EDGE FINISHES

The manner in which a laminated workpiece is edge finished depends upon its use and the desired effect. Counter tops, for instance, generally are edged with the same laminate (especially if a colored, rather than a wood-grain laminate is used). However, a metal edging, applied with screws, may be used — and often is preferred for sink tops, worktables and the like. On the other hand, it generally is preferable to edge fine cabinetwork with matching (or contrasting) solid wood edging (which can be prepared from appropriate workpieces with your router, as told in *Chapter 3*).

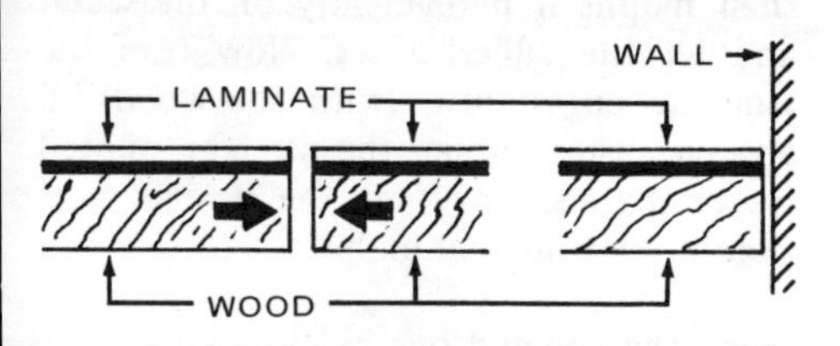

TOP TRIMMED FOR A BUTT JOINT OR REAR SIDE

If two top-laminated pieces are to be butt jointed, or a top-laminated piece is to fit against a wall (or similar) so that the edge will be hidden, the lamination on top is simply flush-finished with the edge. However, if a workpiece is to be laminated on top and also along a visible edge (or end), the "corner" formed by the adjoining edges of the top and side laminates must be finished in one of the three ways illustrated. Method 1 is a squared "corner"; methods 2 and 3 are chamfered "corners" with the bit set at different depths-of-cut.

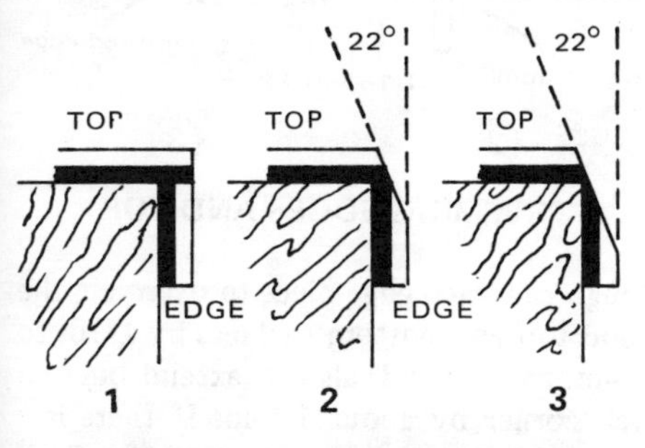

THREE WAYS TO TRIM EDGES

NOTE: Formica and other laminates have a thin layer of "finish" on top with a second, black layer of "body" underneath. If the laminate edge is cut off square, the body will show as a paper thin black line; when the cut off is at an angle, this visible black line will be slightly thicker.

The Accessory and/or Bits Needed

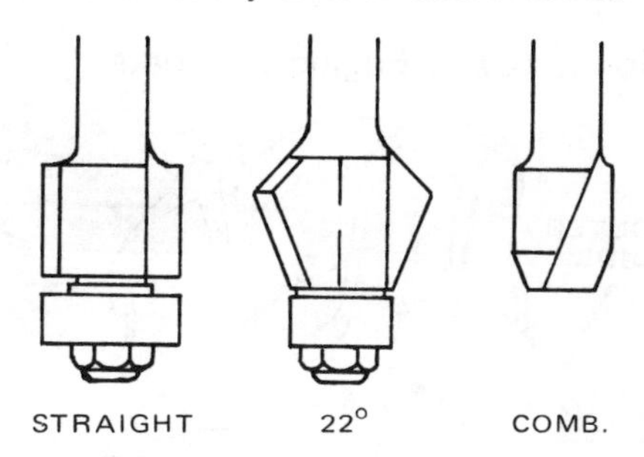

You can use either a piloted bit or the combination bit in conjunction with the Multi-Purpose Router Guide *(refer to Chapter 1)*. A piloted bit is quicker and easier to use, but two separate bits are needed — one for flush and another for bevel-angle edging. The combination bit will make either type of edging, but it must be guided by using the above router guide with its bracket-assembly-arm installed on it. This set-up has the added advantage of allowing you to vary the distance between the bit and the guide bushing — to make

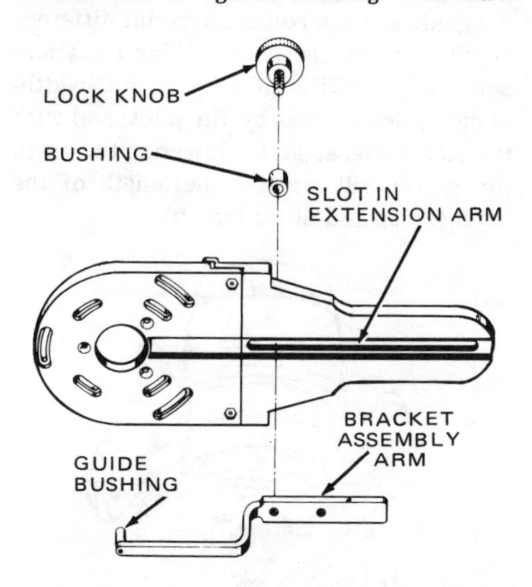

ASSEMBLING BRACKET ASSY. ARM ATTACHMENT TO ROUTER GUIDE

deeper or shallower cuts. If it is advisable to do the edge trimming in two parts (instead of one) because of a large overhang, making first a shallow then a deeper cut causes fewer problems. Also, when bevel edging the deepness of the cut can be more finely adjusted.

Mounting and Edging Laminates

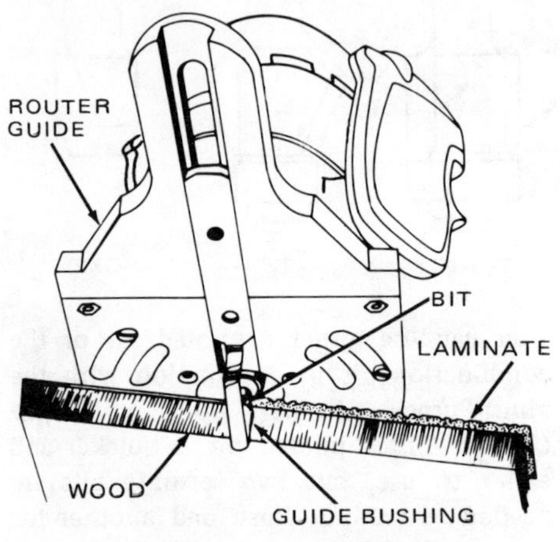

USING THE ROUTER GUIDE FOR FLUSH EDGING

Typical top edging operations are illustrated. For set-up and adjustments of the router guide refer to the Owner's Manual packaged with it. Note that when using the guide and the combination bit different depth settings are required for flush and bevel edging. With either pilot bit, width-of-cut is determined by the pilot; and with the pilot bevel-angle bit lowering the bit in the router will increase the length of the bevel (its up-and-down length).

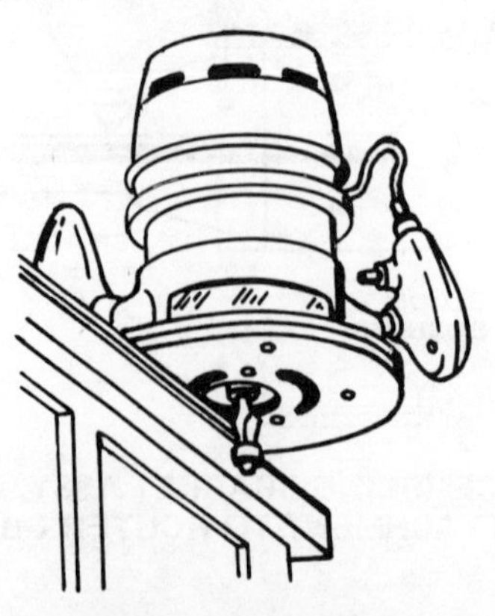

USING A PILOT BIT

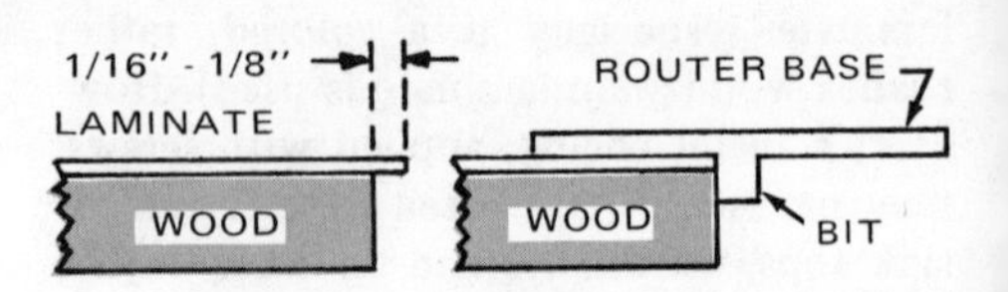

FLUSH TRIMMING A TOP

When the top only is to be laminated, rough saw your laminate to overhang the wood on every side by 1/16- to 1/8-in. then mount it permanently on the wood and let the adhesive set. Now trim the laminate edges flush (with the wood) all around, using either the straight piloted bit or the accessory and the straight portion of the combination bit.

When the top and one or more edges of a square or rectangular workpiece are to be laminated, the edges must be finished first.

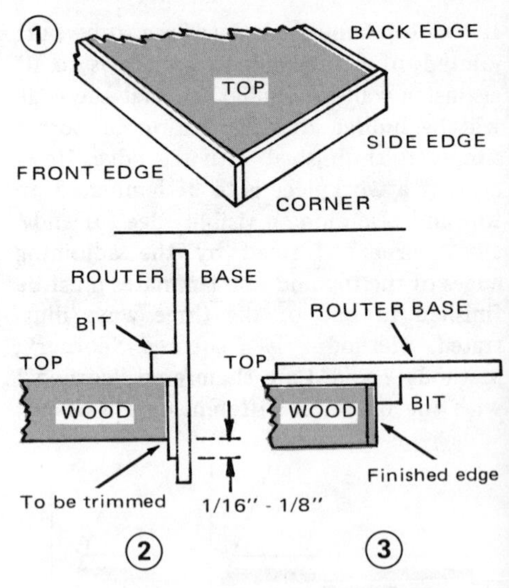

TRIMMING EDGES AND TOP

Rough saw each edge piece to overhang the wood top and bottom surfaces by 1/16- to 1/8-in. each — and, also to extend beyond each corner by about 1/8-in. If there is a back edge piece, mount and trim this flush *on all four sides.* Next, mount and similarly trim both side edge pieces — then mount and trim the front edge piece on all four sides. Finally, mount and trim the top piece on all four sides — either flush (as illustrated), or at a bevel angle (as told preceding).

> *NOTE:* When sawing the top piece to size be sure it will overhang the already mounted edges (*not* just the wood) by 1/16- to 1/8-in. at every side.

If your workpiece top is a triangle, or has more than four straight edges (like a hexagon), the edging pieces cannot be trimmed to fit as shown preceding (only a 90° corner can be so fitted and trimmed). Measure the length of a side, as illustrated, and prepare your edge pieces oversize, as preceding. Cut a scrap board the same (or greater) thickness as your workpiece top, at least 3-in. wide, the *exact length* of a side, and with square (90°) ends. Temporarily securing each edge piece in turn to the scrap board (with clamps or rubber cement), square trim *both* ends. Now, carefully mount all edge pieces on your workpiece, trim their top and bottom edges, then mount and trim the top piece. Finally use a fine-tooth file to flat trim each corner, as illustrated.

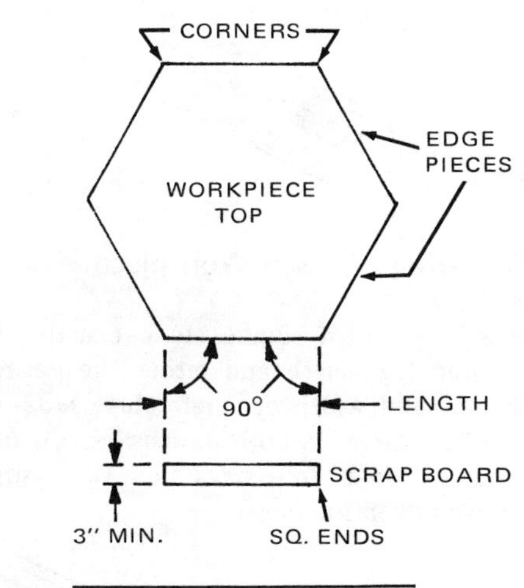

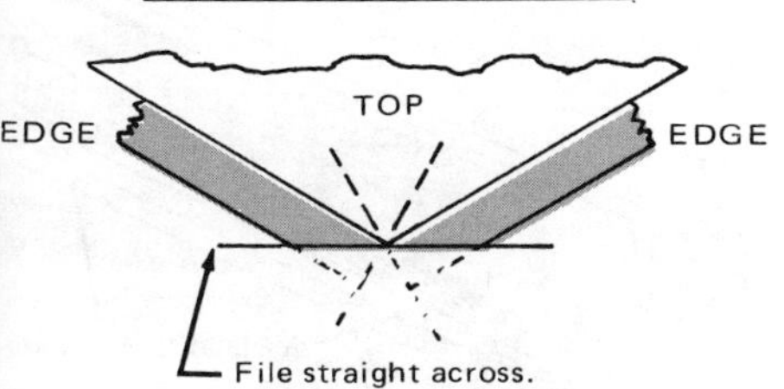

TRIMMING EDGES FOR OTHER THAN FOUR-SIDED FLAT-EDGED WORKPIECES

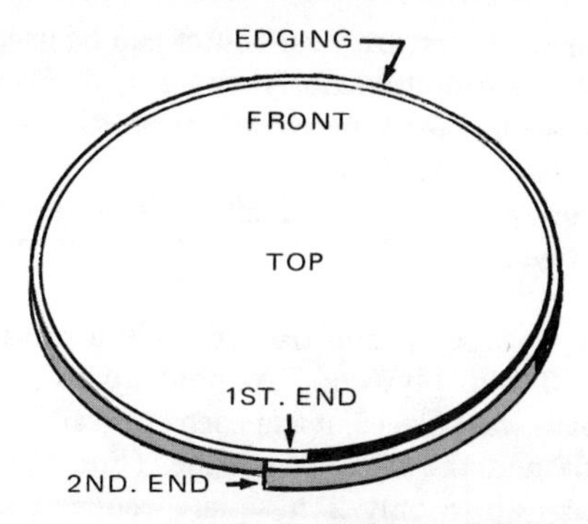

ANY WORKPIECE WITH CURVES OF LARGE ENOUGH RADIUS

Laminating material *cannot* be folded around a sharp corner, but can be bent to follow a curve (inside or outside) with a radius large enough to prevent cracking of the particular material being used (you will have to test this). Therefore, a continuous (rather than a pieced) edge can be applied to any workpiece having "reasonable" curves and no corners.

Measure the perimeter of your workpiece, then rough saw one edge piece to overhang at top and bottom (as above) and to overlap at the ends by 1/4-in. or more. Cut a scrap block, as suggested before, except its length need only be sufficient to work with and only one end need be square. Using this block, flush trim the "1st end" of the edge piece. Now, temporarily — but snugly — mount the edge piece on your workpiece and mark the "2nd end" overlap. Afterwards, reuse the scrap block to trim the "2nd end" flush on the mark — then permanently mount the edge piece on the workpiece and finish it and the top piece as previously told.

SQUARE-LEG TAPERING AND DECORATING

Uses and the Fixture To Make

Tapered square legs for tables, chairs, bed end-boards, etc. are more graceful than straight square ones, and decorative grooving (such as beading, fluting or paneling) gives them a distinctive and professional appearance. With the help of a simple homemade fixture your router can be used, first, to simultaneously taper and plane square-cut workpieces to accurate (and identical) dimensions and, second, to decorate these tapered pieces in a variety of ways.

The fixture is constructed as illustrated. Use 3/4-in. plywood. To hold up to 3-in. square workpieces, make each side rail 4-in. wide and the base 5-in. wide. (For workpieces up to only 2-in. square, reduce both dimensions by 1-in., etc.) Make all three pieces 10-in. longer than the longest workpiece you plan to handle. Use 1/4-in. plywood and cut two pieces 1-in. narrower and 10-in. shorter than the two rails. Glue these to the *inner* sides of the respective side rails so as to be flush at the bottom edges and recessed 5-in. at each end (i.e., centered lengthwise). Permanently attach one ("fixed") side rail, added piece at the inner side, along the top of one edge of the base; use glue and 2- to 2-1/2-in. wood screws spaced no more than 6-in. apart, to assure rigidity.

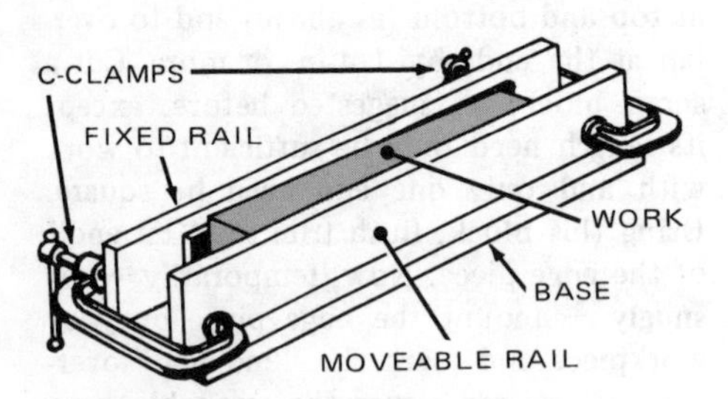

HOMEMADE TAPERING FIXTURE

NOTE: The two side rails must be exactly equal in height; and so must the two 1/4-in. facings. When positioning the moveable side rail, always place the facing at the inner side and align its two ends with the ends of the base.

For tapering you will need two wood wedges; for decorating, four are required. Make these with their large ends approximately half the width and height of your largest workpiece cross-section, and tapered at about 10° on one side to a feather edge (which will determine the length).

NOTE: Making the wedges half the cross-section of your largest workpiece in size will permit their use with workpieces half of the largest workpiece size, etc.

IMPORTANT: The router edge guide (*Chapter 2*), traveled along the outer side of one or the other side rails (while the router sub-base travels on top of the two side-rail edges), is used for all operations as a means of positioning the cut. Two C-clamps, as illustrated, are used to secure the workpiece firmly between the two side rails.

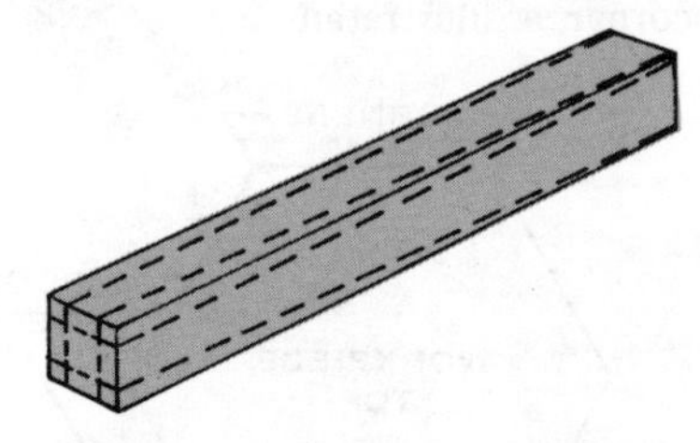

Tapering a Square Workpiece

Use a piece of square stock exactly the desired leg length and either the desired height and width or, preferably, 1/32- to 1/16-in. larger in both dimensions. At one end and on all four sides draw the desired finish dimension lines.

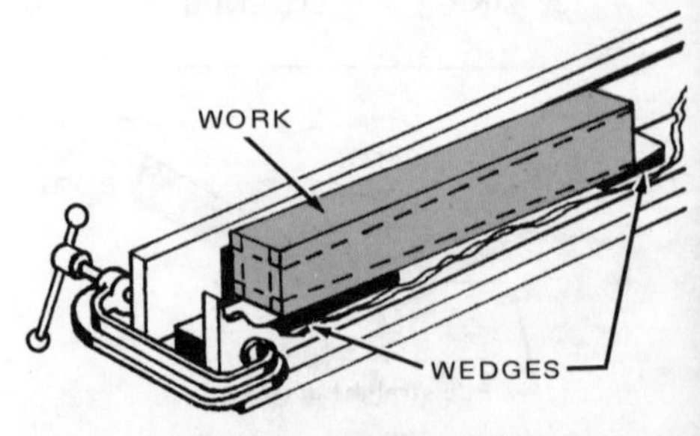

Align end and taper line by adjusting wedges.

Place your workpiece on the fixture base with one end approximately aligned with the fixed-rail facing end. Use wedges, as illustrated, to elevate one (or both) workpiece ends to exactly align your top dimension (taper) line with the top edge of the facing, end-to-end. Securely C-clamp the moveable side rail in place to hold the workpiece firmly — and check to make certain the top dimension lines are still properly aligned with both side-rail facings.

Install the *rabbeting bit (Chapter 2)* in your router. Place the router on top of the two side rails at the fixture end where the workpiece projects up the most, with the bit hanging down clear of the workpiece end. Adjust the depth-of-cut so that the bottom of the bit will just touch — *without* cutting into — the top of one side-rail facing. Adjust the edge guide so the bit will rabbet one workpiece edge *without* cutting into the adjoining side rail. Start the router and make one pass from end-to-end of the workpiece — then readjust the edge guide for as many more passes as are needed to finish planing the whole width of this workpiece side.

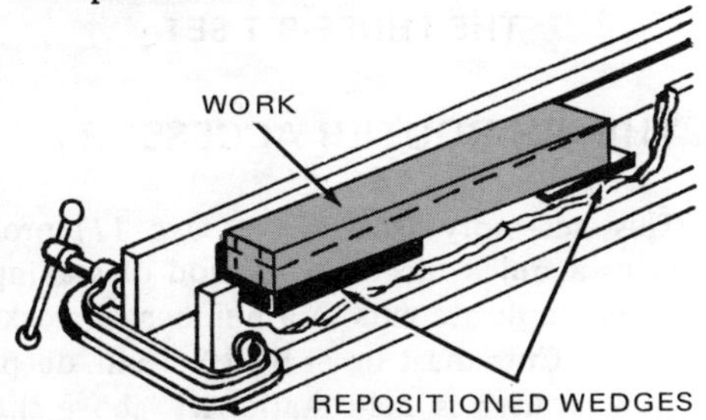

Align end and taper line by adjusting wedges.

For the second, adjacent workpiece side, reposition the workpiece as above after rotating it 90°. Note, however, that the moveable rail, when clamped in position, will no longer be parallel to the fixed rail. This means that, if you set your edge guide to one rail and try to edge along the opposite side of the workpiece, your bit will — when approaching the previously tapered workpiece end — cut into the opposite side rail. To avoid this you must do the cutting along each workpiece edge with the edge guide adjusted for and pressing against the *adjacent* side rail. Any center cut passes needed can be guided from either side rail.

The third and fourth workpiece sides are finished in the same way as the first two. Note, however, that because the workpiece bottom is (in each case) already tapered, the wedges must be positioned farther under each end to properly align the dimension lines with the tops of the facings. Do all four sides with the *same* depth-of-cut setting.

Decorating a Workpiece

Typical examples of the types of decorations that can be added, after tapering a workpiece, are illustrated. Beading is done by using the *point-cutting 1/4-rd. bit*, with cuts spaced to leave equal-width, equally-spaced beads on the surface. Fluting is similarly accomplished either with a straight or, preferably, a veining bit of small-enough diameter. An indented panel, as shown, or a raised panel can be cut with a straight bit of appropriate diameter. Cuts can be run off at one or both ends . . . or can be stopped short of the ends by fastening stop blocks to the ends of the

TAPERED GROOVES

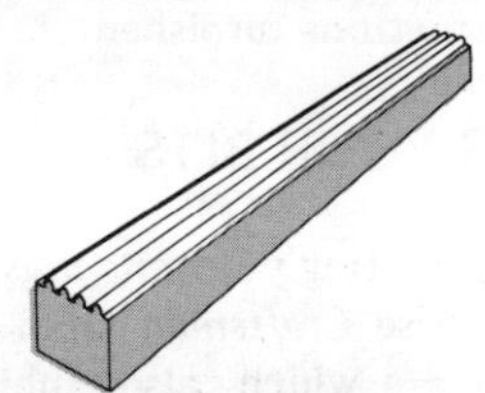
BEADING PARALLEL TO THE RESPECTIVE SIDES

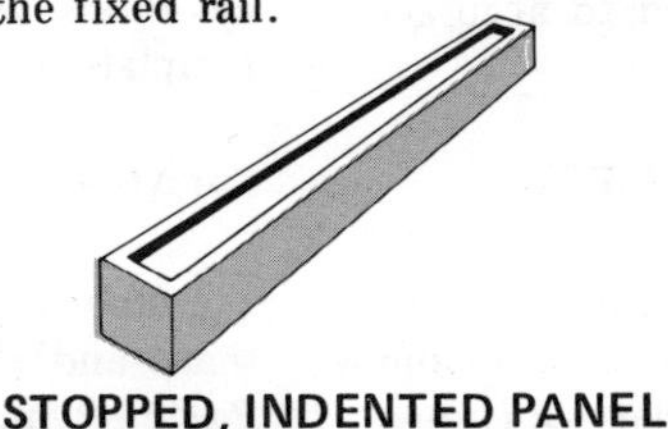
STOPPED, INDENTED PANEL

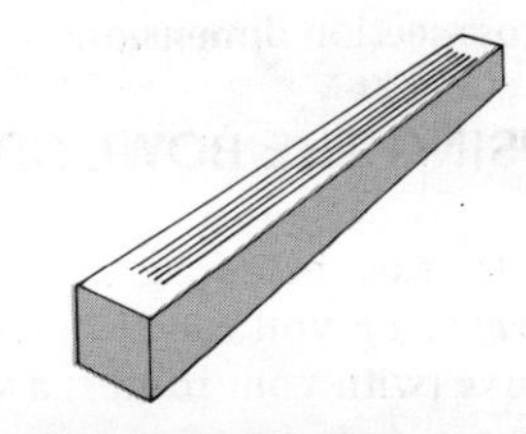
FLUTING, PARALLEL TO C/L AND STOPPED EACH END

fixture on top where the router sub-base will contact (and be stopped by) them. For variation, cuts also can be feathered out to zero depth at one (either) end by wedging the workpiece elevation so that the feathered-out end elevation is below the other end (is, where cut is to end, at an elevation that will produce a zero depth-of-cut).

If the decorative grooves are to be parallel to the respective, already tapered workpiece sides, half of them (all those parallel to one side) are cut with the edge guide against this (same) fixture side . . . and the other half, with the edge guide against the opposite fixture side. If continued far enough toward the workpiece small end, each pair of opposite matching grooves will meet at a V-point, as shown . . . or, if continued beyond this point, will cross.

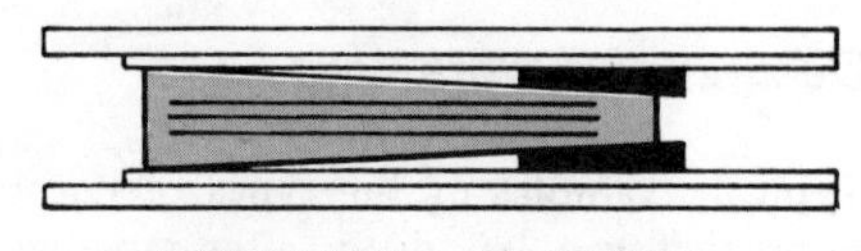

PARALLEL GROOVES

If the grooves are to be parallel to the workpiece centerline, the workpiece must be wedged (at the sides of the small end, as shown) so that the two fixture side rails will be parallel to this centerline. Grooves can now be cut using either side rail to guide the edge guide.

Workpieces having oblong, hexagonal and, even octagonal cross-sections (if each side is wide enough to support the workpiece accurately, without "tilting" to one side or the other, can similarly be tapered and decorated. However, since there is no way of indexing the workpiece rotated position to equalize the spacing of the sides, the workpiece must be pre-sawed to accurate cross-section dimensions.

USING THE BOWL CRAFTER

With this practical, easy-to-use accessory (*page 11*), you can turn (as on a lathe) and carve (with your router) a variety of turned shapes and sizes from as small as 2-1/2-in.

TYPICAL BOWL-CRAFTER SHAPES

dia. (max. 5-1/4-in. high) to as large as 10-in. dia. (max. 3-1/2-in. high). The wood stock is mounted on a faceplate driven by the accessory motor at a very slow (4 rpm) speed. Your router mounts in a carriage that you slide on the 22 x 23-in. accessory table to feed the router bit to the workpiece. Carriage movement is guided by a template secured to the accessory fence; you make any template you need using one of the paper patterns furnished or your own pattern. To do the turning you need three bits, available as a set.

THE THREE-BIT SET

THE PIN-ROUTER ACCESSORY

This accessory (*shown on page 11*) provides a quick, accurate method of making exact duplicate cuts in a number of workpieces. Cuts must be at least 3/16-in. deep. Your router is held stationary above the accessory table by an arm that adjusts it up or down. The table has a guide pin for a template to the top side of which your workpiece is fastened so that moving the template (and workpiece) over the pin will allow the router bit to make the required cut in the workpiece. You make your own template per instructions furnished.

SHARPENING YOUR BITS

For smooth, free cutting your bits *must* be sharp and clean. Use *Craftsman* Gum and Pitch Remover — which also inhibits rusting — for quick, easy cleaning. Use the

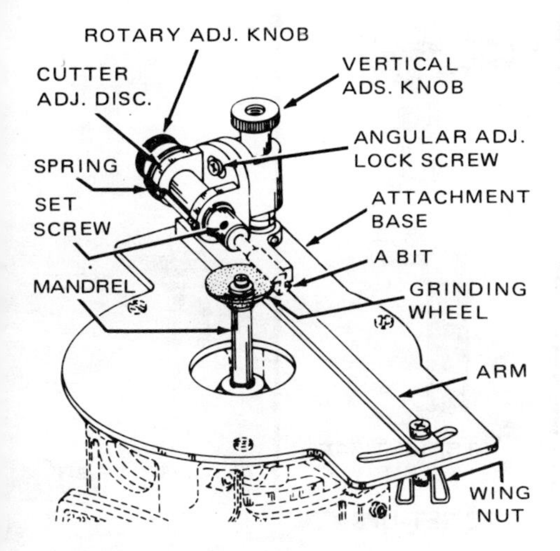

THE ATTACHMENT

Craftsman Cutter Grinding Attachment, which fits onto your router as illustrated, for precision sharpening of *any* of your bits. This attachment is furnished with two grinding wheels: a white-colored wheel for sharpening high-speed steel bits; a green-colored wheel for sharpening carbide-tipped bits.

The attachment Owner's Manual provides complete instructions for setting-up and using the attachment. Following is a general explanation of the bit-sharpening operations.

The attachment is mounted on the router — which powers the grinding wheel — in place of the router sub-base, and the router must be used upside-down. For stability, if necessary, the router can be supported between the jaws of a large-enough wood vise (but do *not* tighten the vise) . . . or in a homemade wooden frame that will prevent it from tipping. Before beginning, make certain to install the *proper* (white or green, as above) grinding wheel on the mandrel held by the router chuck.

Regardless of the bit shape, the attachment can be adjusted so that each bit cutting edge, in turn, will be correctly in contact with the *top* surface of the grinding wheel. Use *only the top* wheel surface; make certain that only the one bit edge to be sharpened is in contact with the wheel. Do *all* sharpening on the *flat* (leading side) of a cutting edge . . . *never* grind the shoulder (outer side) nor the trailing side of a cutting edge.

IMPORTANT: Grinding on the outer or trailing side of a cutting edge will alter the shape of a bit so that it will no longer make the exact cut for which it was originally intended. If an edge is so badly nicked or chipped that grinding on the flat side will not restore the edge, the bit must be discarded.

"Grinding on the flat side" means that the flat side must be positioned *exactly parallel* to the top surface of the grinding wheel (*not tilted*), and positioned so that the wheel edge does *not* cut into any adjoining part of the bit. *Do as little grinding as possible.*

The accompanying illustrations show how typical bit shapes must be positioned. To achieve proper bit positioning, one or more of the following attachment adjustments are required.

Rotate the vertical adjusting knob counter-clockwise as far as possible, to fully elevate the bit holder. Loosen the attachment wing nut then simultaneously move the attachment arm and the router depth-of-cut setting to position the top of the grinding wheel in the approximate desired position with respect to the bit cutting edge. Leave about 1/64-in. gap between the wheel and the bit edge. Retighten the wing nut and the router depth-of-cut setting.

Loosen both the rotary adjusting knob and the angular adjusting screw. Rotate the cutter adjustment disc to engage the spring in a disc notch. As necessary, rotate the bit (by turning the knob and disc) and/or tilt the bit holder up or down until the flat side of its edge is exactly parallel to the grinding-wheel top. Retighten the knob and screw. It may be necessary to hold a hex wrench in the head of the set screw (to

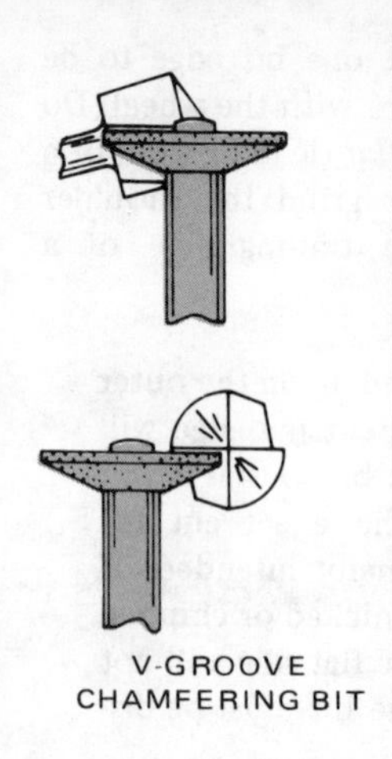

V-GROOVE CHAMFERING BIT

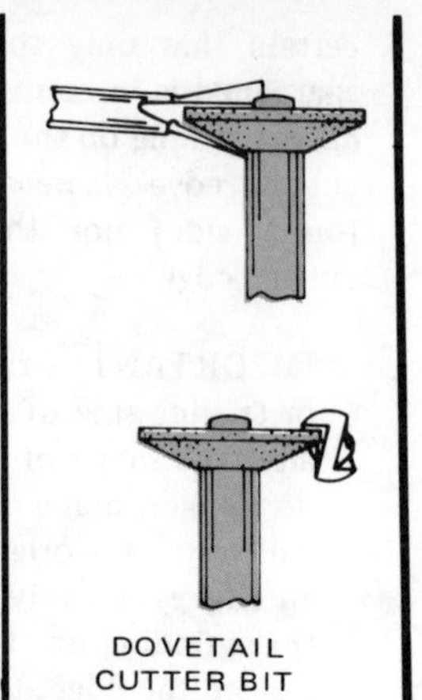

DOVETAIL CUTTER BIT

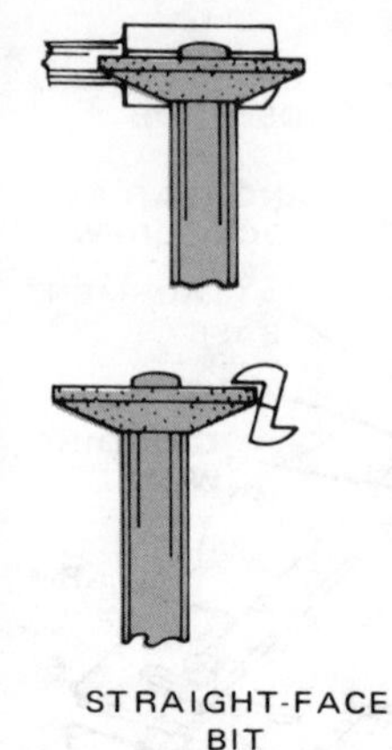

STRAIGHT-FACE BIT

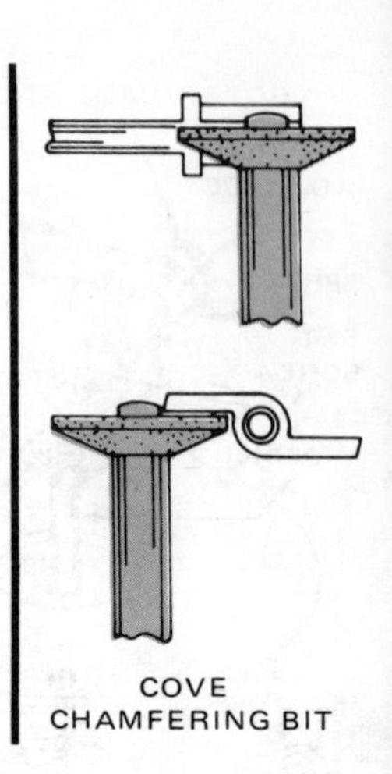

COVE CHAMFERING BIT

TYPICAL SHARPENING SET-UPS

prevent shaft rotation) while tightening the knob. Recheck your adjustments and correct them as necessary.

> *NOTE:* While making the above adjustments it may be necessary to readjust the arm position, to prevent the wheel edge from contacting the bit. If so, retighten the wing nut.

With all other adjustments satisfactorily made, start the router motor then rotate the vertical adjusting knob clockwise to place the bit edge in *light* contact with the grinding-wheel top. Slide the bit forward and back over the grinding wheel until the whole edge has been ground and you can tell (by the cessation of grinding noise) that the grinding action at this setting is finished.

If the edge was but slightly dulled, this one action may be sufficient; but, if more grinding is needed, rotate the vertical adjusting knob to lower the bit a *very small amount* (until you can again hear the grinding action), and repeat sliding the bit over the wheel. Continue in this manner until the edge is satisfactorily sharpened.

The notches in the cutter adjustment disc are for relocating the bit rotation position for grinding a second and/or third bit edge (for two and three edged bits). If your bit has more than one cutting edge, after completing the first grinding action on the first cutting edge — and *before* using the vertical adjusting knob to lower the bit — rotate the rotary adjustment knob to engage the spring with the next appropriate disc notch, to grind the second cutting edge (then, the third cutting edge, if there is one). In short, grind all the bit edges with each vertical adjusting knob setting before regrinding any edge with a new setting. This will assure uniform depth-of-grinding for all the edges (which is necessary to keep the bit cutting uniformly when in use).

After all cutting edges have been ground to desired sharpness, use a fine-tooth file and *very lightly* touch up the outer (unground) side of each edge to remove any burrs.

FOR SAFE OPERATION AND EXACT INFORMATION PERTAINING TO THE MODEL YOU HAVE REFER TO THE OWNER'S MANUAL PACKAGED WITH YOUR TOOL OR ACCESSORY

* * * * * * * *

THE INSTRUCTIONS CONTAINED IN THIS BOOK ARE GENERAL AND MAY NOT BE APPLICABLE TO ALL MODELS

CHAPTER V

THE TABLE-SHAPING, DECORATING, CARVING AND WOOD-TURNING ACCESSORIES

TABLE-SHAPING OPERATIONS

USING A ROUTER TABLE

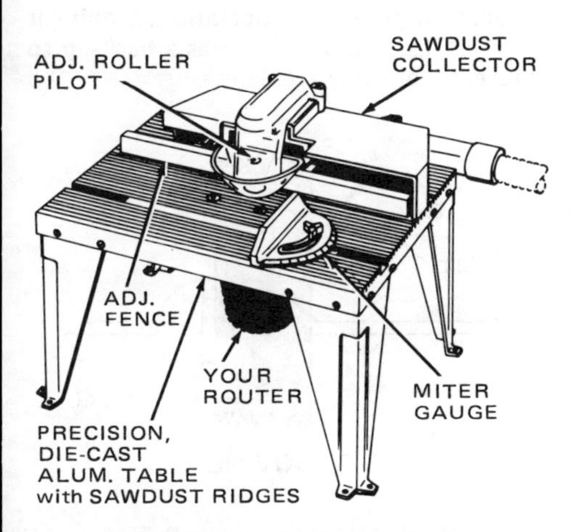

DELUXE ROUTER TABLE

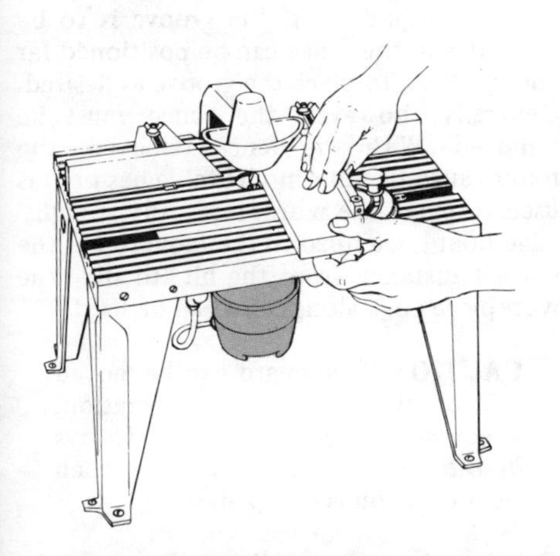

HEAVY-DUTY ROUTER TABLE

The Deluxe Router Table illustrated will convert your router into an excellent high-speed, bench-type wood shaper on which you can do a variety of intricate edge-shaping work, even on small workpieces which are difficult to shape when guiding the router by hand. The adjustable roller pilot serves to guide a workpiece whenever a bit without a pilot is used and the work-piece edge shape is curved so that the fence(s) cannot be used; bits with pilots and without the roller pilot are used for this same purpose; the fences are used for all straight-edged work and can be adjusted separately or together (which saves set-up time). Work can also be guided by the miter gauge (used, especially, for end shaping a board too narrow to be guided by the fences) and, to make this operation even easier to do precisely, we recommend that you purchase and use a Miter-Gauge Hold-Down Clamp (sold separately). All operations are made easier because the ridged table top helps prevent dust build-up that would prevent you from holding the workpiece flat down — and because the dust collector helps keep the area clean for better visibility (to use the latter you must also have a suitable Shop Vac, sold separately).

The Heavy-Duty Router Table is similar to the foregoing, but without the roller pilot and sawdust collector features. For these and other Sears tables and table accessories *refer to a current Sears Catalog.*

With a table you can do accurate jointing — the straightening and smoothing of straight edges to make perfect joints — or you can edge shape the whole or any part of any workpiece edge (straight or curved) that can be fed to the bit. In addition, you can rout through a workpiece to create slots or latticework designs, can carve the under-side of clear (see-through) plastic, can accu-rately cut narrowly-spaced end-to-end or

A TABLE MAKES SMALL-WORKPIECE EDGE SHAPING EASIER

blind grooves – and can do all these operations without the need of special guides or the time-consuming set-ups needed when hand-guiding your router.

GENERAL OPERATING INSTRUCTIONS

IMPORTANT: You must refer to your accessory's Owner's Manual for specific assembly, set-up and adjustment instructions. The following are merely generalized comments regarding table and table accessory uses.

In table shaping the bit is used upside-down. If a pilot is used, it is at top. Bit rotation is, as illustrated, *counterclockwise* when viewed from above the workpiece. To obtain the same edge pattern produced by hand routing with the router on the workpiece top, the workpiece must be placed on the table *bottom-side up.*

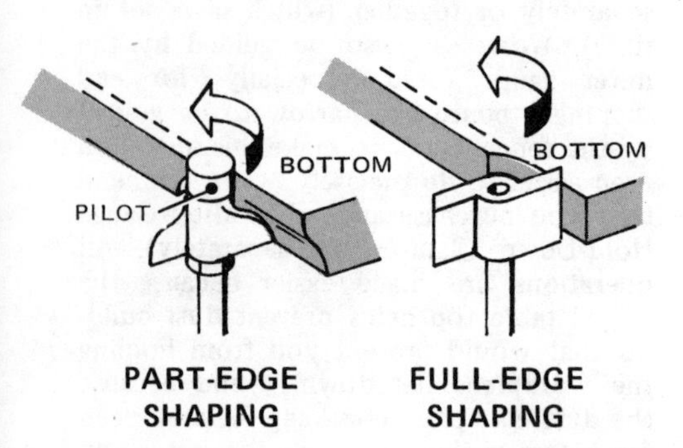

PART-EDGE SHAPING **FULL-EDGE SHAPING**

Full-edge shaping (removal of the entire thickness of a workpiece edge) can*not* be done using a pilot as the guide – the table fence or miter gauge must be used, and the workpiece edge must be straight (a curved or contoured edge cannot be guided in these ways). Most full-edge shaping is done with the rabbeting bit to straighten and plane the edge for making a tight butt joint (and is called "jointing"). Other bits can be used for full-edge shaping if you wish to simultaneously shape the edge and to recess it back to a finished dimension line.

NOTE: If a pattern with a spacer (refer to *Chapter 3*) is secured on top of the workpiece (to the workpiece *bottom* side), the full edge can be shaped using a pilot with the edge of the pattern to ride against it. *Full-end* shaping of a board too narrow to slide against the fence can be done with the miter gauge (if table is so equipped).

Part-edge shaping (which leaves an uncut part at the *top* of the edge thick enough to firmly contact a guide) can be done against the fence (if the edge is straight), or can be (and, generally, is) done using a pilot (or, if table is so equipped, the roller pilot) to guide the edge against. When a pilot is used, the fence should be moved back just enough to permit the operation; keeping it as close as possible serves as a back-up to prevent a possible accident.

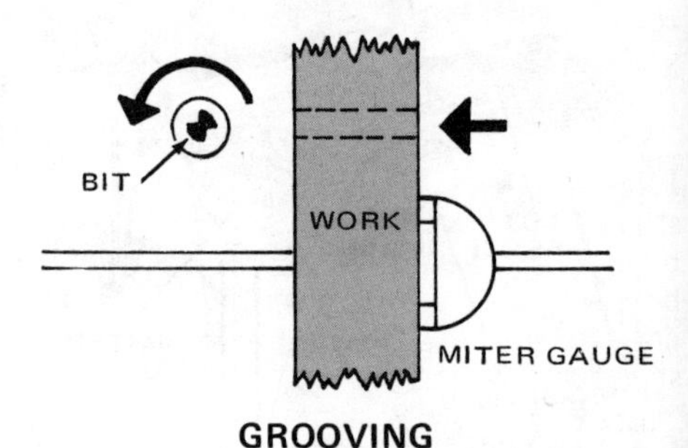

GROOVING

Grooving (which is done on the *underside* of the workpiece) can be done using the fence as a guide – if the groove is to be straight and the fence can be positioned far enough back to place the groove as desired. Generally, however, the fence must be removed. With the fence removed, the miter gauge (if your model table has one) is used to guide the workpiece. Any straight-edge board, clamped to the table top at the correct distance from the bit (to slide the workpiece edge along) also can be used.

CAUTION: The guard can be moved out of the way for an operation, when necessary – but *must always be returned* to proper position when the operation is completed.

Carving (also done on the *underside* of the workpiece) is done entirely by freehand guiding of the workpiece over the bit. Unless the workpiece is transparent (so you can see the bit through it), there is no sure, practical method of guiding.

IMPORTANT: Whenever freehand guiding or using the miter gauge or a straightedge guide, *remove the fence* from the table. Pilots can*not* be used for grooving or carving operations. Guide bushings are never used for table routing operations. A pattern (with a pilot) can be used only for outside or inside *edge* shaping, never for grooving or carving.

When edge shaping, the workpiece must always be fed to the bit *against* the bit rotation, to prevent the bit from hogging the work and pulling it out of your hands. Therefore, whenever the workpiece edge being shaped is between you and the bit (figs. 1 and 2 of the illustration), feed from *right to left* . . . but if the bit is between you and the edge being shaped (fig. 3), feed from *left to right*.

Preferably, use the fence (fig. 1) for straight-edge shaping (although a pilot can be used, if desirable). A pilot (fig. 2) must be used for all outside curved or contoured edge shaping, and (fig. 3) for all inside edge shaping.

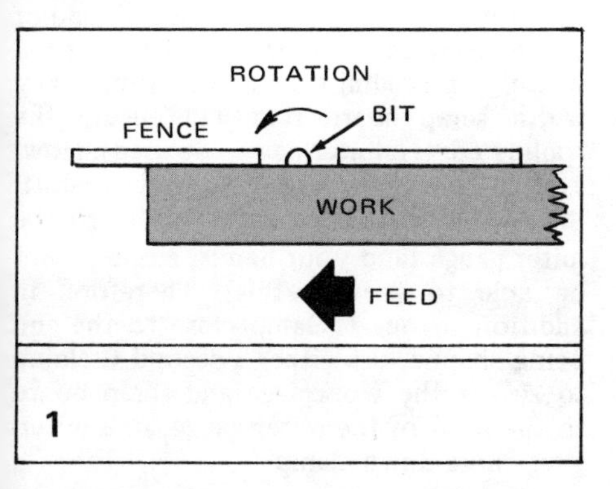

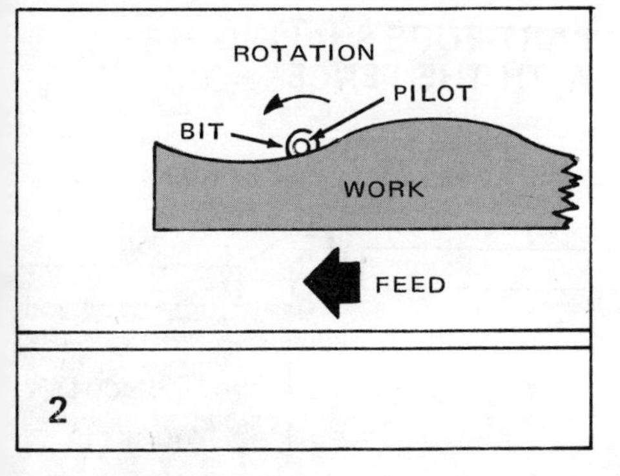

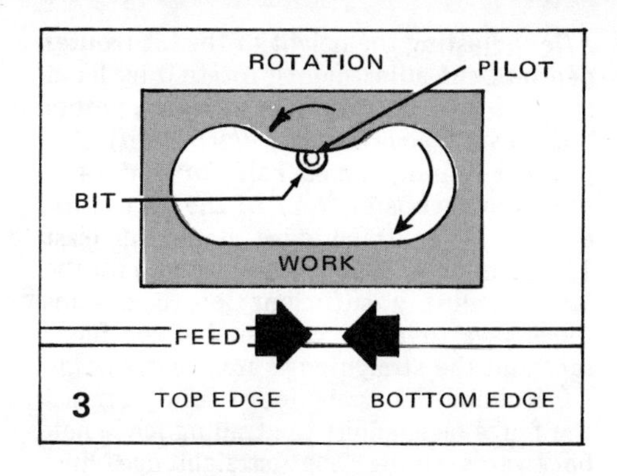

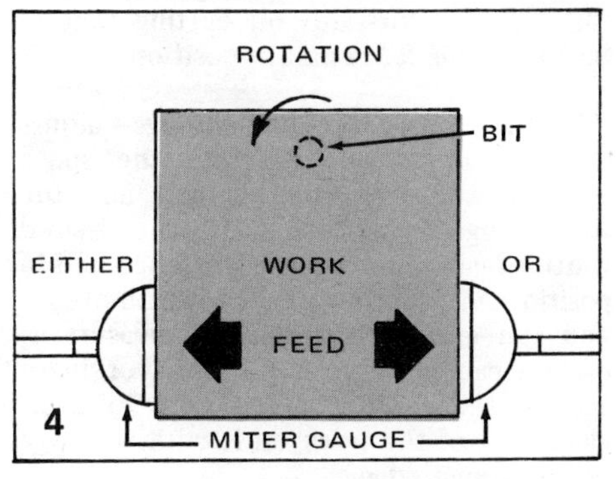

When grooving (or carving) the feed can be from either direction (fig. 4) — and the miter gauge (if used) can be at either side of the workpiece (it is always positioned behind, to *push* the workpiece).

FULL-EDGE SHAPING

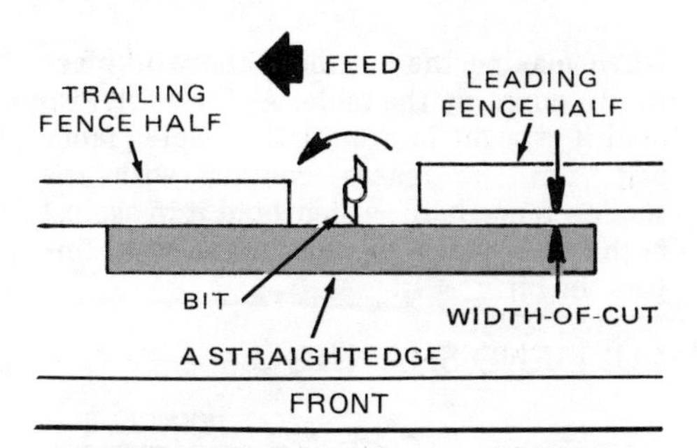

Because full-edge shaping cuts away the whole edge, the *trailing* fence half must be adjusted forward of the *leading* fence half an amount equal to the width-of-cut — to compensate for the removed stock and allow the workpiece to slide in a straight path along the fence.

After adjusting the height of the bit (router depth-of-cut adjustment), rotate it by hand to place one cutting edge at its maximum "out-front" position (*see illustration*). Adjust the trailing fence half forward until the front face is in front of the bit cutting edge. Lay a straightedge board at least 1/4-in. thick and 16- to 18-in. long) on the table against a sufficient length of this fence face to make certain that the fence face and the straightedge are *exactly parallel.* Holding the straightedge firmly against the fence face, adjust the trailing fence half backwards until the straightedge just touches the (forward) bit cutting edge – then lock this fence half in position.

Without moving the straightedge, adjust the leading fence half until the space between the face of this half and the straightedge *exactly* equals your desired width-of-cut – then lock this fence half in position. To determine the width-of-cut, you can either use a ruler to measure it, or you can place your marked workpiece against the leading fence half to sight alignment of the mark on it with the edge of the straightedge.

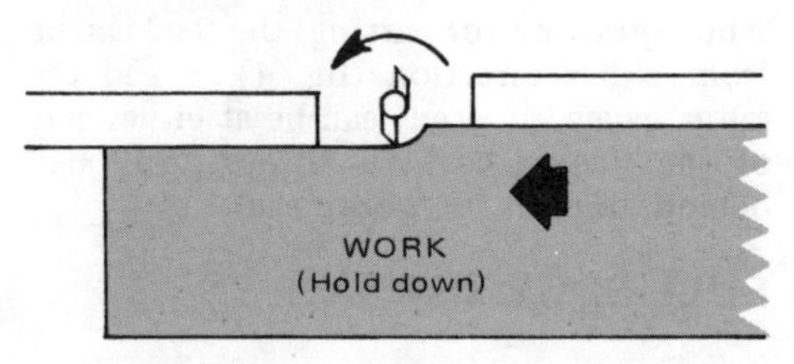

When making the cut, hold the workpiece firmly down on the table. At the start, also hold it straight in against the leading fence half, until it makes contact with the trailing fence half – then hold it in against both fence halves to slide in a straight line past the bit.

FULL-END SHAPING

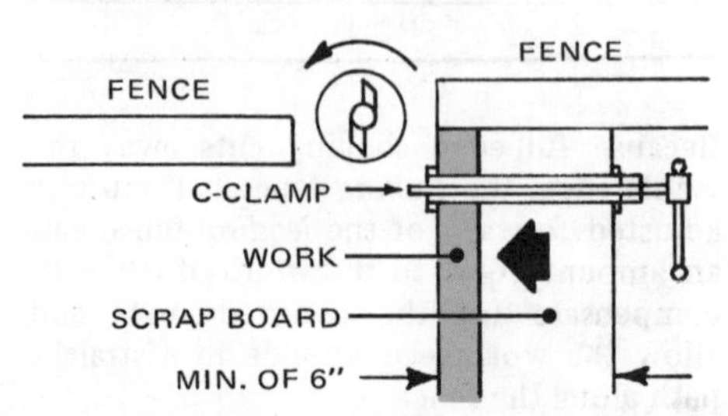

Because the bit will splinter the trailing edge of a board when shaping across the grain, it is advisable to clamp a scrap board *behind* the workpiece, as illustrated, when end shaping. When using the fence, if the workpiece end is less than 6-in. wide, a scrap board wide enough to make the total width a minimum of 6-in. *must* be used. Position the clamp as close to the end being shaped as possible.

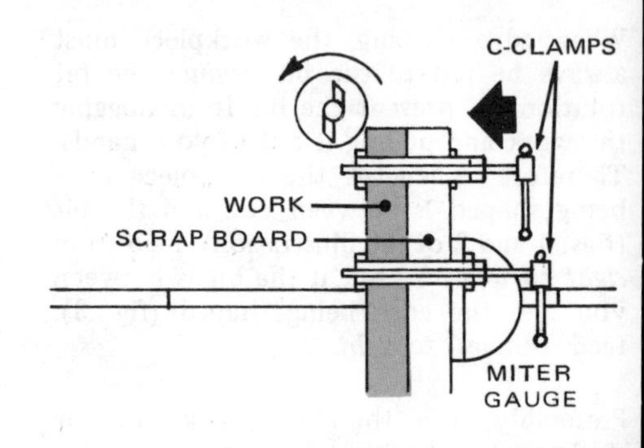

NOTE: This arrangement (use of scrap board) should be used whether full- or part-end shaping.

A miter gauge (if you have one), instead of the fence, can be used – and the "total width" (preceding) is unimportant (any width scrap board that will absorb the trailing edge splintering can be used). However, it is very important to prevent shifting of the workpiece with respect to the miter gauge (and your hands, alone, won't be able to prevent this). Therefore, in addition to one C-clamp close to the end being shaped, use either a second C-clamp to secure the workpiece and scrap board to the head of the miter gauge, or a miter-gauge hold-down clamp.

PART-EDGE SHAPING WITH THE FENCE

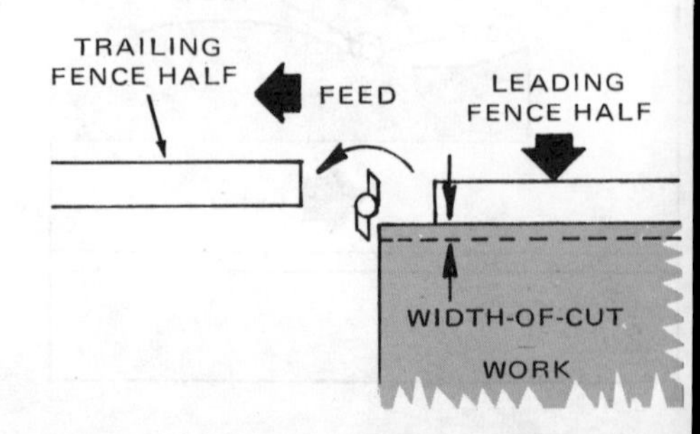

To make an accurate width-of-cut setting, the bit must first be adjusted to the desired height and rotated to position one cutting edge at the front, as previously told. Mark the width-of-cut (dash line, in the illustration) on your workpiece. Loosen and move both fence halves back of the bit. Place your workpiece on the table with the width-of-cut mark aligned with the bit forward cutting edge, and adjust the *leading* fence half forward until its front face just touches the workpiece. The workpiece edge and the fence face must be *exactly* parallel. Lock this fence half.

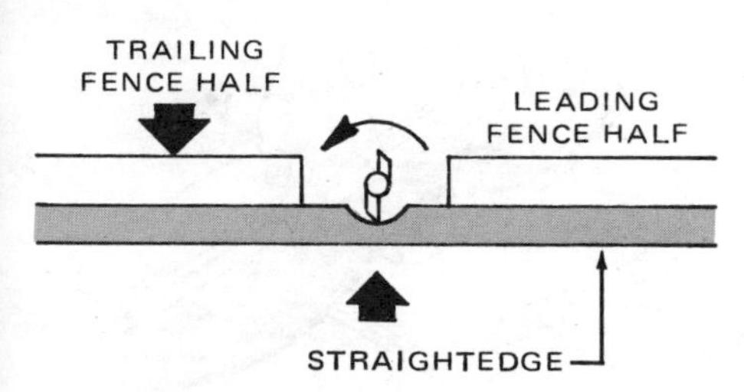

Use a straightedge board, at least 1/4-in. thick and 16- to 18-in. long by 2-in. or more wide (the same one can be used here and for the previous operation). Start your router, lay the straightedge on the table, and push it straight into the bit so that its right half will be up against — and *exactly* parallel to — the leading-fence-half face. Turn off the router and *wait* for the bit to stop revolving. Now, without moving the straightedge, adjust the trailing fence half forward until it also just touches the straightedge — and both fence halves are *exactly* parallel to the straightedge. Lock this fence half and proceed to make your cut.

SHAPING SMALL WORKPIECES AGAINST THE FENCE

WARNING: Do *not* attempt this when using a pilot as a guide.

Small, straight workpieces, down to 1-in. by 3-in. size (*see illustration*), can be shaped against the fence using a straightedge wood block, as shown. Cut the block notch so there will be no end-play of the workpiece in the block. Make the notch to a depth that will recess the workpiece, as shown, flush with the block edge. Adjust the fence either as for a full- or part-edge cut, preceding — then feed the block (with workpiece in it) straight along the fence.

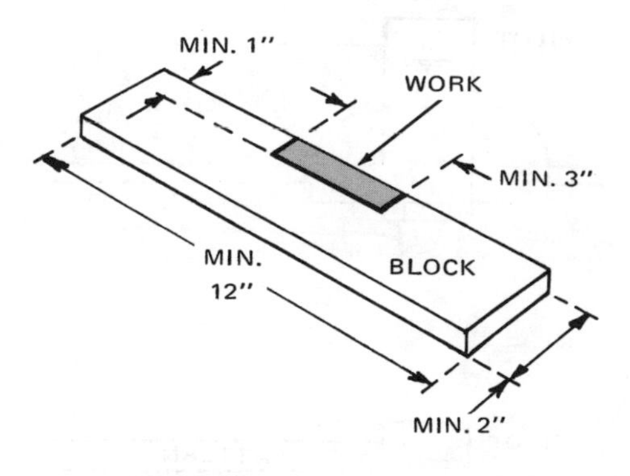

PART- OR FULL-EDGE SHAPING WITH A PILOT

Both the adjusted height of the bit and the size pilot used will determine the actual shape of the cut to be made. If the bit height is to be such that there will not be at least 1/16-in. thickness of uncut wood at the workpiece top (to contact the pilot), a pattern must be secured to the workpiece top (its bottom side) to serve this purpose. Any pattern used must have a contact edge that is either identical to the workpiece edge — or, if the full workpiece edge is to be removed, the pattern edge must be identical to the workpiece "final edge" (*see illustration*). This means that the pattern edge must have the same contour as the workpiece edge (or final edge).

NOTE: It is *not* practical to remove a lot of stock when planning a full-edge cutting operation for shaping an edge. The only good reason for shaping the full edge is to remove slight sawing inaccuracies that may be unavoidable when band- or jig-sawing a contoured edge to shape. When preparing a contoured edge you can "rough-saw" leaving "bumps" up to 1/8-in. *beyond* the desired final edge. By then making an accurate pattern to conform with the exact final edge, and by placing it correctly on top of the workpiece, you can shape the workpiece smoothly to the final-edge line.

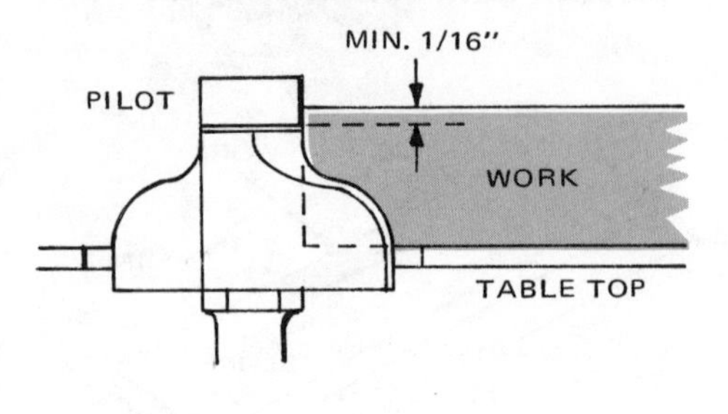

– OR –

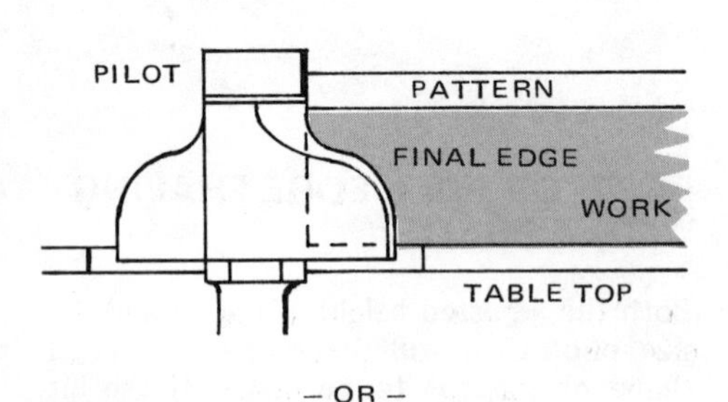

– OR –

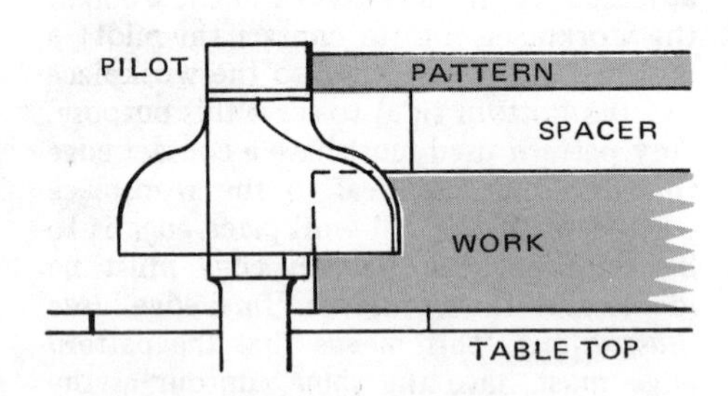

If necessary, because of the bit height adjustment, a scrap-wood spacer of correct thickness can be located between the workpiece and pattern (to elevate the pattern up to the pilot). Any pattern and/or spacer used *must* be secured so it (they) cannot slip. Being on top (bottom side) of the workpiece, these generally can be temporarily nailed to the workpiece.

To make the proper bit height adjustment – and to check on the width-of-cut determined by pilot size and/or pattern position – mark the desired cut shape on a workpiece end. Place the workpiece on the table with this end as close as possible to the bit – then make your adjustments (bit height and pilot size or pattern position) by aligning one bit cutting edge with your marked shape.

While feeding your workpiece to the bit, hold it down on the table – and, also, hold it *squarely* in against the pilot (part of edge being cut as nearly as possible at 90° to the bit centerline) at all times.

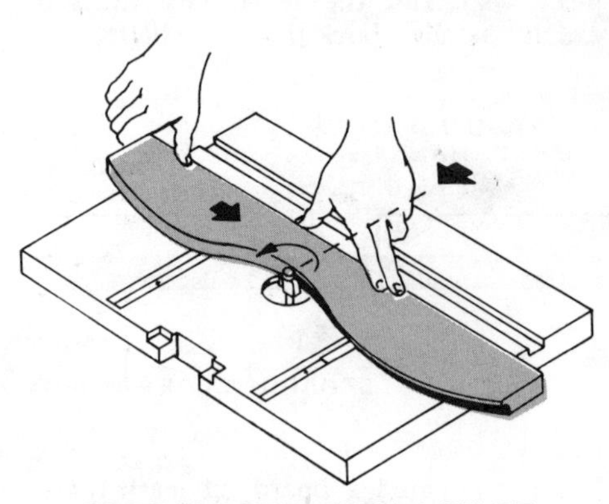

EDGE SHAPING WITH A PILOT

USING A STRAIGHTEDGE FOR GROOVING

For making grooves on the underside (top) of the workpiece, the fence can be used, with the two halves adjusted parallel, if it can be positioned far enough to the rear for your purpose. Otherwise, remove the fence and substitute a straightedge board, as illustrated. In fact, if the table top is not big enough to allow even the required

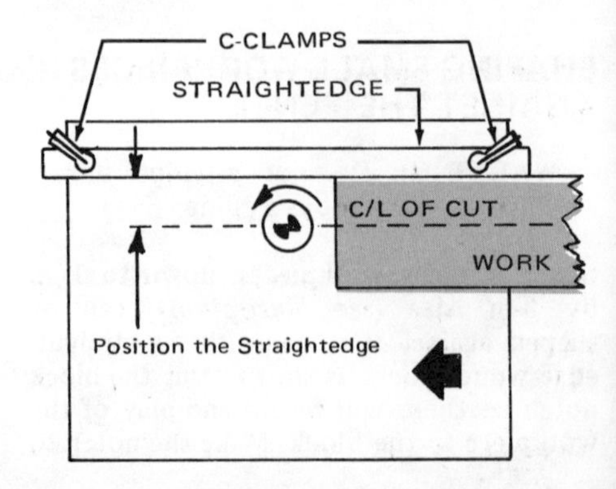

positioning of a straightedge board, you can cover it with a large enough piece of 1/4-in. hardboard (cut-out at center for the bit to project up through it) — and C-clamp the straightedge board to this.

Angled grooves can be made by using a wedge to slide along the straightedge and hold the workpiece at the desired angle. The workpiece must be secured to the wedge so as not to slide along it. Temporarily nail a scrap cross-piece to the wedge and to the top (bottom side) of the work-piece to hold them securely together.

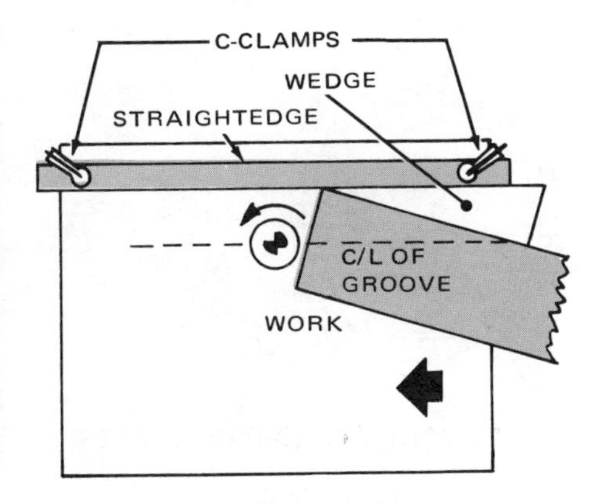

If nailing the workpiece to secure it to the wedge is undesirable, design the wedge so that the workpiece "corner" will contact the fence, as shown — then use rubber cement on wedge and workpiece edges to prevent sliding and/or install a handle on the wedge.

USING A MITER GAUGE FOR GROOVING

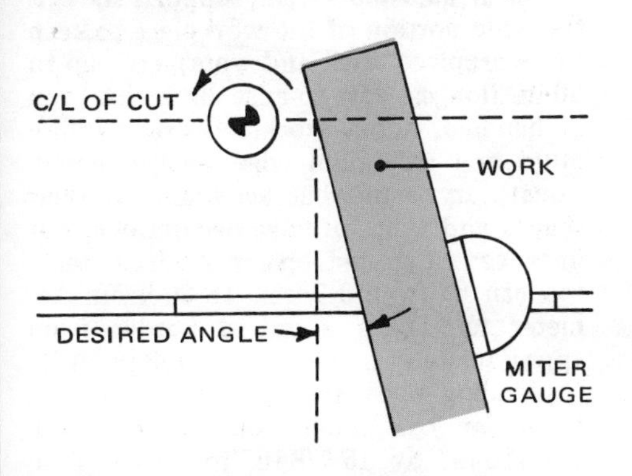

The miter gauge can be used for grooving operations in much the same way already described for "Full-Edge Shaping," preceding. In addition, the miter gauge can be set at any desired angle, to produce grooves at this angle to the workpiece edge that is against the miter gauge.

When grooving (straight or at an angle) the workpiece generally can be held by hand firmly enough against the miter-gauge head to prevent side-slippage . . . on the other hand, you may find it difficult to do this without getting one hand too close to the bit (*always allow at least 6-in clearance between the bit and the path your hand will move along*). Therefore, it is advisable to C-clamp the workpiece to the miter gauge head (as previously shown) or to use a miter-gauge hold-down clamp if the workpiece is too narrow for a safe and sure hand hold.

ON-EDGE SHAPING

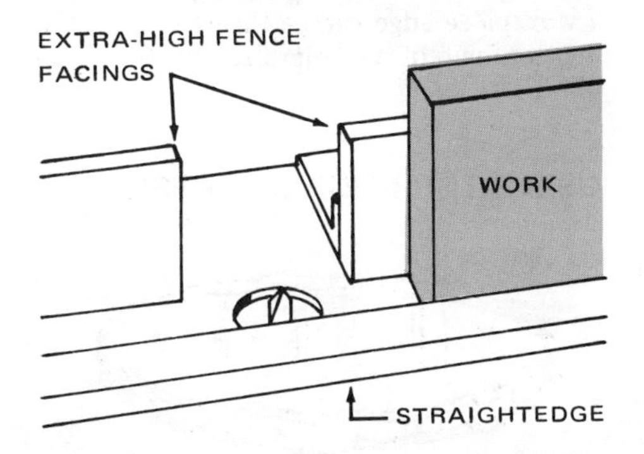

Sometimes it may be desirable to edge shape into either the top or bottom work-piece surface, instead of straight into the edge. Different edge patterns can be provided in this manner. Such an operation, however, presents the problem of holding the workpiece truly upright and in against the bit throughout the cut.

To overcome this problem, set up as illustrated. When attaching wood facings to your fence (refer to the Owner's Manual packaged with your table), use pieces of wood at least two-thirds as high as the width of workpiece to be on-edge shaped. When setting up for the operation, C-clamp a straightedge to the table top, spaced out from the fence so as to provide a channel in which the workpiece will be snugly guided past the bit.

ROLLER-PILOT SHAPING

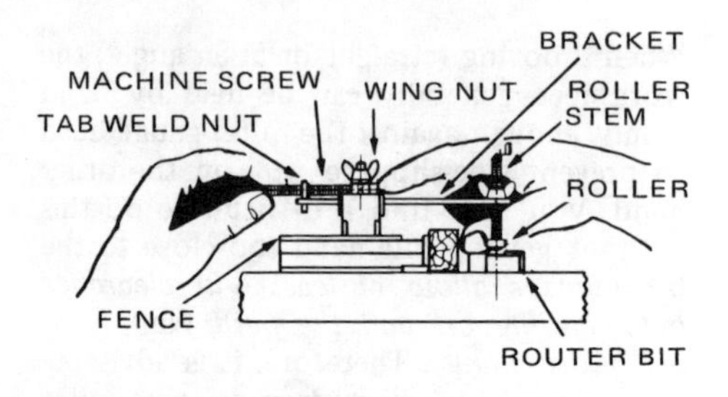

Edge shaping of contoured edges using pilotless bits can be done with the roller pilot (on tables so equipped) properly adjusted to guide the workpiece edge. Refer to your table's Owner's Manual for complete instructions. The guide provides a small-diameter roller (pilot) against which a workpiece edge can be thrust to limit the depth-of-cut of the bit directly below the pilot.

USING THE EDGE CRAFTER

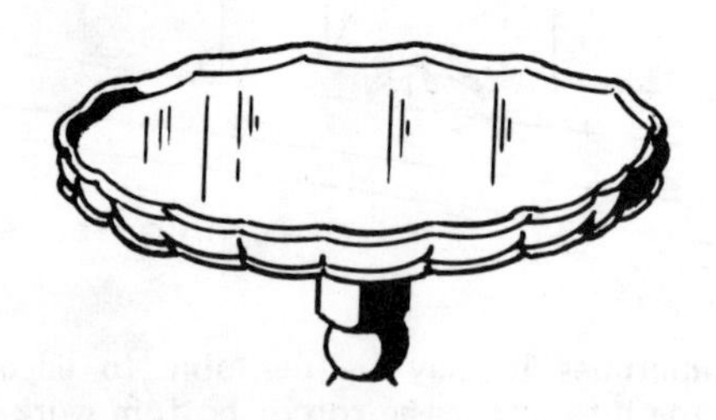

The Edge Crafter Accessory — sold separately to fit on your Router Table — will enable you to produce professional-quality, fancy-edged, flat or piecrust table tops, serving trays, and mirror or picture frames in a variety of shapes and sizes. Workpieces can also be top-surface decorated with grooves that parallel the shaped edges. A bit set, that includes the bits commonly needed and is sold separately, is recommended. Four complete templates, that can be used separately or in combinations to produce different designs, are furnished with the accessory — plus instructions for making as many more templates as desired. *Refer to a current Sears Catalog* for buying information; and *refer to the Owner's Manual* furnished with the accessory for specific assembly, adjustment and operating instructions.

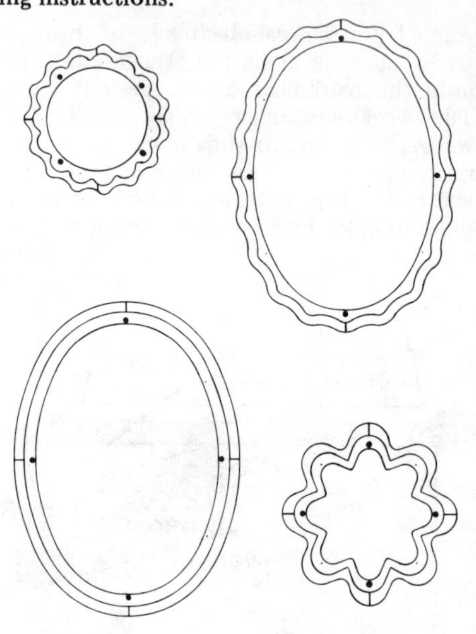

TYPICAL WORKPIECE SHAPES

The typical workpieces shown are some of those produced by the four templates furnished. Combining the use of templates will vary the results. As with all table operations, routing is done on the workpiece underside; and the template and the fixture support guide are attached to the center of the workpiece bottom (which is on top during the operation). A support bracket, attached to the accessory and having an adjustable stem, supports the off-the-table portion of the workpiece to keep the workpiece level, and workpieces up to 30-in. (longest edge-to-edge dimension) can be handled. Actual workpieces sizes (minimum and maximum edge-to-edge dimensions) vary somewhat according to their shapes and types of edge decorations. For instance: A round, piecrust-edged table top can be from 9-3/8-in. to 30-in. in diameter and have a raised border from approximately 1-1/2-in. to 2-1/8-in. wide (depending upon the type of scalloping); a similar oval table top can be from 11-3/16-in. by 15-7/8-in. to 25-15/16-in. by 30-in. with similarly varied raised border widths. The maximum thickness of a finished workpiece, including the height of a raised border, is 1-7/16-in.; minimum thickness is 1/4-in., but minimum thickness at the center where the support guide is attached is 5/8-in., which must be provided, if necessary, by temporarily glueing or nailing on a 1-1/2-in. square wood block to the bottom side.

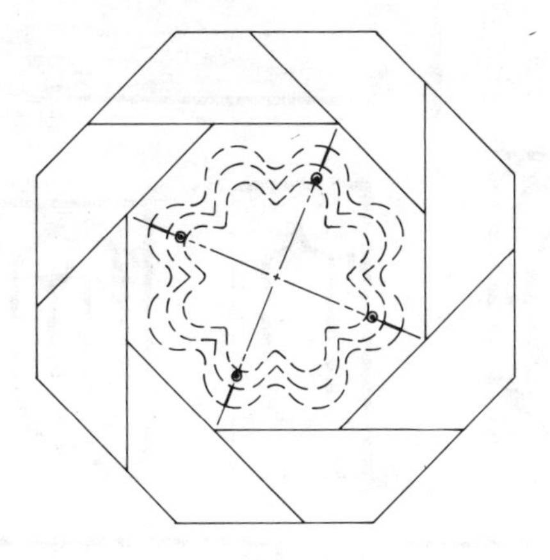

BLOCKING FOR A TYPICAL RAISED BORDER

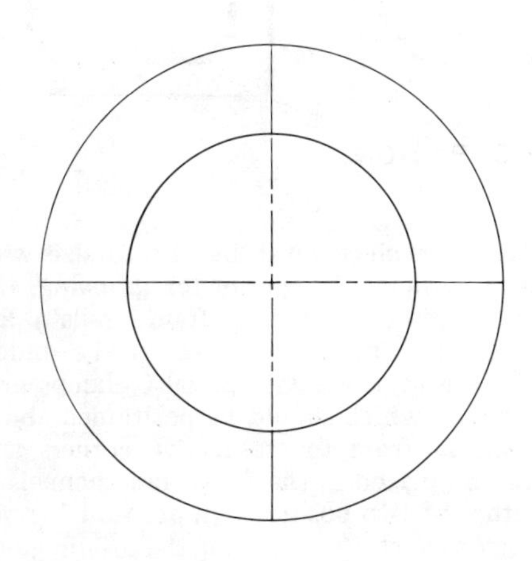

BLOCKING FOR A TYPICAL FRAME

Any flat (without raised border) workpiece can be prepared by rough sawing to shape to leave 1/16- to 1/8-in. stock to be removed by routing. If workpiece is a frame, it can be prepared by glueing together small blocks to form the shape and temporarily attaching these to a backing. Table tops and trays with raised borders are prepared by adding on, around the top edge, glued-on and tightly jointed wood blocks to form the raised border portion. In all cases, it is desirable to have those contours to be shaped such that no more stock than necessary will have to be removed during the shaping operation.

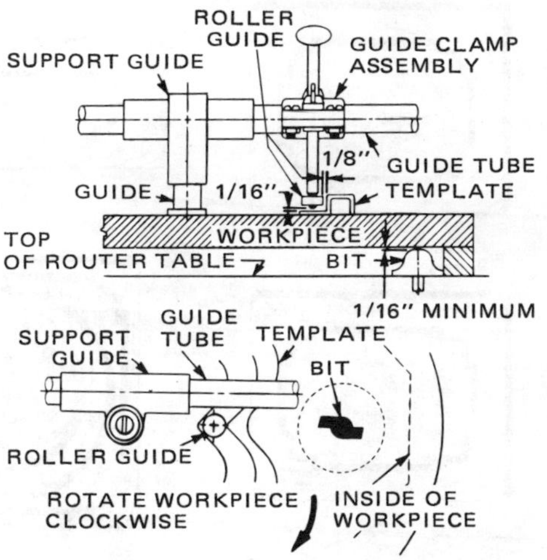

AN INSIDE OF BORDER OPERATION

Perfect-circle table tops with or without raised borders that require only perfect-circle routing can be worked without a pattern, by simply locking the guide arm for the desired depth-of-cut. In all other cases, a pattern must be used — and the guide clamp assembly is locked after properly positioning the roller guide against the template for each successive cut. It is positioned, in each instance, so that a maximum cut of about 1/8-in. will be taken as the assembly slides in and out along the guide tubes to follow the template — and it is reset as many times as necessary for the final cut to accomplish the desired contour. Each time the bit height is changed, or a different bit is substituted, in order to vary the contour, these steps are repeated — and if a different template is later used, the steps are again repeated. All feeding is done against bit rotation: counterclockwise when routing an outside edge; clockwise when routing the inner side of a raised border or frame. Because, when routing the inner side of a raised border, it is not desirable to risk cutting into the table top with the bit top, a fine lip (about 1/64-in.) is generally left at the inner side of the added-on blocks — this can be removed later by sanding it away.

THE DRAWER AND DOOR PANEL DECORATOR

TYPICAL PANEL DECORATIONS

This easily used accessory will make it possible for you to decorate the face of any panel type workpiece – such as a door, drawer front, folding screen panel, etc. – up to 36-in. square by 1-in. thick with a variety of groove-routed perimeter and/or radius designs. The accessory consists of four framing pieces with clamps, which can be assembled to frame a square or rectangular workpiece for surface grooving parallel to the edges, seven corner sets (four templates per set) to snap into place at the frame corners to create decorative corner groovings, and a radius attachment to be used for routing areas from 5-in. to 17-1/4-in. radius. End cutting router bits (for grooving) and a 5/8-in. guide bushing – *refer to Chapter 1* – which must be purchased separately, are also required.

The workpiece must be cut to size with 90° corners. For perimeter grooving, the four framing pieces ("frame rails") are assembled to the workpiece on its underside, using the eight special C-clamps provided – which should be positioned about 1-in. in from the respective corners and can be placed in the frame rail channels in either of two positions. In position 1 (*refer to the illustrations*), using the 5/8-in. guide bushing on the router, the centerline of the router-bit cut can be adjusted (using the C-clamp adjusting screw) from 3/4-in. to 1-7/8-in. in from the workpiece edge; in position 2 this adjusted distance is from 1-7/8-in. to 3-in. After this adjustment is made the C-clamp clamp screws are tightened, the workpiece (with the frame rails attached) is turned rightside-up and

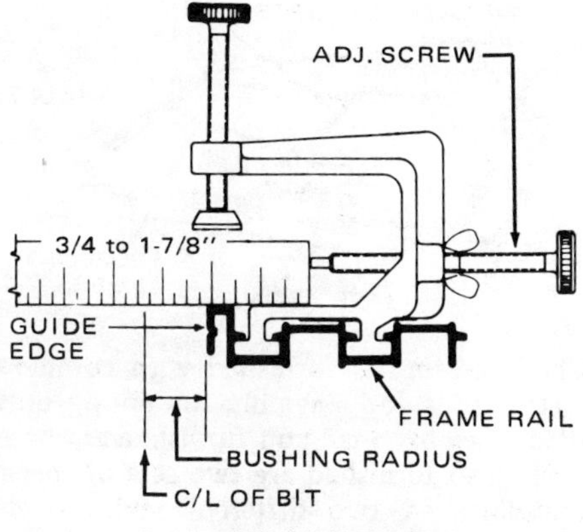

C-CLAMP POSITION 1

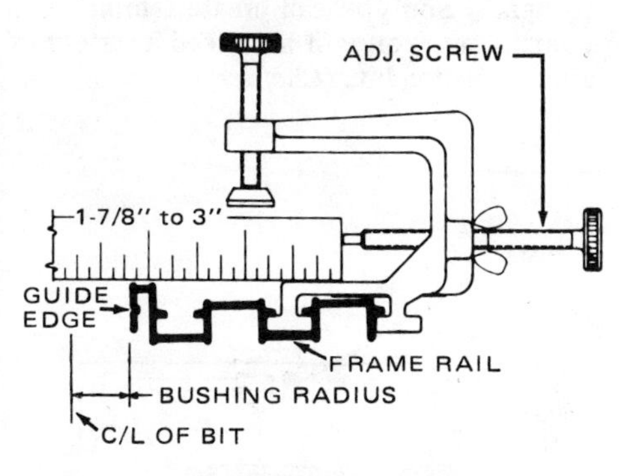

C-CLAMP POSITION 2

placed on a bench or other work surface, and the selected corner-set templates are snapped into place at the four corners of the frame rails.

Routing of the perimeter groove is done by adjusting the router bit for a maximum 1/8-in. deep cut, then traversing the router clockwise around the workpiece against the frame rails and the corner templates. Deeper grooves require two or more passes. Additional "parallel" grooves are made after readjusting the C-clamp adjusting screws.

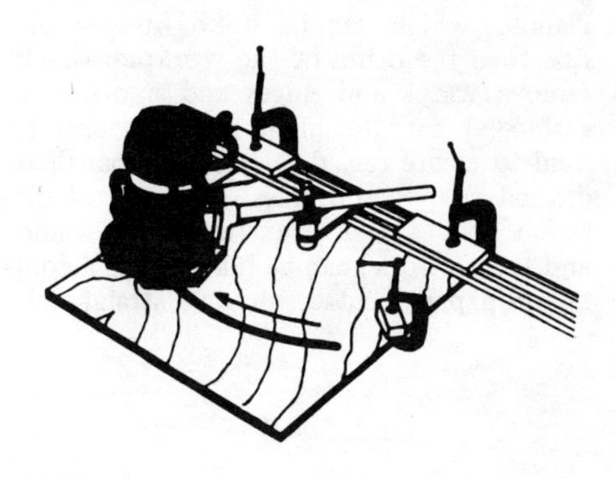

To create groove-cut radius designs the router is mounted on the radius attachment which, in turn, is mounted on one frame rail that is C-clamped in place on the workpiece. Since the rail can be clamped to the workpiece at any desired position and the radius attachment also can be secured to the rail where desired, arcs of a great variety of radii and placement can be created. In addition, homemade templates can be used at the corners to create still a greater variety of designs.

> IMPORTANT: For all accessories, refer to your accessory Owner's Manual for complete instructions and to a current Sears Catalog for buying information.

THE DECOROUT-OR PLANER

This accessory also is used for decorating the surfaces of square or rectangular workpieces, such as doors, drawer fronts and panels. However, because the router is mounted above the workpiece on a carriage that slides freely crosswise on a guiderail assembly which, in turn, slides freely on parallel support tables (*see the accompanying illustration*), designs of your own choosing can be routed anywhere on the workpiece surface in addition to around its perimeter. By varying the router depth-of-cut you can add still other variations to your routed designs. Moreover, with a rabbeting bit (*Chapter 1*) installed in the router, you can plane to a level, either a single board or two or more workpieces glued together to form a large piece. Planing, which can be done first on one side then the other of the workpieces, will remove warps and ridges and smooth the surface(s) for finishing; and can also be used to create raised or indented panels of desired shapes and sizes. Cut-outs of different shapes and sizes (including frames and lattice work) can be made using a combination panel cutter bit or a straight bit.

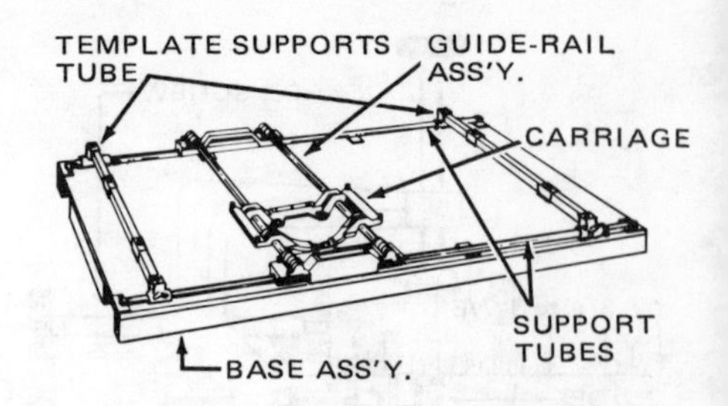

The accessory is furnished with complete instructions for assembly, mounting on a base assembly that you furnish, and operation. Also furnished are two sets of corner templates in two different styles (eight templates); each set makes two different-size corners for a total of four different corners — and you can create templates to your liking. You will also need a variety of groove-cutting bits (*Chapter 1*).

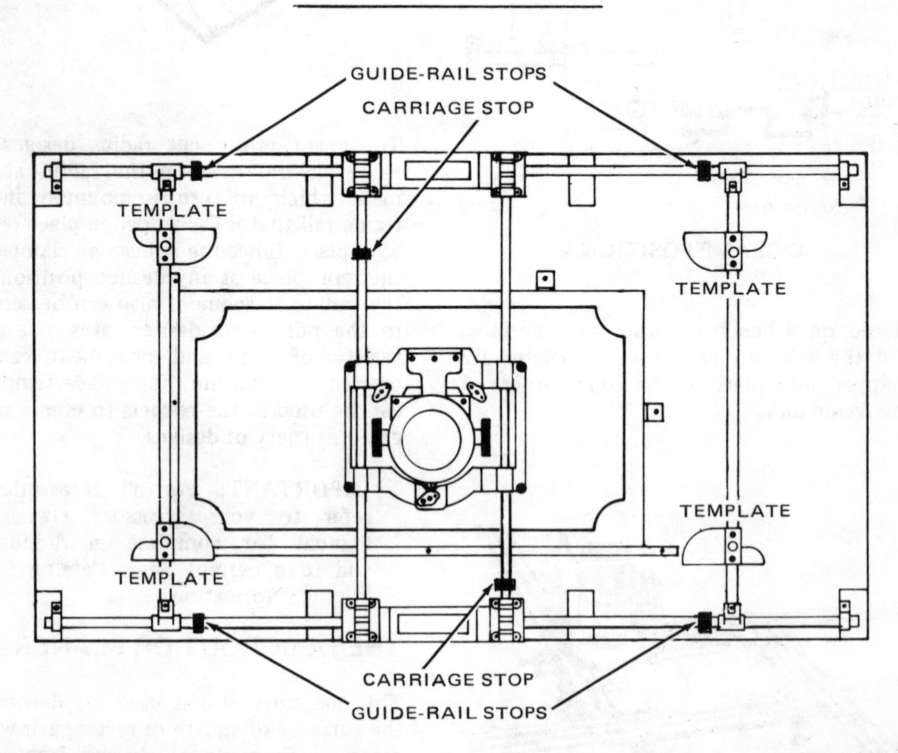

Perimeter grooving, at any desired distance from the workpiece edge, is done by clamping the workpiece into position on the accessory base assembly (clamps are furnished) and by setting the thumb-screw clamped guide-rail and carriage stops to limit guide-rail and carriage movements. Planing is done with a similar set-up. If decorative corners are desired, the appropriate corner templates (four) are fastened to supports on the template-support tubes and positioned as necessary.

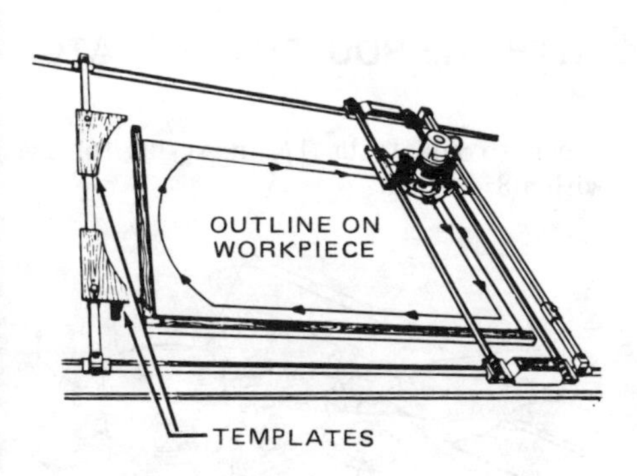

Special grooved designs and/or raised or indented panels or cut-outs can be achieved by using homemade templates to be fastened to the template-support tubes. Workpieces up to 21-in. wide by 42-in. long can be accommodated by the base assembly on which the accessory is mounted — and longer workpieces (to be decorated in two or more sections) also can be handled.

Using homemade templates to guide the carriage and guide-rail assembly there is no limit to the type and sizes of special designs — for grooving, paneling or cut-out work — that can be created. For all work a cut is started simply by rotating the router (while running) downward on its hinged carriage mount, holding it firmly down while guiding the carriage and guide-rail assembly to cut in a clockwise direction, then by stopping the router and rotating it back up off of the workpiece at the finish.

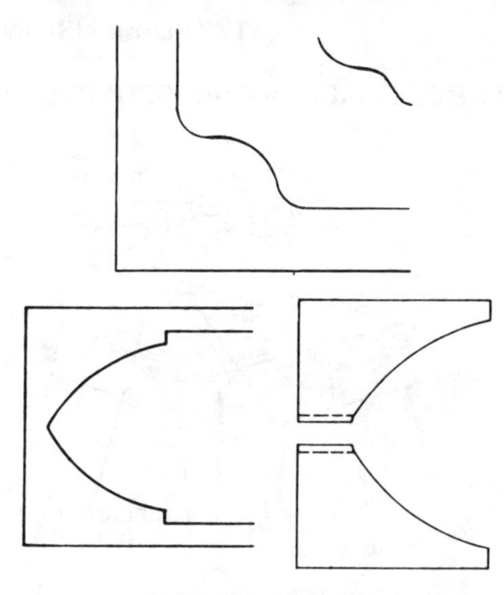

TYPICAL DESIGNS

ALL INFORMATION PROVIDED IN THIS BOOK IS INTENDED SOLELY TO HELP YOU UNDERSTAND THE GENERAL PRINCIPLES OF OPERATIONS OF THE TOOLS, AND IS BASED UPON CURRENT MODELS OF THE TOOLS AND ACCESSORIES. YOU MUST REFER TO THE OWNER'S MANUAL FURNISHED WITH YOUR TOOL OR ACCESSORY FOR PERTINENT, SAFE ASSEMBLY AND OPERATING INSTRUCTIONS

TWO-DIMENSIONAL CARVING AND

THREE-DIMENSIONAL SCULPTURING WITH THE ROUTER RECREATOR

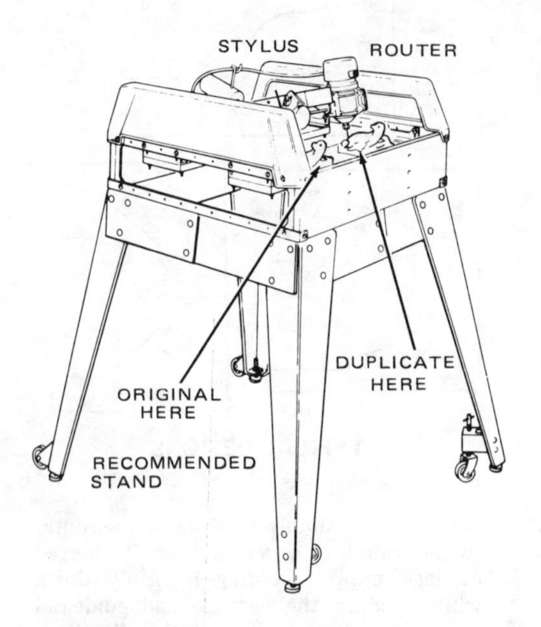

With this accessory, your router (Sears and most other models), and the proper bits (*refer to a current Sears Catalog for recommended bits*) you can duplicate two-dimensional carvings of letters and decorative motifs on workpieces up to 10- by 24-in. from originals or paper tracings and can duplicate three-dimensional originals in sizes up to 8-in. diameter by 8-in. high.

The accessory is furnished unassembled with complete instructions for assembly, adjustment and operation — you *must* refer to the accessory Owner's Manual for these instructions. Most any router with a motor body from 3 to 3-3/4-in. in diameter can be used, but it is necessary to partially disassemble the router to mount it on the accessory. The stand shown in the illustration is sold separately (*refer to a current Sears Catalog*) and is recommended for best use of your accessory. You will also need a selection of router bits, especially the five-piece bit set offered for use with this accessory. Three styluses (1/16-in., 1/8-in. and 1/4-in.) are furnished for use with bits of like diameters — also a 3/4-in. sleeve to adapt the 1/4-in. stylus for use with a 3/4-in. bit.

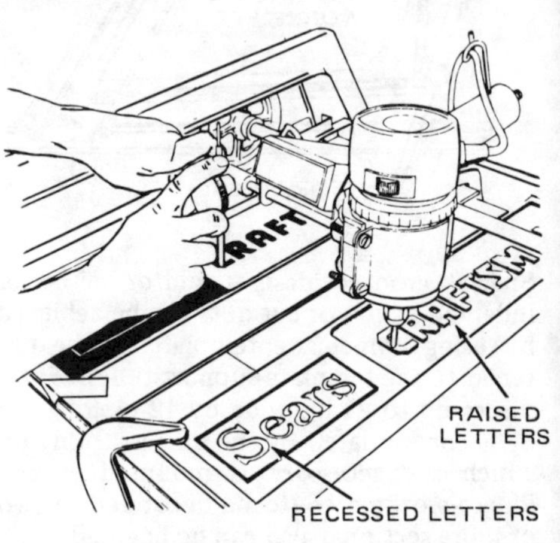

Signs and other two-dimensional decorative works can be duplicated at 100% of size from either originals or from drawings. The original (or drawing) is secured flat on one of the accessory "shelf boards" and the workpiece (for the duplicate) is secured to another shelf board (under the router). A bit of proper diameter for the operation is installed in the router and a like diameter stylus is installed in the accessory stylus mount. After the router is started and lowered to begin work the stylus is used to trace the original (or drawing) — and the router bit faithfully follows all movements of the stylus in any direction (including up and down) to carve the workpiece. Recessed letters and designs can be carved out; raised letters and designs can be created by carving out around them. Varying letter (etc.) heights (or depths) can be created as desired.

Square and rectangular workpieces up to 10-in. by 24-in. can be decoratively edged using this accessory and one of the edging bits (*Chapter 1*) on a shaft with a pilot. The workpiece is clamped in place in the accessory and the stylus guide arm is used to travel the router along the edge for a depth-of-cut established by the bit pilot.

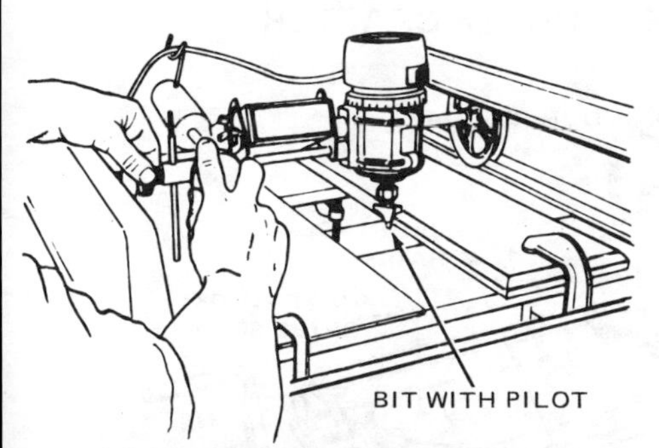

FOR DECORATIVE EDGING

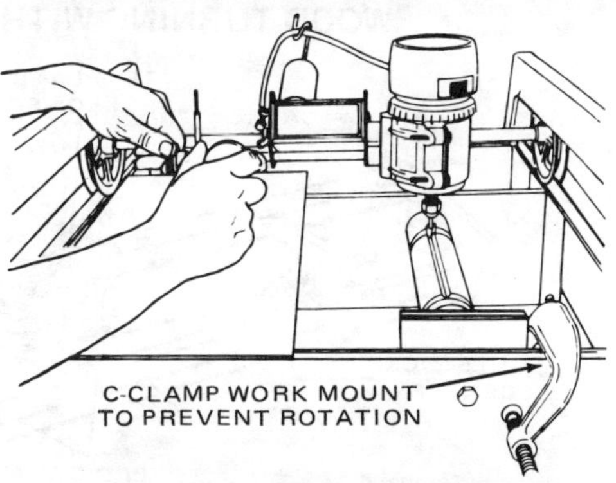

FOR AXIAL DECORATIONS

Spindles up to 24-in. long can be decorated both with circumferential (ring) grooves and with lengthwise (axial) grooves in any patterns that can be cut by one or a combination of the various grooving bits available (*Chapter 1*). These cuts can be made from a drawing (template) or from an original — which means that you can make four or more exact duplicates (as for table legs). The workpiece is mounted in the accessory between a cone-point spindle mount and a work mount (both furnished) so that it will be properly centered and aligned with the router. The template (or original) is mounted alongside to guide positioning or movement of the stylus.

For making a ring the stylus is locked in position and the workpiece is revolved — after lowering the running router — by hand turning the workpiece with a wrench. To make an axial groove the workpiece is correctly positioned (indexed) and C-clamped in position, then the stylus is used to guide the router.

For carving three-dimensional objects from an original (up to 8-in. in diameter by 8-in. tall) it is necessary to prepare a wood block

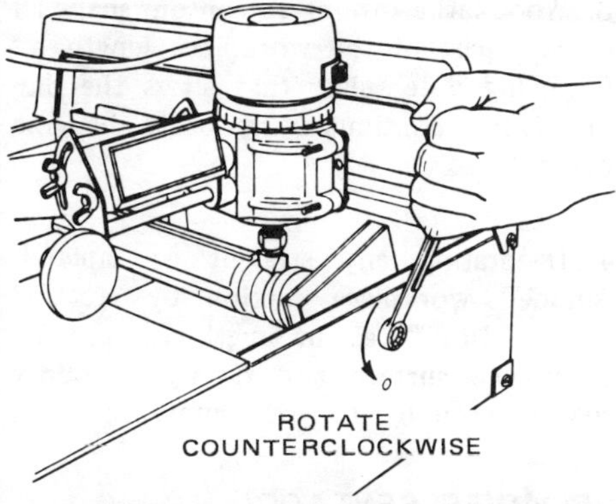

FOR DECORATIVE RINGS

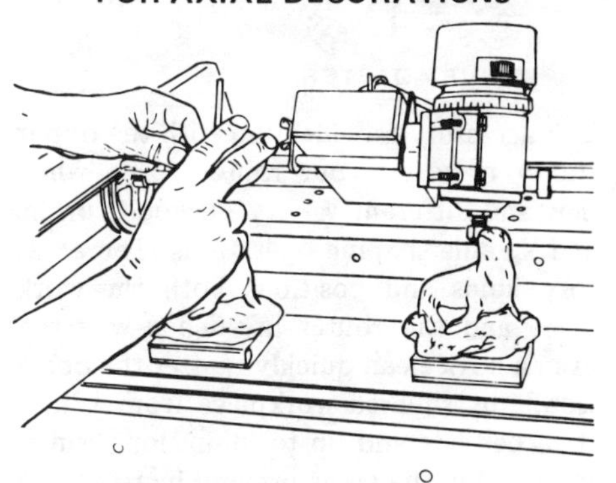

3-DIMENSIONAL CARVING

of the required size — either a solid block or one made by laminating like or different woods — which should be pre-sawed to remove as much scrap as possible (so that carving will require as little wood removal as possible). Both the original and the workpiece are mounted in the accessory on the shelf boards provided on the work mounts (also provided), which allows for various positioning of the two so that all sides can be carved (all carving is done by the router straight downward into each of the five workpiece sides that must be shaped). With the original and workpiece both positioned for the carving of one (of the five) sides, the stylus is used to guide the router position and depth-of-cut. If deeper than 1/8-in. cuts are needed a succession of cuts is used to achieve the final depth. Each of the five sides are finished, in turn, so that the final shape is achieved. Afterwards, it may be necessary to finish very fine details by sanding and/or carving with a hobby tool — but details down to 1/16-in. surface diameter can be carved by the router using a 1/16-in. bit; and any detail that is not recessed so as to be inaccessible from above with a straight-shafted bit can be carved.

WOOD TURNING WITH THE ROUTER CRAFTER

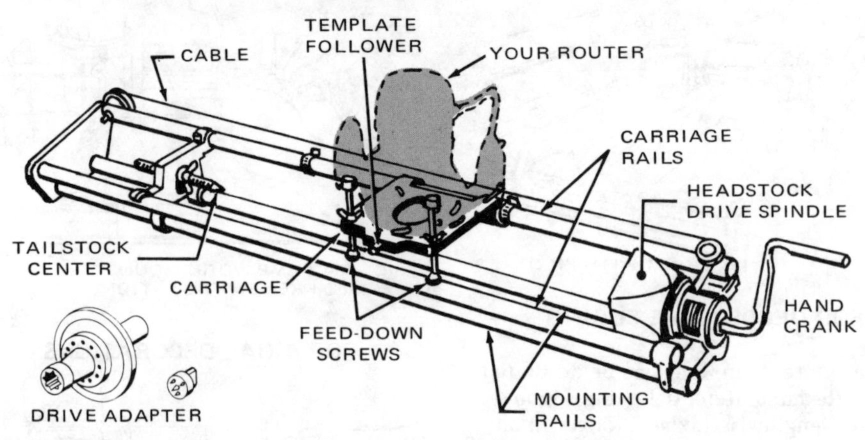

This accessory provides you with the opportunity of using your router for a whole new and different variety of wood turning and spindle shaping operations. The accessory holds and positions both the workpiece and the router in such a way that even a novice can quickly master the operation. Any squared workpiece from 1-in. to 3-in. per side and up to 36-in. long can be mounted in the accessory and be rotated or held stationary while the router is traveled as needed to make a desired cut. The accessory is furnished complete but you will also need a selection of router bits. Our recommendation is the 11-piece bit set offered; and we also recommend the Drive Adapter attachment, which can be used to replace the accessory spindle to allow cuts over the full length of a workpiece. *Refer to a current Sears Catalog* for buying information — and *refer to the accessory Owner's Manual* for all detailed set-up, adjustment and operating instructions.

For operation, your router is mounted on the accessory carriage, which can be travelled end-to-end of the workpiece or be held stationary, and is controlled by hand or by a hand crank synchronized with the workpiece rotation. Depth-of-cut can be preset or can be guided by a template (prepared by you) attached to the accessory.

Because cuts can be made whether the workpiece is rotating or not, you can duplicate almost all of the spindle shapes that can be made on a wood lathe — and can also create a number of decorative effects that can*not* be done with an ordinary (homeshop-type) wood lathe. The only wood-lathe cut that cannot be duplicated is a bowl-cut (one made horizontally into a cross-section area or the workpiece end). The types of work you can do (to be further explained, later) are as follows:

1. Wood-lathe turning (rotating the workpiece) to round all or any part of the workpiece length, to the same or different diameters — with all or any portion of each turned section cut straight (sides parallel to workpiece centerline) or tapered (narrower at one end than the other).

2. Wood-lathe turning to produce beads, coves and steps around the workpiece circumference.

3. Wood-lathe turning to contour shape all or any part of the workpiece length by following a template that alters the diameters in a continuous, smoothly changing manner.

4. Decorating any straight or tapered, rounded workpiece section by creating reeds and/or flutes cut lengthwise into the workpiece surface and evenly or oddly spaced around the circumference in a

variety of choices that allows for one to 24 parallel beads (or flutes). Reeds and flutes can be shaped to depths that parallel the workpiece surface or are tapered with respect to this surface . . . and flutes can be cut down to or past the workpiece centerline so that the cuts from various sides will meet at center to produce a hollowed-out or "see-through" effect.

5. Decorating any straight or tapered, rounded workpiece section that is approximately 5-1/2-in. or more from the workpiece headstock end by creating "roping" (spiraled reeds) or "spiraling" (spiraled flutes). Like straight reeds and flutes, these can be evenly or oddly spaced around the circumference; can be at straight or tapered depths; and flutes can be cut for a "see-through" effect. In addition, the spiraling can be made left-hand or right-hand . . . or a combination of both to produce a "diamond-cut" effect.

6. A spindle also can be turned to be oval at one (the tailstock) end, with the oval feathering into a circular cross-section at the other (headstock) end.

OPERATING ADJUSTMENTS THAT YOU WILL USE

IMPORTANT: *Never* change bits or a set-up without first unplugging your router — to avoid the possibility of an accidental start. Refer to the router-crafter Owner's Manual for assembly and mounting of the router crafter and other pertinent instructions.

Centering The Bit

A bit will make different cuts when it is exactly at 90° to the surface being cut and when, instead, it is at some other angle. In order to keep all cuts consistent, all work should be done with the bit at 90° . . . that is, with the vertical centerline of the bit pointing exactly at the workpiece center. The accuracy with which you center the

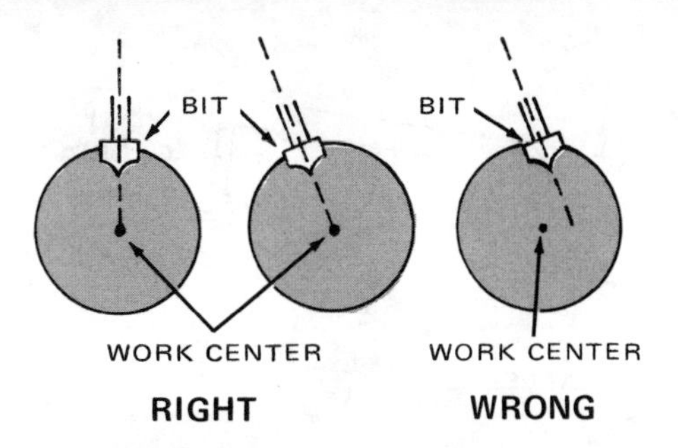

bit is not so important when the operation is reducing a square to a round or to a rounded contour. It becomes more important when you are turning beads and coves — because of the different cut shapes that angling will produce. It can be *very* important when cutting reeds, flutes, roping and spiraling because any difference in cut shape may be quite apparent, and might spoil the desired effect.

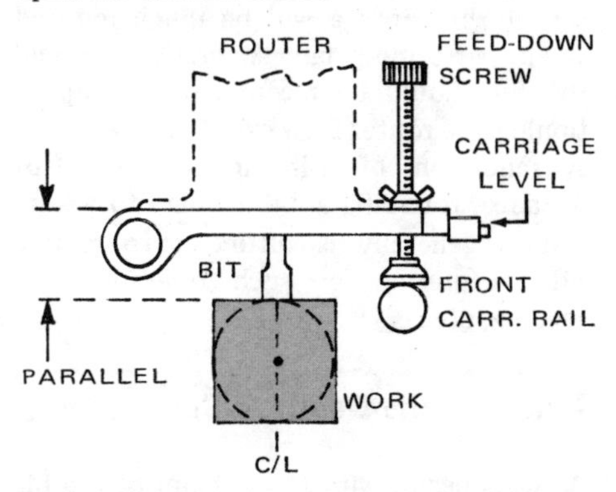

The carriage on which your router is mounted is provided with mounting slots that permit positioning of the router forward or backward. When the feed-down screws are adjusted so that the carriage is level, positioning the router with the bit at the center of the round opening in the carriage will "point" the bit correctly at the center of any workpiece mounted in the fixture. However, as the carriage is tilted up at front, this bit position will progressively "point" the bit farther and farther forward of the workpiece center. To compensate, and correct the "aim" of the bit, the router must be moved farther back on the carriage.

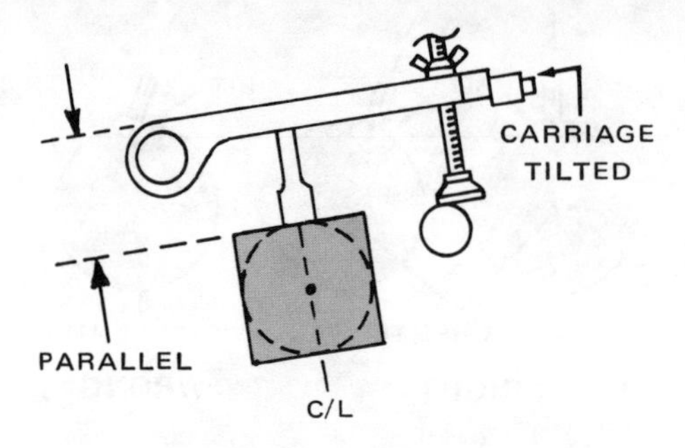

When setting up a square workpiece, center the bit as illustrated (by rotating the workpiece to position its top parallel with the carriage, as shown). The bit will now remain centered for all later operations made after rounding this workpiece, *if the diameter remains approximately the same dimension* as the square. On the other hand, if the diameter is much reduced, the tilt of the carriage will be much reduced when performing later operations — and the bit should be recentered (by repositioning the router forward on the carriage). A reduction of 1-in. in diameter (for instance, rounding a 3-in. square to a 2-in. round) generally is sufficient to require bit recentering for such operations as reeding, etc.

Adjusting the Depth-of-Cut

A cut is begun with the bottom of the bit resting on the workpiece surface into which the cut is to be made . . . then, when the router is turned on, the carriage is allowed to pivot downward until the bit penetrates the workpiece to the desired depth-of-cut. Afterwards, the cut is completed by moving the carriage along the carriage rails and/or by rotating the workpiece.

The rear carriage rail is the axis on which the carriage pivots; and its downward movement is limited by adjustment of the feed-down screws, which rest on the front carriage rail. The router depth-of-cut adjustment is used *only* for convenient positioning of the bit *prior* to adjusting the feed-down screws (except, if desired, when rounding a square, as told later).

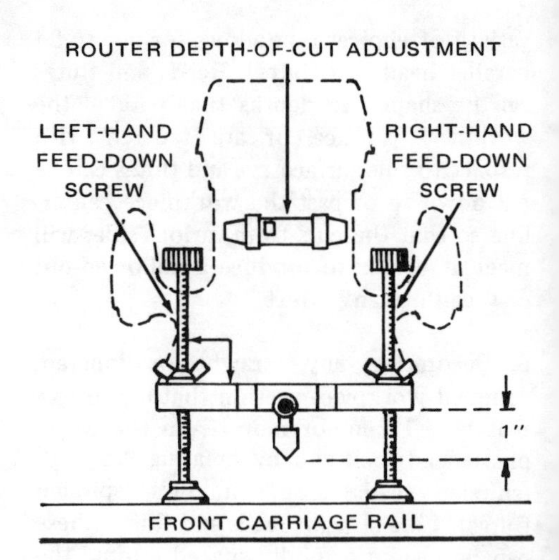

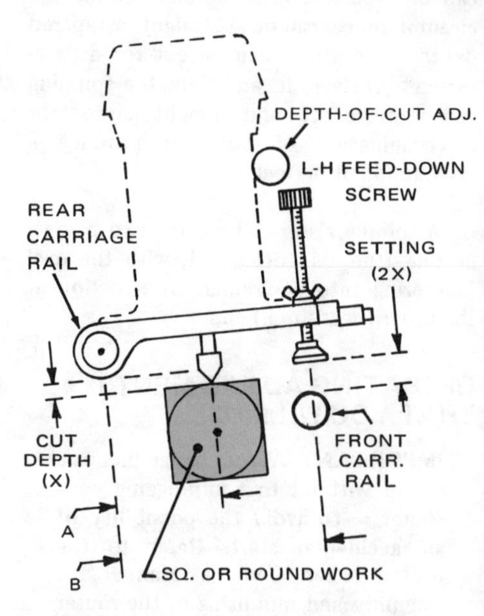

ADJUSTING LEFT-HAND SCREW

With the workpiece mounted between the tailstock and headstock (as told later), begin with the bit installed in the router and adjusted (router depth-of-cut adjustment) to project *no more* than 1-in. below the carriage — and with both feed-down screws positioned (by screwing them up or down) with *one-half or more* of their lengths projecting below the carriage. The bit should *not* touch the workpiece, and additional downward adjustment of the feed-down screws may, accordingly, be needed.

Adjust the bit downward until it just touches the workpiece, as illustrated — using, first, the router depth-of-cut adjustment, then (if necessary) the feed-down screws. Center the bit (preceding) and tighten the router mounting screws — then recheck to make certain the bit is *just touching* the workpiece. Now, decide the cut depth ("X" in illustration) desired.

Because the distance ("A") between the carriage pivot axis and the bit centerline is approximately half the distance ("B") from this axis to the feed-down screws' contact points, the feed-down screws' setting ("2X") must be approximately twice the desired cut depth ("X"). The *left-hand* feed-down screw, only, is used to establish this setting. The *right-hand* feed-down screw is needed only when the cut depth is too great to make in one pass, and intermediate depth settings are needed for one (or more) passes preceding the final pass.

Adjust the *left-hand* feed-down screw for the setting ("2X"), then tighten the wing nut on this screw while holding the screw knob to prevent turning of the screw. Each full five revolutions of the screw counterclockwise will elevate it 1/4-in. To make the setting, you can either measure the distance between the screw pad and the rail with a ruler . . . or you can start with the pad just touching the rail and count the revolutions.

After adjusting the left-hand screw — and if *only one pass* will be required to make the cut — adjust the right-hand screw so the distance between its pad and the rail will *be greater* than the setting ("2X"), to make certain this screw won't alter your setting.

> *NOTE:* The right-hand screw can, if desired, be set *exactly* like the left-hand screw. Setting both screws the same, whenever practical, provides a firmer contact on the front carriage rail — which may produce a more perfect cut.

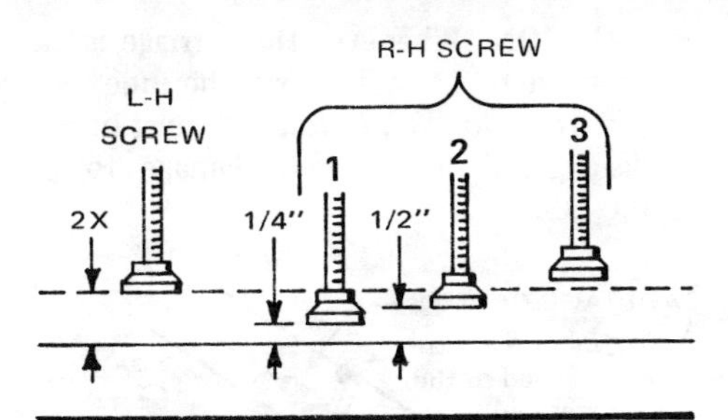

TYPICAL LEFT- AND RIGHT-HAND SCREW ADJUSTMENTS

If the desired cut depth exceeds 1/8-in., two or more passes, each to a depth of about 1/8-in., should be made. In this case, after adjusting the left-hand feed-down screw to "2X", adjust the right-hand screw so its pad is approximately 1/4-in. above the front carriage rail (position "1" in the illustration). This will limit the cut to about 1/8-in. Make the first pass then, if necessary; readjust the right-hand screw for another 1/8-in. pass (position "2") . . . and so on, until its final adjustment (position "3") is above, or the same as, that of the left-hand screw (which will then determine the depth for the final pass).

> *NOTE:* When using a template and the template follower, either feed-down screw can be used, as above, to limit the depth-of-cut per pass. Otherwise, the feed-down screws are not used, and should be adjusted up, out of the way. *Refer to "Contour Shaping", following.*

The Cable and Carriage Position Controls

1. For some cuts the carriage must be mechanically secured in a stationary position on the rails. Do *not* attempt to hold it in position by hand; any slight sideways movement will spoil the cut. After positioning the carriage *always* move both carriage clamps up against their respective sides of the carriage, and tighten these clamps.

CAUTION: Whenever the carriage is clamped to be stationary, the index pin (*refer to "3", following*) must be *dis*-engaged, to prevent damage to the cable.

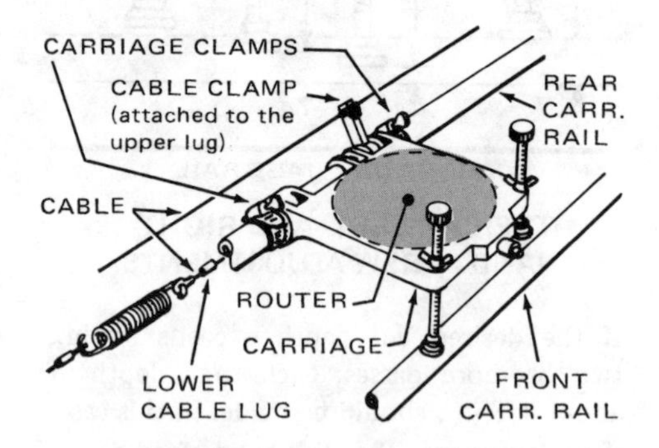

2. The carriage can be moved along the rails by hand, to position it or for making some cuts. To move the carriage by hand, loosen the two carriage clamps and move them out of the way. If the cable clamp is attached either to the upper cable lug (as illustrated) or to the lower cable lug, detach it. If the desired carriage movement is to be the full length of the fixture, position the two carriage clamps at their respective extreme ends of the rear carriage rail, and tighten them to secure them thus. On the other hand, one or both of these clamps can be secured at any other position required to limit the extent of carriage movement along the rails.

IMPORTANT: Whenever the carriage is to be moved along the rails by hand *for making a cut*, the index pin must be *engaged* and the drum clamp must be *tightened (refer to 3" following; also to "Indexing")* . . . otherwise the workpiece may rotate to spoil the cut. Also, the carriage must be *detached* from the cable (attempting to hand move the carriage with the cable attached can result in snarling of the cable turns around the drum).

Preferably, always travel the carriage from *left to right* when moving it by hand to make a cut. Doing it the same way every time will help you to obtain more uniform cuts.

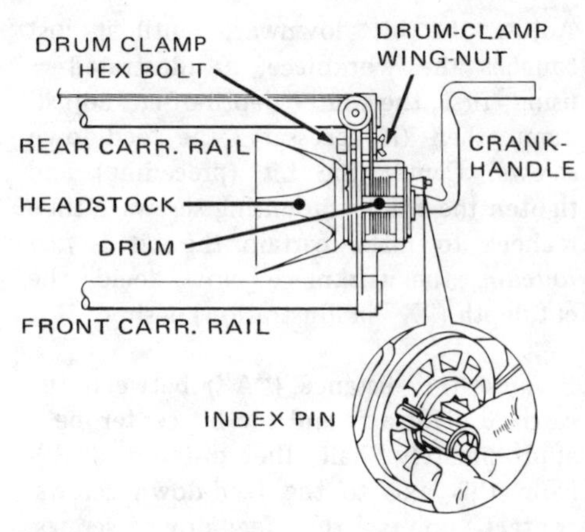

3. The carriage also can be moved along the rails, with the cable, by turning the hand crank. To use the cable for moving the carriage: a) The drum clamp must be *loose.* b) The index pin must be *engaged* so that the cable drum will be rotated by the hand crank. c) The carriage must be *attached* to one or the other of the two cable lugs. d) The hand crank must be rotated *correctly* (either counterclockwise or clockwise, depending upon which cable lug the carriage is attached to) *to move the carriage from left to right.*

a) To loosen the drum clamp, use a hex wrench to hold the hex bolt stationary, and turn the drum-clamp wing nut counterclockwise.

b) To engage the index pin, hold it out and rotate it until the "wings" at the pin end are aligned with the slots in the drum, then release it to allow it to recess within the drum end. When fully engaged, the pin head will be practically up against the drum end. It may be necessary to rotate the hand crank slightly in one direction or the other to allow the pin to become fully engaged.

NOTE: When later disengaging the pin, simply pull it out, rotate it one-quarter turn, then release it. Check to make certain it has not slipped back into its recess.

c) To attach the carriage to one of the cable lugs, use the cable clamp on the carriage. This clamp can be rotated up, to engage the upper cable lug — or down, to engage the lower cable lug. Position the carriage by hand to align the cable clamp with the desired cable lug, seat the lug in the clamp recess, then tighten the clamp hex nut *just enough* to secure the lug in position.

d) Whenever the hand crank is used to propel the carriage for making a cut, the resulting cut will be a spiral. A spiral cut can be either *left-hand or right-hand.* The left-hand spiral is wrapped clockwise around the workpiece — is made by attaching the carriage to the *upper* cable lug and by rotating the hand crank *counterclockwise.* The right-hand spiral is wrapped counterclockwise around the workpiece — is made by attaching the carriage to the *lower* cable lug and by rotating the hand crank *clockwise.*

IMPORTANT: *Never* attempt to make a spiral cut by turning the hand crank so as to move the carriage from right to left. In the first place, when the carriage is (correctly) being moved from left to right, the torque of the bit tends to assist, rather than oppose, workpiece rotation — and results in more uniform cutting. Second, and more important, if carriage travel is reversed (from right to left) cable force is transmitted through the cable spring, and any stretching of this spring will cause an erratic carriage movement that will spoil your cut. You *must* attach the carriage to the proper lug and rotate the hand crank in the proper direction.

When correctly done, moving the carriage by turning the hand crank results in advancing the carriage (left-to-right) approximately 6-3/4 inches for each full revolution of the workpiece. If you are *not* making a cut it doesn't matter whether you rotate the hand crank to move the carriage one way or the other.

Indexing

As previously told (*item "2", preceding*), whenever traveling the carriage by hand *to make a cut* lengthwise of the workpiece, the index pin must be engaged, the drum clamp must be tightened, and the carriage must be detached from the cable. If you are to make a single lengthwise cut, it doesn't matter how the headstock is positioned with respect to the drum; but to make two or more spaced cuts you will use the indexing numbers on the headstock.

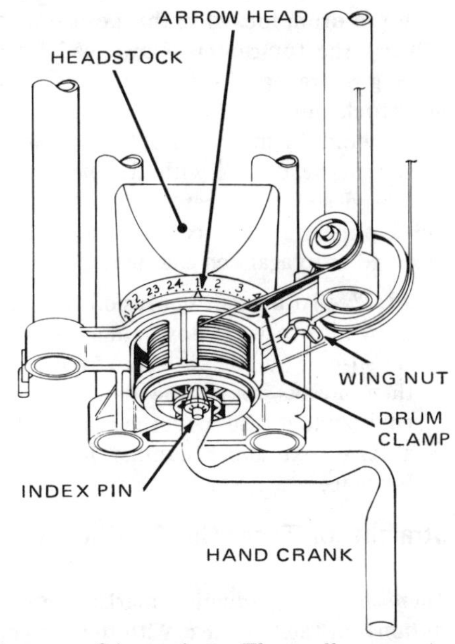

There are 24 numbers. These allow you to position the headstock (and, thus, the position to which the workpiece is rotated and locked) in any one of 24 positions. By selecting the numbers at which the headstock is to be locked for a sequence of lengthwise cuts, you can equally space 2, 3, 4, 6, 8, 12, or 24 parallel cuts around the workpiece. You can also step space cuts (i.e.: 1, 2, 4, 5, 7, 8, etc.) or can unequally space them (i.e.: 1, 3, 7, 8, 14, 17, etc.) to form a variety of parallel-cut patterns.

There are four arrow heads on the drum, spaced 90° apart. To obtain desired spacing it is essential that you use the *same* arrow head for reference throughout an operation. For this reason, it is best to begin every spacing sequence with the drum and headstock positioned as illustrated. To do this, *before* tightening the drum clamp, rotate the hand crank counterclockwise until the cable spring is near the tailstock end, and the index pin is at the top-center of the drum end. One of the drum arrow heads will also be at top-center. Now, tighten the drum clamp — and do *not* loosen it until after completing your spacing operation.

With the drum locked in this position, you will use the top-center arrow head for *all* spacing references. To turn any one of the headstock numbers to this arrow head, simply hold the index pin out (disengaged), rotate the headstock with the hand crank to the desired number, then release the index pin (and make certain it seats in its recess so as to again be engaged).

NOTE: To prevent confusion, it is a good idea to write down, in advance, the spacing numbers selected for use — then always rotate the hand crank counterclockwise to set the headstock at the next *larger* number in your sequence.

Straight- or Taper-Cut Setting

There are five graduation marks (*see illustration*) on the tailstock. With the top edge of the center bushing positioned directly over the *lowest* mark (*as illustrated*), the tailstock center is approximately in line with the center of the headstock so that the centerline of a workpiece mounted between the headstock and the tailstock is parallel to the carriage rails. Any cut that is made by traveling the carriage along the rails while the bushing is at the setting will, therefore, be a uniform distance from the workpiece centerline, from end-to-end of the workpiece. This is called "straight (or zero-taper) turning".

Raising the center bushing to place its top edge over any one of the other graduation

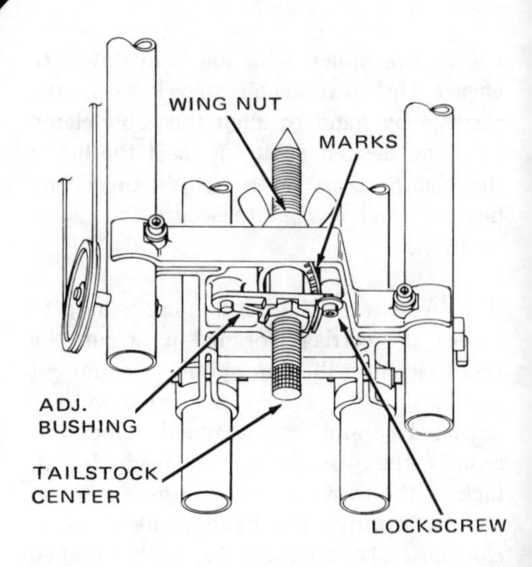

marks will elevate the tailstock above the headstock. Now, when the carriage is traveled along the rails to make a cut, the cut will be closer to the workpiece centerline at the tailstock end than at the headstock end. This is called "taper turning". A workpiece that is rounded by taper turning will be smaller in diameter at the tailstock end; any beads or similar cut at the tailstock end will be smaller in circumference — and any lengthwise flutes or similar will be deeper at the tailstock end than at the headstock end.

Setting the bushing at the first mark above the bottom mark elevates the tailstock center approximately 1/8 inch, and each mark above this adds approximately another 1/8 inch so that the top mark elevates the tailstock approximately 1/2 inch. To adjust the bushing, first loosen the wing nut on the tailstock center. Also, loosen the hex-head lockscrew. Place the bushing *top* edge on the mark selected — then securely retighten the lockscrew. Afterwards, the wing nut is retightened when mounting the workpiece, as told later.

Since elevating the tailstock reduces the distance between the bit and the workpiece centerline at the tailstock end, any cut made *without* revolving the workpiece will be deeper at the tailstock end by the *same* amount that the tailstock has been elevated. On the other hand, any cut made *by revolving* the workpiece will result in reducing the workpiece diameter by *twice* the amount that the tailstock has been elevated. Lengthwise grooves (referred to as "tapered reeds, flutes, ropes, etc.") can be planned to start, at the tailstock end, at a certain depth — and to feather out to zero depth (or nearly so) at or before reaching the headstock end. Circular grooves (referred to as "step-tapered beads, coves, etc.") can be planned to have a certain circumference at the tailstock end, with progressively larger circumferences towards the headstock end. Rounded or contoured workpieces can be produced with end-to-end tapers, or with tapers only in certain selected areas.

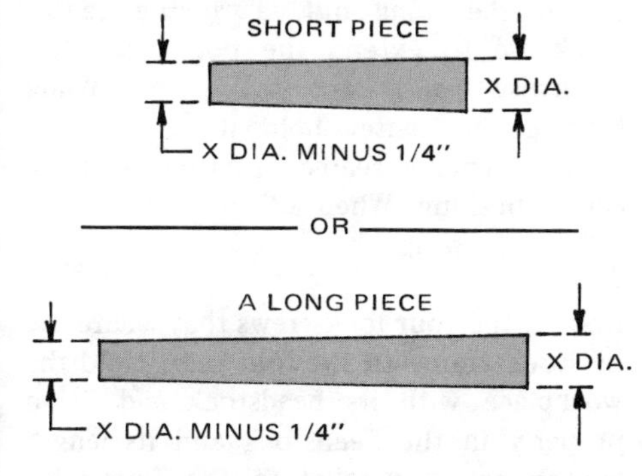

A 1/4" TAPER

The abruptness of the taper slope at any setting of the bushing will depend upon the workpiece length; the shorter the workpiece, the more abrupt the slope will be (*see illustration:* "A 1/4-in. Taper"). For this reason you can*not* exactly predetermine a taper by relying solely upon the setting of the bushing (the marks are useful for reference only). To exactly set the bushing for a desired taper, first mark the two ends of the workpiece section to be tapered. Position the carriage, with the router installed on it, so the bit is directly above the mark nearest the tailstock end — and with the feed-down screws adjusted to place the bit end 1 inch or more above the workpiece surface. Now, elevate the tailstock center and measure the distance between the carriage and the workpiece surface — then move the carriage to locate the bit directly above the workpiece mark nearest the headstock end, and again measure the distance between the carriage and the workpiece surface. Repeat adjusting the tailstock elevation and making these same two measurements until you obtain the desired difference between the two measurements.

GENERAL OPERATING INSTRUCTIONS

Mounting a Workpiece

A workpiece *must be square at the headstock end;* it can be square, round or any other shape at the tailstock end. Generally, it will be square and the same size end-to-end . . . but there may be reason to use one that is square only at one end, and round or differently shaped at the other (tailstock) end.

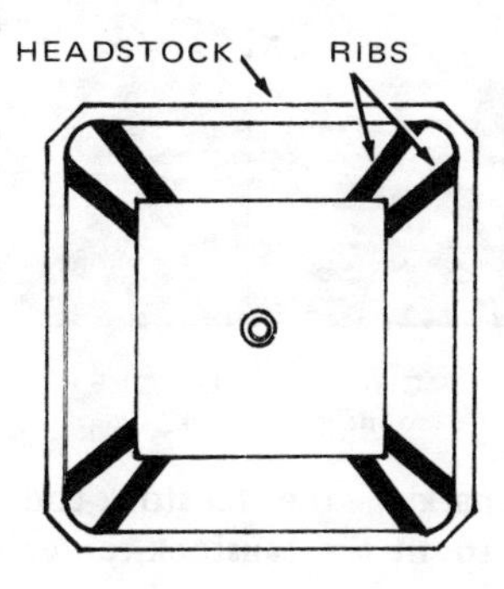

The workpiece must be square at the headstock end because the headstock construction will accept (and correctly center) only square pieces (from 1-in. up to about 3-in. sq.). This workpiece end is fitted into the headstock, with its four corners recessed in the (respective) four pairs of headstock ribs.

The tailstock end is mounted on center to the point of the tailstock center. For a

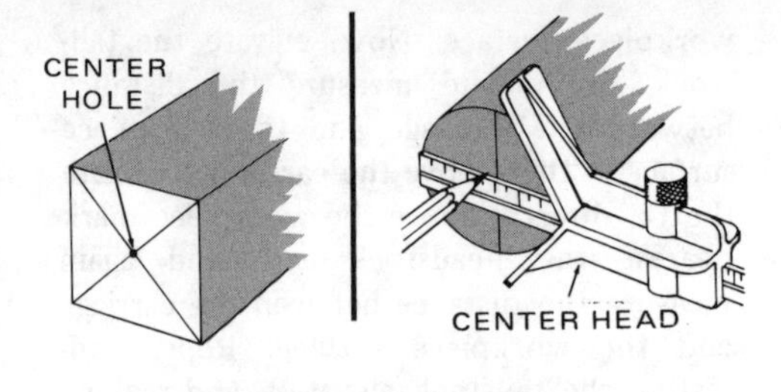

square-end workpiece the exact center is found by drawing two diagonal lines, as illustrated, and marking where they cross. For a circular-end workpiece, use the center head of a combination square to draw two lines, and mark their intersection. Other end shapes can be centered by using either a center head (for elliptical shapes) or a carpenter's square (for flat-sided shapes) — and by drawing as many close lines as possible, then "spotting" the center among them.

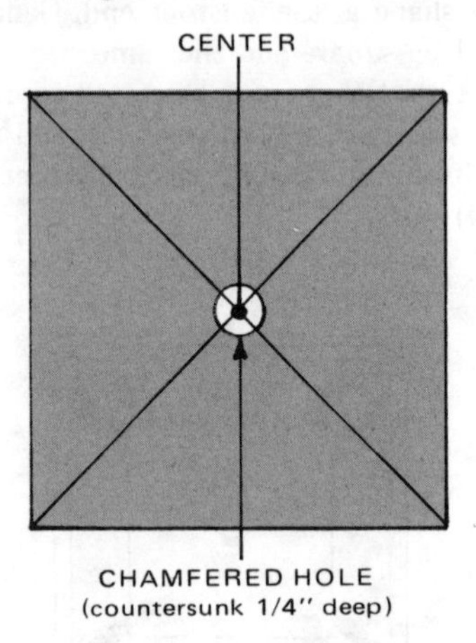

After marking the tailstock-end center, drill it to fit the tailstock-center pointed end. Either use a center drill, to a depth of 1/4-in., or drill a hole (1/16-in. to 3/32-in. diameter), then countersink it (with a standard wood countersink bit) to a depth of 1/4-in. Lubricate the hole with wax, petroleum jelly or some other suitable grease.

Loosen the two cable clamps (*refer to "The Cable and Carriage Position Controls", preceding*), and position the carriage to be approximately where the middle of the workpiece will be when mounted (so it will be out of the way).

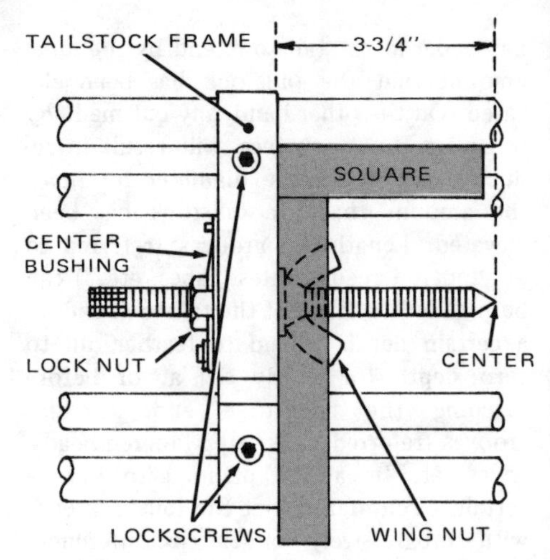

If necessary, readjust the tailstock center so its point is approximately 3-3/4-in. out from the tailstock frame. To do this, loosen the wing nut. Turn the center clockwise to extend the point; counterclockwise to retract the point. While turning the center hold it so that the locknut remains seated in its recess in the center bushing. When adjusted, *lightly* retighten the wing nut.

Loosen the four lockscrews that secure the tailstock frame to the four rails. Hold the workpiece with its headstock end fitted properly in the headstock and its length approximately parallel to the four rails. Slide the tailstock to the right on the rails until the point of the tailstock center just touches the workpiece end, *without* entering the drilled hole. Release the workpiece and *lightly* tighten the one lockscrew that holds the tailstock frame to the rear carriage rail, then hold a tri-square (or any suitable right-angle) against the rear carriage rail and tailstock frame to square the frame with the rail. When it is squared, tighten the two top lockscrews, then the bottom two.

CAUTION: Do *not* overtighten the lockscrews; doing so could dent the rails. They need only be snug.

NOTE: When using the tri-square make certain its sides are firmly up against both the rail and the tailstock frame. Every time the tailstock frame is moved on the rails it must be re-squared in this manner.

Lift the workpiece tailstock end up to align its center hole with the tailstock center. Check to be certain the headstock end is still properly in the headstock. Turn the tailstock center clockwise until its point is firmly, but *not* tightly, seated in the workpiece center hole. Be sure the locknut is still seated in the center bushing, then tighten the wing nut — firmly, but *not* excessively.

Now, check the workpiece mounting. The workpiece *must* be firmly enough supported to prevent end play at either end; but you *must* be able to rotate it freely by hand. If the mounting seems sloppy, readjustment of the tailstock center 1/8- to 1/4-turn clockwise should make it properly firm; or, if the workpiece is too tight, readjust the center 1/8- to 1/4-turn counterclockwise.

Cutting Procedures

There are four different procedures for making a cut.

1. Around the Workpiece and Continuing to the Right. This procedure is used for rounding a square, reducing the diameter of a rounded section, and for all contour shaping. The carriage must be *detached* from the cable and the two carriage clamps must be positioned (and tightened) so as to stop carriage travel when the bit reaches the (respective) desired horizontal ends of the cut. The hand crank is used to revolve the workpiece, and the index pin must be *disengaged* so the cable won't be moved. The bit should be centered.

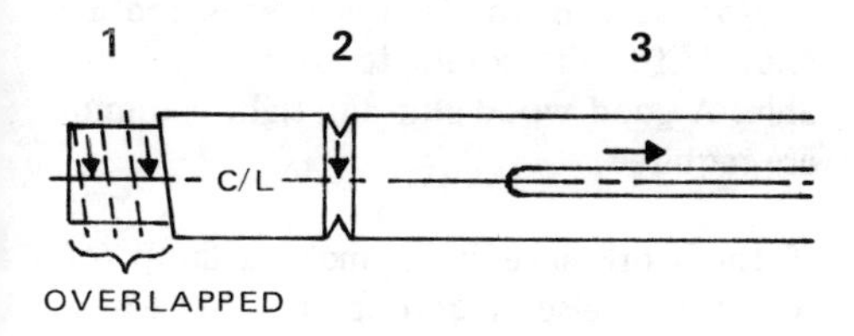

Always start at the left end of the area to be cut and *work toward the right.* After completing the depth-of-cut adjustment for the cut (or the first pass), lift the front of the carriage until the bit is above the workpiece — then turn the router on. Without turning the hand crank, carefully lower the carriage onto its feed-down screw(s). Turn the hand crank *counter-clockwise* to over-complete one revolution, then continue to turn it while slowly moving the carriage to the right. Carriage movement must be such that the resulting spiral cuts *overlap by at least one-quarter*— and crank movement should be at a steady pace, *just fast enough* for the bit to cut smoothly. At the end of the cut, lift the carriage up before turning the router off.

2. Around the Workpiece. This procedure is used for making beads, coves and reduced diameter flats (shoulders). The carriage must be *detached* from the cable and the two carriage clamps must be positioned (and tightened) to hold the carriage *stationary* at the location for the cut. The hand crank is used to revolve the workpiece, and the index pin must be *disengaged* so the cable won't be moved. The bit should be centered.

After completing the depth-of-cut adjustment for the cut (or the first pass), lift the front of the carriage until the bit is above the workpiece, then turn the router on. Without turning the hand crank, carefully lower the carriage onto its feed-down screw(s). Turn the hand crank *counter-clockwise* to over-complete one revolution, then lift the carriage up and turn the router off. Hand crank movement should be at a steady pace, *just fast enough* for the bit to cut smoothly.

3. Lengthwise of the Workpiece. This is the procedure used for making reeds and flutes. The carriage must be *detached* from the cable and the two carriage clamps must be positioned (and tightened) so as to stop carriage travel when the bit reaches the (respective) desired horizontal ends of the cut. The hand crank is *not* used, and should be removed after using it to rotate the workpiece into position for the cut. The index pin must be *engaged* and the drum clamp must be *tightened.* The bit must be centered (unless purposely off-centered to produce a different cut shape).

Start at the left end of the cut to be made and work toward the right end. Begin with the drum locked in position as told under "Indexing", preceding — and with the index pin engaged at the headstock number selected for this particular lengthwise cut. After completing the depth-of-cut adjustment for the cut (or the first pass), lift the front of the carriage until the bit is above the workpiece, then turn the router on. Make certain the carriage is against the left-hand carriage clamp, then carefully lower it onto its feed-down screw(s). Move the carriage by hand toward the other end at a steady pace, *just fast enough* for the bit to cut smoothly. At the end of the cut lift the carriage up, then turn the router off.

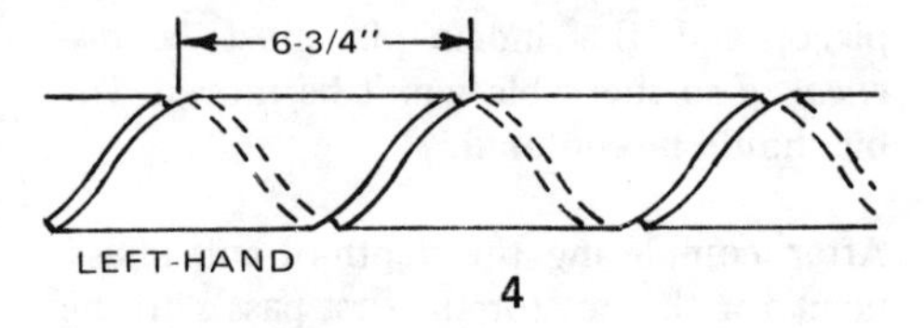

4

4. Around the Workpiece and Proportionately Advancing (to the Right). This is the procedure used for cutting ropes and spirals. Advancement is *always* at the fixed ratio of one complete spiral per 6-3/4-in. of workpiece length, and is controlled by cable movement (as it winds or unwinds on the drum). The carriage must be *attached* to the cable, and the two carriage clamps must be positioned (and tightened) so as to stop carriage travel when the bit reaches the (respective) desired horizontal end(s) of the cut. The hand crank is used both to revolve the workpiece and (through cable movement) to travel the carriage. Therefore, the drum clamp must be *loosened* and the index pin must be *engaged.* The bit must be centered (unless purposely off-centered to produce a different cut shape).

For a left-hand rope or spiral cut (*illustrated*), attach the carriage clamp to the *upper* cable lug and start at the left end of the desired cut. For a right-hand rope or spiral attach the carriage clamp to the *lower* cable lug and also start at the left end of the desired cut. This requires revolving the handcrank *counterclockwise* for a left-hand spiral — or, *clockwise* for a right-hand spiral.

After completing the depth-of-cut adjustment for the cut (or the first pass), lift the front of the carriage until the bit is above the workpiece, then turn the router on. Make certain the carriage is against the starting-position carriage clamp, then carefully lower it onto its feed-down screw(s). Next, turn the hand crank at a steady pace, *just fast enough* for the bit to cut smoothly. Continue to the end of the cut, then lift the carriage up and turn the router off.

> **IMPORTANT:** When using any of these procedures, if it is necessary to stop the operation before the cut is completed, lift the carriage *before* turning the router off. To restart the cut, it is best to return to the original starting position, and begin again.

WORKPIECE PREPARATION

As previously told, the workpiece must be square, at least at the headstock end. It may be unnecessarily expensive to obtain a large enough piece (especially, if a rare wood is to be used) to make a square of the desired size. In such case, smaller pieces can be sandwiched together to form the desired square, as shown — or, even, can be assembled in any fashion that will produce the desired square. It is necessary, only, that adjoining faces be accurately planed and/or sanded to fit together smoothly enough for the joints to be unobjectionable. A good wood glue and tight clamping are required.

If the workpiece is to make a lamp (or, something else requiring an end-to-end center hole), the center-hole problem is easily solved by leaving a center opening

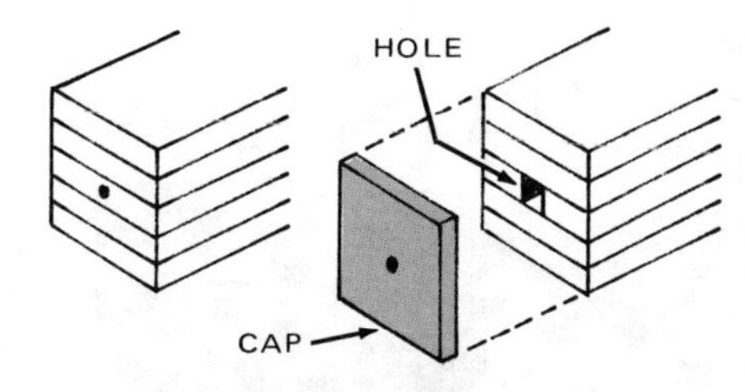

TWO WAYS OF ASSEMBLING A WORKPIECE

when assembling the pieces to form the square. However, because the tailstock end must be center drilled and held by the tailstock center, this (one, only) end must then be capped (to provide a solid, drillable end). The cap needn't be a permanent part; it can be temporarily nailed or glued in place — but it should be 1/4-in. or more thick.

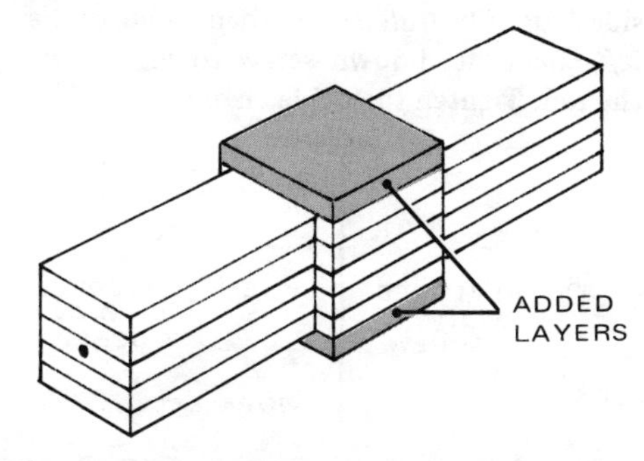

If a finished workpiece is to have considerably different diameters (or square sections) at different areas (like a lamp pedestal that is bigger at bottom), it isn't necessary to waste wood building up the maximum dimension throughout. You can build-up the dimension needed only at each area in which needed, as indicated by the illustration.

Another method of preparing a spindle is called "post-blocking", and calls for gluing pieces together, as illustrated, to form the beginning square. This method is particularly desirable when two or more woods of different characteristics are to be combined to provide the appearance of an inlaid workpiece. As illustrated, different wood pieces can be assembled so that, after finishing, they will result in a spindle having different wood characteristics in different areas.

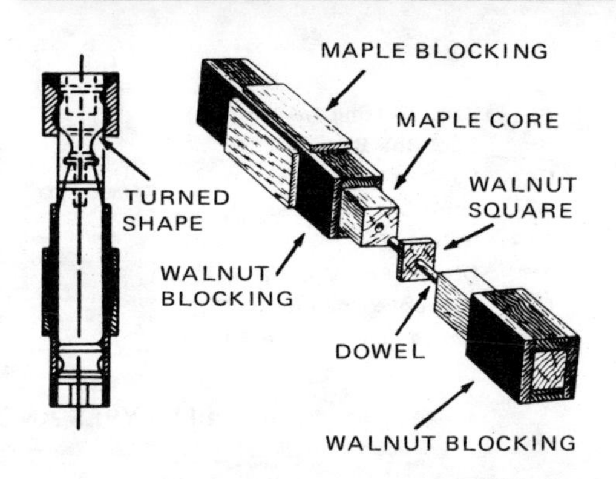

Wood turnings also can be produced in sections, to be assembled later (with centered dowels) to make up the full length desired. If one section, like the base of a pedestal, is to be quite large in diameter, this section may best be turned on a wood lathe. But if the next section is to be small enough (not over 3-in. dia.) and is to be roped or similarly decorated in a manner that can't be done on a wood lathe, it must be done on the router crafter. If both sections are started as squares their ends can be accurately centered; after turning, the joining ends can be center drilled and joined together with a glued, suitable-diameter wood dowel (recessed 1/2-in. or more into each section).

THE BITS TO USE

Any *end-cutting* bit can be used. This includes all of the shafted bits (*Chapter 1*) and the rabbeting/surfacing bit (which is used *without* a pilot). *None of the side-cutting* bits (which includes all the other arbor-held bits) can be used; and the rabbeting/surfacing bit can*not* be used with a pilot.

Particularly recommended, because of the desirable shapes they produce, are the 9/32-in. point-cutting ogee bit, the 1/2-in. core-box bit, and the 15/16-in. rabbeting/surfacing bit (which bits are sold as a set together with the arbor and pilots for the rabbet bit). These and other very useful bits are shown in the accompanying illustration.

(See next page for illustration.)

A – Point-Cutting 1/4-Rd.
B – Core-Box Bit
C – Straight Bit
D – Point-Cutting Ogee
E – Veining Bit
F – Double-End V-Groove
G – V-Groove Chamfering Bit
H – Rabbet and Surface Bit

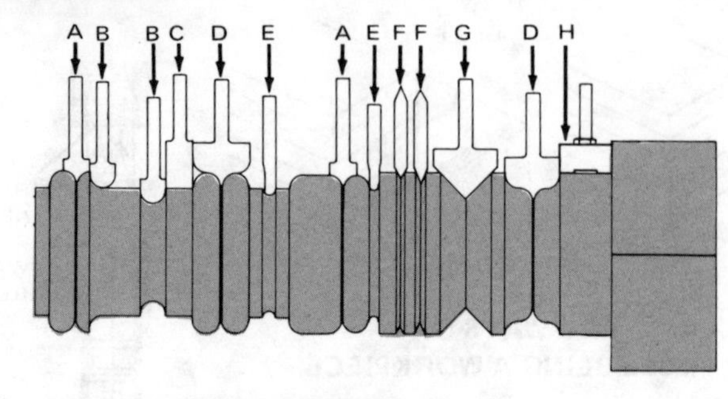

BIT TYPES AND CUT SHAPES

ROUNDING FROM A SQUARE

This is the first operation for making a turned spindle. Every section of your workpiece that is not to be left in its original square shape should be rounded prior to performing any other operation on it. Rounding is *always* done with the rabbeting/surfacing bit (without a pilot).

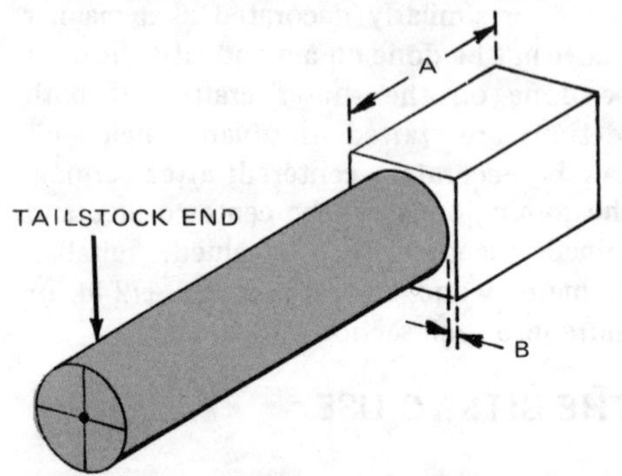

The illustration shows a typically rounded spindle. Section "A" is the unworked part at the headstock end. Dimension "B" can be zero, if the rounded part is to have a diameter exactly equal to a side of the square; but it generally is more practical to plan some measurement (at least 1/32-in.) for "B", thus making the rounded diameter slightly smaller (and more certain to be smooth and true).

There are two methods of rounding. For the first, generally preferred, method you will begin by using "Cutting Procedure No. 3", preceding – then finish with "Cutting Procedure No. 1". The second method is to use "Cutting Procedure No. 1" throughout.

To set up for procedure No. 3, begin with the index pin at top-center and engaged so that headstock number "1" is also at top-center. The carriage must be detached from the cable. Turn the hand crank slightly *clockwise* until the (centered) bit can be rested flat against one workpiece side (*as illustrated*) – then adjust the *left-* hand feed-down screw to *just touch* the rail. Tighten the cable clamp.

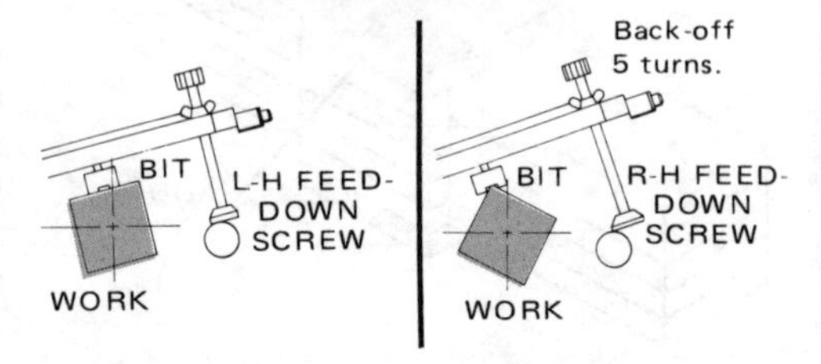

Now, disengage the index pin, hold the carriage up, and rotate the headstock to number "4" – then reengage the index pin. Adjust the *right*-hand feed-down screw to just touch the rail, then back it off (counterclockwise) to elevate it approximately 1/4-in. (5 full turns) and lock it.

Position the two carriage clamps as required, then travel the carriage (*procedure no. 3*) to make the first cut. This cut will remove approximately 1/8-in. from one workpiece corner. To do the same for the other three corners, reset the headstock, in sequence (by simply disengaging then reengaging the index pin) to numbers 10, 16 and 22 – and make a cut at each setting. This completes *one sequence of cuts.*

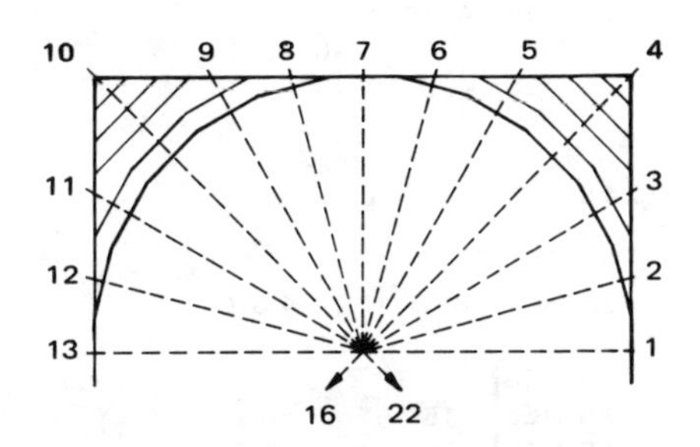

FIVE 1/8" CUTTING SEQUENCES FOR A 3" SQUARE

For each remaining sequence of cuts that is needed, reset the right-hand feed-down screw by backing it off an additional 5 turns. Continue making cutting sequences until the *left*-hand feed-down screw (instead of the right-hand one) contacts the rail. For a second and third sequence of cuts, also use headstock settings of numbers 4, 10, 16 and 22 — but for a fourth sequence use numbers 3, 4, 5, 9, 10, 11, 15, 16, 17, 21, 22 and 23 . . . and for a fifth sequence (if needed) use all 24 numbers, making a cut at each.

The foregoing will produce an approximate cylindrical shape having up to 24 flat sides. To complete the rounding, switch to "Cutting Procedure No 1" — with the right-hand feed-down screw up (out-of-the-way) and the *left*-hand one readjusted to produce the dimension "B" first mentioned. Backing this screw off (counterclockwise) 1/2 turn will make dimension "B" about 0.025 in. This will result in a cylinder approximately 1/20-in. smaller, in diameter, than the original square.

If, instead of the above, you decide to use the second method of rounding, set up for "Procedure No. 1" at the beginning. To start, adjust both feed-down screws as for the first method. Make the first cut — then readjust the *right*-hand screw 5 turns counterclockwise, make a second cut — and so on, finishing by finally readjusting the left-hand screw (as for the first method). While making each cut — especially at the start, when the corners are sharp — rotate the workpiece *slowly* and hold the carriage down firmly (so the bit won't kick it up). Be sure to overlap the spirals as you move the carriage.

> *NOTE:* Whichever method you use, hand sanding may be required to produce a desirable final appearance.

REDUCING A ROUND DIAMETER

This is accomplished by using "Cutting Procedure No. 1" and, preferably, the panel-raising bit. The two feed-down screws are used as told under "Adjusting the Depth-of-Cut", preceding — always using the *right*-hand screw to limit each pass to a 1/8-in. cut. Make as many passes as necessary to reach your final diameter — which will be reached when the *left*-hand feed-down screw (instead of the right-hand one) contacts the rail. While making a cut, rotate the hand crank *rather rapidly* . . . but move the carriage *slowly*. This will assure a smoother, easier operation.

> *NOTE:* If the workpiece section to be reduced in diameter is too short to use either the panel-raising or the rabbeting/surfacing bit, use an appropriate-size straight bit and "Cutting Procedure No. 2", instead. That is, do the reduced section like a bead, cove or shoulder.

FLAT-SIDE SHAPING

Using "Cutting Procedure No. 3" as preceding, an originally square workpiece can, instead of being rounded, be reduced to a 4-, 6-, 8-, 12- or 24-sided spindle, which can then be decorated in any of the ways in which a round spindle can be decorated. However, the fewer the number of sides in the final spindle, the smaller in cross-section this final spindle will have to be (as shown by the illustration). The reason for this is that the maximum width of any one side that can be smoothly and accurately shaped is limited to 15/16-in. (the width of

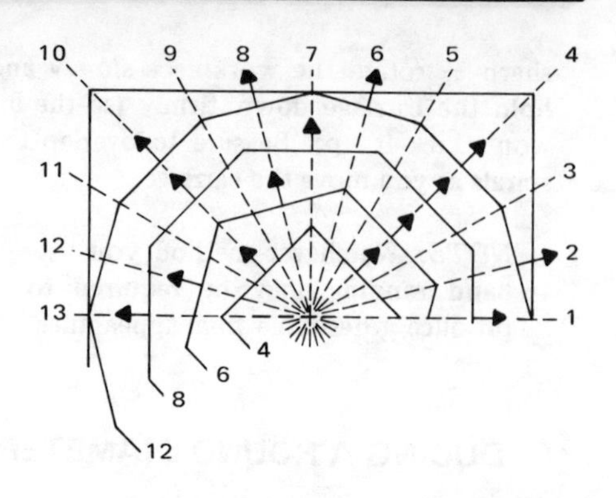

FINAL CUT SEQUENCE SETTINGS:

4 SIDES: 4, 10, 16, 22
6 SIDES: 4, 8, 12, 16, 20, 24
8 SIDES: 4, 7, 10, 13, 16, 19, 22, 1
12 SIDES: 4, 6, 8, 10, 12, 14, 16, 18, 20, 22, 24, 2
24 SIDES: All 24 numbers

MAXIMUM WIDTH OF A SIDE:

4 SIDES, 6 SIDES, 8 SIDES: 15/16"
12 SIDES: Approx. 3/4"
24 SIDES: Approx. 3/8"

REDUCING A 3" SQUARE TO FLAT-SIDED SHAPES

the rabbeting/surfacing bit). Sides can be smaller, if desired (in the illustration, the 12-sided shape has sides approximately 3/4-in. wide, which is the minimum width of a side for this shape).

Cutting sequences should begin (as explained in the preceding) at the corners — that is, with the settings 4, 10, 16 and 22. Beginning with a 3-in. square, for 24 sides, do two sequences at these settings, then make a final sequence using all 24 headstock numbers. For other shapes with sides as shown the sequences are:

12 Sides: 4 at the 4, 10, 16 and 22 settings — then finish at the 12 settings shown.

8 Sides: 4 at the 4, 10, 16, 22 settings — then finish at the 8 settings shown.

6 Sides: 4 at the 4, 10, 16, 22 settings, 4 at settings 4, 7, 10, 13, 16, 19, 22, 1 — then finish at the 6 settings shown.

4 Sides: 5 at the 4, 10, 16, 22 settings, 5 at settings 4, 6, 8, 10, 12, 14, 16, 18, 20, 22, 24, 2 — then finish at the 4, 10, 16, 22 settings.

IMPORTANT: If you start with a workpiece smaller than 3-in. square, the number of sequences prior to the final setting sequences must be reduced, accordingly.

TAPER ROUNDING

A taper can extend from the workpiece tailstock end to as close to the headstock end that carriage movement will allow . . . or, it can start and end anywhere else you want. There can be a single tapered section, or two or more tapered sections of the same or different lengths. When there are two or more tapered sections the tailstock adjustment setting can be the same or different for each (to produce identically or differently sloped tapers).

Adjust the tailstock center bushing for your desired taper as previously explained (*refer to "Straight- or Taper-Cut Setting", preceding*). To establish the depth-of-cut setting, position the carriage with your bit over the *finish* mark for the taper (mark on workpiece nearest the headstock). If the taper is to feather out at this mark, set the left-hand feed-down screw so the bit end just touches the workpiece surface at this mark. Adjusting this feed-down screw higher will result in a taper which, instead of feathering out, ends up with a smaller diameter (or greater depth) than the remainder of the workpiece to the right of this mark.

After adjusting the left-hand feed-down screw to establish the final depth-of-cut, use the right-hand screw to limit the depth of each pass, as already explained. Make these adjustments with the carriage positioned to locate the bit over the taper *start* mark (one nearest the tailstock end). Start

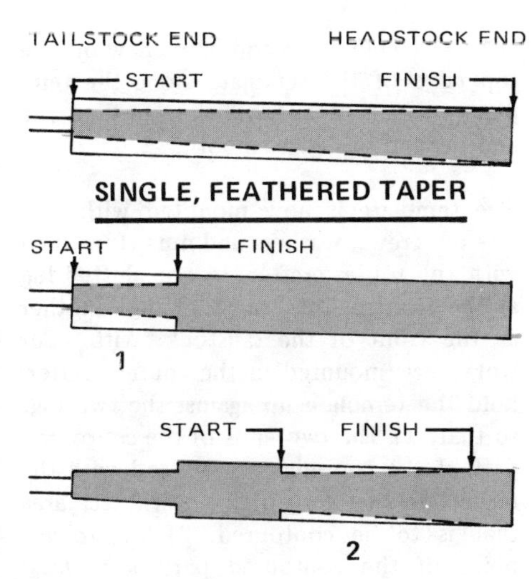

each pass at the tailstock end of your marked taper by lowering the (revolving) bit into the workpiece at this point, then moving the carriage to the right.

CONTOUR SHAPING

Any workpiece area that is to be shaped (instead of straight- or taper-rounded) and cannot be completed with the carriage stationary (as for beading, etc.), must be contour shaped. Therefore, if your workpiece is to have one or more areas with curved profiles that cannot be done in the following manner (refer to "Beading, Coving, Etc."), these areas require contour shaping. When required, contour shaping is the second operation to perform (after rounding or taper rounding).

> *NOTE:* It is *not* practical to reduce a square by the contour-shaping method. The square should first be rounded. However, if a square is to be only partially rounded (at the corners, leaving flats between) while simultaneously contouring the partially rounded profile, this method can be used to reduce the square as desired.

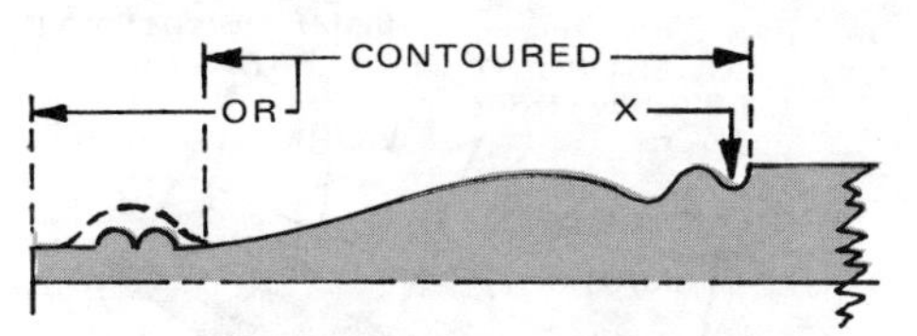

A TYPICAL CONTOURED SHAPE

Contour shaping is done with the 1/2-in. (dia.) core box bit (*Chapter 1*), and by using the (also, 1/2-in. dia.) template follower on the front of the carriage. Consequently, the smallest concave curvature ("X" *in the illustration*) that can be contour shaped is one with a 1/4-in. radius, and neither Vs nor square shoulders can be shaped in this manner (must be shaped by beading, coving, etc.). However, (*as indicated by the illustration*), when contour-shaping a workpiece, it may be time-saving to include reduced-diameter areas that will later be beaded, etc., and to do so in a manner that will leave just enough stock for the (later) beading, etc. operation(s).

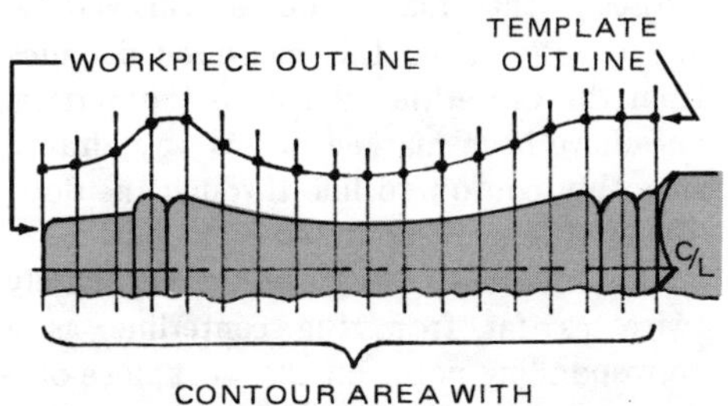

A TYPICAL TEMPLATE

The typical template illustrated is designed to finish shape the tapered area at the tailstock end, to leave "humps" for later shaping of the beads required, and to shape the balance of the workpiece up to the remaining square at the headstock end. *Before* the template is used, all the area covered by the template should be straight rounded ("*Rounding From a Square*", *preceding*) down to the maximum diameter of the area covered by the template.

To prepare your template, first make an *exact-size* outline drawing on paper of your

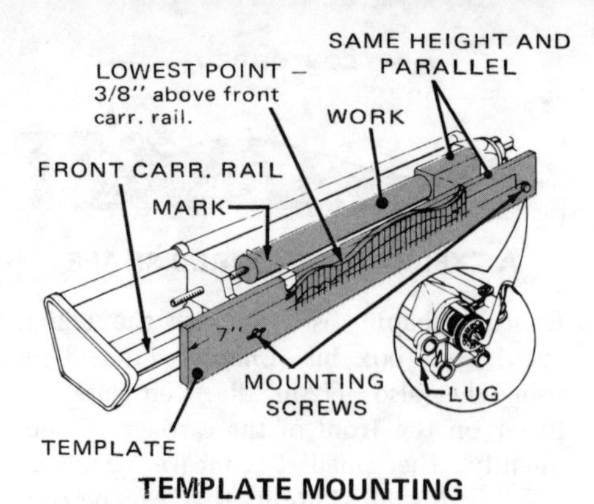

TEMPLATE MOUNTING

workpiece as you want it to be after it is contoured. As shown by the accompanying illustration, this drawing must show the workpiece centerline, and only the half above the centerline needs to be drawn. Now, divide the centerline into equal parts by drawing vertical lines (at 90° to the centerline) 1/8- to 1/4-in. apart. On each vertical line measure the distance from the centerline to where your workpiece outline crosses it, then make a dot on this vertical line *exactly twice* this measured distance from the centerline. When all the vertical lines have been marked in this way, draw a smoothly contoured line through the dots. This last line is your template outline – and every point on it should be exactly twice as far from the centerline as a corresponding point on the workpiece outline.

> *NOTE:* Doubling the template-outline distance above the centerline is necessary because the up-and-down movements of the template follower are, like those of the feed-down screws previously explained, approximately double the resulting up-and-down bit movements.

For a template, use 1/4-in. hardboard or 1/2- or 3/4-in. plywood. The piece used must be 5-in. wide by 10 inches *longer* than your *whole* workpiece. Glue or tape your finished drawing on the template with: 1) Its left end approximately 7-in. from the template left end. 2) The drawing centerline parallel to the template top edge. 3) The highest point of the drawing at or just below this top edge. Saw off the top edge of the template along the template outline of the drawing – then file and/or sand this edge smooth.

The template is now mounted with two sets of screws, washers and nuts (furnished with the router crafter) to one slotted lug at the front of the headstock and another at the front of the tailstock. With your workpiece mounted in the router crafter, hold the template up against the two lugs so that: 1) The two ends of the contoured part of the top edge are aligned with the respective two ends of the workpiece area that is to be contoured. 2) The *lowest* point of the contoured part is *at least 3/8-in. above* the top of the front rail. 3) The centerline of the drawing on the template is parallel to the top of the front rail (which also makes it parallel to the workpiece centerline). Mark (on the template back) the location for the tailstock mounting screw.

Drill a 1/4-in. hole for the tailstock mounting screw – then extend this 1/2-in. to right and left to make a 1/4-in. x 1-in. long slot parallel to the top edge. Temporarily mount the template on the tailstock and recheck its position per the above, sliding it to right or left as required. When it is properly positioned, mark the location for the headstock screw, remove the template and drill a 1/4-in. hole at this mark – then remount the template with both screws.

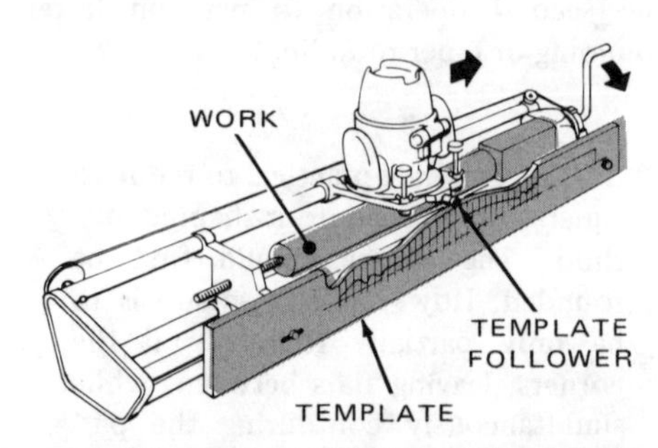

A CONTOUR SHAPING OPERATION

Position the two feed-down screws high enough to be up out-of-the-way – so that carriage up-and-down movement is controlled *only* by the template follower resting on the top template edge. Use "Cutting Procedure No. 1", preceding, to do the contour shaping. During the operation, turn the hand crank (counterclockwise) rather rapidly while advancing the carriage (left-to-right, by hand) rather slowly. If a cut has to be more than 1/8-in. deep at any point, use the right-hand feed-down screw (as previously explained) to limit the cuts for two or more passes.

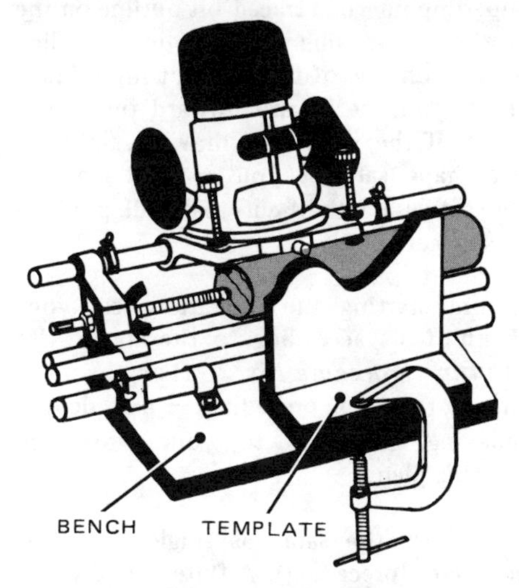

A SMALL TEMPLATE

If only a short workpiece section is to be contoured, a small, bench-mounted template can be used, as illustrated. The same rules apply for preparation as already explained.

BEADING, COVING, ETC.

Both the point-cutting 1/4-round and the point-cutting ogee bits can be used to cut quarter-round shapes, two of which (side-by-side) will result in a half-round, raised bead (as illustrated). Other than half-round shapes can be produced by using a straight or veining bit in addition, and by making two or more spaced cuts at the same or different depth-of-cut settings. Indented cove-, vee- and square-groove shapes can be made in one cut (or, if desired, a series of parallel, overlapped cuts) with the appropriate veining, V-grooving or straight-cutting bits, etc. By combining the shapes produced by all these various bits, there is a practically unlimited variety of banding (around-the-workpiece) decorations available to an imaginative operator.

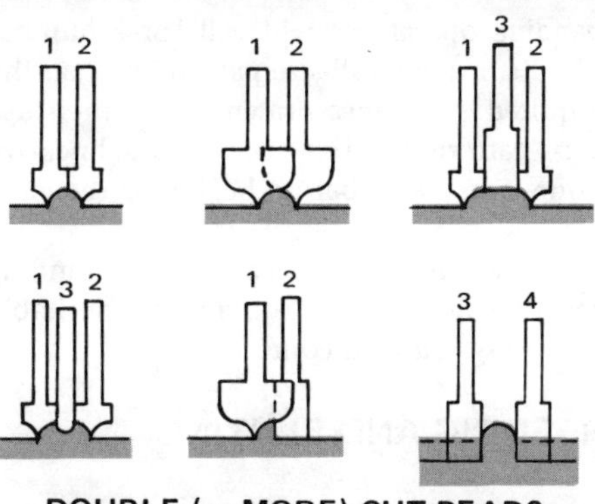

DOUBLE-(or MORE) CUT BEADS

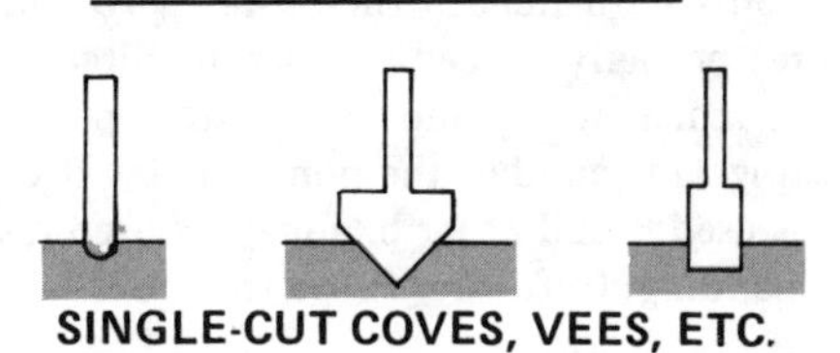

SINGLE-CUT COVES, VEES, ETC.

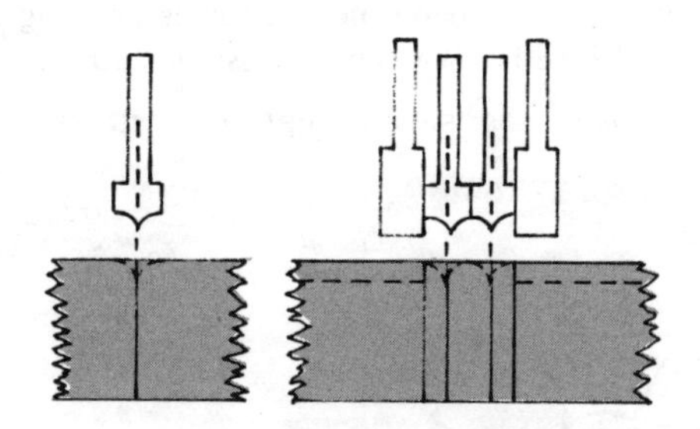

TYPICAL GUIDELINES FOR BANDING CUTS

All banding cuts are made by using "*Cutting Procedure No. 2" (Around the Workpiece), preceding.* The bit must be accurately positioned for each cut before setting the carriage clamps to hold the carriage stationary. This is most easily done by first drawing a pencil guideline on the workpiece to mark the location of the bit center. To draw this guideline, hold the pencil point against the workpiece while revolving it with the hand crank. When banding operations will call for a number of cuts, make a full-size pattern with all the required guidelines drawn on it, then use this pattern to draw these guidelines on your workpiece, before beginning the cuts.

After cutting beads, some light sanding may be necessary to obtain the desirable smoothly-rounded contours.

REEDING AND FLUTING

Reeds are simply beads cut lengthwise instead of banded. Therefore, two (or more) properly spaced cuts are required to make each reed, and either the point-cutting 1/4-round or the point-cutting ogee bit is used — and other bits may be used (as for banding) to further shape the reeds.

Both the cut spacing and the depth-of-cut help to determine the final reed shapes. To plan the shapes, make a full-size cross-section drawing of your workpiece as it is (ready for reeding). Also, on tracing paper, make an outline of the bit to be used.

You can now divide the workpiece drawing into 12 (30°) segments (*as shown at the left in the illustration*), into 24 (15°) segments (*as shown at the right*) — or into 8 (45°), 6 (60°), 4 (90°), 3 (120°) or 2 (180°) segments. Or, if a "stepped" type reeding is desired, you can (for instance) divide it into 24 15° segments then block out every third segment line to leave a spacing of 15°, 30°, blank, 60°, 75°, blank, etc.

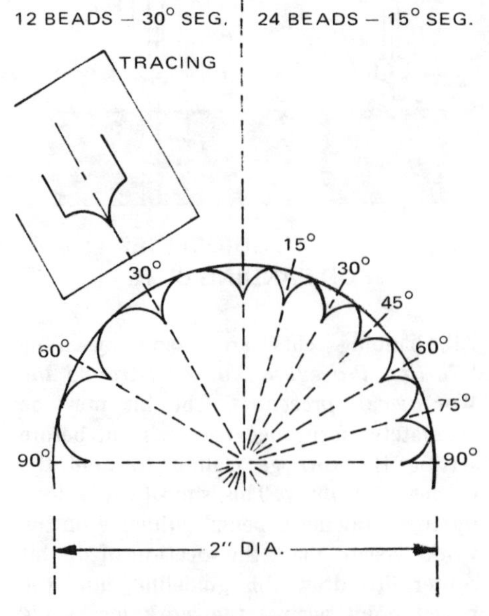

PLANNING REEDS

Having drawn the segment lines as desired, superimpose your traced bit outline on the workpiece drawing with the bit centerline exactly on one of the segment lines. Move the bit outline inward, toward the center point of the workpiece drawing, until the cut shape satisfies you — then measure the actual depth-of-cut that will produce this effect.

Before starting the operation, set your depth-of-cut according to the above. Use "*Cutting Procedure No. 3*" (Lengthwise of the Workpiece), preceding — and do the indexing according to your workpiece drawing plan.

Flutes are the same as single-cut coves, vees, etc. (preceding). A flute is cut with a veining or core-box bit, a vee-groove bit, a straight bit, or any bit that will provide the desired grooving effect. These should be laid-out (by drawings) and planned in the same way reeds are planned. The only difference is that it is the shapes of the cut bottoms that are important, rather than the top shapes left by the cuts.

Before cutting reeds or flutes be sure to set the carriage stops to limit the lengths. After cutting reeds, some light sanding may be necessary to obtain the desired smoothly-rounded contours.

ROPING AND SPIRALING

In cross-section, roping is much the same as reeding — and spiraling is similar to fluting (i.e.: if you were to saw a finished workpiece in two at any point, the cut-off end

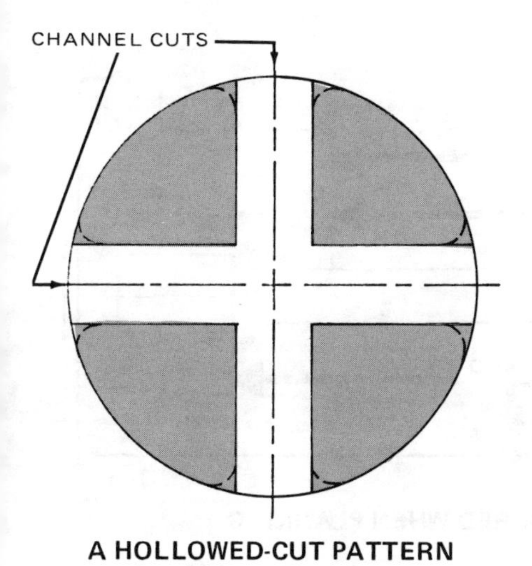

A HOLLOWED-CUT PATTERN

of a roped piece would look like that of a reeded piece, except that the ropes will be wider . . . etc.). In short, the spacing (indexing) of the cuts and the depth-of-cut are planned just as they are for reeding and fluting.

The only difference is that "*Cutting Procedure No. 4*" *(Around the Workpiece and Proportionately Advancing), preceding* is used for the operation. Just keep in mind whether right- or left-hand roping (or spiraling) is desired. Sanding may also be required, as for reeding.

HOLLOW CUTTING

Either fluting or spiraling cuts (preceding) can be made to a depth (by repeated passes at the same setting) that will cause them to meet at the workpiece center so that a "see-through" (hollowed-out) effect will result. The illustration shows a 2-in. diameter workpiece hollow-cut with a 3/8-in. veining bit, then rounded-off (at the outer cut edges) by additional cuts made with a point-cutting 1/4-round bit. Each channel cut (done by making five 1/8-in. deep passes at each set-up position) must be deep enough to meet the adjoining cuts at the inside. These can be done with a straight bit, veining bit, or any suitable-width bit that will make channels to suit your layout.

Just keep in mind that the wider the bit, in proportion to the workpiece diameter, the greater the "see-through" effect will be. To obtain a desired result you should make a scale cross-section drawing of your workpiece, then superimpose on this channels that are to be cut at the selected index positions with the selected (width) bit.

After the "see-through" channels are cut, the outer edges can be shaped (as for reeding or roping) as desired, by making additional spaced cuts with other bits. Sanding, as preceding, may also be required.

PLANNING A WORKPIECE

The first step in planning a project is to determine the size workpiece needed. As previously explained, the workpiece must be square at the headstock end, and it is generally most practical to make it the same size square throughout. Each side of the square must be at least as wide as the largest diameter of the finished turning — and, to allow for a smooth, uniform turning, it is best to have each square side 1/8-in. or more wider than the largest diameter.

When planning the workpiece length, allowances must be made as shown by the illustration on next page. With the tailstock center screw extended approximately 3-3/4-in. (enough to allow shaping all the way from the tailstock end — dimension "A" in the illustration), the maximum allowable length for a 1-in. square workpiece is approximately 36-in. About 2-1/2-in. of this (dimension "B") will be inside of the headstock. If the workpiece is 3-in. square, its maximum length is only about 34-1/2-in., of which approximately 1-in. will be inside the headstock. In short, the maximum length of workpiece between

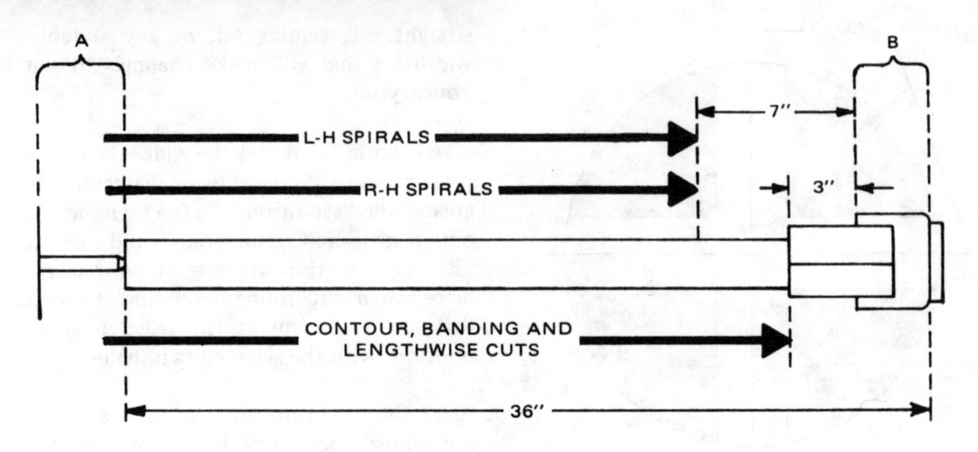

DIMENSIONS TO BE CONSIDERED WHEN PLANNING

the tailstock center and the *outside* of the headstock is approximately 33-1/2-in. (with tailstock center screw so extended).

Because the carriage will allow the bit to come only as close as 3-in. from the headstock, an added 3-in. must be reserved (from turning operations) at the headstock end. This means that a maximum length of approximately 30-1/2-in. (regardless of workpiece square size) can be reduced to a round, contour shaped, banded or lengthwise cut. And there are further limitations when using the cable to make spiral cuts. The closest to the headstock that either a left- or a right-hand spiral can end is 7-in. That is, maximum spiral-section length is approximately 26-1/2 inches, measured from the tailstock end.

Of course, if shaping must be done end-to-end of a workpiece, you can do part of the shaping with one end in the headstock, then do the rest with the opposite end in the headstock (providing you leave, or can nail or glue on, a square part to fit inside the headstock).

Having allowed for the above limitations, the next step is to plan the actual cuts. Draw, full size, as accurate a "picture" of the finished project as you can, keeping in mind the kinds of cuts that your various bits will make so that you can depict these with reasonable accuracy. All straight- or taper-rounded or contoured areas should be drawn exactly as you will want them to be. In addition, all banding cuts should be accurately drawn so that you can determine which bits to use and the depth-of-cut settings required.

Lengthwise cuts should be shown, as illustrated, with the number (around the workpiece) to be made. Remember: the spacing (in degrees) of lengthwise cuts is 360 (degrees) divided by the number of cuts — and the size of bit used will determine the appearance (cut widths).

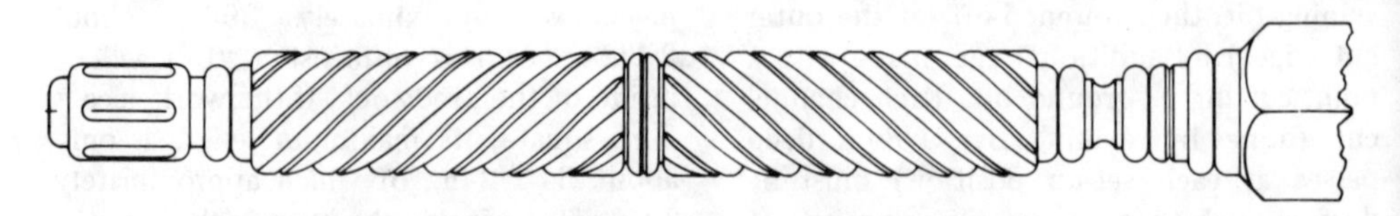

A WORKING PLAN – Shown 20% of Actual Size

TAKE TIME TO PLAN – MAKE EVERY SET-UP CORRECTLY

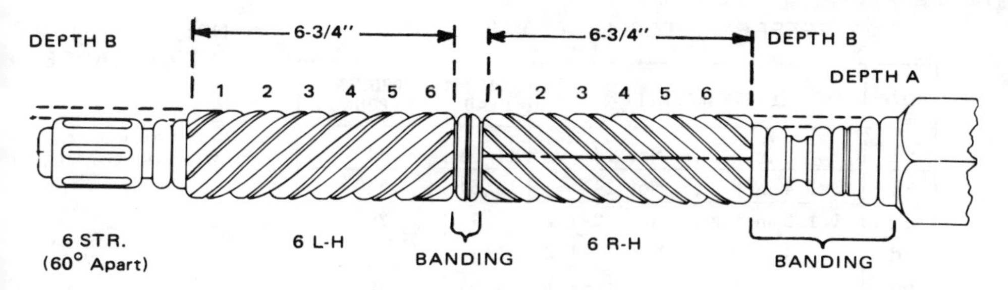

SOME HELPFUL PLANNING FACTORS

When planning spiral cuts, keep in mind that each spiral, in one full revolution, will extend 6-3/4-in. If, as shown in the illustration, you plan to have six (indexed) spirals, the silhouettes (as shown along top of workpiece) of those six spirals will be spaced 1/6 of 6-3/4-in. apart (approx. 1-1/8-in.) For eight (indexed) spirals the spacing is 1/8 of 6-3/4 equals .84375 in.; for 12, 1/12 of 6-3/4 equals .5625 in., etc.

In short, to "picture" the roping or spiral cuts desired, mark off distances of 6-3/4-in. from the left side (start) of each spiraled section . . . then divide each distance into 6, 8, 12, etc. equal spaces according to the number of indexed spirals you plan to have. Each space will represent the top center of a spiral cut.

After making a reasonably comprehensive full-scale drawing of your project, the next step is to plan the sequence of cuts. If there are *no* tapered areas, your first cuts will be simply to reduce the square to required round (diameter) dimensions. To save time, mark your drawing to show the required minimum diameters ("Depth A", "Depth B" in the illustration) for various areas. When reducing the square to a round, reduce it to these marked diameters — then proceed with the banding, lengthwise and roping cuts, as needed.

If there will be a taper-rounded area, draw it to scale and indicate the approximate tailstock setting (1/4-in., 1/2-in., etc.) you will use when setting up (as previously explained).

If there will be a contoured area, draw it to scale — then project (as illustrated) the required template shape to achieve this contour (as previously explained).

If properly completed, your finished (full-scale) project drawing should not only show the final workpiece outline, it should also indicate to you each step of the turning operations together with the bits and depths-of-cut to be used — and how to set the tailstock (for any taper needed) and/or how to shape any template needed for a contoured area. Of course, to make such a drawing takes some time and calculations . . . it may be more fun and less tiring simply to start cutting and let chance determine the outcome (but you *can't* very well make duplicates — such as four matching table legs — in this manner).

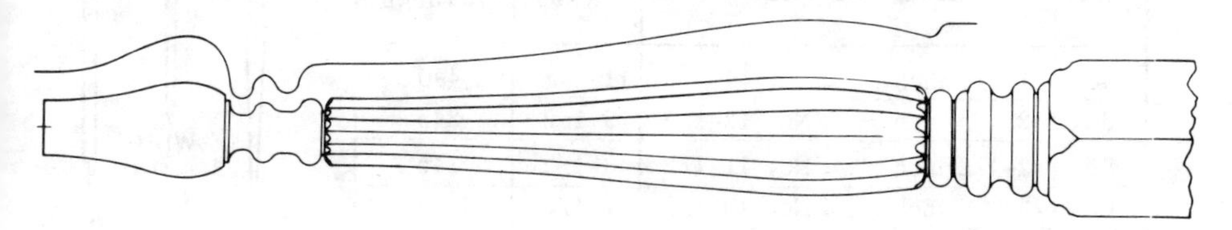

WORKING PLAN THAT REQUIRES A TEMPLATE

CREATING TURNED SHAPES IS A FASCINATING PASTIME

REFERENCE TABLE – COMMON NAILS

SIZE	LENGTH and GAUGE	DIA. HEAD	APPROX. NO. TO POUND
2d	1 inch . . . No. 15	11/64	845
3d	1-1/4 inch . . . No. 14	13/64	540
4d	1-1/2 inch . . . No. 12-1/2	1/4	290
5d	1-3/4 inch . . . No. 12-1/2	1/4	250
6d	2 inch . . . No. 11-1/2	17/64	165
7d	2-1/4 inch . . . No. 11-1/2	17/64	150
8d	2-1/2 inch . . . No. 10-1/4	9/32	100
9d	2-3/4 inch . . . No. 10-1/4	9/32	90
10d	3 inch . . . No. 9	5/16	65
12d	3-1/4 inch . . . No. 9	5/16	60
16d	3-1/2 inch . . . No. 8	11/32	45
20d	4 inch . . . No. 6	13/32	30
30d	4-1/2 inch . . . No. 5	7/16	20
40d	5 inch . . . No. 4	15/32	17
50d	5-1/2 inch . . . No. 3	1/2	13
60d	6 inch . . . No. 2	17/32	10

REFERENCE TABLE – FINISHING NAILS

SIZE	LENGTH and GAUGE	DIA. HEAD	APPROX. NO. TO POUND
3d	1-1/4 inch . . . No. 15-1/2	12-1/2	880
4d	1-1/2 inch . . . No. 15	12	630
6d	2 inch . . . No. 13	10	290
8d	2-1/2 inch . . . No. 12-1/2	9-1/2	195
10d	3 inch . . . No. 11-1/2	8-1/2	125

REFERENCE TABLE – CASING NAILS

SIZE	LENGTH and GAUGE	DIA. HEAD	APPROX. NO. TO POUND
4d	1-1/2 inch . . . No. 14	11	490
6d	2 inch . . . No. 12-1/2	9-1/2	245
8d	2-1/2 inch . . . No. 11-1/2	8-1/2	145
10d	3 inch . . . No. 10-1/2	7-1/2	95
16d	3-1/2 inch . . . No. 10	7	72

NAIL DIAMETER 1 TO 20 GAUGE

USE A DRILL SMALLER THAN NAIL DIAMETER

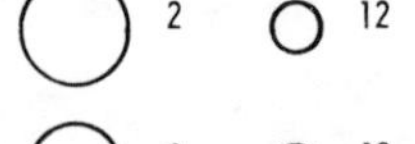
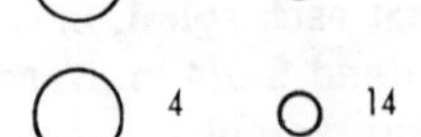
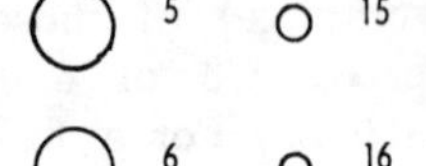
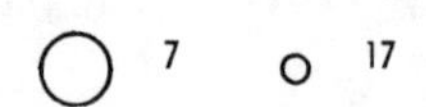

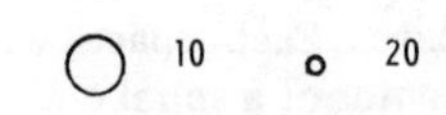

RUST-PROOF NAILS

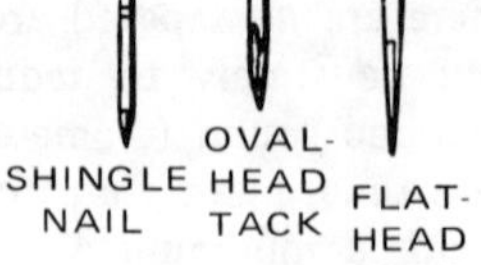

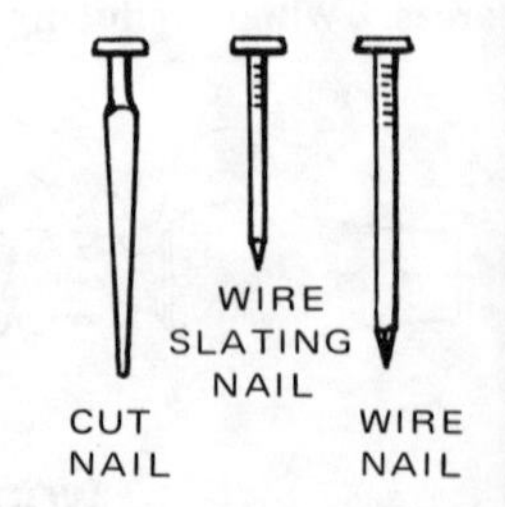

USE THE CORRECT NAIL FOR EACH JOB

SECTION II

SCROLL, SABRE & RECIPROCATING SAWS

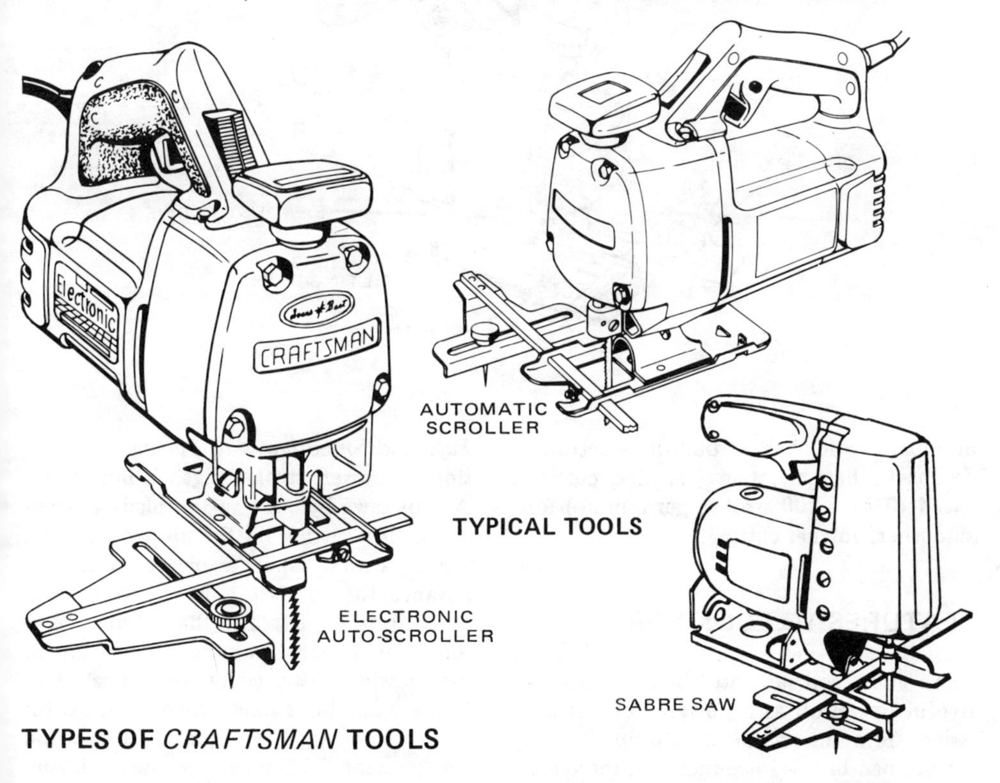

TYPICAL TOOLS

TYPES OF *CRAFTSMAN* TOOLS

For hobby work, shop or general handyman use a sabre (or the improved scroller-type) saw is one of the most useful tools you can own. Even the simplest and most economical type of saw serves the purposes of a hand-held, powered jig saw, with which straight or intricately curved and/or angled pattern lines can be cut in workpieces of wood and other materials.

Sabre saws are available in "sizes" ranging from 1/6- up to 1/4-hp, in one-speed, two-speed and variable-speed models. This type is guided — to cut along a pattern line — by turning the *whole tool* in the direction desired. Your hand positions and placement of the tool cord must be taken into account when sawing along lengthy and intricate pattern lines.

Scroll saws are available in three types: manual, automatic and electronic. All types have variable-speed controls and "sizes" are from 1/4- to 1/2-hp. The blade chuck of the three types is swivel mounted to permit 360-degree blade rotation while cutting. With the manual scroller, blade swiveling is accomplished by hand-turning the knob at tool top, which can be locked in four different positions for straight-line cutting. With the automatic scroller, the same manual control can be used . . . or swiveling (with the knob unlocked) can be done simply by using slight directional pressure of the hand guiding the tool. In either case, there is *no* need to turn the tool, itself . . . the blade, alone, will follow your pattern line forward, sideward or even backward. The electronic model is also

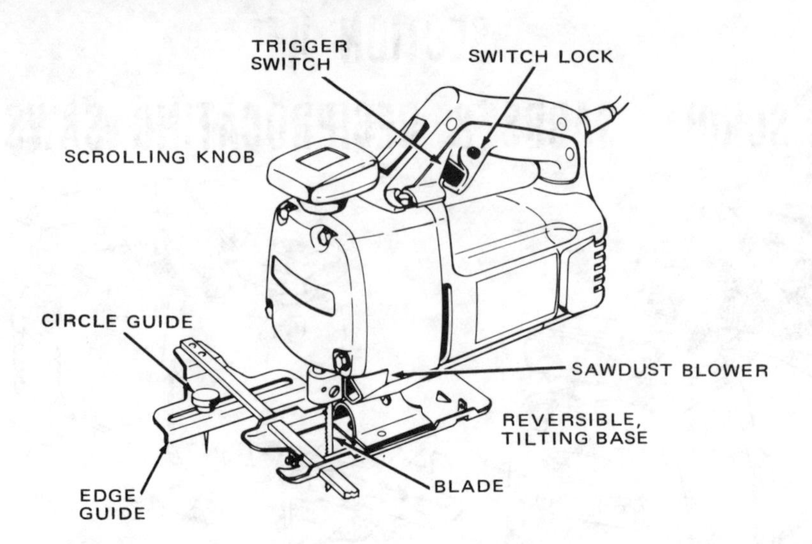

automatic and has a built-in electronic feedback that maintains selected cutting speed (0 to 3,000 strokes per minute) for smoother, quicker cutting.

FEATURES TO LOOK FOR

Sabre and scroll saws are about as hazard-free in operation as a power tool can be. Aside from the *double-insulation feature* (mentioned in the Introduction), there are no significant differences among tools with regards to operator safety. There are, however, a great many differences that affect the type and quality of work to be done, and the ease and rapidity with which it can be done. *Before* selecting a tool, consider which of the following features are important to your particular work requirements.

Power. To great extent, the motor hp determines the thickness and/or hardness of the wood that can be sawed without overloading the tool and tiring the operator. A small hp tool is quite satisfactory for thin-wood hobbywork and occasional odd jobs; but cabinetwork and rough carpentry require power — generally, the more the better, especially for any prolonged project on which the tool will be used continuously.

Ease and Smoothness of Sawing. In addition to power, stroke-length is important. A tool saws by moving the blade up-and-down, for cutting on the up-stroke, and a longer stroke takes a bigger "bite" to advance the cut faster. When sawing thin wood (up to 1/2-in.), the advance produced by a short stroke is fast enough for easy sawing — especially for intricate pattern sawing; but a long stroke is needed for sawing thick (and, especially, hard) wood (in fact, the 6-in. long, fast-cutting blades can be used only in a 1-in. stroke tool).

Stroke Speed. Slow speeds are necessary for sawing metals and other hard materials — too-fast a speed quickly dulls the blade. A slow speed may also be desirable when precisely sawing an intricate pattern. On the other hand, the faster the speed the easier it is to saw accurately along a long straight or gently curved line. Less expensive tools offer only one or two no-load speed(s); better tools have trigger-controlled variable speed (from 0 to maximum). Moreover, a trigger-controlled tool should be fitted with a full-on lock with quick release, so that finger pressure isn't required for full-speed operation.

Scrolling Feature. As previously explained,

WITH AUTOMATIC SCROLLING YOU CAN GUIDE IN ANY DIRECTION

this feature makes it easier to cut along pattern lines, especially if your workpiece is too large to reposition or to walk around as may be necessary if using a (non-scrolling) sabre saw. Any scroller, however, should be fitted with a lock to hold the blade in one position when desired. Better tools permit locking the blade in any of four positions: forward, right, left or backward. Manual scrolling requires two-hand tool guidance; an automatic scroller can be guided with one hand.

Bevel-Angle Sawing. Some tools have a base that can be tilted in *one* direction and secured so that the blade will saw a bevel angle on the workpiece edge being cut. The best is a base that can be tilted in *either* direction for sawing bevels up to 45 degrees, right or left.

Straight-Line and Circle Sawing. Tool guidance generally is free-hand, or by sliding the tool base along a straightedge guide. For many jobs, however, it is handy to have an adjustable edge guide that can be positioned to slide along the workpiece edge for making a cut at the desired distance in from this edge. Better edge guides also have a center point — which can be held on center to swing the tool for cutting a perfect circle of the (adjusted) diameter.

Serviceability. Better construction makes a more durable, easy-to-service tool. Important details are: ball-, instead of sleeve-bearings; an impact-resistant handle; a sturdy base; and an impact-resistant tool body.

Conveniences. A tool's overall usefulness to you can depend upon some added feature, like a built-in sawdust blower to keep the cutting line clean and visible . . . or upon the types of blades and accessories available for various types of work.

SABRE- AND SCROLL-SAW BLADES

Craftsman blades are available for a variety of operations. Refer to a current Sears Catalog for an up-to-date listing — and to your tool's Owner's Manual for types recommended for use with your model tool. Typical blades illustrated are shown in the accompanying table. Blades are available in 14 and 50 blade assorted kits.

TYPICAL BLADES AND USES

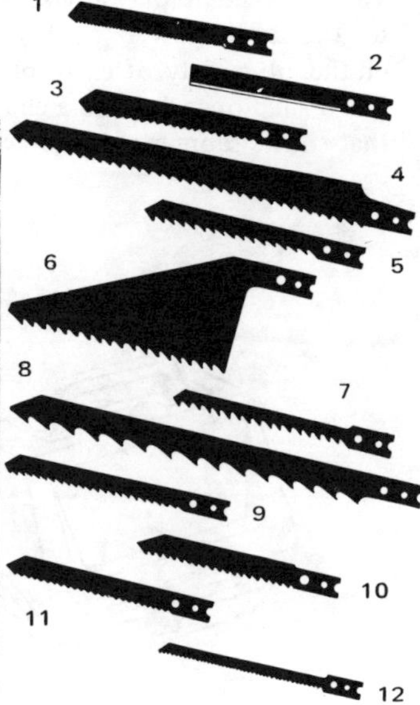

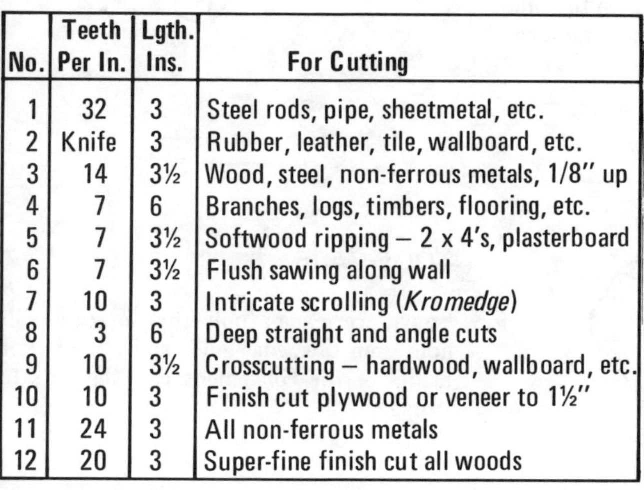

No.	Teeth Per In.	Lgth. Ins.	For Cutting
1	32	3	Steel rods, pipe, sheetmetal, etc.
2	Knife	3	Rubber, leather, tile, wallboard, etc.
3	14	3½	Wood, steel, non-ferrous metals, 1/8" up
4	7	6	Branches, logs, timbers, flooring, etc.
5	7	3½	Softwood ripping – 2 x 4's, plasterboard
6	7	3½	Flush sawing along wall
7	10	3	Intricate scrolling (*Kromedge*)
8	3	6	Deep straight and angle cuts
9	10	3½	Crosscutting – hardwood, wallboard, etc.
10	10	3	Finish cut plywood or veneer to 1½"
11	24	3	All non-ferrous metals
12	20	3	Super-fine finish cut all woods

REFER TO A **CURRENT** *SEARS CATALOG FOR BLADES AVAILABLE*

CRAFTSMAN ACCESSORIES

CIRCLE-CUTTING EDGE GUIDE

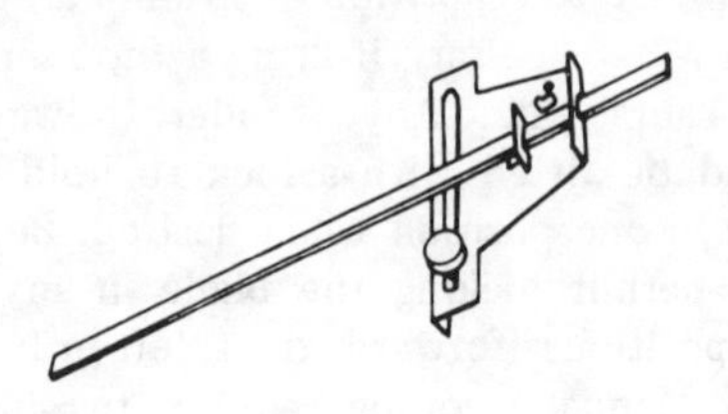

For any tool not already equipped, this is the same guide previously described. Can be adjusted to various distances out from the tool base to slide along a straight edge. The pivot point is also adjustable in the slot shown for sawing differently centered circles.

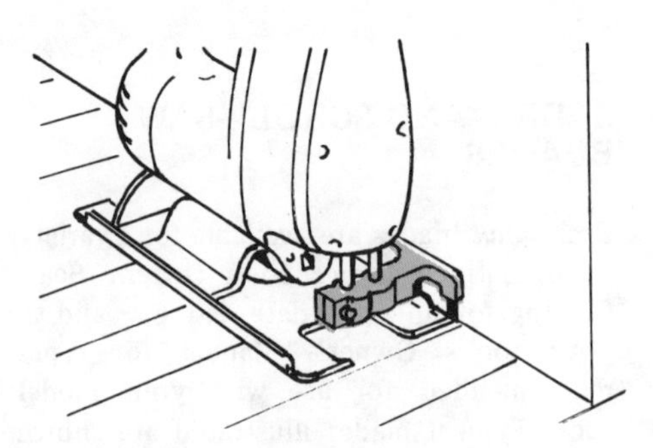

SIDE-CUTTER ATTACHMENT

When attached to the saw bar this extension holds the blade vertically at one side of the saw base so that cutting can be done flush along any wall or other vertical construction against which the base is guided. Can*not* be used with all tool models; check your Owner's Manual.

BLADE AND DRILL-BIT HOLDER

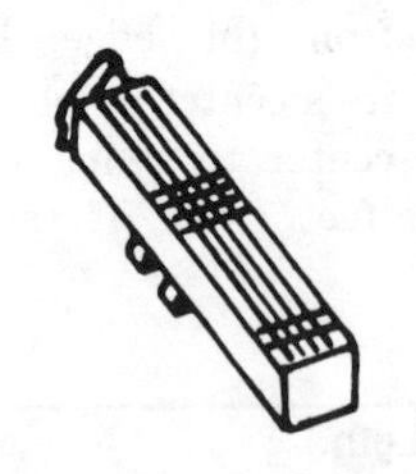

This convenient plastic container attaches to the tool power cord to provide an on-the-job supply of extra blades and bits. Has a snap-open lid and a chart on the side that shows sabre-saw blade types and uses.

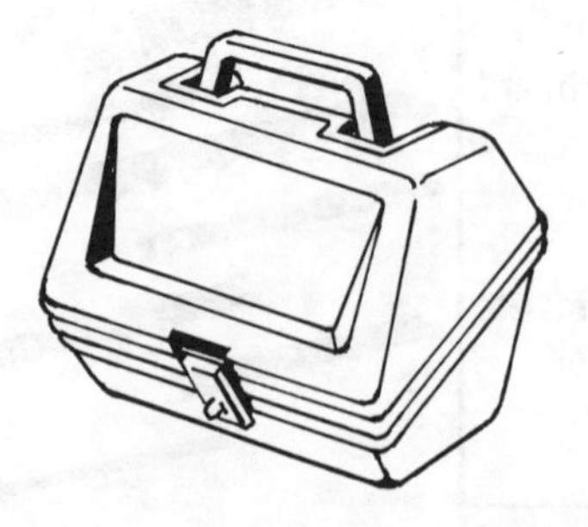

TOOL CASE

Tough Permanex polyethylene case will hold your saw, edge guide and a number of blades — for convenient carrying or safe storage.

A TOOL CASE ADDS TO THE LIFE AND CONVENIENCE OF YOUR TOOL

TYPICAL OPERATIONS

Long straight lines not too far in from a workpiece straightedge are most easily cut with the help of the edge guide. Feed your tool steadily, *only* at the rate of advance at which it will continue to cut freely. This rate depends upon workpiece thickness, hardness and condition (damp, knotty, etc.). A convex edge, or a concave one that the guide face can uniformly follow, can also be used for guiding a like-shaped cut.

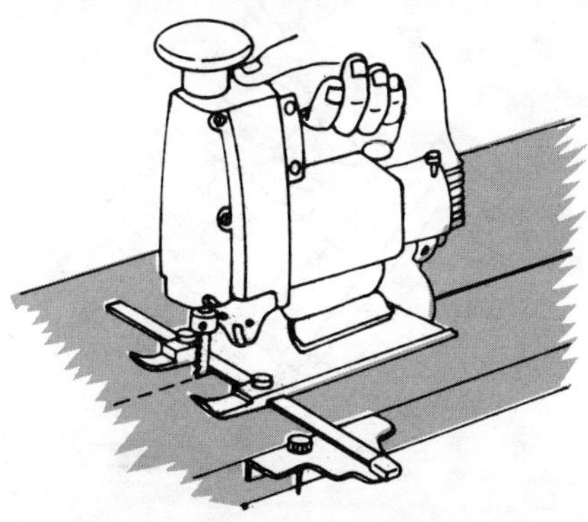

RIPPING A LONG, STRAIGHT LINE

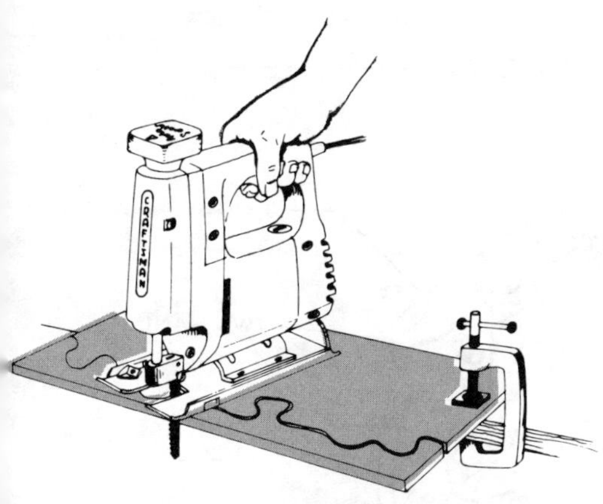

SAWING AN INTRICATE DESIGN

Any design line having curves or angles in which the blade can turn while advancing can be freehand sawed. Advance the tool carefully, as above – and do *not* try to turn the blade on itself (it must advance as it turns so as not to bind at the sides). Corners and curves must be sawed by backing then advancing, repeatedly, to widen the saw kerf as necessary. Sharp angles are best cut by approaching from the two sides, with separate cuts.

Narrow metal sections and pipes are best cut, as illustrated, with the blade reversed to allow the tool to hang on the workpiece. Very light feeding pressure is then needed to keep the blade cutting uniformly – and there is no problem of holding the tool in place on the workpiece. Wide enough sections can be sawed in either preceding manner. When sawing sheetmetal it must be laid flat on scrap wood to be sawed with it – and must be clamped firmly in position close to the cutting action (to prevent the blade from pulling it up and buckling it). Be very careful *not* to advance too fast.

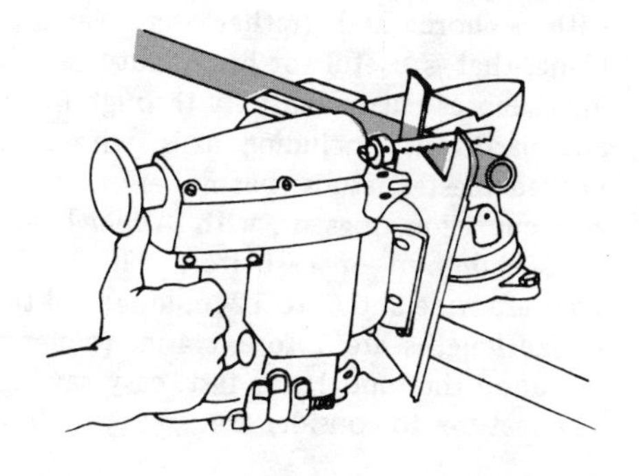

CUTTING OFF METAL TUBING

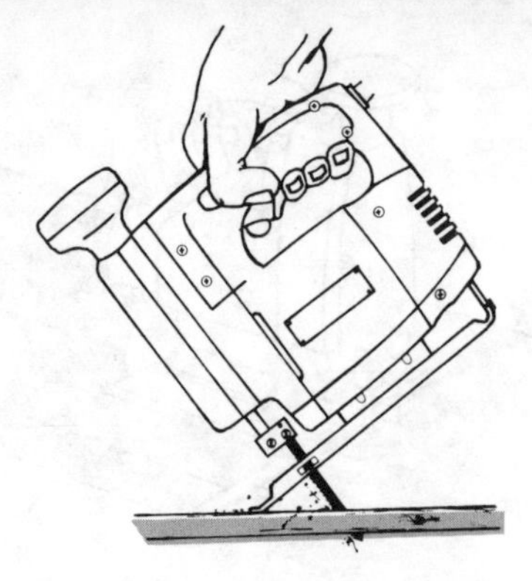

STARTING AN INSIDE CUT

One of the most useful features of this type tool is its ability to start a cut anywhere on the workpiece surface — without the need of drilling a starting hole. Simply rest the tool (on the workpiece) on the toe-end of the base with the blade end aligned with your cut line. Start the motor then, while pressing firmly down on the base toe to prevent side wobble, rock the saw to lower the moving blade into the workpiece. After the base is flat on the workpiece, advance the tool to cut in the usual manner.

RECIPROCATING SAW

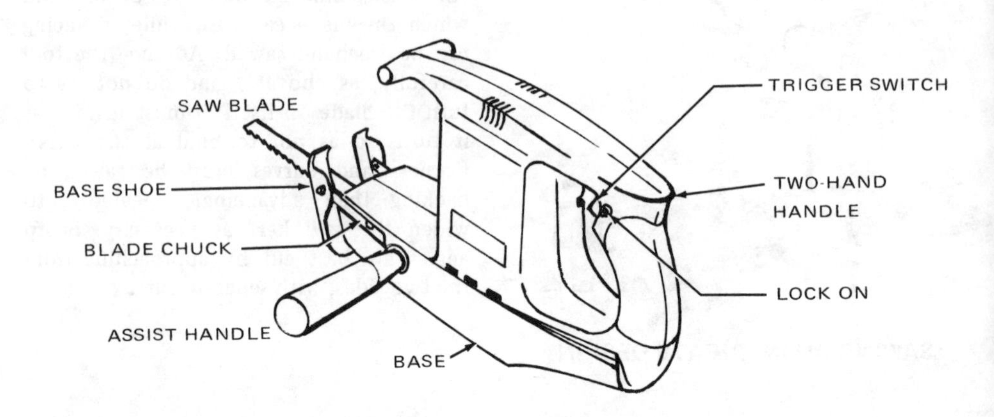

USES AND TOOL FEATURES

This is an extra-powerful sabre-type saw with a horizontal (rather than vertical) blade, that is useful for heavy-duty sawing jobs such as cutting entirely through floors and partitions (including nails, wire-mesh backed plaster, studs, beams, etc.). It can also cut 12-in. logs or, with proper blade, 1-in. aluminim or cast iron. The blades used are wide and 6- to 12-in. long; and the stroke lengths are 1 to 1-1/4-in. (depending upon the model) for fast, easy sawing. The features to consider are:

Power and Stroke. More hp and a longer stroke make for faster, easier, smoother sawing through heavy beams and such — but may not be needed for lighter-duty or occasional use.

Speed of Cut. As with sabre saws, the strokes-per-minute are important. Slower speed is better when cutting through metals (floor-board nails, lathing wire, etc.) or when cutting along a much-curved or angled line. Therefore, a variable-speed model provides more versatility (and longer blade life in general use) than a single-speed model (which is designed for general wood-cutting). A trigger "ON" lock with quick release (with a variable-speed model) is also helpful when doing full-speed work.

Conveniences. To do sawing *both* straight down (as for floor cutting) *and* sideways (as for sawing at floor level sideways through a partition) you need a tool with a blade clamp on which the blade can be horizontally installed (to face right or left) and a reversible base shoe. Straight-down sawing is done with the saw vertical, resting on its base shoe; for flush cutting the saw is held horizontal with the base shoe against the wall (partition, etc.) to be cut. A properly designed base shoe also makes plunge cutting (starting a cut at workpiece center) easy. A *two*-hand handle makes all work easier.

Serviceability. Longer-lasting construction features include: a) Quiet-running helical gears and all ball- (rather than sleeve-) bearings; b) Easy to replace, etc. motor brushes; c) A high-impact, non-glare housing and handle.

Safety. Check for double insulation.

CRAFTSMAN ACCESSORIES

Craftsman blades for a variety of operations are as shown in the accompanying table.

> *NOTE:* A tool case, similar to the one for sabre saws, is available.

No.	Teeth Per In.	Lgth. Ins.	For Cutting
1	7	6	All except metal – smooth and plunge cuts.
2	3	9	Fast, rough cuts in wood over 1" thick.
3	24	6	Steel – other metals – to 2" thick.
4	7	6	Flush cuts, wood, plastic, nails, etc.
5	7	12	All except metal – smooth, deep cuts.
6	14	6	Rough-cut wood; nails.

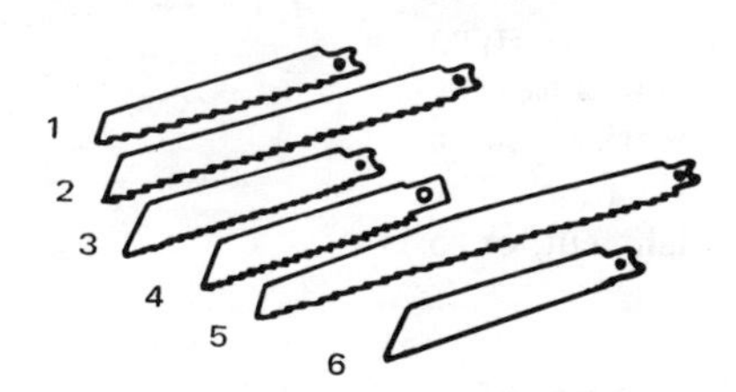

TYPICAL OPERATIONS

General sawing is done, as shown, with the blade horizontally in front of the tool and upright so that the tool weight applies most of the thrust needed to keep the blade advancing through the workpiece. The base shoe is installed with the closed side at bottom — so that it surrounds the blade — and can be positioned inward or outward, to expose more or less of the blade as required by the workpiece width.

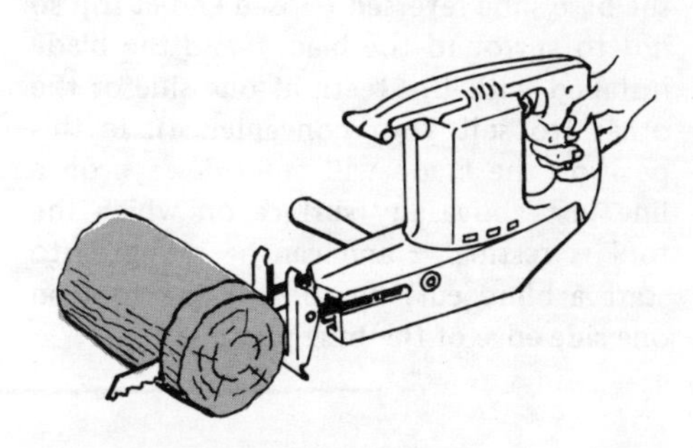

STARTING A BLIND CUT

To start a blind cut in a workpiece the base shoe is moved inward, as close to the tool as possible, to form a rocker at the tool front. With the power on, the tool is then rotated on the base-plate front edge from a horizontal to a vertical position — so that the moving blade plunges into the workpiece at the desired start of the cut.

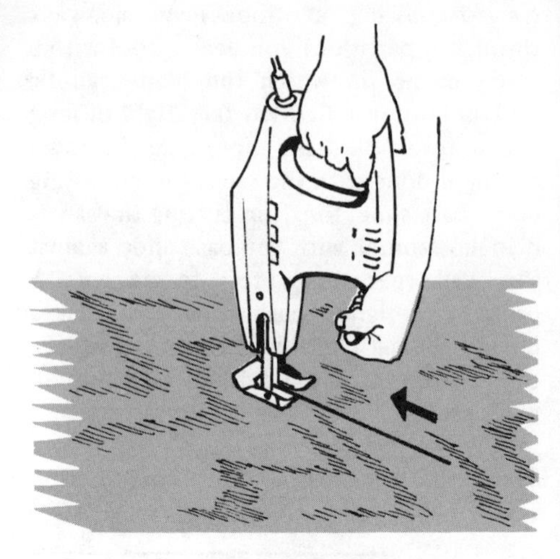

DEEP SAWING

Sawing through a floor is done with the tool resting on the base shoe, as it will be after completing the start of a blind cut (as above). It can be held vertically, as shown, or at any convenient angle that is steep enough for the blade to penetrate the material being cut. Upright work — like a partition — is sawed in similar manner. The tool can be guided for a straight cut, or to follow curves, etc. as desired.

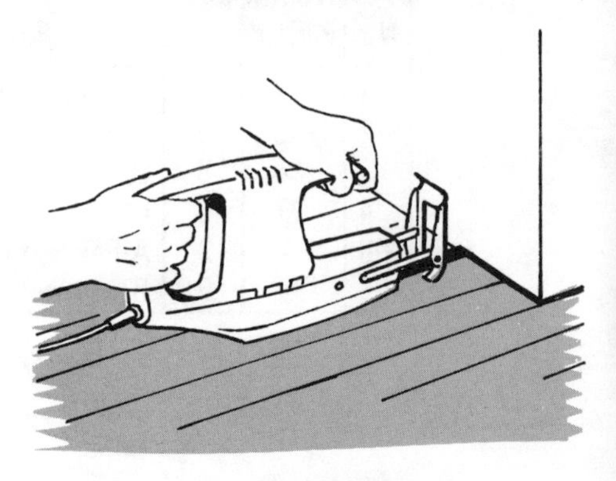

FLUSH SAWING

Flush cutting — along the base of a partition, as shown, or along the floor at the bottom of the partition — is done with the base shoe reversed (closed end at top so *not* to surround the blade), and the blade installed with the teeth at one side or the other (to suit your convenience). In this position the blade will cut sideways on a line just above any surface on which the tool is resting — and can be plunged (to start a blind cut) by rocking the tool on one side edge of the base plate.

Thick metal sections are cut like wood — but at much slower speeds of operation. Blade lubrication is recommended, to prolong blade life and improve the cutting action. Use a generous amount of light oil for cutting non-ferrous metals, iron or steel. Support the workpiece and the tool firmly to prevent vibration and/or blade twisting. To cut sheetmetal, preferably sandwich it between scrap pieces of plywood (or similar) to prevent tearing.

WHEN SAWING THROUGH FLOORS OR WALLS
BE CAREFUL **NOT** *TO SAW INTO ELECTRICAL WIRES OR PIPES*

SECTION III
ELECTRIC HAND DRILLS

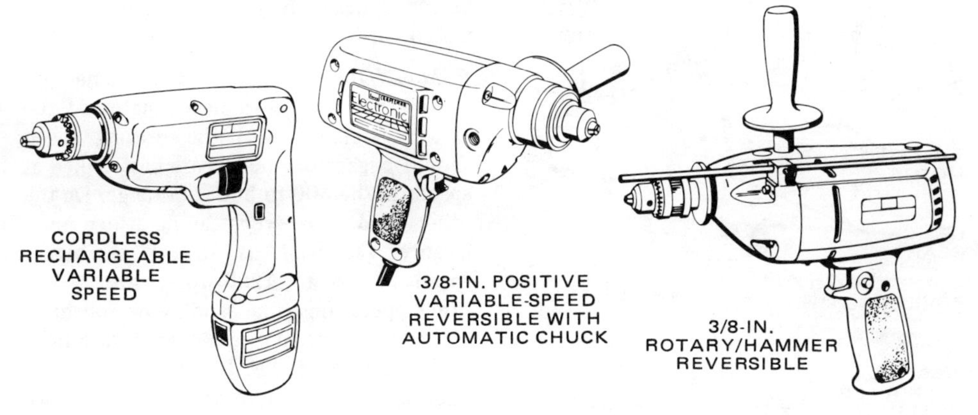

TYPICAL POPULAR DRILLS

A DRILL MAY BE YOUR MOST-USED POWER TOOL

An electric hand drill is, for most shop- and/or home-owners, the number one power tool to acquire — because of the many maintenance, repair and construction projects that can be more easily accomplished with a power drill than by hand-drilling methods. In fact, a power hand drill is not only useful for drilling holes in a variety of materials (including masonry and metal as well as wood), with proper accessories it can also be used for such operations as buffing, sanding, etc. Drilling — even if only to prepare holes for nails, screws and bolts — can be done in so much less time and so much better with a power tool that any adequate power drill is a very good investment.

There is a wide selection of tools for powered hand drilling, and the model tool that will be your best buy depends mostly upon the type of useage that you will expect from your tool. "Useage" relates principally to the size (diameter and depth) of holes to be drilled and the materials (wood, plastic, iron, steel, etc.) in which they will be drilled. In short, your first consideration when buying a drill should be, simply, what sizes of holes in what kinds of materials you will want to drill. A tool that has the capacity to do what you want (or more) will make your work fast, easy and pleasant; one with too-little capacity may eventually finish a job, but will tire you and, possibly, spoil the workpiece and/or the drill bit in the process.

FEATURES TO LOOK FOR

SAFETY. Because a drill is taken to wherever it is convenient to do the job, double insulation is a considerable safety factor for any 110V (or higher voltage) tool.

CAPACITY. Drills are rated in terms of the maximum size full-shank twist drill (one having a shank the same size as the holes it will make) that the drill chuck will hold. The popular sizes are 1/4-in., 3/8-in. and 1/2-in. Although some twist-drill sizes are available with turned-down shanks (i.e.: a 1/2-in. drill with a 1/4-in. shank), generally speaking a power drill's chuck capacity is a good *first* indication of the maximum size hole the drill can "comfortably" bore through hard metal.

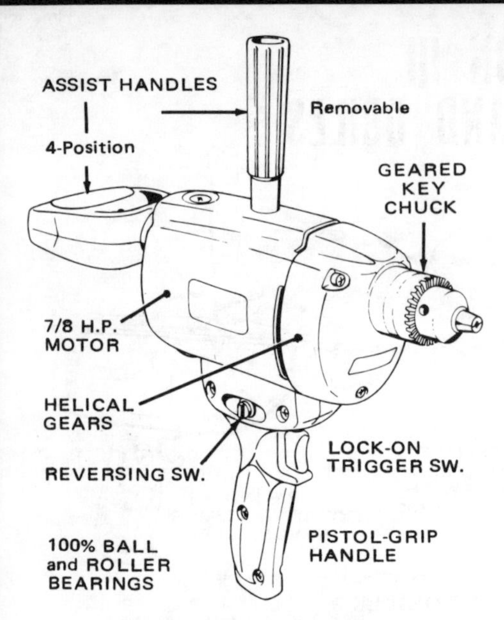

POWERFUL 1/2-IN. DRILL

POWER. Drills are also rated according to maximum hp developed by the motor. This is the *second* (and, often the most important) indication of a power drill's work capacity. It doesn't matter what the chuck capacity may be, if a tool is underpowered it can*not* "comfortably" do the work its chuck size indicates. Before buying, compare the hp ratings. If you will work only with light, relatively thin materials, a light-duty drill will probably suffice; but if you need to drill heavy or hard materials or deep holes and expect a lot of use from your drill, a higher-hp rated drill will be worth the extra cost.

> *NOTE:* A wattage rating indicates the efficiency of a motor; is *not* a reliable indicator of motor hp.

KIND OF POWER. Most power drills are made to operate on 110-120V AC (or, for industrial useage, on 220-240V AC). Such drills require cords to be plugged-into an outlet (or extension) convenient to the work location. However, drills having real usefulness are also available in models that operate on rechargeable batteries — refer to a *current* Sears Catalog for listings. These "cordless" drills, when "charged", can be used anywhere — and the power-pak can be recharged quickly. Such drills are excellent for use in out-of-way places (where current outlets are not at hand), but the power available in one charge is limited so that you cannot expect to be able to use such a drill as long at a time or for as heavy-duty work as you can one with a cord.

RPM AND VARIABLE SPEED. Generally, the harder the workpiece material, the slower (smaller rpm) the drilling speed should be; ferrous metals are best drilled at speeds in the 300 to 500 rpm range. On the other hand, most work can be drilled more cleanly (as well as faster) at higher speeds . . . up to 1200 rpm. Also, some other operations, like sanding or polishing, are better done at the higher rpm. Single-speed drills may be designed to perform excellently for certain operations, but not for others. The best way to obtain all possible drilling-speed advantages is to purchase a variable-speed tool (usually, the speed is variable from 0 to 1200 rpm). This type of tool also makes it easier to start holes (at very slow speed), run-in screws (at low to zero speeds), and is useful for many other operations.

ELECTRONIC CONTROL. The electronic model drill incorporates a circuit that senses need for power and instantly provides it — drill rpm remains constant at speed selected by your finger pressure on trigger.

REVERSIBILITY. All drill bits are designed for clockwise rotation, the same as needed for driving-in a screw. On the other hand, unscrewing a screw (or bolt), or using a screw extractor requires counterclockwise rotation. This feature, therefore, makes a drill useful for these two additional operations, especially if the speed is variable. Also, reversing the rotation will make it easier to release a bit that becomes jammed (by its chips) in the hole it is drilling.

TRIGGER CONTROL. Because drilling and other tool operations are most easily accomplished with precise control, a convenient trigger-type (squeeze-on) switch is desirable. In a variable-speed model, trigger-switch control of the speed is especially desirable. The best trigger switches have a lock-on feature (in a variable-speed model the switch can be locked on at top speed) — that prevents tiring of the trigger finger during lengthy operations — together with a quick release (another squeeze of the finger) for instant stopping.

CHUCK TYPE. The most reliable, easiest to use, all-purpose chuck is a 3-jaw self-centering type that will securely hold any size round shank. Most have a geared key lock but the electronic drill is fitted with a keyless (automatic) chuck that is tightened by running the drill forward — loosened by running the drill in reverse. Use of some accessories requires chuck removal.

EASE OF HANDLING. A lightweight tool with convenient hand holds is less tiring to use than a heavy, awkward one. The most popular type of handle for the guiding hand is the center-balanced handle (with a trigger switch). Additional assist handle(s) — at the rear and/or on top — are very useful for heavy-duty and/or continuous work.

SERVICEABILITY. Such features as permanently-lubricated ball or roller bearings, smoothly quiet helical or spur gearing and a high-impact non-glare housing all add to the durability and/or usefulness of a tool.

IMPORTANT: In addition to a complete selection of power drills as noted above, the Craftsman line includes a *Reversible, Rotary Hammer Drill.* This tool operates as a standard drill for most operations, but can also be adjusted to operate as a percussion tool (21 hammer-like impacts per revolution; up to 25,200 per minute) for much easier drilling into brick, tile, stone or concrete.

TYPES AND USES OF DRILL BITS

With the proper bit you can drill a hole in wood, composition boards, plastic, most metals, stone, tile or concrete. Following are the *Craftsman* bits used for these purposes.

Twist Drills are most used for drilling metals, but can also be used for drilling plastics and woods (though the brad-point drills are better for wood drilling). Lower cost carbon-steel drills are not as satisfactory as the high-speed steel drills, which will drill all except the harder steels (such as stainless) and stay sharp much longer. Most twist drills are available singly or in sets in "jobber lengths", meaning that the length is determined by the diameter according to trade custom — and most are the same diameter end-to-end, though "turned-down-shank" bits in larger sizes are available (these have shanks to fit the drill chucks). There are four standards for bit sizes:

1) Fractional sizes range from 1/16-in. to 1/2-in. in increments of 1/64-in. — a total of 29.

2) Wire-gauge sizes range from no. 60 (smallest) to no. 1 — a total of 60.

3) Lettered sizes range from A (smallest) to Z — a total of 26.

4) Metric sizes commonly range from 3.3 mm. to 14 mm. — a total of 15.

Special, 18-in. long (electricians') bits are also available in popular fractional sizes.

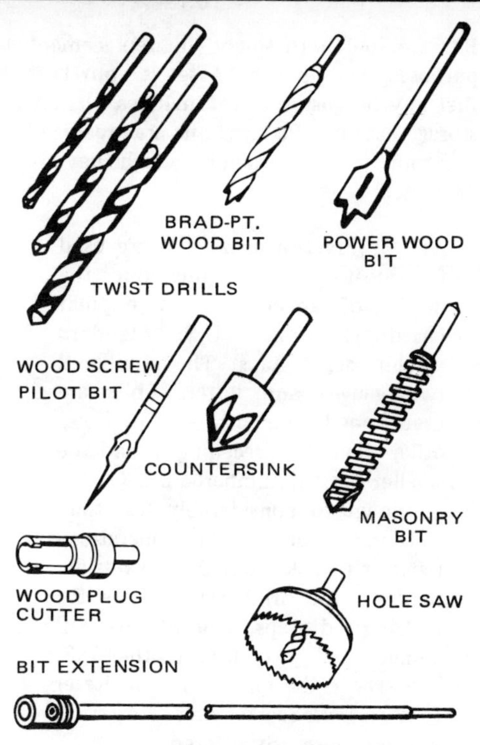

TYPICAL HOLE-DRILLING TOOLS

Bits are sold both singly (for replacement purposes) and in sets. A set is your best first buy because each set includes a handy storage case in which the bits are organized according to sizes – and by which they are protected.

NOTE: Fractional-size bits are used for most purposes, including the drilling of tap holes for the popular (hardware items) U.S. Standard machine-screw taps. The numbered (wire-gauge) and lettered bits are used mostly for drilling tap holes other than the preceding – and the smaller sizes of numbered bits (which go down to considerably less than 1/16-in.), for special operations (jeweler's work, etc.). Metric bits are required for drilling tap holes for metric-sized taps, and these will come more into use as the U.S. converts to the metric system. Refer to a *current* Sears Catalog for sizes, kits, etc. currently offered.

Brad-Point Wood Bits have a center spur that keeps the bit from "walking" and two cutting spurs that accurately "round-the-hole", for wood drilling. Flutes are designed for rapid chip ejection. There are eight sizes: 1/4-, 5/16-, 3/8-, 7/16-, 1/2-, 5/8-, 3/4-, and 1-in.

Power Wood Bits are specially designed for fast, clean boring through all types of wood and firm composition-wood products. Sizes range from 1/4-in. to 1-1/2-in., in 1/8-in. increments, and all have 1/4-in. shanks.

Wood-Screw Pilot Bits are (each) made to bore a shaped and sized hole for one of the standard-size wood screws (nos. 4 through 12 in lengths from 1/2- to 1-1/2-in.). The two workpieces to be joined are drilled simultaneously and the bit produces a countersunk hole for the screw shank in the top piece and a smaller-diameter hole for the screw core (threaded part) in the bottom piece. All have 1/4-in. shanks.

Countersinks are used to shape the top of a previously bored hole to receive the head of a flat-head screw that is to be sunk flush with the surface. The tool cuts an 82° cone, has a 1/4-in. shank.

Masonry Bits have tungsten-carbide cutting tips designed for drilling stud-bolt holes, etc. in concrete, stone, brick, plasterboard, cast-iron and non-ferrous metals. Popular sizes are 3/16-, 1/4-, 5/16-, 3/8-, 1/2-, 5/8- and 3/4-in. with shanks ranging from 3/16- to 3/8-in. diameter. Bit lengths are similar to jobber lengths, except that the 1/4-, 5/16-, 3/8- and 1/2-in. sizes are also available in 13-in. lengths for piercing masonry walls.

Hole Saws are used for drilling large holes (3/4-in. to 2-1/2-in.) by removing a "plug" from the workpiece. A different saw is needed for each size hole, and workpiece thickness is limited to the height of the saw blade. To remove a "plug" the workpiece must be drilled through. A mandrel is required – to provide a central shank and, also, a pilot bit, to keep the hole saw drilling on center. Hole saws are available both in high-speed steel types and in carbide-tipped steel types (which last up to five times longer) – in individual sizes and in kits. The carbide-tipped saws can be used for cutting holes in ceramic tiles, cement and asbestos board.

Wood Plug Cutters are used to make screw, bolt or decorative plug holes. They are "self-extracting" – that is, designed to remove the cut plug without prying, and are available in single 1/2-, 5/8- and 3/4-in. diameter sizes or in a set.

Bit Extension. This is a 12-in. rod with a 1/4-in. shank and a 5/8-in. outside diameter socket that will hold any 1/4-in. shank bit. It can be used to extend the reach of any bit it will hold – or to increase the drilling depth of any 1/4-in. shank bit that will drill a hole 5/8-in. or larger in diameter.

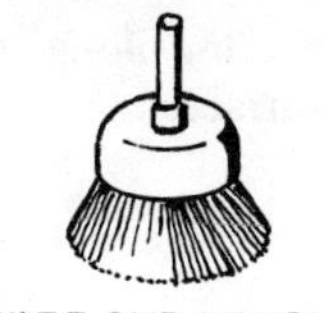

ACCESSORIES FOR OTHER WORK

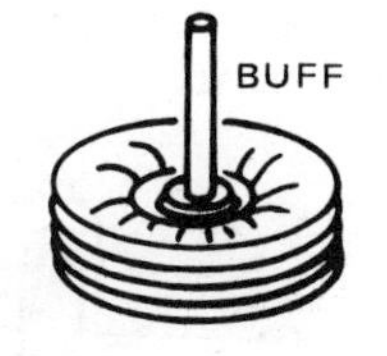

OTHER-WORK CHUCKED ACCESSORIES

With the following accessories your electric hand drill can be used for a number of labor-saving operations in addition to boring.

Screw Extractors are used for removing the ends of machine screws and bolts broken off in a workpiece — by first drilling a hole in the screw-stub center, then inserting the extractor and revolving it counter-clockwise. This 5-piece set (in its own plastic case) includes sizes nos. 1-5 (for screws approximately 1/8-in. diameter, up) — with square-end rounded shanks that can be used both for hand turning (with an end wrench) or in a reversible electric drill. (A 3/8-in. tool is needed to hold the largest extractor.)

Drum File. This 2-in. diameter, hollow, steel rasp makes quick work of stock removal from wood, plastic or soft metal. It is useful for preliminary shaping of a workpiece. The shank is 1/4-in.

Wire Brushes. These stiff wire brushes are all exceptionally useful for fast rust, scale or paint removal or for cleaning and smoothing a pitted or burred surface. All have 1/4-in. shanks. The 3-in. diameter wheel brushes and 1-3/4-in. diameter cup brushes are available in fine or coarse wire. There is also a 2-3/4-in. coarse-wire cup brush. One carbon-removal brush is 1-in. diameter; the other, 1-1/8-in. diameter with twisted wire ends for extra-heavy-duty work.

Sanding Drum with Sleeve. The 1/4-in. shank, expanding-rubber drum holds replaceable sanding sleeves available in various grits for a range of on-the-job sanding operations. Drums are available in two sizes: 1-1/2-in. diameter and 2-3/16-in. diameter — both with a 1-in. high face.

Buff. This 1/4-in. shank tool, 3-in. in dia. made of 50-ply muslin is excellent for rubbing out scratches, etc. when used with buffing compound.

Mini-Stripper. Furnished as a strip-and-sand kit the five flexible wheels (two fine grit, two medium and one coarse) size 1x2-1/2-in. are excellent for sanding wood crevices or smooth finishing of wood, plastic or metal.

Sander-Polisher-Buffer Set. This set provides the accessories you need for finishing or refinishing of wood or metal using a 1/4-in. or 3/8-in. power drill. Included are a convenient angle drill head that threads onto a 3/8-in. by 24 thread chuck spindle, a chuck adapter (for a 1/4-in. spindle), a 5-in. diameter, flexible rubber back-up pad, a lambswool polishing bonnet and six assorted sanding discs (extra discs available in packages). The angle head has a two-position side handle for easy holding and guiding along straight or curved workpiece surfaces.

Heavy-Duty Contour Sanders. A flap-type sander with cushioning brushes that force the attached abrasive discs into, around and over workpiece corners — for quick sanding of small openings and curved surfaces. The 6-in. diameter wheel has an abrasive coil, a 1/2-in. reducer bushing and an adapter to fit a 1/4-in. or a 3/8-in. power-drill chuck. The 1-in. wide abrasive strips are available as replacements in coarse, medium and fine grades.

Screwdriver and Nutdriver Set. This 12-piece set (in its own plastic case) converts any 1/4-in. (or larger) variable-speed, reversible electric drill into a power screwdriver or socket wrench — for both installing and removing wood screws, machine screws and nuts. The set includes two spade bits for slotted screws nos. 6-10, two Phillips bits (nos. 1 and 2) and seven 6-point nut drivers sizes 3/16- to 7/16-in. with shafts.

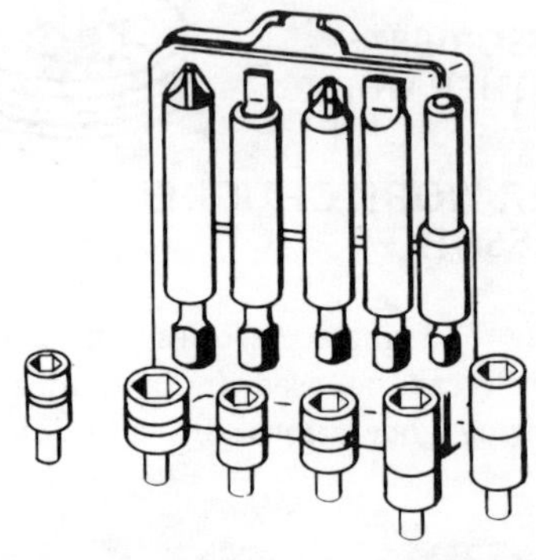

SCREWDRIVER and NUTDRIVER SET

Other sets, including a 31-piece set for professional useage, are also available — as are replacement bits. Refer to a *current* Sears Catalog for buying information.

REFER TO A **CURRENT** *SEARS CATALOG FOR LATEST BUYING INFORMATION ON ALL ACCESSORIES*

ELECTRIC-DRILL ACCESSORIES

Angle Drill Head

This attachment replaces the chuck on any 1/4-in. or 3/8-in. power drill having a 1/4 by 24 or 3/8 by 24 chuck spindle to provide two important advantages: 1) A 90-degree approach angle that makes it easier to hold and use a sanding pad with abrasive disc or polishing bonnet. 2) An approach angle that places the bulky drill out of the way so you can drill in narrow spaces, such as sideways between wall studs. The attachment has a 2-position handle for convenient holding, and provides a 1:1 gear ratio.

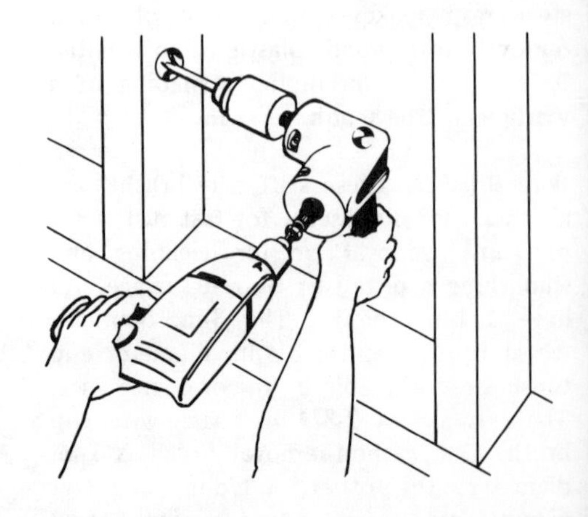

Nail Spinner

This attachment chucks into any 1/4-in. or 3/8-in. power drill to firmly grip a finishing nail and allow the drill to spin the nail into your workpiece. It accommodates 4, 6, 8 or 10 penny size finishing nails. By driving a nail in this manner you eliminate the need for predrilling the hole to avoid wood splitting. Spinning leaves the nail about 1/2-in. extended, to be set by hammering in the usual manner. Excellent for all fine cabinetwork, picture-frame assembly and other fine-finishing jobs.

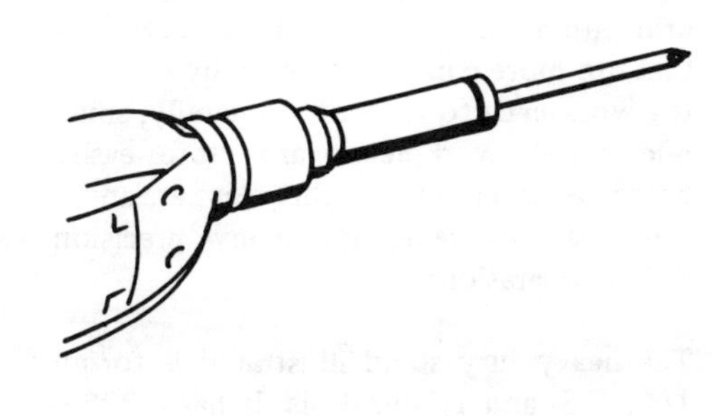

Impact Drill Attachment

Any 1,000 rpm (or more) reversible 1/4-in. or 3/8-in. power hand drill can be converted into a power impact wrench with this attachment and the necessary drive sockets (*not* furnished; for available drive sockets *refer to a current Sears Catalog*). Two sizes are offered: for 1/2-in. or for 3/8-in. square-drive sockets. Chucked in your drill the attachment makes it possible to loosen rusted and "frozen" nuts and bolts or to quickly and properly tighten nuts or bolts in places difficult to reach with an ordinary wrench. Excellent for wheel changing and other automotive work.

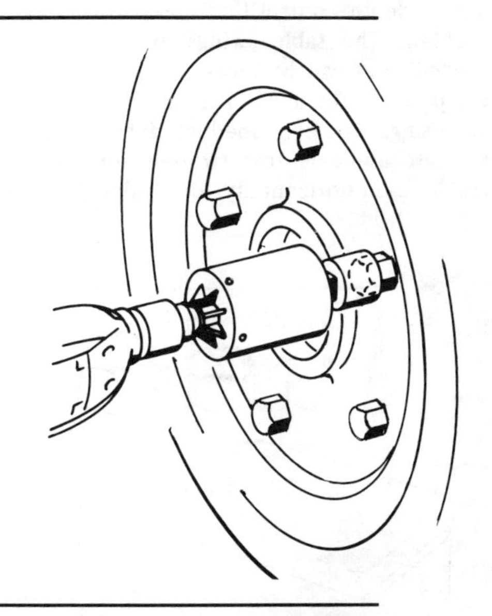

Doweling Jig

This accessory makes it easy to accurately position the holes in two workpieces to be joined together by the use of dowel pins. Designed for easy set-up to exactly duplicate hole locations in the two workpieces, the jig has a revolving turret with guide holes for 3/16-in. to 1/2-in. drills to accommodate dowels of like diameters — and will accept workpieces up to 4-in. thick (or wide). Refer to a *current* Sears Catalog for available dowel pin sets.

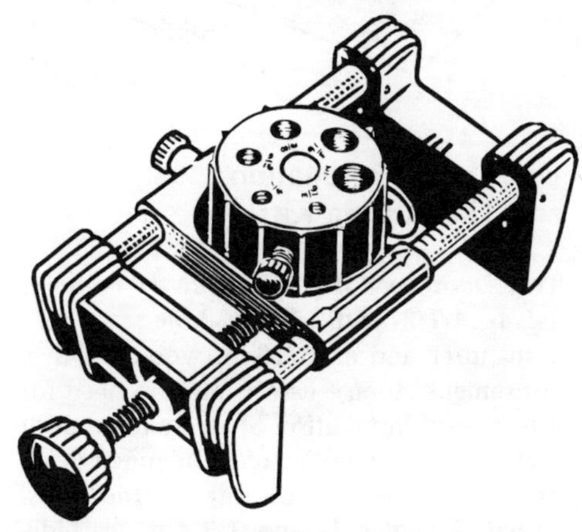

Drill Stands and Vise

A drill stand converts your power hand drill into a bench tool for those operations that are more convenient to do by carrying the workpiece to the drill. Generally, small odd-shaped workpieces are more easily bored, polished, etc. in this manner, and a stand is invaluable for many precision drilling operations.

The heavy-duty stand illustrated is for all 1/4-, 3/8- and 1/2-in. drills. It has a 20-in. column, a 6-in. throat depth, a 7-1/2-in. square base, and an adjustable rack and pinion depth control that locks from 0 to 2-1/2-in. The table swings away (if not needed) and can be locked in any desired tilt position for angle drilling. Other two- and single-position medium-duty stands also are available (the two-position stand can be used horizontally for sanding, buffing, etc.).

The vise shown is for use with most drill stands. It can be bolted to the stand base to hold a workpiece; has 4-in. jaws with a 2-in. opening. Small workpieces can be drilled more safely and accurately using a vise than by attempting to hold them by hand or with pliers, etc.

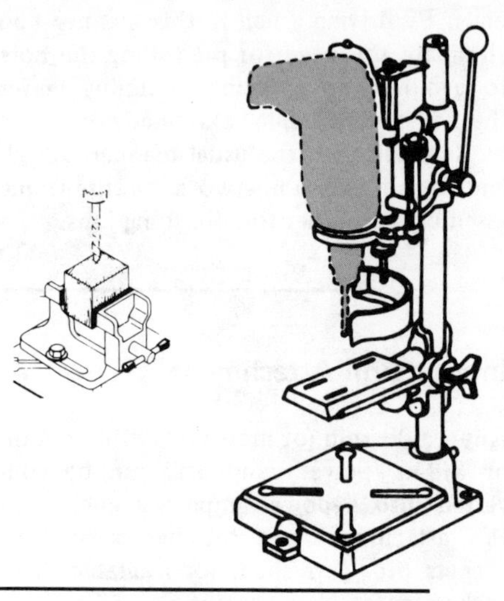

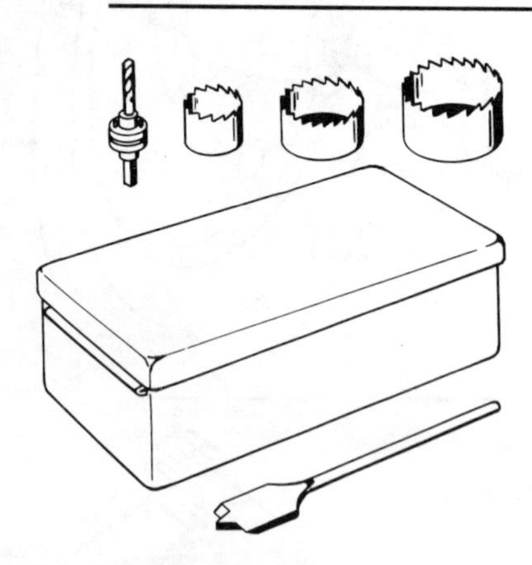

Door-Lock Installation and Tile-Cutting Kits

The Door-Lock Kit (*illustrated*) contains 1-1/4-, 1-7/8- and 2-1/8-in. hole saws with a mandrel and a 15/16-in. wood bit in a convenient storage case — all you need for quick, easy installation of all standard door locks, including police-recommended dead-bolt locks. The Tile-Cutting Kit (*not illustrated*) includes 1- and 1-3/4-in. carbide-tipped hole saws, a mandrel and 1/8- and 1/4-in. masonry drills in a case — for cutting holes through ceramic tiles, brick, concrete, etc. for lighting fixture and plumbing installations.

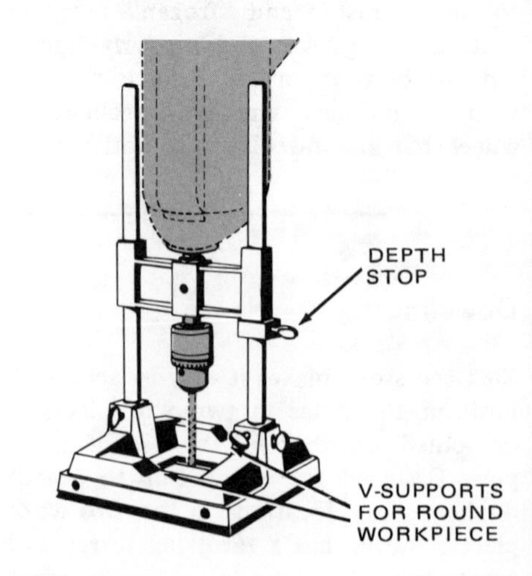

Drill Guide

This Portalign® attachment fits most 1/4-in. and 3/8-in. drills and is lightweight enough for hand holding to be used both for guiding the drill bit and for accurately adjusting the depth-of-cut. It is excellent as a guide for such operations as installing door locks, or for precise drilling of holes in round stock — also for angle drilling at any angle up to 90 degrees to a surface. With proper other accessories it also enables you to use your drill for sanding or shaping, or as a drill press.

Wood-Turning Attachment

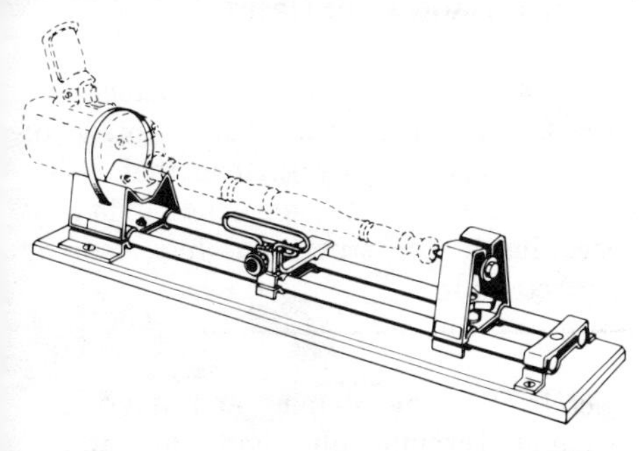

For use with most 1/4-in. or 3/8-in. electric drills this attachment will enable you to turn wood workpieces up to 16-in. long by up to 3 or 4-1/2-in. in diamater (the maximum diameter depends upon the power of your drill). The drill is strapped into place on the headstock; the workpiece is held between the headstock and the sliding tailstock, which can be securely locked in position. Both headstock and tailstock have leveling adjustment screws for perfect alignment. The tool rest is adjustable in-and-out, horizontally and vertically. Regular wood-turning chisels and/or knives, rasps and sandpapers, etc. are used for the turning operations.

Sturdily made and mounted on a 6 x 30-in. 3/4-in. fiberboard base that can be clamped to a workbench.

Drill Bit Sharpeners

A bit sharpener can save you time and money. Too often, twist drills are dulled or broken off by continued or abusive use, and replacement is costly. Usually, reshaping and/or resharpening can salvage any bit that still has at least half of its original length of flutes remaining.

Two types of drill-bit sharpeners are illustrated, one that is self-motorized for independent operation; the other, which is exactly the same but is designed to be motorized by your drill (any pistol-grip 1/4- or 3/8-in. drill). Both are for sharpening twist drills (*no other* types of bits) of carbon-steel or high-speed steel construction.

The (either) sharpener has eleven sized openings for drill sizes 1/8-, 9/64-, 5/32-, 11/64-, 3/16-, 7/32-, 1/4-, 9/32-, 5/16-, 11/32- and 3/8-in., and is used in much the same way (and as easily) as an electric pencil sharpener. When the simple instructions (in the Owner's Manual) are followed, the sharpener will simultaneously sharpen and shape the bit to center the point and provide the correct angles for the point and lips. (Obtaining correct angles when hand sharpening on a grinding wheel is extremely difficult.)

Also available is a heavy-duty professional-type sharpener that has a wheel-dressing system, a diamond-type dresser, and a calibrated feed control.

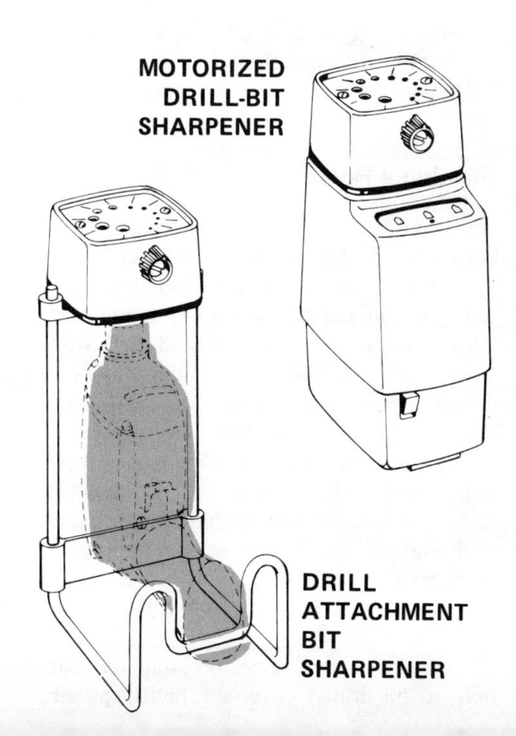

Drill Bit Cases

Drill bit cases both of all-steel and polystyrene plastic construction are available for 21-, 29- and 60-bit storage, for fractional or wire-gauge twist drills. The spaces are coded to make it easy to find the drill size needed.

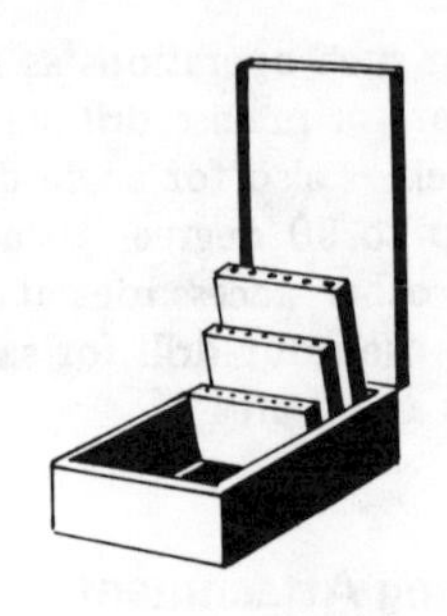

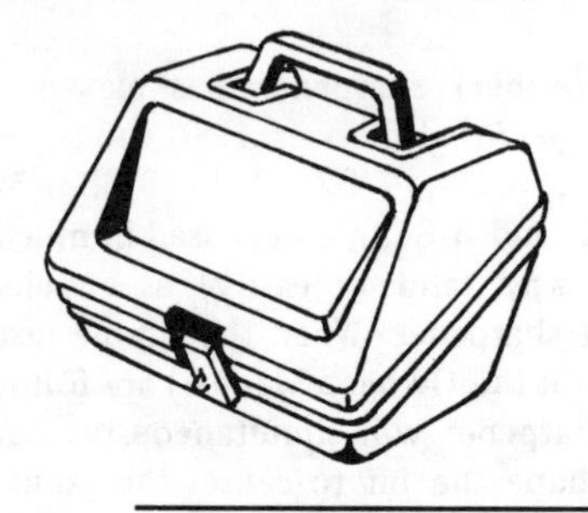

Electric Hand Drill Cases

There is a sturdy, convenient storage and carrying case for your tool – made of tough Permanex polyethylene that resists oil, acid and alkaline substances. There is space inside for storage of bits, sanding discs, etc., too.

IMPORTANT NOTE: In addition to the preceding Sears also offers a complete line of electrical and air-drive impact drills, wrenches, staplers and nail drivers – for a multitude of operations such as drilling into concrete, bending, shaping and severing metal, torquing nuts and bolts and driving roofing staples or nails, etc. Refer to a *current* Sears Catalog for items available.

TYPICAL HAND-DRILL OPERATIONS

Following are a few of the very many different work operations that you can do with your drill and the accessories available.

Starting a Hole

Whenever practical – and, especially, if a large twist drill is to be used – start a hole in wood or plastic by first indenting the spot with an awl to leave a depression just large enough for the drill end to enter. Always start a hole in metal by using a center punch. For a small (up to 1/8-in. diameter) hole, make the dent just large enough to hold the drill end; for a larger hole, mark and drill a small hole at least large and deep enough to hold the (larger) drill end. A small drill or, preferably, a countersink can be used for this latter purpose.

If exact precision is desired, lay out the hole to be drilled as shown, lightly punch marking four spots around the outer diameter to use as a guide while drilling.

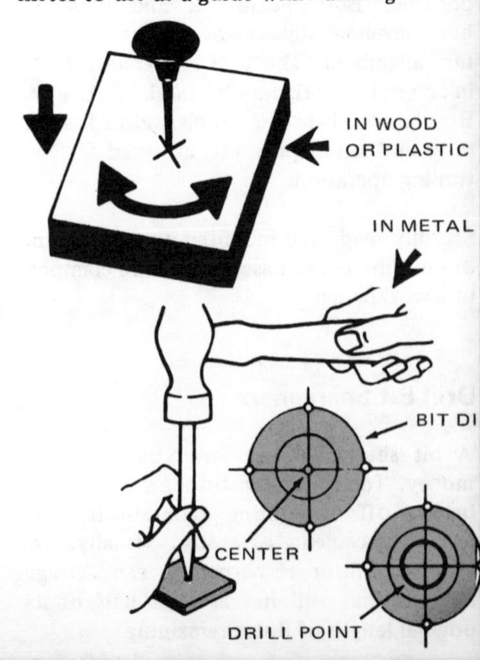

NOTE: Drill wood, plastics and similar materials dry, except, use water to cool the work and bit when deep drilling in a thermoset plastic; use turpentine to keep the chips moving out when deep drilling a dense, gummy non-ferrous metal; and always lubricate the bit point by maintaining a few drops of light to medium oil on the work (in the hole) when drilling iron or steel.

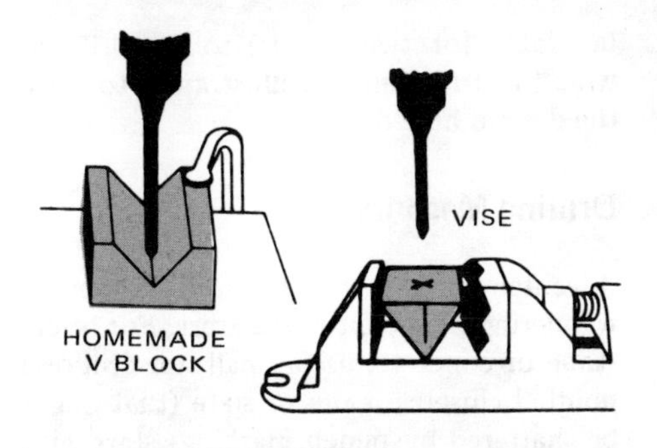

TYPICAL WORK-HOLDING ARRANGEMENTS

Drilling a Hole for Tapping

Holes that are to be tapped must be cut exactly 90-degrees to the workpiece surface, else the screw, when tightened, may be broken (head popped off) by the strain imposed by an angled hole. Also, the heads of countersunk flat-head screws won't recess properly unless the hole and countersink recess are drilled squarely. To assure squarely-drilled holes use the *Drill Guide*, shown preceding, or a drill stand.

Using the Drill Stand

When using your drill with a stand (as a drill press) provide some mechanical means of securing the workpiece in place on the table. *Never* attempt to hold a small piece with your fingers or pliers. Three typical holding arrangements are illustrated.

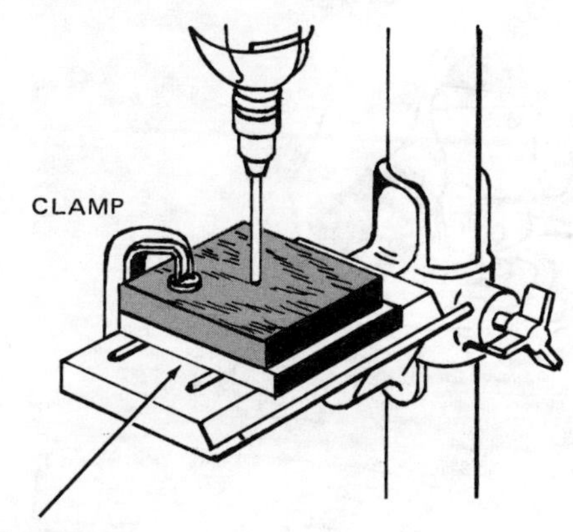

Drilling to Depth

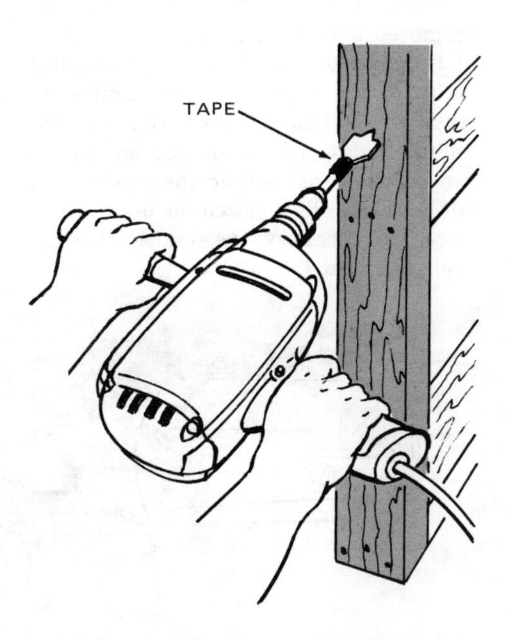

If you are using a drill stand depth-of-hole (if not through) can be predetermined by setting the depth gauge. When not using a stand, you can either attach a drill stop (available for twist drills) to the drill, or wrap the drill shank (as illustrated) to mark the desired hole depth.

Drilling Masonry

A center mark should be used to prevent wandering of the bit at the start. For brick, stone or concrete, use a small star drill or a pointed chisel; for tile or slate (that might be shattered by punch marking) start with the smallest diameter bit possible and hold the drill very steady — or, better, dimple the spot by first using a cone-shaped grinding point.

Materials, like stone or mortar, that are the same hardness throughout can be drilled as desired, with little effort. Concrete, on the other hand, contains pebbles that are extremely hard. If your bit point strikes such a pebble very considerable "push" may be required to break through it (in fact, if the surrounding material is loose, the bit may be moved aside to spoil the hole). Instead of trying to drill through the pebble, it is better to use a star drill and hammer to crush the pebble — then continue the drilling (unless, of course, you are using a hammer drill that will do the crushing for you). When drilling glazed tile use no more force than necessary; the surface layer can easily be cracked.

Sanding, Buffing, Etc.

Disc sanding and buffing operations are done easily with the angle-head attachment, as illustrated. When sanding, always tilt the disc so that its trailing half side only contacts the work surface — and keep advancing the disc steadily. Other operations like buffing, drum sanding, wheel polishing (of metal), and wire bushing do not require use of the angle head — can be done by holding the drill at the desired angle to the workpiece. Grinding with a grinding wheel over 1-1/2-in. diameter *must* be done only with the drill secured in either the bench stand or the drill stand accessory (with grinding guard). Safety glasses or goggles *must be worn* for all grinding, sanding and wire-brushing operations.

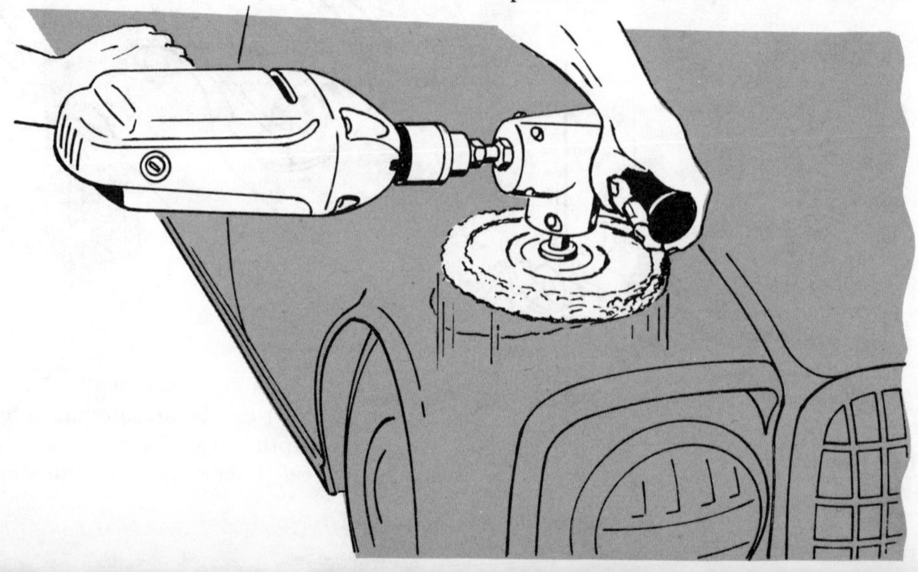

SECTION IV
CIRCULAR SAWS

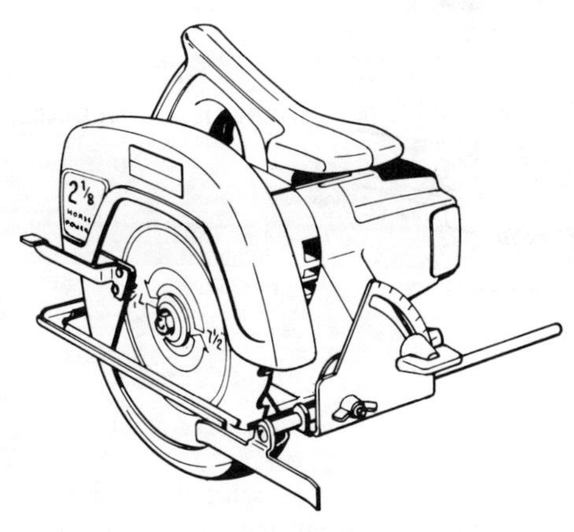

A 7-1/2 IN. SAW

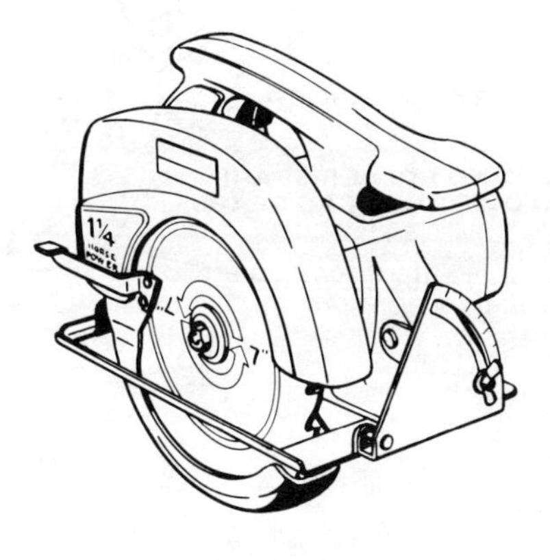

A 7-IN. SAW

ADVANTAGES AND TYPES OF CIRCULAR SAWS

Practically every construction job, regardless of size, and all cabinetwork requires the sawing to size and/or shape of wood structural members, sheeting or siding, etc. In fact, the principal tools of any carpenter are his hammers, nails and saws; and for a cabinetmaker, his saws are also of prime importance.

Though some sawing still must be done with hand saws or other types of power saws, most of the tiring, time-consuming work can be far more easily and swiftly accomplished with a circular saw designed to be used on-the-job. The fact that a compact, reasonably lightweight circular saw can be used under nearly all the same circumstances in which a carpenter's hand saw is used makes this type of saw more advantageous to use for general carpentry work than a bench-type tool.

Circular saws are classified, principally, by the blade size — which determines how thick a workpiece can be cut through. However, motor hp is just about as important; a large diameter blade is of no value if the tool lacks the power to drive it through large and tough wood sections. Safety features, also, are *very important* . . . a fast-whirling blade can be extremely hazardous if the tool is not well built, for safe handling.

NOTE: A 7-1/2-in. blade will make a 2-3/8-in. 90° cut or a 2-1/8-in. 45° cut. For a 7-1/4-in. blade the cuts are, respectively, 2-1/4 in. and 2 in.; for a 7-in. blade they are 2-1/8 in. and 1-5/8 in.; for a 5-1/2-in. blade, 1-3/4 in. and 1-1/8 in.

Craftsman circular saws are available in sizes from a lightweight, 5-1/2-in. (blade size), 3/4 hp. tool to a large 7-1/2-in. tool with a 2-1/8 hp. motor designed for heavy-duty shop use. When selecting your tool, first determine the size and power you will need for the work you will expect it to do. Next — and of equal importance — consider the advantages of the following *Craftsman* features, and select a model having those features you desire.

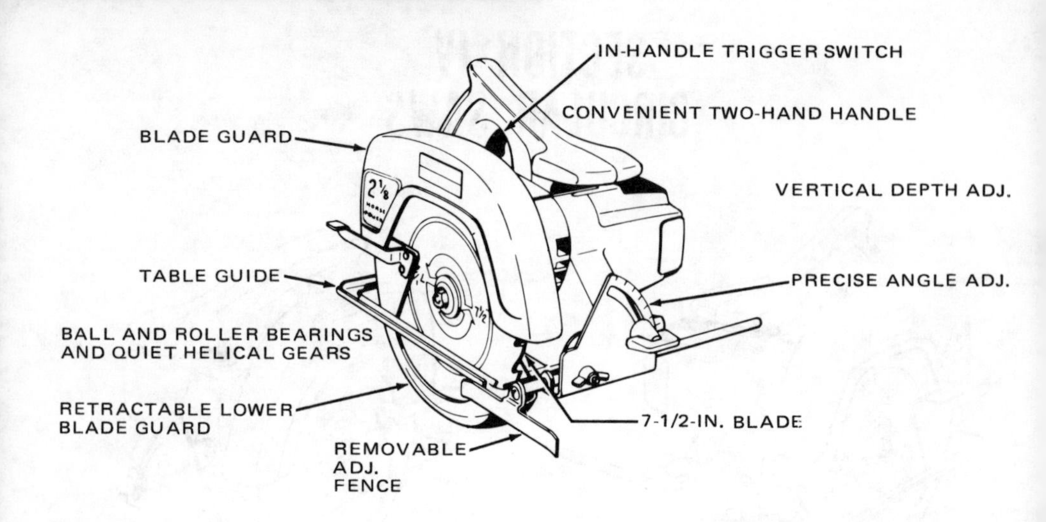

SAFETY:

1) *Double Insulation* is a safeguard against electrical shock.

2) A substantial, permanent *Upper Blade Guard* together with an equally substantial, *Retractable Lower Blade Guard* that stays closed (to enclose 85% of the blade) except when blade is actually in use — but does not interfere with sawing operations because of its free pivoting action.

3) A balanced, centered *Two-Hand* Handle that makes it easy to properly guide the saw for cutting.

EASE OF SAWING:

1) Blade no-load speeds range from 4000 to 5400 rpm. Combined with ample power, a faster turning blade makes a faster, smoother cut than one geared-down to a slow speed.

2) A wrap-around, wide, firm-support base with an easy-to-see blade port that helps you to keep the saw tracking accurately along a cut line. Base width, when sufficient, makes it easy to rock the blade down to start a blind cut and to hold to the line when bevel sawing or sawing in an awkward position.

3) A depth-of-cut selection made by *moving the saw up or down* instead of by tilting it. This keeps the handle in the same convenient position for *all* depth-of-cut settings.

4) Easy-to-read bevel-angle scale with *small* increments for accurate settings.

5) An adjustable, strongly-built rip fence with a *wide contact face* that will slide smoothly and truly along the workpiece edge, without allowing the saw to wander off the cut line.

6) *A push-button arbor lock* that will allow you to change blades with only *one* wrench (instead of two) very quickly and easily.

DURABILITY AND CONVENIENCE

Best *Craftsman* saws have such features as: A quiet-running power transmission with 100% ball and/or roller, permanently lubricated bearings and precision helical gears. A high-impact handle and non-glare, die-cast aluminum guards. Easily accessible motor brushes. A 6-ft. cord with bend relief at point of stress. A full assortment of blades.

CIRCULAR-SAW ACCESSORIES

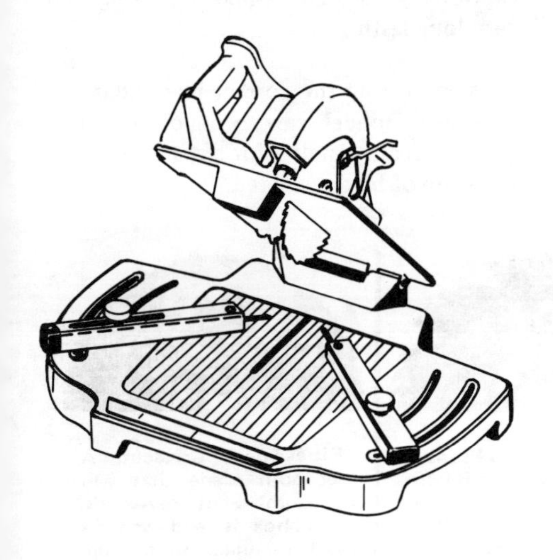

Miter Maker

This portable accessory (it can be bolted to a bench or set up on any level surface) allows you to use your circular handsaw for quick, easy and extremely accurate sawing of miter angles to produce picture framing and like workpieces. Mitering can be done right- or left-handed by simply setting the adjustable fences as desired. Will accept stock up to 2-in. thick. Has provision for repetitive cuts and built-in safety features for setups and operations.

Saw Case

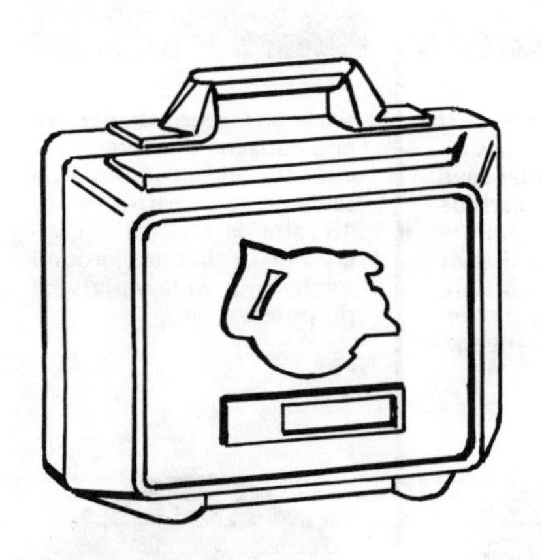

A durable Permanex® polyethylene case with sturdy double-wall construction and a split, integral handle. Two heavy latches. Stores your saw and rip guide with extra space for wrench and blades. Size 17 by 14 by 8 in.

Circular-Saw Table

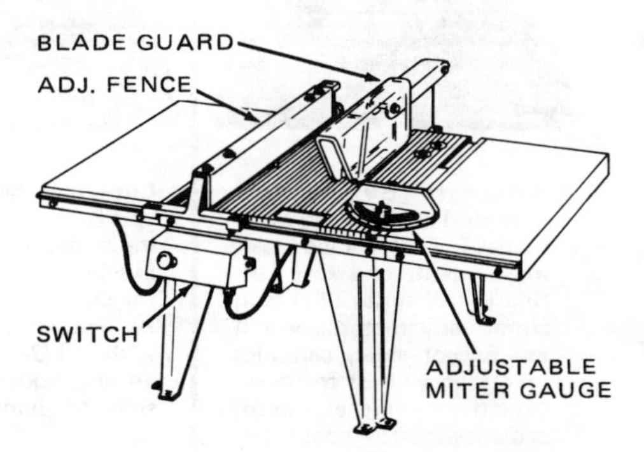

With your circular saw mounted beneath this sturdy die-cast aluminum table with two steel side extensions provides a big 19- by 29-in. surface on which to do bench-saw type work. Ridged table top prevents sawdust build-up under workpiece; table has an adjustable fence and adjustable miter gage for accurate rip and straight or angled crosscutting — also, a see-through blade guard. There is a convenient on/off switch so that saw switch can be locked at on.

CIRCULAR-SAW BLADES

Typical *Craftsman* blades available in various sizes are illustrated. The *Kromedge* blades are made of chrome-nickle-molybdenum steel that holds a keen edge, and are chrome plated to resist rust and pitch build-up much better than ordinary steel blades. The *carbide-tipped* blades are exceptionally fast and smooth cutting, and very long lasting.

Be sure to buy the correct blade diameter for your model saw – and consult a current Sears Catalog for sizes available in the style of blade selected.

Chisel-Tooth Combination. An all purpose, set-tooth blade for fast – but not real smooth – ripping or crosscutting of solid woods. An excellent contractor's framing blade.

Hollow-Ground Planer. Deep hollow-ground with extra stability for glue-joint sawing. Designed for fine-finish woodworking; accurate, quiet crosscutting or ripping operations.

Fine-Tooth Crosscut. A set-tooth blade that will smoothly cut plywoods, fiberboards and veneers with minimum splintering; also for crosscutting solid woods.

Alternate Bevel-Ground Carbide-Tipped. King of all blades . . . *very* long lasting, smooth and fast cutting for all types of cuts in almost any material you'll use except steel, ceramics or masonry. Best for hardboard, particle board, cement-asbestos board and similar abrasive materials.

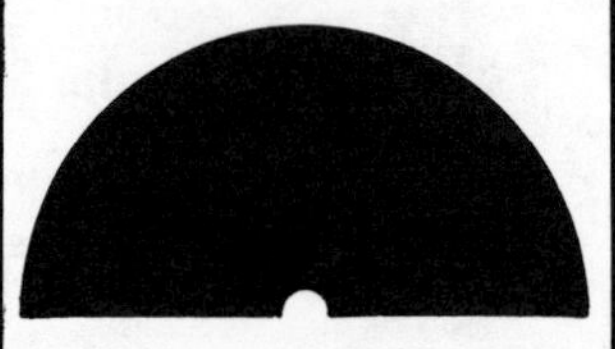

Cut-Off Wheel. In 6-, 7- and 8-in. dia. both in aluminum oxide for metal sawing and in silicon-carbide for cutting stone or masonry. For circular hand saws with 1/2- and 5/8-in. arbors. Adds a new dimension to hand-saw useage.

Carbide-Tipped Blades. In circular-saw diameters for cut-off and combination sawing uses with 14 to 48 alternately top bevel-ground or flat top-ground teeth for a wide variety of purposes.

Master Combination. Teeth are set for fast and precise ripping or crosscutting in all solid woods.

Flattop-Ground Carbide-Tipped. A very durable combination-type blade for use on most building materials and non-ferrous metals. For fast ripping, regular and finish sawing.

Steel Slicer. A special-design blade that burns through ferrous sheetmetal up to 3/32-in. thickness, for fast, clean, easy sawing.

REFER TO YOUR OWNER'S MANUAL FOR BLADES RECOMMENDED FOR YOUR SAW

Table Guide

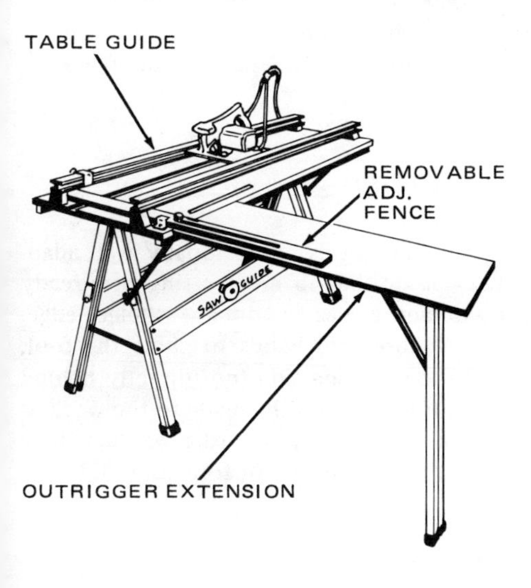

With this portable accessory (it can be carried to any location and be quickly set up) your circular hand saw is transformed into a very safe, convenient to use and accurate bench-type tool especially designed for crosscutting (straight or at any desired miter and/or bevel angle up to 45°) long or short boards up to 2-in. thick by 50-in. wide, for ripcutting straight or at a bevel angle any length board, and for cutting panels up to 4 by 8-ft. in size. It is also excellent for cutting tongues and rabbets at board ends and for notching and grooving board surfaces (or edges, if boards are not too wide).

The table guide is shown with the outrigger extension (sold separately), which can be attached at a number of places and is recommended to support panels and other large workpieces. Bevel angling and depth-of-cut are controlled by the saw adjustments; mitering is controlled by setting the removable, adjustable fence to the desired angle on a scale affixed to the table guide. Your saw is attached to a saw guide that slides between two rails for crosscutting — or, with the saw repositioned 90°, is fixed in place for feeding the work under the rails for ripcutting.

IMPORTANT: This accessory can also be used to guide your router.

Saw Guide

This Portalign® accessory can be mounted on your saw shoe to adapt your saw for quick, easy and very accurate cut-off of boards at 90° or at any desired miter angle up to 45° right or left. Bevel (and, therefore, compound) angles can also be cut as provided for by your saw design. This is an excellent attachment for use in preparing rafters and like, on-the-job construction lumber up to approximately 12-in. wide supported on saw horses or similar.

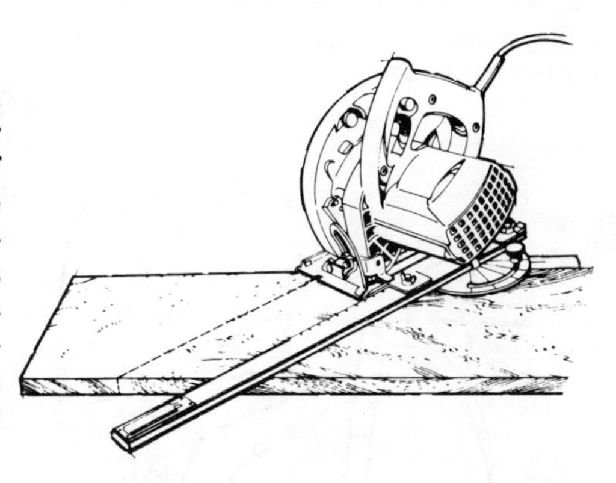

REFER TO YOUR OWNER'S MANUAL AND BE GUIDED BY THE INSTRUCTIONS THEREIN IF THESE DIFFER IN ANY WAY FROM THE GENERAL INSTRUCTIONS IN THIS BOOK.

IF, FOR ANY REASON, YOU DO NOT HAVE AN OWNER'S MANUAL, DO **NOT** *OPERATE YOUR TOOL UNTIL YOU DO OBTAIN ONE.*

TYPICAL OPERATIONS

IMPORTANT: Always support your workpiece, if necessary, so it can't move during an operation — and so that the saw blade can*not* cut through it into something (like the ground) that will damage the blade.

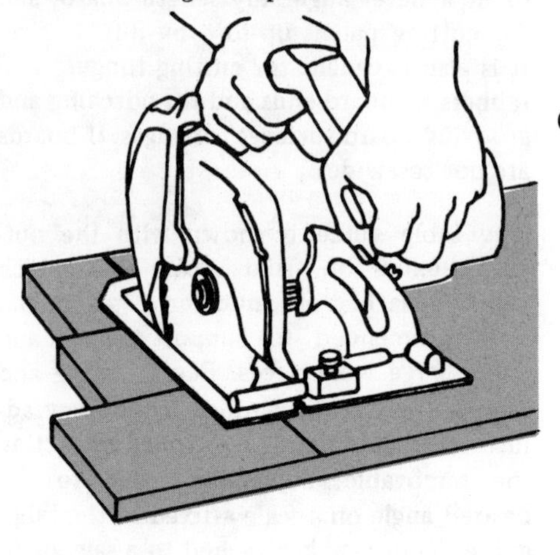

CROSSCUTTING

A circular saw is exceptionally well adapted for on-the-job crosscutting of already assembled pieces to trim a workpiece edge. Always use two hands to guide the tool, and stand to one side (*not* directly behind the cut line). Feed the blade to the work as fast as it will cut in order to keep to a straight line, but do *not* force the tool.

BEVEL RIPPING

Whenever possible, use the edge guide for ripping, as shown. The guide is exceptionally useful for holding the blade on the line-of-cut when bevel edging. Stand to one side behind the work (as illustrated) if the cut is short enough to reach its full extent . . . otherwise, stand at the outer side and walk your saw the length of the cut while holding the guide in against the workpiece edge.

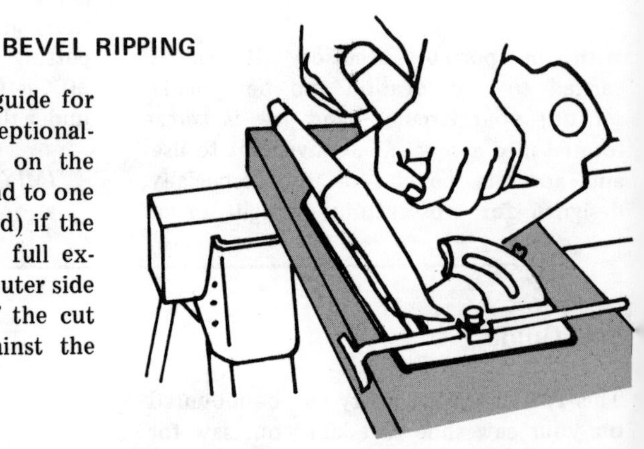

BLIND CUTTING

A blind cut can be started anywhere in a workpiece surface by rocking the (rotating) blade into the work, as shown. Be sure to align the blade with the cut line, and to allow room behind the blade so as not to overcut in this direction. Do *not* pull the saw backwards to meet a desired starting point; if you have started too far out, finish the cut forward — then remove the blade from the kerf, turn the saw 180 degrees to reenter the kerf, and saw in the opposite direction, back to the desired starting point.

REFER TO ACCESSORY OWNER'S MANUAL FOR COMPLETE INSTRUCTIONS

MAKING A CUT-OFF THROUGH METAL TUBE

The metal-cutting blade allows you to size copper, brass, aluminum and other non-ferrous metal workpieces — such as pipes, tubing, window and screen framing, etc. Support the workpiece securely, and advance the blade slowly. Also, best keep it lubricated (with tallow or similar wax). When using the steel-slicer blade, be sure the workpiece is flat and secured so it cannot buckle during the operation. This (steel-slicer) blade will also saw plastics such as Lucite and Plexiglas, without the chipping and cracking produced by a toothed blade — but cutting should be done as fast as possible to prevent over-heating (and marring) at any one spot.

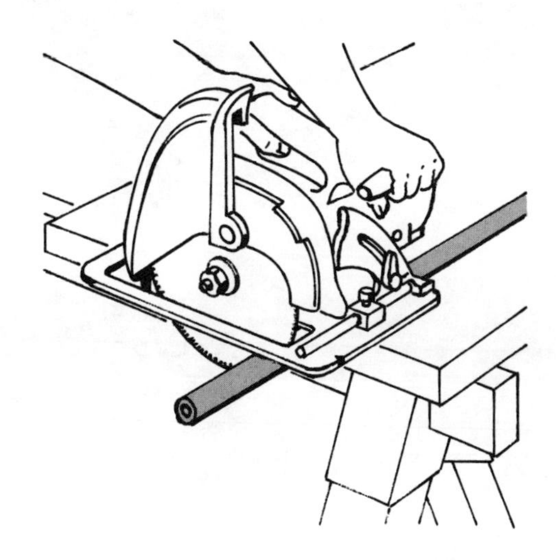

REFER TO YOUR OWNER'S MANUAL FOR CORRECT BLADE TO USE

USING A CUTTER'S EDGE

Straight-line sawing on any width work-piece is much facilitated by use of the Cutter's Edge, shown — which is over 8-ft. long and can quickly be clamped into place to guide your circular hand saw, sabre saw or router, or even a cutting knife. Excellent for working with wallboard, linoleum and similar products.

MITERING WITH THE TABLE GUIDE

With the adjustable fence set to a desired angle, the workpiece is positioned against this fence then cut-off at the established miter angle by pushing the saw (in its saw guide) along the accessory guide rails to make the cut.

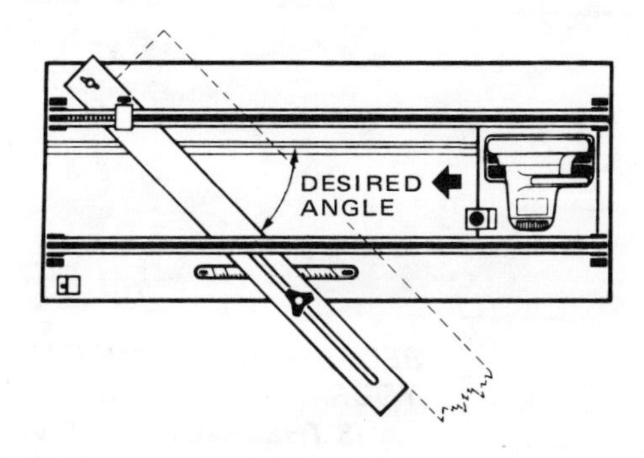

NOTES

BECAUSE THIS BOOK CANNOT COVER SPECIFIC MODELS YOUR OWNER'S MANUAL (FOR A TOOL OR ACCESSORY) IS THE **ONLY** *POSITIVE AUTHORITY FOR SAFETY PRECAUTIONS WITH REGARDS TO OPERATIONS AND/OR ACCESSORIES, ETC. RECOMMENDED FOR USE WITH YOUR TOOL.*

SECTION V
THE POWER PLANER

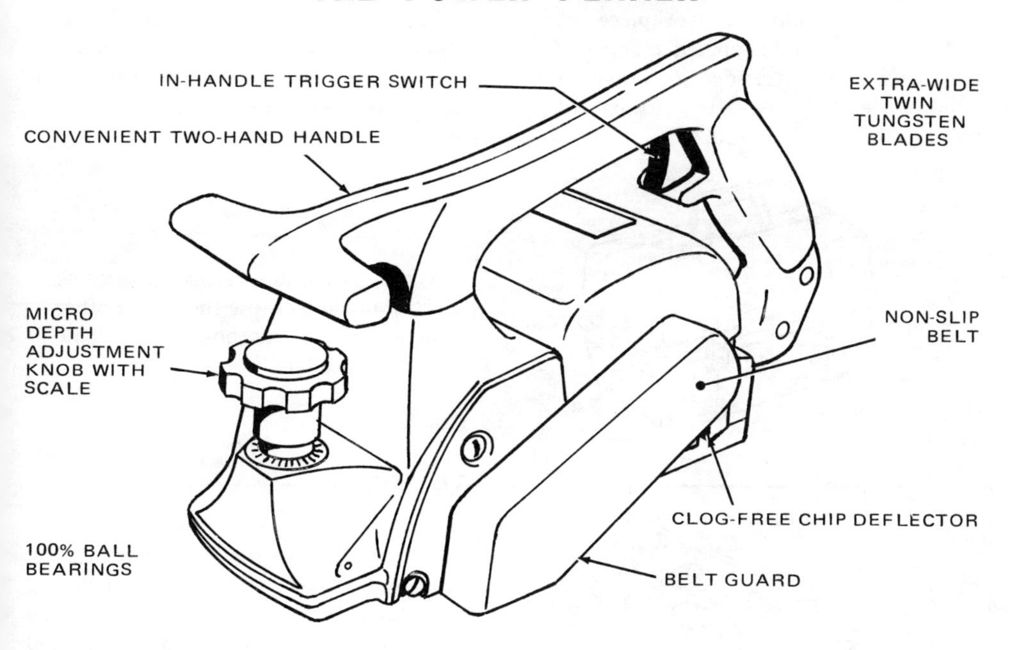

DESCRIPTION AND FEATURES OF THE *CRAFTSMAN* TOOL

Accurate planing of board surfaces and edges and, especially, bevel-edge planing requires considerable effort and experience if done with a hand plane or similar non-powered tool. However, this compact, lightweight tool, powered with a 3/8 hp., high-speed motor, makes light work of such projects as surface planing, sizing, butt-jointing and the bevel-edging of doors, windows, shutters, drawer slides and other workpieces. There is considerable advantage in the fact that this is a hand tool and can be carried to the work, wherever it is. Moreover, very little practice is needed to acquire sufficient expertise for most any job.

Cutting is accomplished by two planer knives, in a rotary head, that will plane a swath up to 3-5/8-in. wide by up to 1/16-in. deep. The head revolves at 15,000 rpm (no-load speed) for clean, glass-smooth cutting. Features that make this an exceptionally useful tool are as follows:

Safety. Double insulation and a fully-enclosed belt drive.

Ease of Handling. Large, two-hand handle designed for positive guidance . . . built-in, positive-control trigger switch . . . non-marring base (doesn't mark workpiece) . . . lightweight, glare-free housing. Also, a clog-free chip chute.

Ease of Cutting. High-speed twin *tungsten-steel* knives cut a full 3-5/8-in. swath, enough to plane wide side of a 2x4 in one pass — or to plane a wider board in several passes. Handy knob provides micro depth-of-cut adjustment from zero to 1/16-in. and has easy-to-read scale for positive settings.

Versatility. With appropriate accessories, *furnished with the tool*, you can do accurate 45° bevel-edge planing, accurate rabbet-edge planing (up to 3/16-in. deep by 11/32-in. wide in three passes, each 1/16-in. deep), accurately-guided (for width) surface planing along a workpiece edge, and accurate 5° relief-angled planing of a door or window, etc. edge (to provide the relief needed for close-fitted closing of the outer (swinging) door, etc. edge).

Service and Durability. Easy-to-reach motor brushes, for service or replacement . . . 100% ball bearings, for quiet, trouble-free operation . . . a non-slip, long-life drive belt . . . high-impact polyester housing, polymer handle and die-cast aluminum base. Cutting knives, in matched sets, readily available for replacement when needed.

NOTE: A durable Permanex carrying case, similar to those shown for other hand tools in this book, is available for your planer.

TYPICAL OPERATIONS

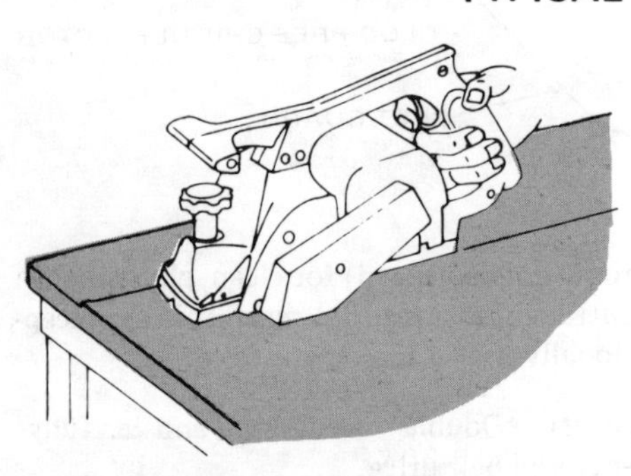

PLANING A WIDE SURFACE

To plane a wide surface, plan your cut passes (each is 3-5/8-in. wide) to overlap about 1/16-in. If the surface is rough, adjust the depth-of-cut to be from 1/32-in. to 3/64-in. maximum, and plane the entire surface (with overlapping passes) at this setting. If the surface is still rough, repeat this whole operation as many times more as necessary to reduce the surface to a level plane that is within 1/32-in. of absolute smoothness all over. Afterwards, readjust the depth-of-cut to 1/64-in. or 1/32-in. (maximum), then go over the whole surface again to perfect it.

If you are sizing a board for thickness, decide whether only one or both surfaces need planing to reduce the board thickness as desired. If both surfaces need planing, plane one surface, as above, removing as *little* stock as possible – then do the second surface to required smoothness and depth. If only one side needs planing, continue planing with the larger depth-of-cut setting until the thickness is reduced to within 1/32-in. of desired final dimension – then finish this side with the smaller depth-of-cut setting, down to final dimension.

Edge planing – for butt jointing and/or sizing – is accomplished in the same manner. When planing an end (across grain) clamp a scrap block to the far end so that the knives won't splinter this end of the cut. Also, at the starting end of an edge cut, be sure to hold the tool firmly up parallel to the edge, so not to dip in below the cut depth at the start. In fact, a scrap block at this end, also, will help keep the depth-of-cut uniform (no rounded end).

Because guidance isn't important – if tool wanders off path you can pull it back and set it straight, so long as all of the surface is covered – one hand (as illustrated) can be used (leaving other hand to hold workpiece) . . . or you can use both hands on the tool for better guidance.

The *edge guide*, when attached to the tool, allows you to accurately guide the planer along a board edge — by holding the tool in against the outer side of the edge — so that the swath cut by the planing operation will be a straight-line uniform distance in from the guiding (outer) side. Cut width, when using the guide, will always be the maximum (3-5/8-in.) because, to use the guide, it must be pressed firmly against the outer, guiding workpiece side. This accessory is especially useful when planing the surface around an edge to raise a center panel, or when planing the edges of long, unevenly surfaced boards.

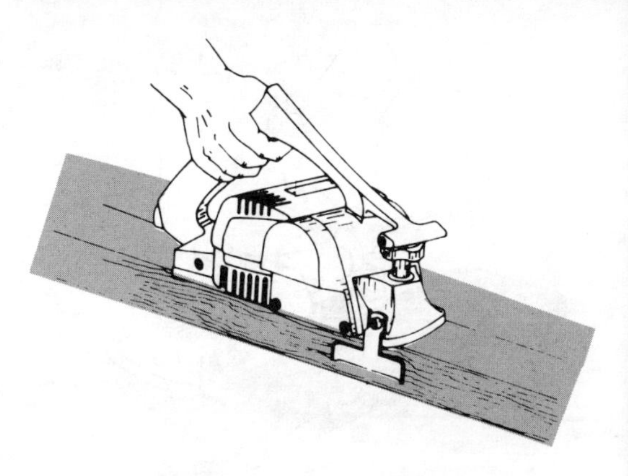

USING THE EDGE GUIDE

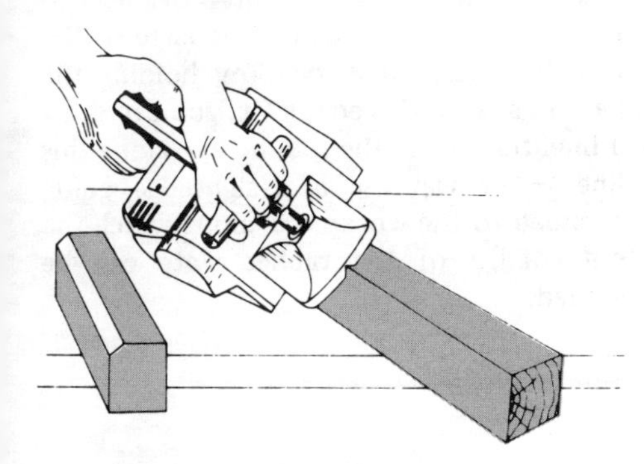

BEVEL-EDGE PLANING

Bevel-edge planing at exactly a 45-degree angle is done without an attachment — simply by using the groove built into the tool base. With the tool held as illustrated (groove centered over workpiece corner) a perfect 45-degree angle is obtained . . . for easy chamfering of the edge. For setting the depth-of-cut, best try different settings on scrap before doing the required cut. If necessary, several passes can be made.

Perfect closing of a door (or swinging window, etc.) requires the outer (opposite hinge) edge to be offset at about a 5-degree angle to allow for the swing when closing. This is a very difficult angle to saw or plane accurately without mechanical guidance. However, with the *door bevel fence* accessory attached, your plane will produce a door (etc.) edge to this exact relief angle. As illustrated, the accessory is used on the planer side which will be at the *same* side of the door (etc.) as the door hinge pin. Simply set the depth-of-cut to take a 1/32-in. bite, then plane the edge by making as many passes as needed to reduce it to a flat (side-to-side) surface. Or, if the door is too wide, continue planing until the door width is reduced as necessary.

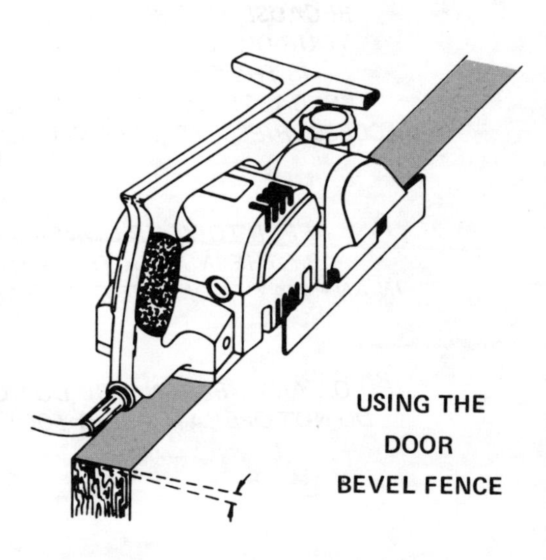

USING THE DOOR BEVEL FENCE

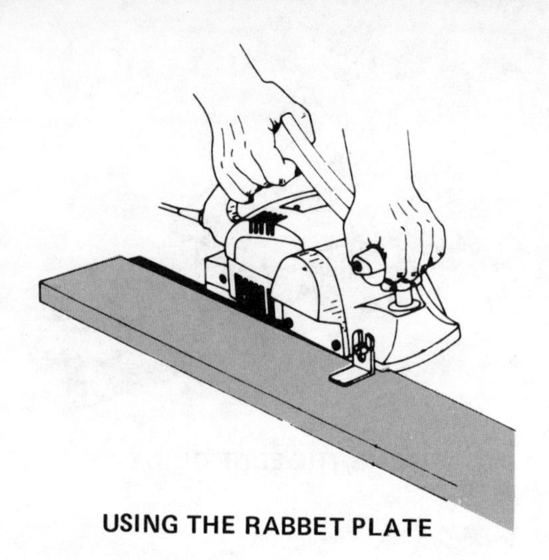

USING THE RABBET PLATE

With the adjustable *rabbet plate* attached, you can plane a rabbet edge of up to 11/32-in. width and of up to 1/16-in. depth in one pass (or up to 3/16-in. depth in three passes). Adjust the plate for maximum depth by sliding it up or down before tightening the holding screw. Best do this with the tool flat on a board so you measure the space between the board and the bottom of the plate. If this distance exceeds 1/16-in., set your tool depth-of-cut for 1/16-in. to make the first pass. Readjust tool depth-of-cut as needed for subsequent passes to end up with the final desired depth-of-cut.

This accessory does *not* guide the width-of-cut (only the depth). You can use the edge guide (preceding), if width is to be 3-5/8-in. For a lesser width rabbet, the rabbet must be pre-cut (with router or saw) to form an edge along which the edge of the tool base can be guided (by holding the base in against this edge). Or, you can draw a line, then guide the tool by eye along this line — or can use a straightedge guide clamped to the workpiece, along which the outer edge of the rabbet plate can be guided.

BECAUSE THIS BOOK CANNOT COVER SPECIFIC MODELS YOUR OWNER'S MANUAL (FOR A TOOL OR ACCESSORY) IS THE **ONLY** *POSITIVE AUTHORITY FOR SAFETY PRECAUTIONS WITH REGARDS TO OPERATIONS AND/OR ACCESSORIES, ETC. RECOMMENDED FOR USE WITH YOUR TOOL.*

REFER TO YOUR OWNER'S MANUAL AND BE GUIDED BY THE INSTRUCTIONS THEREIN IF THESE DIFFER IN ANY WAY FROM THE GENERAL INSTRUCTIONS IN THIS BOOK.

IF, FOR ANY REASON, YOU DO NOT HAVE AN OWNER'S MANUAL, DO **NOT** *OPERATE YOUR TOOL UNTIL YOU DO OBTAIN ONE.*

SECTION VI
PORTABLE ELECTRIC SANDERS

THREE TYPES OF SANDERS

There are three entirely different types of portable electric sanders, as illustrated — each designed for a specific kind of use.

Pad Sander

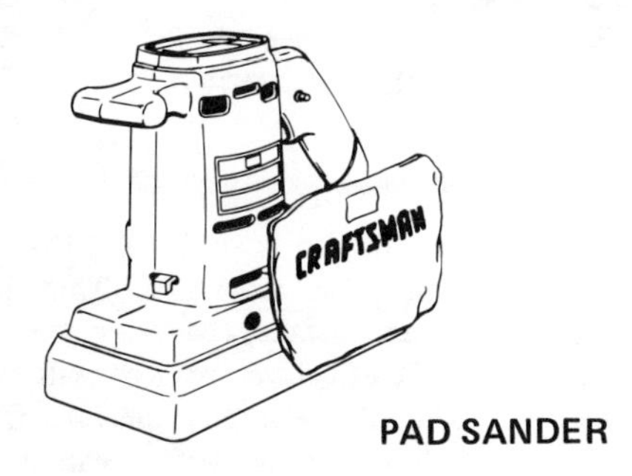

PAD SANDER

This is primarily a tool for the cabinetmaker and wood finisher. Depending upon design, its action may be a reciprocating in-line motion, desirable for with-the-grain, fine-finish sanding — and/or a reciprocating orbital motion that circles across-the-grain for faster stock removal. Because cutting action is easily controlled, this tool can be used for sanding veneers and plywoods, as well as solid woods of all kinds. It can be used for any type of work, including limited paint removal, ordinarily done with a hand-sanding pad . . . and, with a lambswool pad, for all the types of polishing that require firm rubbing. Pad sizes range from 3-5/8 x 7-in. (1/3 sheet) to 4-1/2 x 9-in. (1/2 sheet). Many light- and heavy-duty models are available (refer to a *current* Sears Catalog).

Rotary Sander/Polisher Or Grinder

The high-speed revolving flexible pad of a rotary sander makes this an excellent tool for rapid sanding of surfaces and board edges or ends. With one, you can quickly reduce to shape a preassembled work project made of roughly sized lumber . . . or can edge and end shape coarse-sawed boards. It can also be used to finish sand surfaces to be painted, for sanding curves, most metals, stones, slates and the like materials — and for paint or rust removal. The Grinder shown (with built-on guard) uses a 4-1/2-in. wheel for finishing welds and similar work — or can also be used as a sander with the accessories available. Refer to a *current* Sears Catalog for models and uses — and the sanding and polishing discs, wire brushes and grinding wheels available for carpentry, auto body and other work.

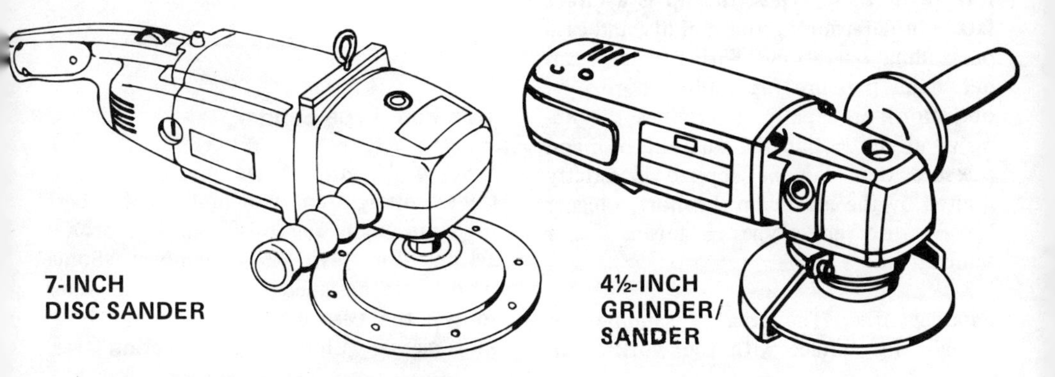

7-INCH DISC SANDER

4½-INCH GRINDER/ SANDER

FOR SAFEST OPERATION READ YOUR TOOL OWNER'S MANUAL

Belt Sander

The sanding action of this type tool (of which there are several models – refer to a *current* Sears Catalog) is powerful; it is a high-speed, flat-surface sander designed for rapid finishing of floors and other large-area surfaces. It is excellent for leveling and smoothing large, rough-sawed, knotty or warped boards . . . or for rapid paint removal and sanding of metals, tiles, etc. Replaceable belts are available in various grits. With the Finishing Stand, shown following, this tool can be converted into a bench-type sander to which workpieces can be fed for quick, easily controlled sanding.

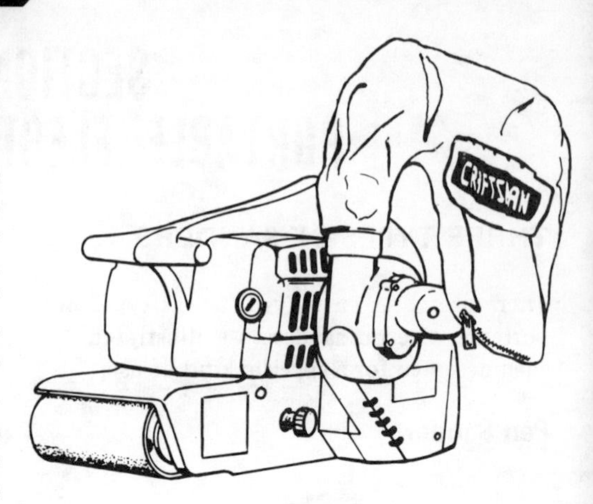

BELT SANDER

FEATURES TO LOOK FOR

In All Types of Sanders:

Safety: Double insulation, a fully-enclosed drive mechanism, and a snap-action trigger switch with a lock "ON" and instant safety release.

Power: A powerful enough motor to accomplish the work intended. Pad sanders range from 1/16 to 1/2-hp., rotary sanders from 3/8 to 1-1/2-hp., and belt sanders from 3/4 to 1-1/2-hp. With pad and belt sanders, the (pad or belt) size and tool weight should be designed for the most (possible) effective result based upon the tool weight (which is calculated to afford all of the sanding pressure required). Therefore, with these types, the hp is a direct factor in determining the rapidity and ease of sanding operations. With a rotary sander, hand pressure (as applied during an operation) principally determines the abrasive effect – but the amount of hand pressure that can be applied is strictly limited by the motor hp. In short, a bigger hp – with any type – means faster sanding.

Sanding Area: The area of sanding grit actually in contact with the work determines (providing hp is sufficient) the rapidity of workpiece coverage. That is, a larger sanding surface (pad size, disc diameter or belt effective surface) will – all else being equal – complete an area faster than a smaller sanding surface can do. In addition, a larger sanding surface makes it easier to prevent gouging or grooving of a workpiece surface. On the other hand, with a pad or rotary sander there are types of work for which it is easier to control a smaller (pad or disc size) tool, especially when finish sanding small areas.

Durability and Serviceability: Ball and/or roller bearings (as opposed to sleeve bearings), die-cut helical or bevel gears rather than stamped gears, die-cast and/or high-impact housing and handles – these are the features to look for.

In a Pad-Type Sander

Sanding Versatility: As previously mentioned, straight-line pad movement is best for with-grain fine-finish sanding; orbital action, for fast stock removal. Some models are designed for one or the other (only); the best models incorporate both movements, with a flip-type selection lever.

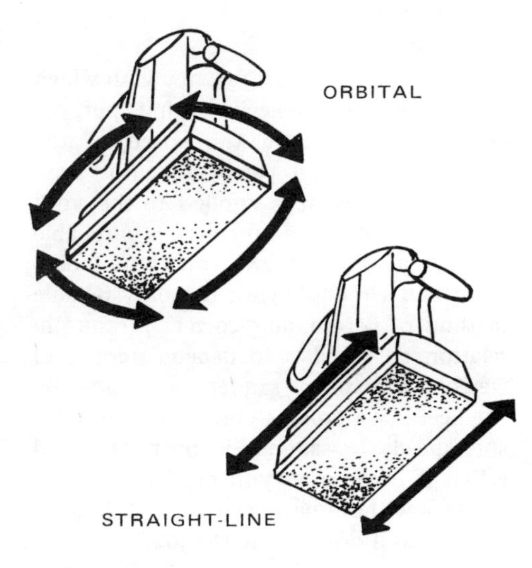

TYPES OF PAD-SANDER ACTIONS

Sanding Control: Ease of handling depends upon the handles, and the smoothness of motor operation. *Craftsman* tools have two convenient handles (for two-hand guidance), and the drives are counterbalanced to reduce vibration and hand fatigue.

Sandpaper Changes: A quick-change, lever-operated sandpaper clamp makes it easier to replace the sandpaper, when needed.

Litter Control: A built-in, fully-enclosed dust pick-up (with easy-to-empty dust bag) keeps the work surface — and the area — dust free.

In a Rotary Sander

Surface Sanding Usefulness: It is not practical to sand with the sandpaper disc flat on the workpiece surface; either one or the other disc half must be used so that you can hold the tool against the thrust generated by the contact friction, and control the sanding operation. Therefore, a stiff tool disc would be impractical . . . and the usefulness of a tool disc depends upon a combination of firmness (to provide proper sanding pressure) and flexibility (to allow you to hold it so that only one half (approximately) will contact a flat surface.

The most useful type of tool disc is comprised of a flexible fibre back-up pad that supports the entire sandpaper sheet (disc), together with a much smaller rubber back-up pad that serves both as a support and the connection to the drive shaft. Too large or stiff a rubber back-up pad reduces the effective flat-surface sanding area; too stiff a fibre back-up pad will make sanding control difficult . . . and if this pad is not substantial, the proper sanding pressure cannot be easily applied. All *Craftsman* sanders have correctly engineered tool discs.

Sanding Control: This tool requires two-hand holding, both for proper support (to control sanding pressure) and for guidance. The best models have one rear pistol-grip

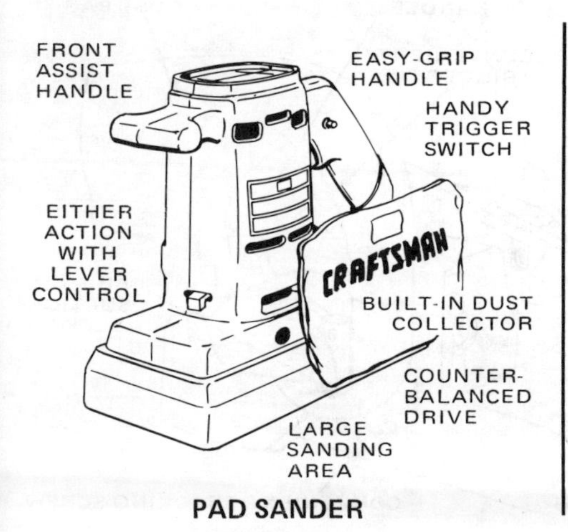

PAD SANDER

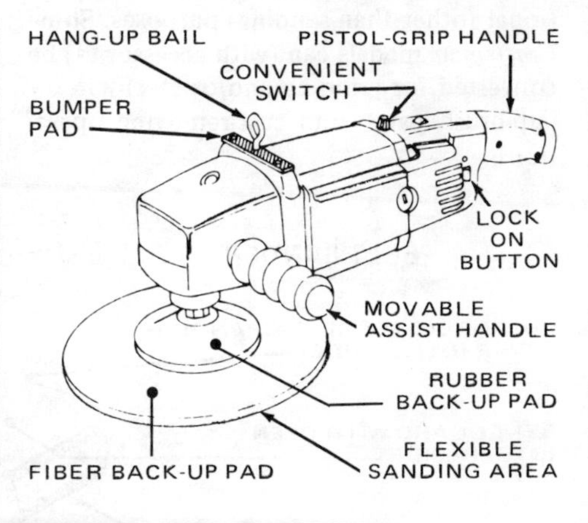

ROTARY SANDER

BUY ONE FOR CABINETWORK – ONE FOR CARPENTRY WORK

handle for either hand plus a forward (guiding-hand handle) that can be installed *at either tool side* (for right- or left-hand use).

Operating Versatility: Two-speed selection is desirable — a high speed for fast, rough sanding and a slow speed for polishing, grinding and smoother, better controlled finish sanding.

Conveniences: Desirable conveniences are: A bumper pad, on which tool can be rested during pauses in an operation; and a hang-up bail, for storing the tool when not in use.

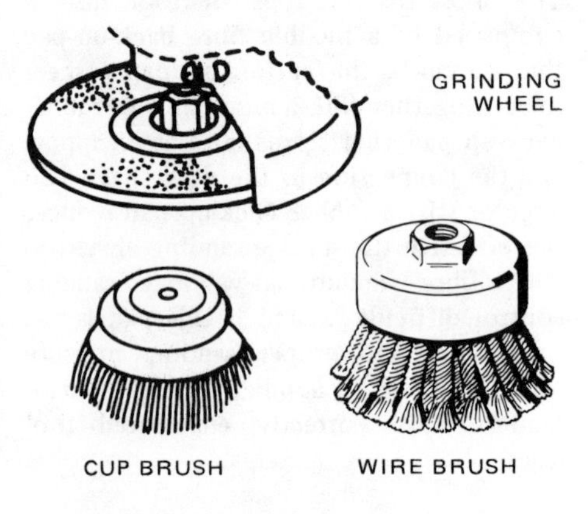

ROTARY-SANDER ACCESSORIES

Other Uses: Greater usefulness is provided by a tool that can be adapted for additional (other than sanding) purposes. Some *Craftsman* models can (with accessories) be converted for grinding and/or steel-wire or cup-brush paint- and rust-removing operations.

In a Belt Sander

Ease of Sanding: The efficiency with which the sanding grit will accomplish its purpose depends partly upon the speed of the sanding action and partly upon the pressure with which it is applied to the work surface. Hand-applied pressure is unreliable because it will vary with different individuals and circumstances; the only reliable method of determining correct pressure in relation to speed is to depend upon tool weight. *Craftsman* sanders are carefully engineered to provide correct tool weights and speeds — sanding is both easy and efficient because all you need do is guide the tool without having either to hold it up or to press it down to do the job.

In addition, the housing is open at one side to expose the belt edge. You can sand right along the base of a vertical partition or wall. Two convenient handles are provided for easy guidance.

Belt Changing: With the best sanders no parts need to be removed because the belt can be quickly and easily changed. Belt tracking — to keep the belt running true on its rollers for longest life — is also easily accomplished with a readily accessible, hand-operated tracking screw.

BELT SANDER

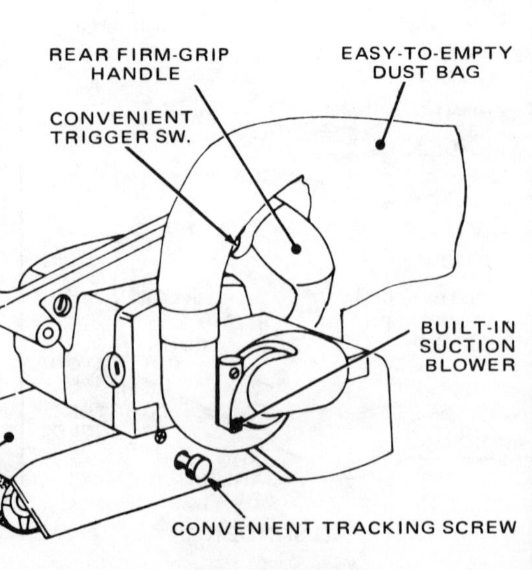

Litter Control: Craftsman belt sanders are available in models equipped with a suction blower and dust bag that will pick up most of the sawdust created. The pick-up not only keeps the work surface clean and visible, it prevents undesirable dust saturation of your breathing air and the surroundings.

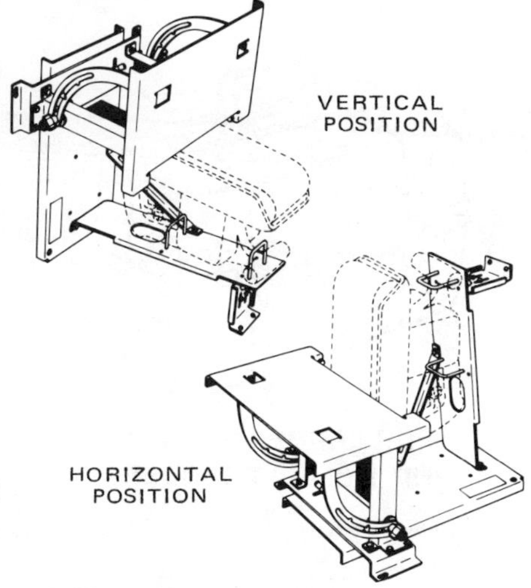

BELT-SANDER FINISHING STAND

Other Uses: A *Finishing Stand*, available as an accessory, will convert your *Craftsman* sander into a bench-type belt sander that can be used in either a horizontal or a vertical position. With this stand you can both surface sand (horizontal position) and edge or end sand (vertical position) any workpiece that can be hand held. It is excellent for both fast, rough sanding and for finish sanding.

ABRASIVES TO USE

Pad Sanders use flat sheets which may be cut to size from 9 x 11-in. hand-sanding sheets or may be purchased in the size required for your model sander. Both standard and special non-clogging (zinc-stearate coated) pre-sized sheets are available in fine, medium and coarse grits (also, extra-coarse in some sizes). The 9 x 11-in. sheets are available in a wide range of types and grits for all the different sanding requirements.

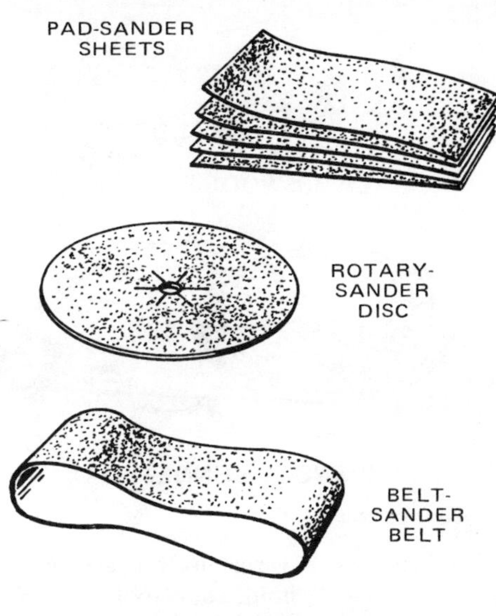

TYPES OF ABRASIVES

Rotary Sanders require pre-cut and center-punched sanding discs of a diameter to fit your model tool. These are available in a variety of grit sizes with aluminum oxide abrasive on paper backing and on longer-lasting fiber backing.

Belt Sanders use cloth-backed or longer-lasting, faster-cutting Polyester-backed, one-piece belts which must be of proper width and length for your sander. The abrasive is aluminum oxide available in extra-fine, fine, medium, coarse and extra-coarse grits for wood and metal sanding.

OTHER ACCESSORIES

As previously mentioned (refer to "Features to Look For", preceding), major accessories for the rotary-type sander are a grinding wheel with guard and a wire cup brush; for the belt sander, a finishing stand. In addition:

Both the pad sander and the rotary sander can be used for polishing with the (respective) lambswool accessory illustrated. Order the correct size for your model tool.

(See next page for illustration.)

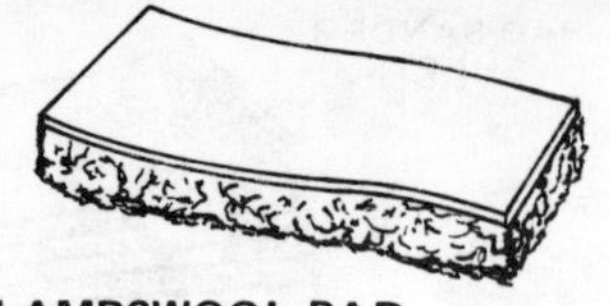

LAMBSWOOL PAD

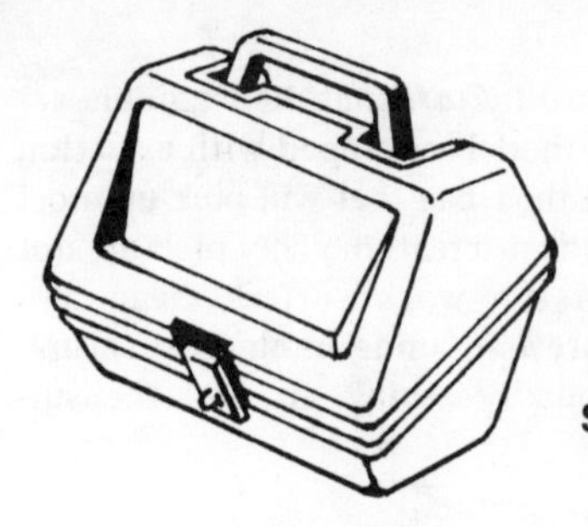

FOR PAD OR 6-IN. ROTARY SANDERS

LAMBSWOOL BONNET

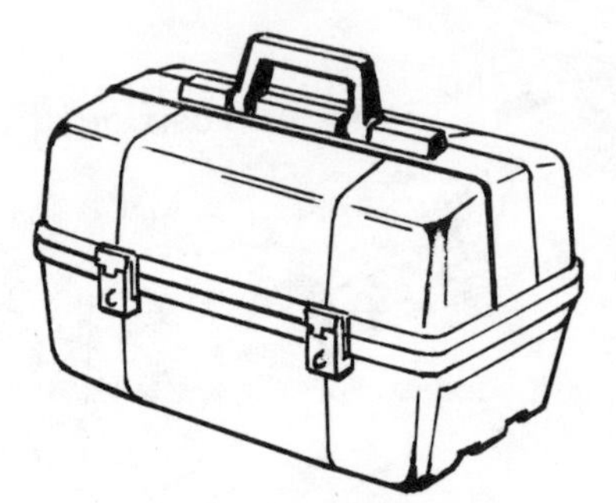

FOR LARGER ROTARY AND THE BELT SANDERS

One of the tough Permanex polyethylene cases shown will hold your tool and an ample selection of abrasives. The case is excellent both for safe storage of your tool and for carrying it to a job.

HELPFUL SUGGESTIONS FOR USING YOUR SANDER

Don't ruin scissors or shears cutting sandpaper. Crease and tear it along a hard and straight enough edge.

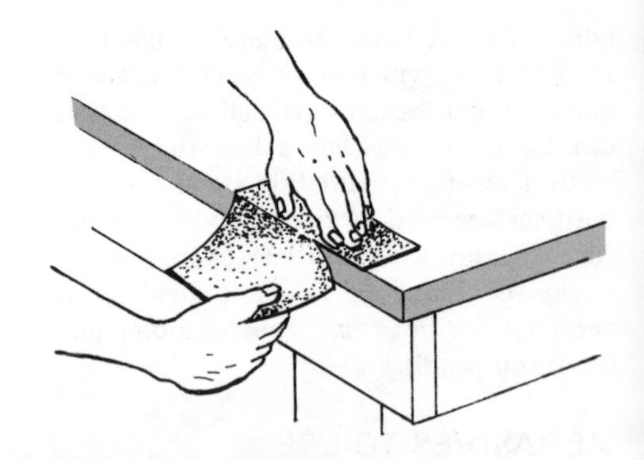

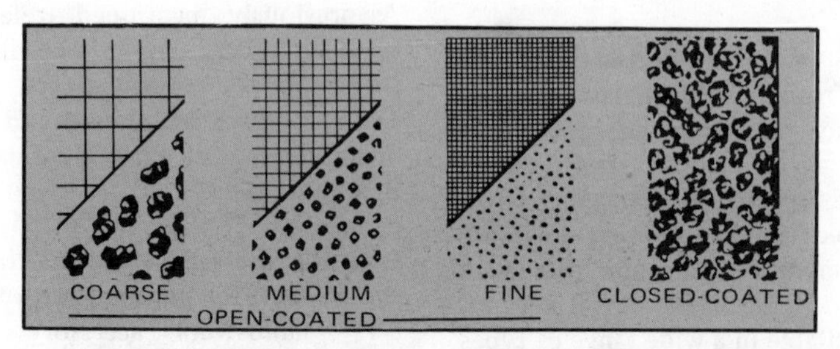

TYPES OF GRITS AND COATINGS

USE THE RIGHT SANDPAPER FOR EACH JOB

Sandpapers are available in a variety of abrasive types. Most used for all power sanding operations is aluminum-oxide, a processed mineral that is a form of corundum, second in hardness only to the diamond. Emery, also, is a coarse, granular form of corundum. Other abrasives hard enough for power sanding operations are the synthetics such as silicone-carbide and tungsten-carbide. The natural abrasives, garnet and flint, are considered too soft for power sanding applications — will quickly lose their cutting edges.

Grit sizes are actually rated by numbers (the smaller numbers designating the coarser grits), but for practical purposes are generally referred to by terms such as "super-fine", "fine", "medium", etc. The quantity of grits per square-inch of sheet is determined by the grit size, and by the density of the coating. Hence, abrasive sheets may be "open-coated" or "closed-coated" (tightly packed). Open-coated abrasives do not "load-up" (become clogged) as readily as closed-coated ones — therefore, are best for practically all wood (and similar material) sanding operations.

The type of sheet (backing) to which the grits are applied — and the bonding agent used — also varies, generally, in relation to the quality of the product. For power sanding good quality is important — a thin paper, lightly-bonded abrasive (such as may be used for hand sanding) will not withstand the rigors of power sanding. Heavy paper backing, at a minimum, is required, and cloth or fiber backing is much better for most uses.

When sanding a thin edge (or end) it is very difficult to prevent the tool from dipping down and rounding one side or the other and, especially, to prevent rounding at the end. If an absolutely flat, squared-edged and cornered workpiece is desired, the only way to assure this is to clamp the work between two scrap boards, as illustrated. If the work is too large to be held in a vise, use C-clamps, instead.

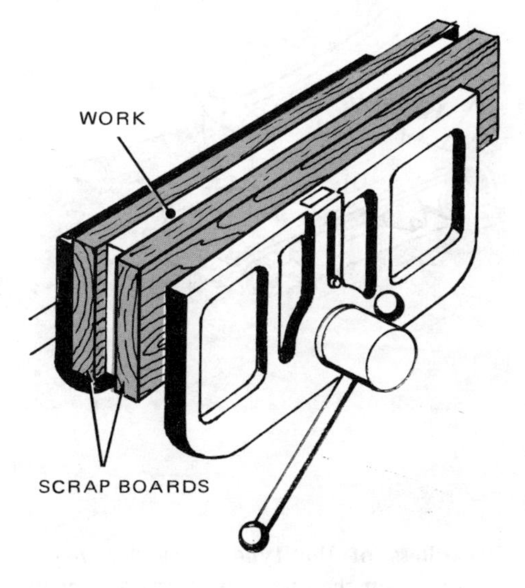

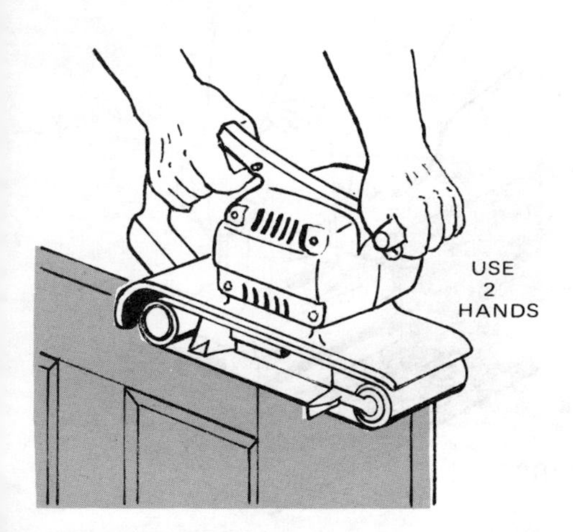

If the preceding method is not practical, be sure to hold your tool with *both* hands so you can balance it squarely on the edge being sanded. When sanding at an edge end, use one hand to slightly lift this end of the sander up so it will not dip down to round off the work end.

POWER SANDING CUTS QUICKLY – WATCH YOUR CONTROL

Never attempt to scrub the work with your sander. Excessive pressure does *not* make the work faster – instead, it might burn or gouge the work, will certainly wear out the abrasive quickly, and could overload and damage your tool. When using a pad sander, apply *very light* pressure; when using a belt sander, do *not* apply any pressure at all (let the tool weight do the job). In either case, keep your tool moving at a steady pace at all times (holding it in one spot will produce a low spot or ripple in the work). The speed with which the tool should be moved depends upon how fast the abrasive is cutting – which can be determined by the "feel" of the resulting friction and the amount of sawdust created. Too fast a motion will stop the cutting action and increase the wear of the abrasive; too slow a motion may remove more stock than desired. Experience will help you to judge the rate of movement required. Carefull attention to the progress of the work will also help.

Regardless of the type of sander, *never* start or stop the motor with the sander in contact with the workpiece. Always start the sander while holding it up, then lower it to start the operation. Always lift it away from the workpiece at the end of an operation, then turn the motor off. Doing otherwise will only result in scarring the workpiece surface.

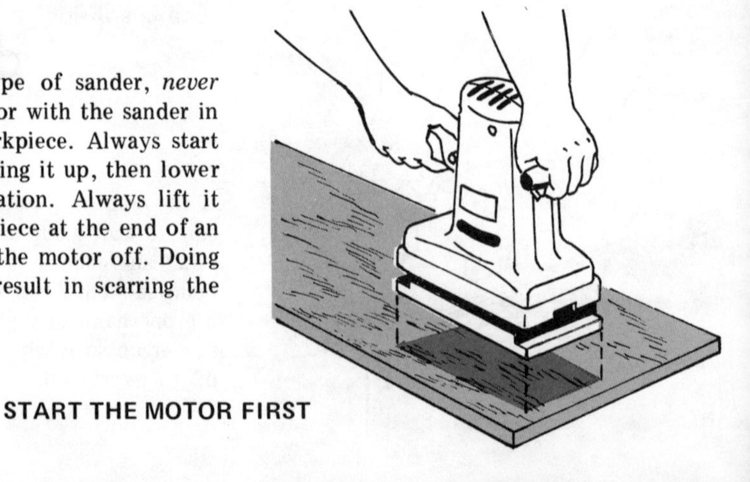

DON'T USE FORCE – LET THE SANDER DO THE WORK

SPECIAL USES OF A PAD SANDER

To sand finish paint, varnish or lacquer use your pad sander with a fine-grit, non-clogging sandpaper pad — and sand with as little downward pressure as possible until you obtain the desired satiny finish. For even smoother finishes you can make pads from extra-fine standard sandpaper sheets.

Removal of thick coats of old paint, varnish, etc. by sanding is not very practical — the abrasive is quickly clogged and made useless, and the amount of abrasive needed may therefore prove to be too costly. Best use a wire brush or a good paint remover to strip off the bulk of the material. After the surface is completely dry you can sand it clean for refinishing. If it is very rough, start with a disc sander using a coarse-grit, open-coat sandpaper. To smooth it for refinishing, use a pad sander with a medium-to-fine-grit, open-coat sandpaper. In all cases, keep the sander moving as rapidly as possible, with light downward pressure.

Metal Finishing

Light clean-up of all kinds of metals (such as knocking off flash, weld finishing, deburring, surfacing fills, and breaking hole edges) can be done with aluminum-oxide abrasives (for high tensile metals) or silicone-carbide abrasives (for low tensile metals). Use 50 (very coarse) to 80 (coarse) grit.

For rust removal and polishing use emery paper, nos. 1 to 3/0. Special effects (to simulate frosting or peening) can be done with grits ranging from 50 (very coarse) to 180 (fine), depending upon the metal and the finish desired. Very high polishes can be achieved — if surface is reasonably smooth at the start — using grits up to 500 (super-fine). Do all work dry and with as little pressure as possible, moving the tool slowly about the surface.

Glass Finishing

Use a silicone-carbide abrasive in grits from 80 (coarse) to 120 (medium) on a pad sander for glass edging and edge beveling. Glass frosting is done in the same way. Surface blemishes, if not too deep, can be rubbed out using 500- to 600-grit (super fine) abrasive. In all cases use light pressure stopping frequently to avoid overheating at any one spot.

Plastic Finishing

Generally, plastics can be sanded in the same way as glass. For clear plastics, however, use a pad made of outing flannel (instead of an abrasive), coated with Simonize or a similar *gritless* cleaner to remove the scratches left after a sanding operation. Finish by polishing with tallow (only) on this pad. Because the surface of a clear plastic is usually soft and easily affected by heat, take extra care to avoid grinding dust or lint into the surface, and to prevent overheating.

Etching Designs on Metal, Glass or Plastic

Use masking tape to form a stencil of the design on the workpiece surface. As an abrasive, use valve-grinding compound mixed with a light oil. Coat the open areas of your stencil design with the compound. Place a thin sheet of metal over this area, then use your tool to agitate this sheet. The masking tape will last long enough to do the job if you use very light pressure.

SPECIAL USES OF A ROTARY SANDER

When using a rotary sander tool weight alone can*not* be used; sanding pressure depends entirely upon the way you hold the tool. As previously explained, the disc can*not* be held flat against a workpiece, it must be tilted and held so that you can travel it along the surface being sanded in a manner to prevent the rotational thrust from bouncing the disc over the surface. The direction of this thrust depends upon which side of the disc contacts the work; your holding force must be in the opposite direction – therefore, it is easiest if you also plan to *travel the tool in the direction opposite to this thrust.*

For best results, tilt the disc at a 5- to 8-degree angle, just enough to be certain the opposite side cannot contact the work. Too great an angle may result in gouging the work. Carefully hold the same angle throughout a stroke (period during which disc contacts work). Limit each stroke to *one* direction of travel only (don't attempt to change direction without lifting the tool off the work and starting over). If practical during a stroke, let the tool weight determine sanding pressure; otherwise, hold the tool to apply light pressure, only. Determine speed of travel as above. Sanding action is quite fast; keep a sharp eye on the progress of your work.

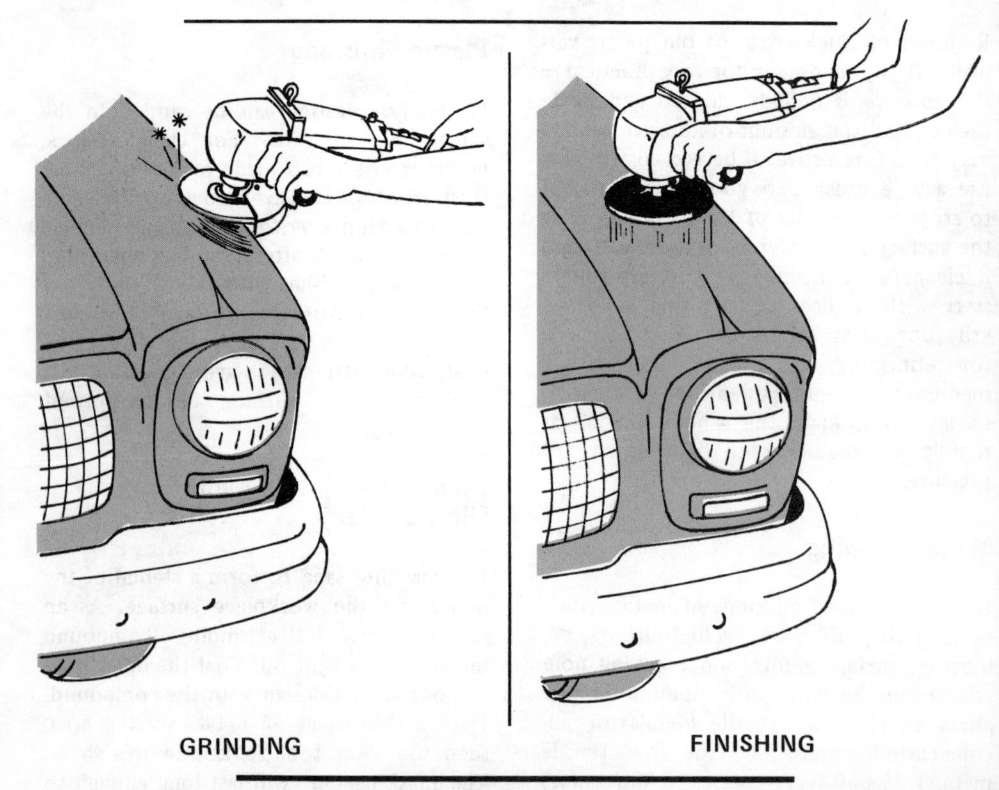

GRINDING FINISHING

AUTOMOTIVE BUFFER/POLISHER

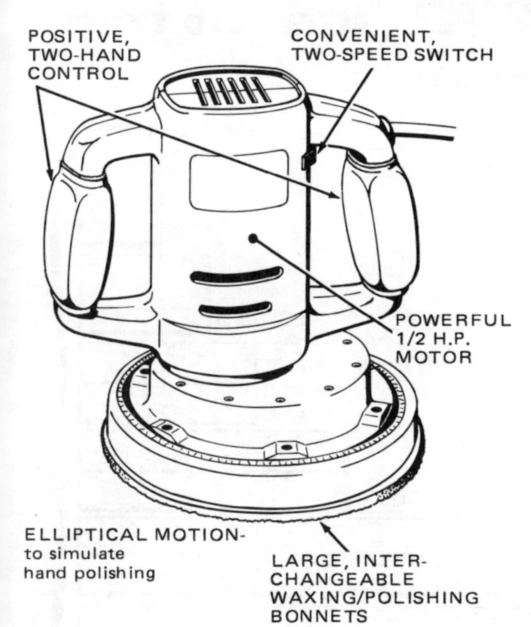

Automotive Buffer/Polisher

This specially designed power tool saves hours of hard labor and does a better-rubbed job of polishing cars, vans, boats . . . even airplanes than you are likely to do by hand. It is excellent for use with most leading liquid or paste waxes. Accessories furnished are two waxing bonnets and one buffing bonnet. Wax is applied at the motor no-load speed of 1700 rpm; the 1900 rpm speed is used for removing wax and polishing. The large-orbit elliptical pad motion simulates hand movements to better spread and polish the wax.

Extra bonnets and a sturdy Polyethylene carrying case are available.

Extra fine, durable car finishes are produced by careful, time-consuming applications of wax and additional time-consuming buffing and polishing to bring the wax to an overall thin, hard coating of desired lustre. With this powerful, easy-to-use tool almost every surface can be properly rubbed — much, much faster and with much less effort than by hand rubbing. The work that might have been a chore becomes a short and profitable light task that can save money and preserve the beauty of your car.

POPULAR WOOD - SIZES AND TYPES

DRESSED LUMBER

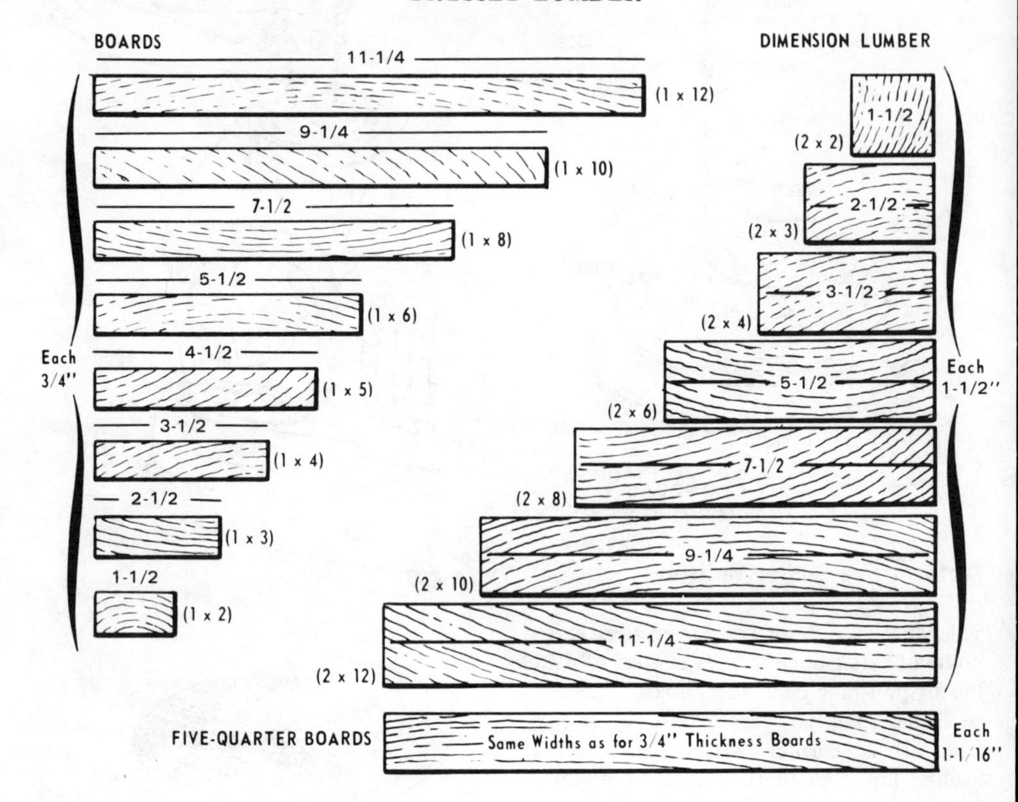

The accompanying chart shows popular homeshop dressed (surfaced four sides) lumber, together with the nominal and the average actual sizes (which may vary slightly in different areas). Nominal thicknesses and widths of boards (at left above) are shown down the center; actual widths are given above the respective boards; and the actual thicknesses are given in the side brackets. The "five-quarter" thickness boards are available in the same widths as the "3/4-inch" boards. Nominal and actual measurements of dimension lumber (at right above) are similarly shown. Only the actual sizes of timbers (at right) are shown; increase each fractional number to the next whole number — for nominal size (that is: 1-1/2x2-1/2 = 2x3).

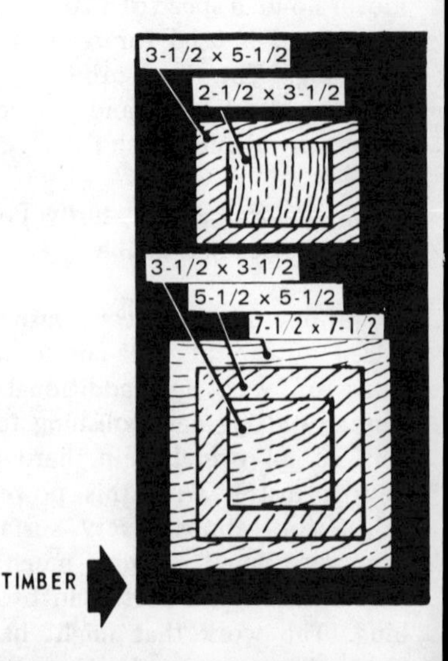

SECTION VII
THE ROTARY GRINDERS/CARVERS

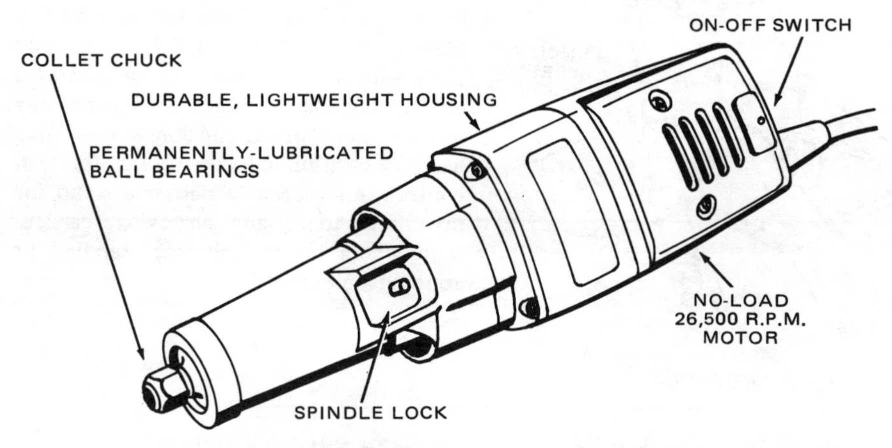

SINGLE-SPEED ROTARY GRINDER

CRAFTSMAN ROTARY GRINDER

This heavy-duty production-type tool has a 1/4 hp high-speed motor, a collet chuck for 1/8-in. and 1/4-in. shank cutters, and is lightweight and easy to handle. With it a tool and diemaker can precisely shape to size cast-metal molds; a model-maker can create wooden models; artists can carve or polish wood, plastics or metals. It is designed for continuous work. The *Rotary Cutters, Solid Carbide Burrs* and *Grinding Points* used with this tool are shown on *pages 3 and 4*.

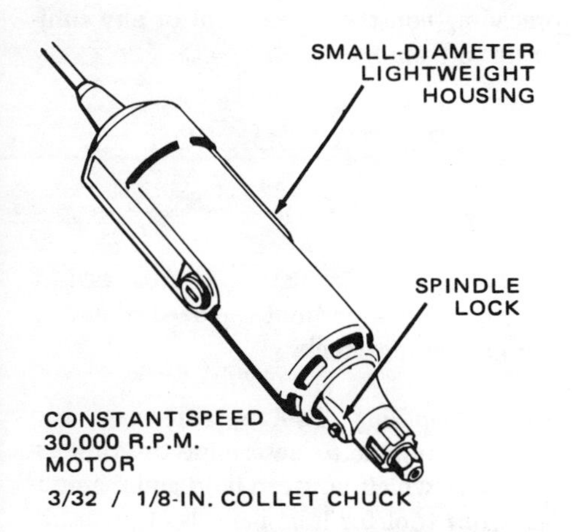

CRAFTSMAN ROTARY POWER TOOLS

These lightweight, comfortably hand-held tools develop the high rpms needed to let you drill, cut, grind, sharpen and polish a variety of hobbycraft materials. A variety of 3/32-in. and 1/8-in. shafted tools (*Pages 5 and 6*) are available. The power tools are especially useful for home improvement projects as well as for hobby work with wood, plastics, ceramics, glass, iron and non-ferrous metals — for such operations as carving, engraving, embossing and damascening, grinding and polishing.

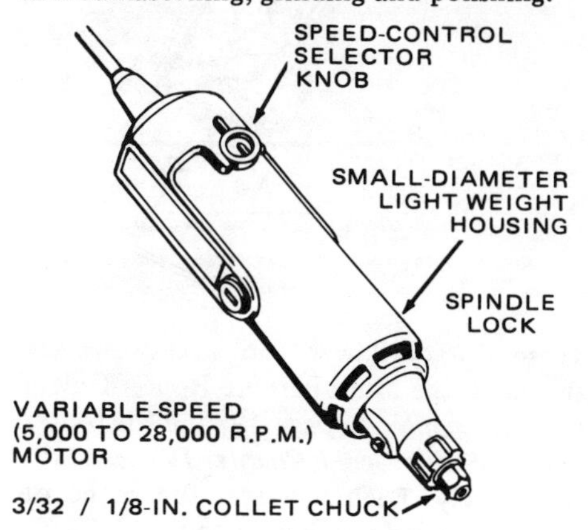

FOR SAFEST OPERATING INSTRUCTIONS REFER TO YOUR OWNER'S MANUAL

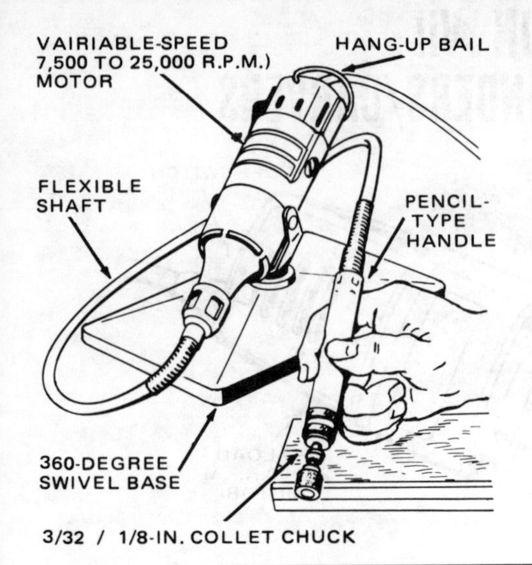

FLEXIBLE-SHAFT MODEL

This *Craftsman* tool is similar to the preceding *Rotary Power Tool* but is mounted on a swivel base (or can be hung by the hang-up bail provided) and has a flexible shaft with a collet chuck at the end of a holder that can be held like a pencil for precise guiding of the chuck-held tool. Also has a 3-position selector switch for rpm control. An especially desirable setup for precision carving and engraving, particularly where internal shaping, sanding or grinding are required.

ROUTER AND PANTAGRAPH ATTACHMENT

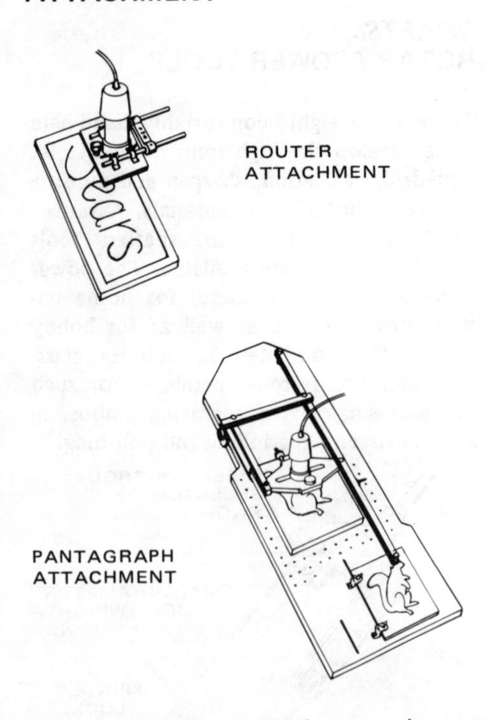

These Rotary Power Tool accessories are similar to the Multi-Purpose Router Guide, (*Sec. I, Chapter 2, page 19*) and the router Rout-A-Form (*Sec. I, Chapter IV, page 50*), respectively. Each increases the scope of work you can do with your tool.

MOTOR SPEED CONTROL

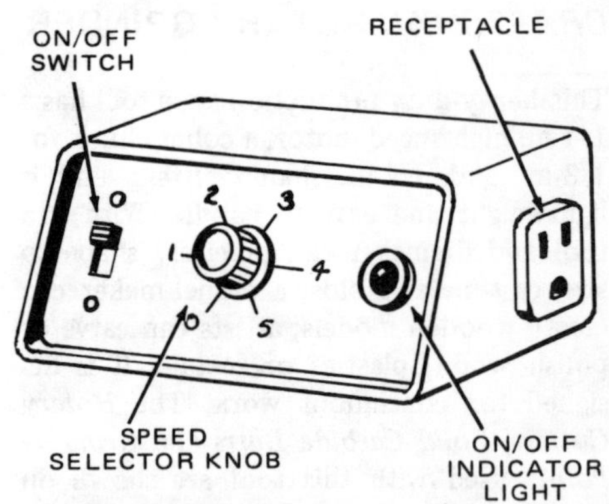

A solid-state variable speed control for the preceding constant speed tool or any similar up to 5 amp. tool.

FEATURES TO LOOK FOR

In Any Rotary Tool

Safety. Double insulation guards against electrical shock without the need of having a grounded receptacle.

Ease-of-Handling. Tool weight, shape and balance combine to determine the tirelessness with which you can hold and manipulate your tool for long periods of precision work. *Craftsman* tools have very lightweight, but strong, plastic housings contoured and balanced for a comfortable grip.

Temperature Rise. Motor heat can be a problem with a closely-held, necessarily compact tool of this type. During an extended period of operation a tool that is not efficiently cooled can become too hot to hold. *Craftsman* tools are properly designed to dissipate most of the motor heat under normal operating conditions.

In A Professional-Type Tool

Durability. The *Craftsman* professional tool is durably constructed for continuous duty — with a 1/4-hp, permanent-magnet motor and lifetime-lubricated ball bearings. The shock-resistant housing is constructed of lightweight aluminum and heat-resistant polyester.

Versatility. No tool is better than the cutters available to do the many jobs needed. Your *Craftsman* tool is accompanied by a wide range of 1/4-in. shank rotary cutters and solid-carbide burrs for all possible types of metal and wood shaping operations. There is also a stand for mounting the tool on a bench — for work that can better be hand held.

Convenience of Use. Changing cutters is made easy by a spindle lock that allows the chuck to be quickly opened or closed with a single wrench. The collet chuck will accept either 1/8-in. or 1/4-in. shank bits and cutters.

In a Hobby-Type Tool

Durability. Each *Craftsman* tool has a lightweight but strong (impact resistant) plastic housing and a motor designed especially for the type of usage intended.

Conveniences. The models illustrated each have a two-collet chuck for 3/32-in. and 1/8-in. shafted cutters, etc. — with a lock pin for quick, easy cutter changes. One also has a hanging bail for convenient tool storage on the wall or bench side.

CUTTING, ETC. ACCESSORIES AND THEIR USES

Professional-Tool Accessories

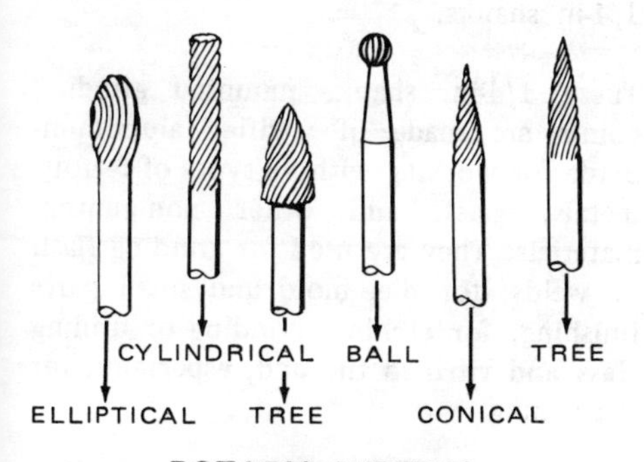

ROTARY CUTTERS

These 1/4-in. shank, high-speed steel cutters are designed for paring, shaving, grooving or shaping of wood, plastic and any metal except hardened steel. The shapes illustrated are those popularly used for cast-metal diemaking, graphic-arts engraving and model- or pattern-making.

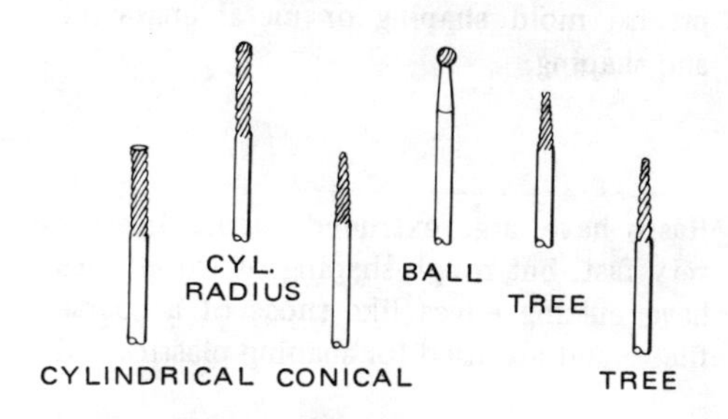

SOLID CARBIDE BURRS

The toughest cutters made, these 1/8-in. shank burrs are of top industrial quality, designed for cutting hardened steel or fast,

REFER TO A **CURRENT** *SEARS CATALOG FOR ACCESSORIES AVAILABLE*

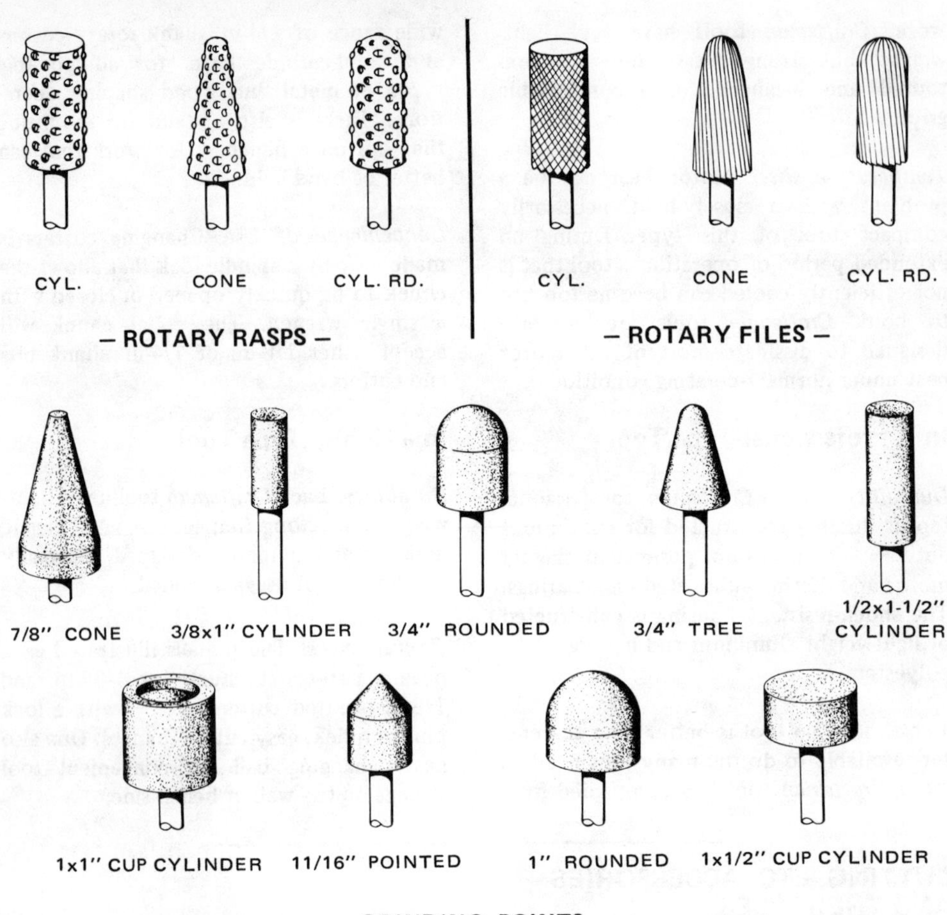

easy cutting of all other commonly used die and mold metals. Their small heads reach into tight places for exceptionally precise mold shaping or metal engraving and shaping.

Rasps have large extruded cutting lips for very fast, but rough shaping of wood; files have cutting edges like those of a coarse file — and are used for shaping plastics and finish shaping of hard woods. All have 1/4-in. shanks.

These 1/4-in. shank, mounted grinding points are made of vitrified aluminum-oxide for working with all types of ferrous metals, glass, and other non-gummy materials. They are used for grinding flash or welds, for die, mold and small parts finishing, for etching, grinding or drilling glass and vitrified tile and, especially, for sharpening.

NOTE: All of the 1/8-in. shafted (or mandrel-mounted) accessories following can also be used with the professional tool.

Hobby Tool Accessories

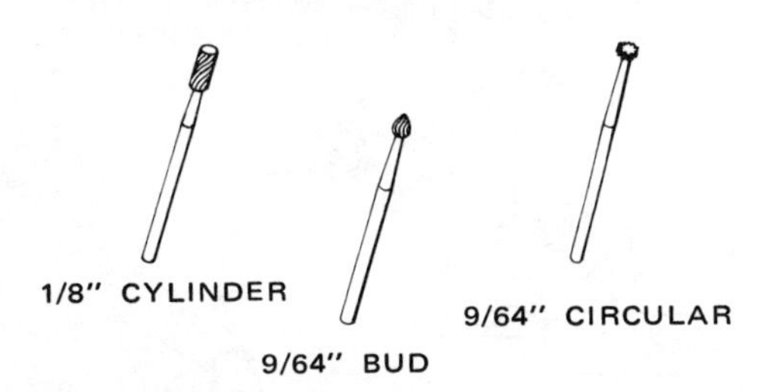

STEEL CUTTING BURRS

These 3/32-in. shafted burrs of hardened steel are for carving, routing, grooving and shaping of wood, plastic and all non-ferrous metals (copper, aluminum, etc.). They are *not* made for cutting hard or brittle materials.

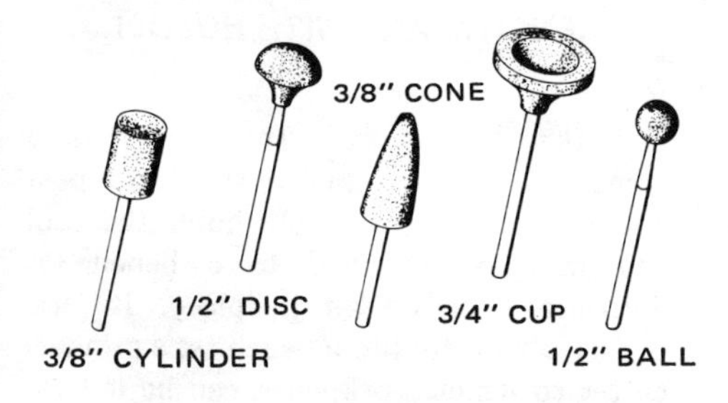

MOUNTED ABRASIVE POINTS

All 1/8-in. shanked, these vitrified aluminum-oxide abrasives are excellent for grinding, shaping, etching and finishing of hard (non-gummy) metals, glass, tile and similar materials. The different shapes enable you to work to various contours.

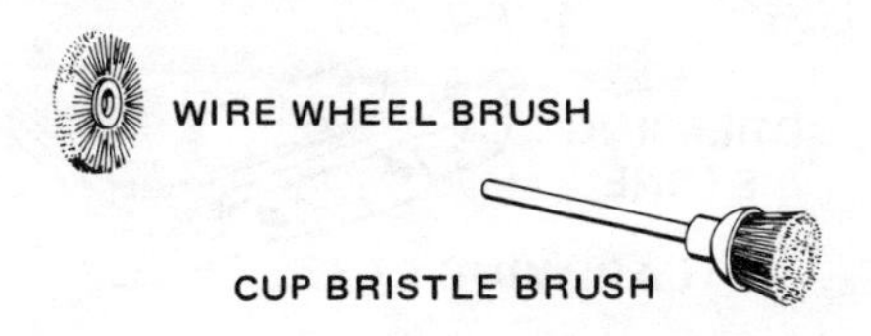

The 3/32-in. shafted bristle brush is 1/2-in. diameter — is useful for cleaning cavities in, or the surface of any hard material. The wire brush requires a 1/8-in. mandrel and is 3/4-in. diameter. It is used for matte finishing soft metals and the tougher metal-cleaning jobs (such as solder joints).

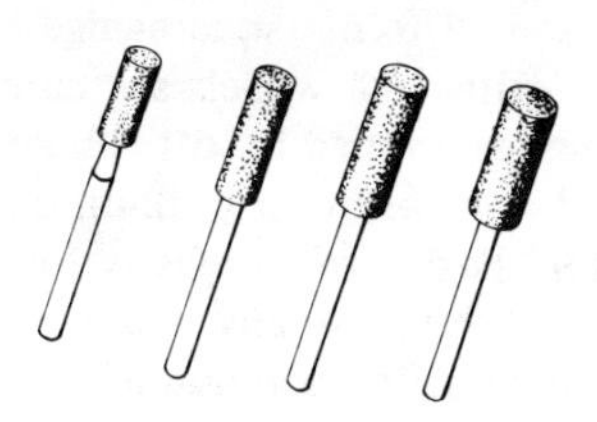

SET OF FOUR SHARPENING POINTS

Sold especially for chain-saw sharpening this set of vitrified aluminum-oxide grinding points is also excellent for a wide range of tool sharpening operations. The different sizes provide a selection for each different application. All have 1/8-in. shanks.

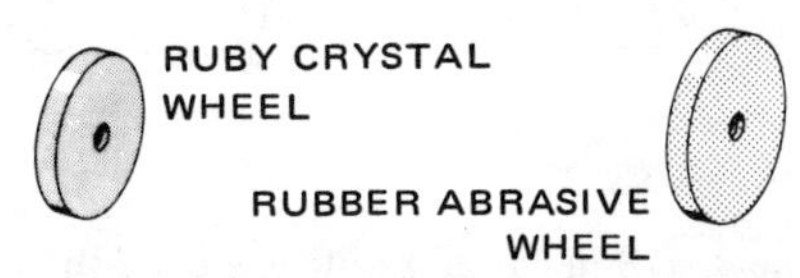

Both of these wheels require a 3/32-in. mandrel. The 1-in. ruby wheel is composed of a special abrasive and is excellent for the finishing of hard metal, glass and other hard materials to ready them for polishing. The 7/8-in. rubber wheel serves the same purpose when used for finishing softer metals and materials.

This is a 16-ply, 1-in. diameter muslin wheel with which you can apply a high-luster to properly finished metal or plastic or to waxed or oiled wood. Use with a buffing compound for metal polishing, with rouge powders (progressively finer) for clear plastics; with pumice followed by wax for other plastics. The wheel can be mounted on either a 3/32-in. or a 1/8-in. mandrel.

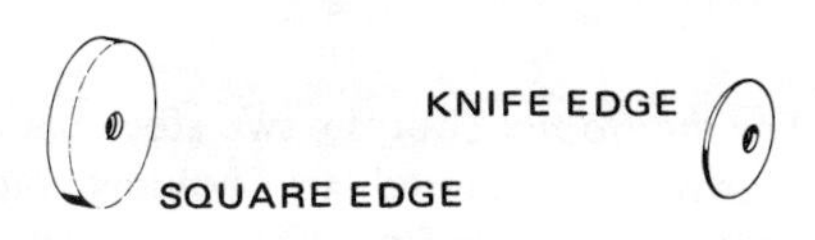

PUMICE WHEELS

Both the 7/8-in. square-edge and the 5/8-in. knife-edge wheels are composed of fine pumice bonded in soft rubber, and can be used with either a 3/32-in. or a 1/8-in. mandrel. Both are excellent for the fine-finish polishing of any metal – without need for a buffing compound.

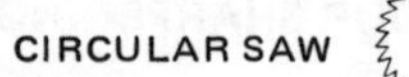

CIRCULAR SAW

This 3/4-in. diameter steel saw is excellent for slitting, cutting-off or grooving of any wood, plastic or soft (non-ferrous) metal. It requires a 1/8-in. mandrel.

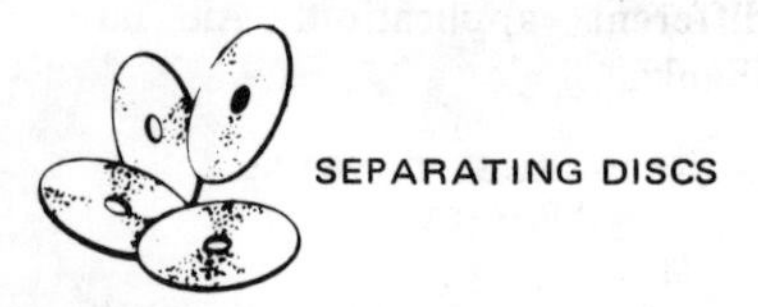

SEPARATING DISCS

These 7/8-in. discs require a 3/32-in. mandrel. They are extremely thin and flexible and are made of hard-rubber bonded silicon-carbide abrasive. Their special purpose is the cutting of glass, vitrified tile and similar hard, brittle materials; and they can also be used for slicing the harder non-ferrous metals.

OTHER ACCESSORIES

NOTE: Any twist drill or wood bit having a correct size (3/32-in, 1/8-in. and/or 1/4-in.) shank may be used with your tool. The cutters, etc. for each of the tools, as listed above, are sold singly and in sets which also include the tool-related accessories following. Refer to a *current* Sears Catalog for up-to-date information.

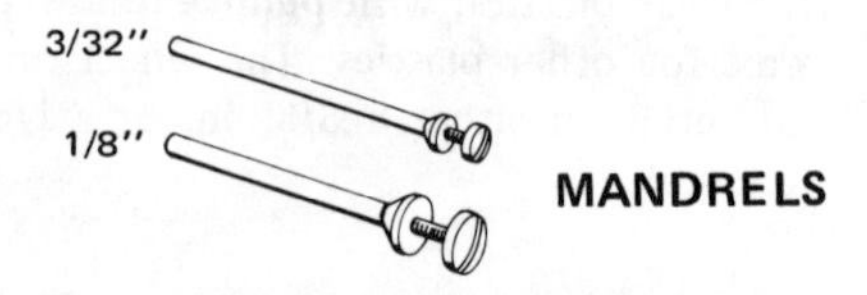

MANDRELS

For the Hobby Tool the two steel mandrels shown are required for holding various ones of the preceding wheels, brushes, etc. as already explained.

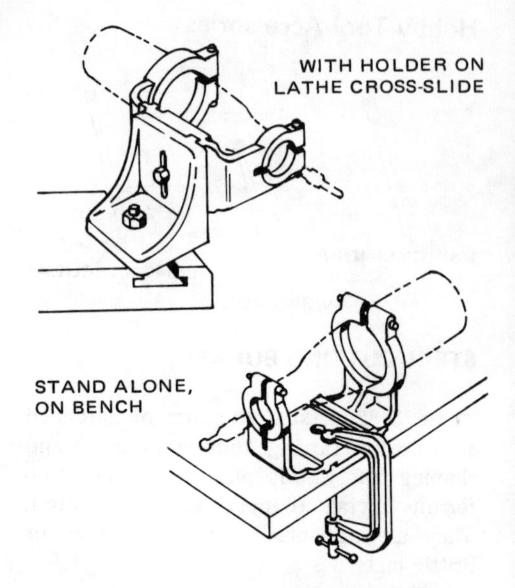

BENCH STAND WITH HOLDER

For the Professional Tool there is a combined bench stand with tool-post holder. The stand securely holds the tool and may be clamped to a bench (as illustrated) or bolted in place. Its use converts your tool to a bench-type grinder/ cutter to which workpieces can be fed for rapid production and/or better control of accuracy. When attached to the tool-post holder this stand can be mounted on a metal-lathe cross-slide for precision internal or external milling, grinding, etc. of a workpiece centered on the lathe.

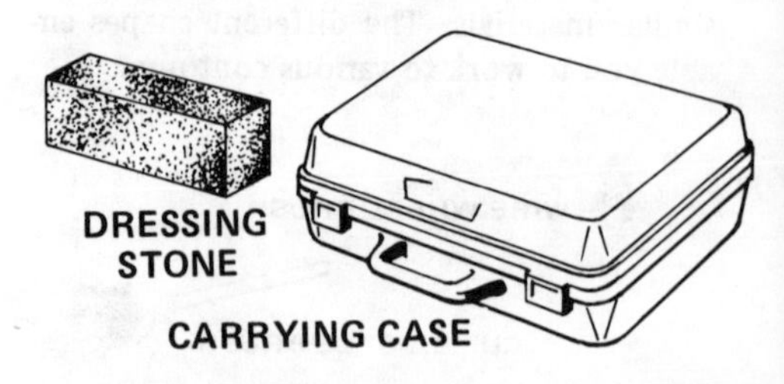

DRESSING STONE

CARRYING CASE

For Either Type of Tool there is a sturdy Permanex polyethelene carrying case in which your tool and a complete set of accessories can be safely and conveniently stored or carried to the job. The dressing stone illustrated is needed for occasional reshaping and cleaning of grinding points.

TYPICAL TOOL OPERATIONS

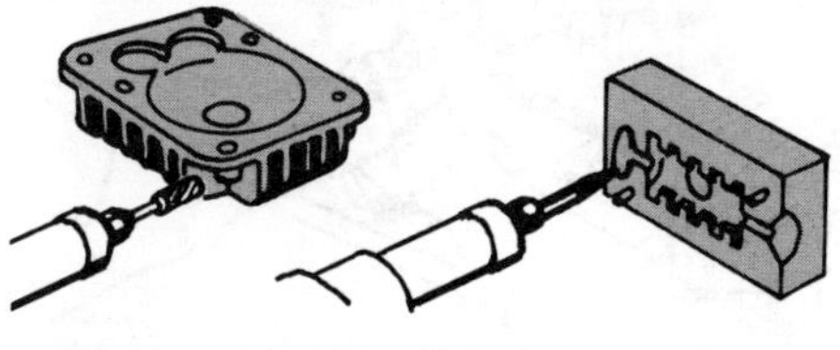

DIEMAKING

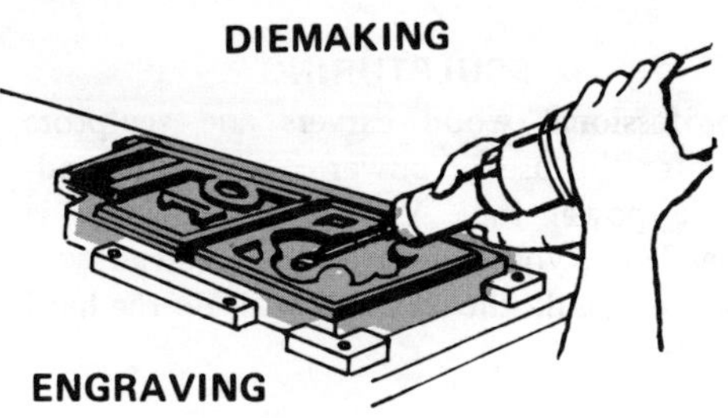

ENGRAVING

There are dozens of ways in which the *Craftsman* professional tool can be used for the precision working of diemaking and engraving metals. With this powerful tool and the accessories you can do any work required faster and with less effort than with an inferior tool.

PRODUCTION WORK

Because it is built for continuous, heavy-duty work, the *Craftsman* professional model makes an excellent bench or lathe cross-slide tool for innumerable shop jobs, such as those illustrated. The stand and holder accessory (preceding) is shown holding the rotary tool.

Every professional who takes pride in his work knows the value of a powerful but lightweight tool like the *Craftsman* professional model. With it you can easily shape wood to close tolerances or do the most intricate carving.

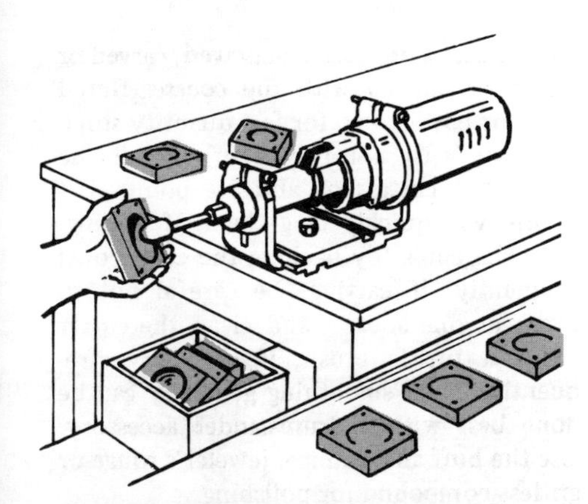

BENCH GRINDING SMALL PARTS

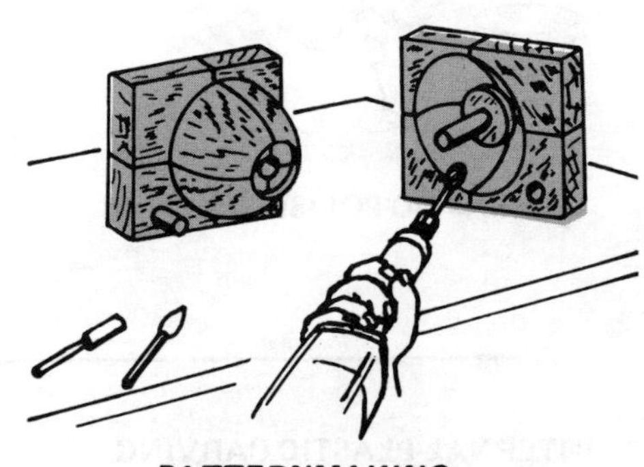

PATTERNMAKING

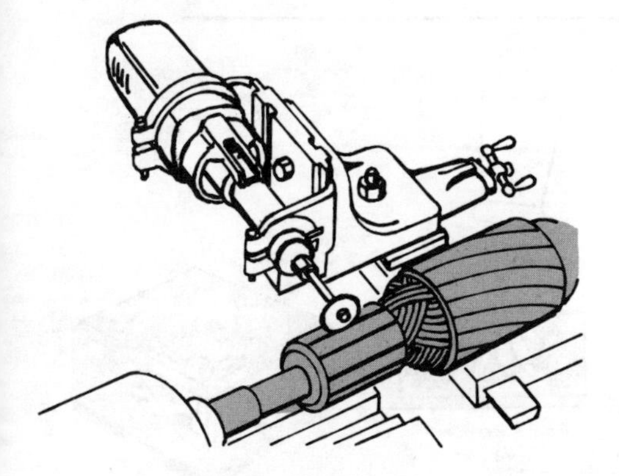

TYPICAL PRECISION SET-UP ON A LATHE

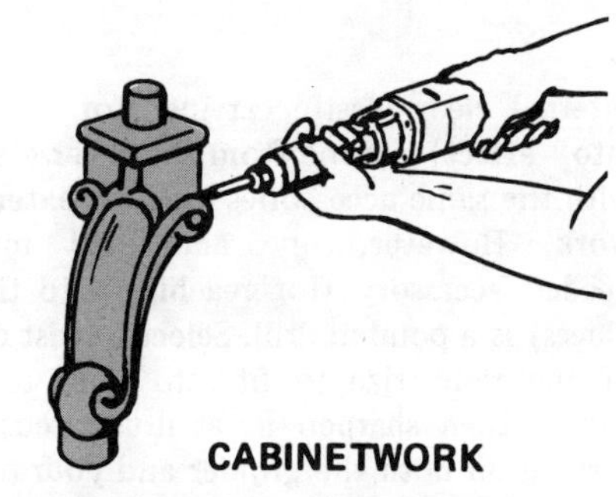

CABINETWORK

USE THE **CRAFTSMAN** *PROFESSIONAL TOOL FOR SHOP-TYPE WORK*

CARVING

SCULPTURING

When operating at top speed with a 16 flute cutter a 24,000 rpm rotary tool takes 384,000 "bites" of wood every minute. Compare this with the action of a hand-held knife and it is obvious why most professional wood carvers and sculptors prefer the use of power — and a dependable power tool. Very little "muscle" is needed — you don't use force; instead, you simply guide the tool and let it do the hard work.

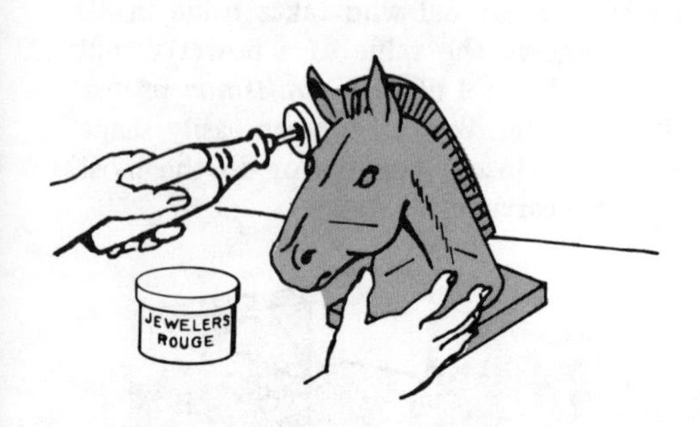

PLASTIC POLISHING

Most plastics are easily engraved, carved or otherwise shaped with the *coarser* fluted burrs or cutters (or, for fast quantity stock removal, with a rotary rasp). Don't use fine-fluted cutters or abrasive points; the plastic will quickly clog them. If drilling, clear the chips (by backing the cutter out) frequently; if carving, be careful not to overheat one spot — and clean the cutter (with a bristle brush, if necessary) frequently. Final smoothing generally can be done best with a drum-sander accessory. Use the buff and pumice, jeweler's rouge or gritless compound for polishing.

INTERNAL PLASTIC CARVING

Internal clear plastic carving (for a "see-into" effect) is done from the reverse side with the same accessories used for external work. However, one additional much needed accessory (for reaching into tight places) is a pointed drill. Select a twist drill of the right size to fit into your tool's chuck, then sharpen it, as illustrated, by turning on both the grinder and your tool.

For a high-gloss carved-surface finish, cover the area with acetone — just enough to make it glisten — and let the acetone evaporate. By dissolving and fusing the surface layer, it will produce the finish desired. Afterwards, clear dyes can be used for coloring. Mixing acetone, water and dye — or die and dry Plaster of Paris — will produce interestingly different effects.

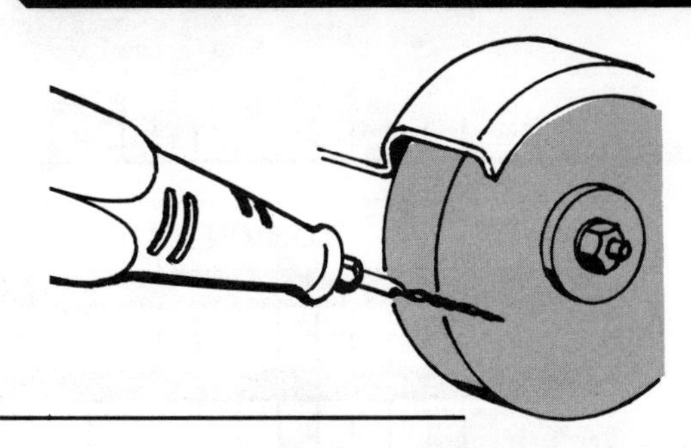

GLASS ETCHING

Etched glass becomes permanently frosted. This frosting can be colored, if desired, by applying colored lacquer and wiping off the excess. Draw your design on paper and rubber-cement this to the opposite glass side. Use one of the pointed grinding points (abrasive) — or, if appropriate, the disc, cone or ball. For frosting or beveling an edge, use one of the cylinders (on its side).

Any non-ferrous metal — including the precious metals used in jewelry — is easily engraved (or, if necessary, shaped) using the rotary files, cutters or burrs, as required by the task at hand. Most soft metals, like plastic, tend to clog the cutter, so care must be taken to keep your cutter clean and free-cutting. Damascening is done with the flat end of a cylindrical grinding point (abrasive) and a flow of water or kerosene (to help keep the abrasive from being clogged). A brushed effect can be obtained by using a wire cup or wheel brush. For polishing, first use a rubber-bonded abrasive wheel — then finish with the buff and a polishing compound.

METAL ENGRAVING

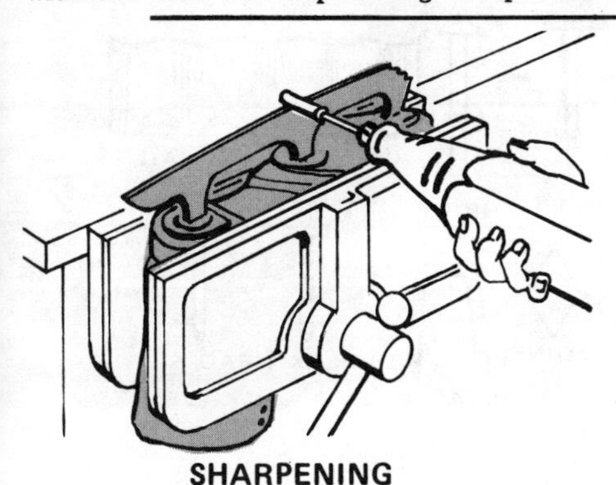

SHARPENING

Fitted with a grinding point of appropriate shape (and/or size), your rotary tool can't be beat for any number of sharpening jobs for which a bench grinder cannot be conveniently used. It is so much faster and less tiring than using a hand file or stone. In addition, with the proper accessories, your tool makes light work of countless jobs. To mention a few, it will remove rust spots, clean blackened pots and pans, scrub dentures, clean golf clubs, or polish switch plates, doorknobs, silverware, jewelry, etc.

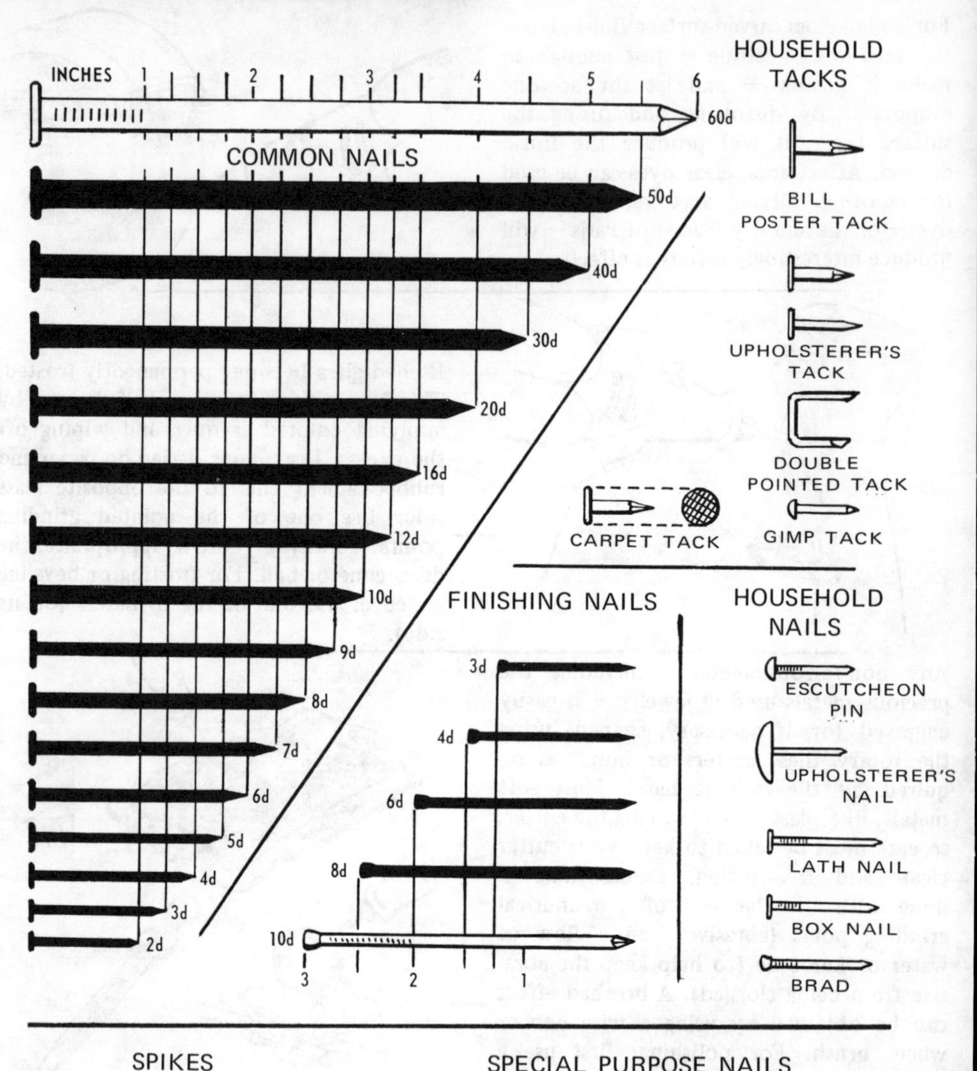

SPIKES

ROUND WIRE SPIKE

FLAT-HEAD GUTTER SPIKE

ROUND-HEAD GUTTER SPIKE

BOAT NAIL

SPECIAL PURPOSE NAILS

SCREW NAILS

HINGE NAIL

CORRUGATED NAIL

WALL-BOARD NAIL

GLAZIER'S POINTS

STAPLE

DUPLEX HEAD

NAILS – SIZES AND TYPES

SECTION VIII – WOOD JOINTS

This section describes 33 commonly used wood joints that can be made with your router and a bench-, radial- or band-saw for the long, straight cut-offs. In order to use your router for some of the required cuts, you must either have a *Trim-A-Form Accessory* (*Chapters 1 and 4 of Section I*) to hold small workpieces, or you must make the homemade work holders described here. Also refer to *Chapters 2 and 3 of Section I* for general routing instructions that are applicable.

TWO USEFUL HOMEMADE HOLDING FIXTURES

Small Workpiece Holder

This adjustable fixture will help you to rout on the surface of a small workpiece by affording a means of clamping it securely to the bench. You can use 1/2- to 1-in. lumber as desired . . . and can size the pieces to suit your requirements. Make identical rabbets on the two sliding pieces and the two rails so that adjustment will be smooth and free. Drive 1-1/2-in. finishing nails about 1-1/4-in. deep into the sliding pieces as shown – then cut off the heads to leave sharp points. These will grip the workpiece, and the holes can be patched afterwards.

On-Edge Workpiece Holder

Preferably make the two rails (which should be identical in size) of 1- to 2-in. lumber and the base of 1-in. lumber. Make the fixture length and the base width to suit your requirements. Support the stationary rail as shown – it *must be rigid*. For use, clamp in the workpiece and clamp the fixture to your bench as illustrated. Having the tops of the two rails identical (and flat) will not only provide a support for the router base to slide along . . . it will also allow you to set your edge guide to measure in accurately from the two sides of the workpiece.

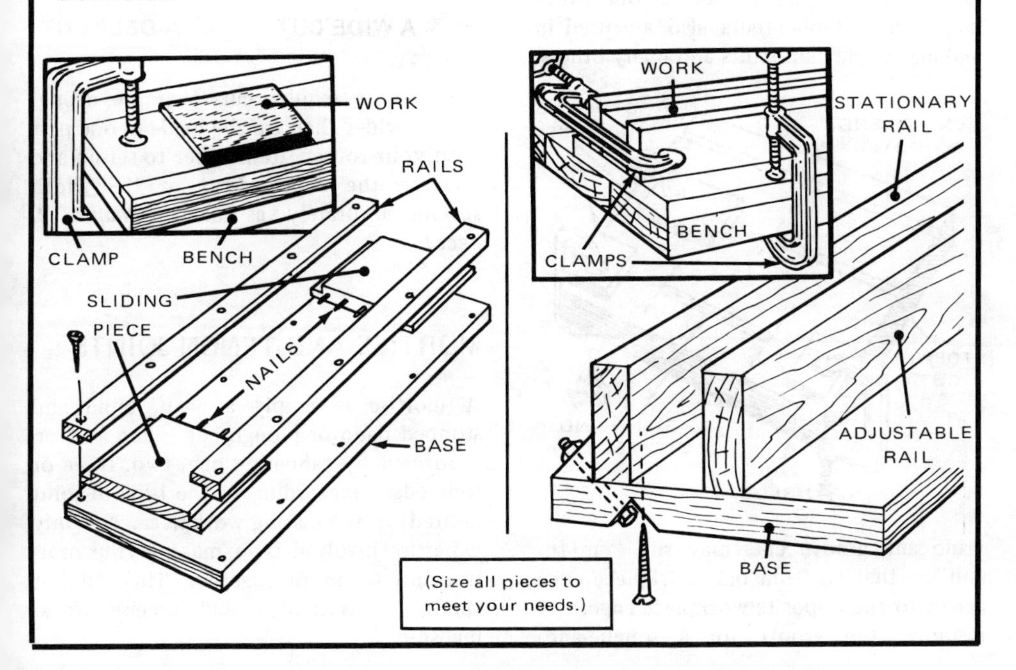

(Size all pieces to meet your needs.)

DADO, GROOVE AND RABBET CUTS

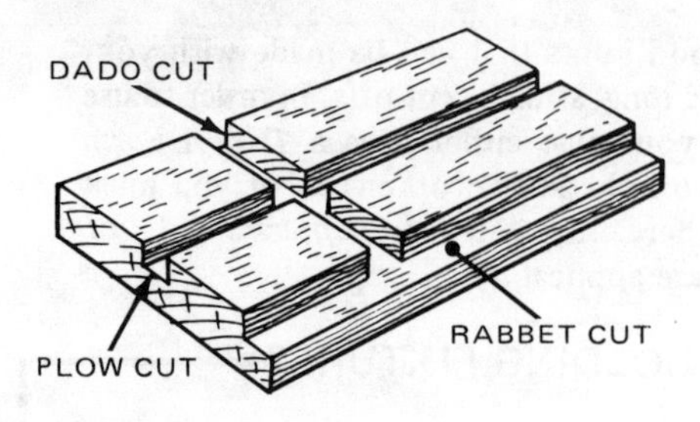

A "dado" is a square groove cut *across* the grain — and similar cuts made *with the grain* are called "grooves" or "plough" cuts. These cuts may be made into the workpiece surface at any location, but they always have two sides and a bottom to form a channel in the wood. Many joints require this type of a dado or groove cut (in one workpiece), together with a mated "tongue" (in the other workpiece).

If a groove (or dado) cut is made at a workpiece edge or end so that it has only one side and a bottom it is called a "rabbet" cut. The "tongue" mentioned above is, for instance, made by making two rabbet cuts at opposite sides of one workpiece edge. Rabbet cuts also are used in making tenons, lap joints and many others.

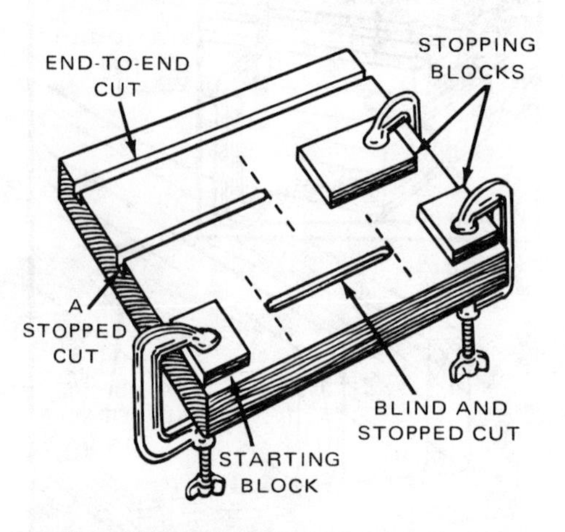

Dado and groove cuts may run "end-to-end" — that is, from one workpiece edge across to the opposite workpiece edge. For instance, the groove for a tongue-and-groove joint is made end-to-end into the workpiece lengthwise edge. Such cuts also may be either "stopped" cuts or "blind and stopped" cuts, as used for making some types of tenon-joint mortises.

To make neat, tight-fitting joints, all the necessary router cuts must be set-up accurately and guided throughout (*no* free-hand cuts). If the workpiece is not large enough to clamp to your workbench or to hold in a vise, you must use the Trim-A-Form Accessory (*Chapter 1, Sec. I*) or one of the holders on the preceding page. And some type of guide must be used. Refer to *Chapter 2, Sec. I* for general set-up and cutting procedures and to *Chapter 4, Sec. I* for use of the Trim-A-Form Accessory. In addition, long cuts — such as needed for most tongue-and-groove joints — are most easily accomplished using the Shaper Table Accessory (*refer to Chapters 1 and 5, Sec. I*).

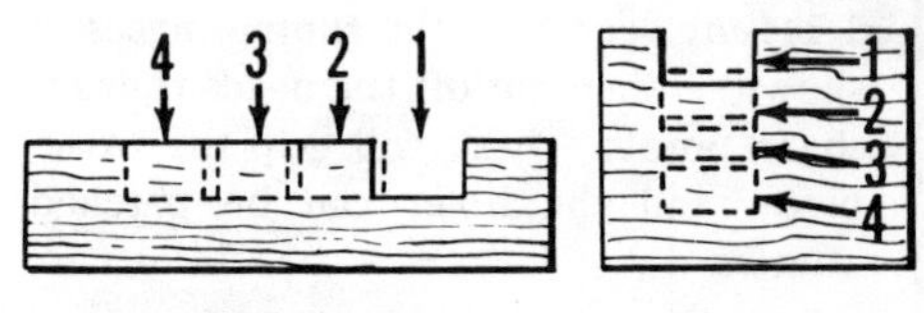

A WIDE CUT   A DEEP CUT

Most joints require cuts that are deeper and/or wider than can be made in one pass with your router. Remember to set-up and increase the depth-of-cut or the width spacing accurately, as told in *Chapter 2, Sec. I.*

MORTISE-AND-TENON JOINTS

A mortise is simply a deep, blind and stopped dado or plough cut — and a tenon is formed by rabbeting one, two, three or four edges (according to the type of joint desired) of the mating workpiece. The only expertise involved is in making your mortise and tenon fit together. This requires careful measurement and precise workmanship.

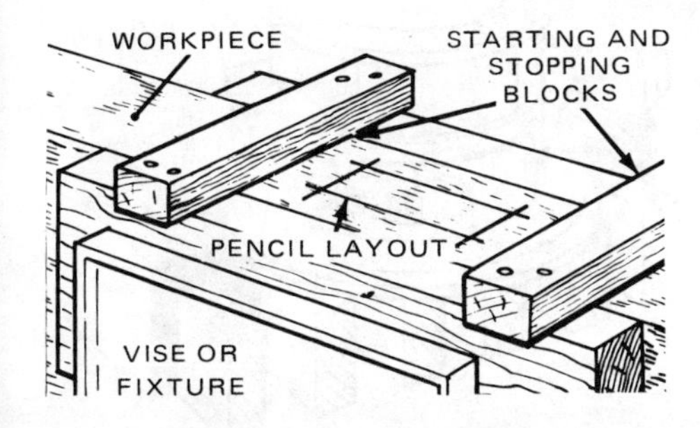

SET-UP FOR MORTISING

A Centered Mortise

Select a bit about 3/4 the size of the width of cut to be made. Adjust it to a reasonable depth of cut. Set your workpiece up in your holding fixture or a vise, using equal thickness scrap blocks at each side of it if this is necessary to provide an overall width on which the router base can slide without wobbling. Carefully measure and mark the mortise area in pencil on the workpiece.

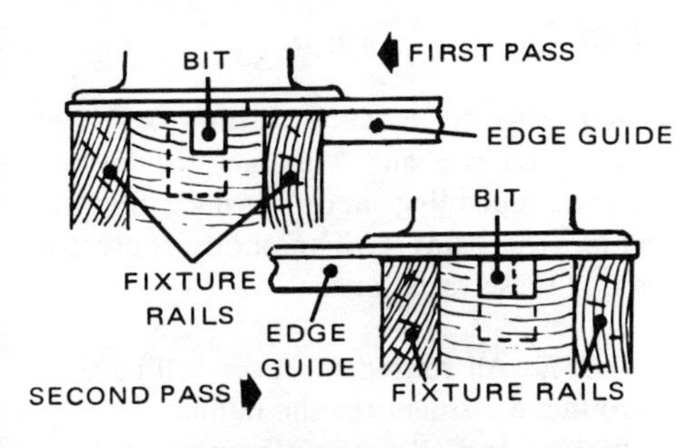

CUTTING THE MORTISE

Now, clamp starting and ending stop blocks in place as for a blind-and-stopped cut. Next, install and adjust your edge guide so that one side of the first pass will be properly located along one side-line of the mortise area. Start the router and make this first pass . . . then make a second pass with the edge guide pressing against the opposite side. You'll now have a shallow cut covering the whole mortise area and exactly centered between the workpiece sides. Proceed to deepen it, as required, in the usual manner.

An Off-Center Mortise

This is cut in exactly the same manner excepting that it is better to do it by using the edge guide along one side only, if possible. If it isn't too wide, use a bit the exact width of the mortise so that one pass at each depth setting will suffice. If it is too wide for this, you'll have to make two or more passes at each depth setting, readjusting the edge guide for each pass.

A Centered, Four-Faced Tenon

This is the most commonly used type because it completely hides the mortise cut when the joint is assembled. There are two methods of setting up to make the cuts.

For the first method start with the same set-up as for the centered mortise. If possible, select a bit wide enough to exceed the width of cut required by 1/16 inch or more. Adjust your edge guide so that the cut will travel along your marked tenon line at one side (and overlap into the scrap boards at the side). Make one pass at each side — leaving a perfectly centered shallow tenon . . . then proceed to deepen this cut as required. You now have a two-faced, centered tenon. To make the other two faces, turn the workpiece edgewise in your holding fixture . . . and repeat the preceding steps. *(see next page)*

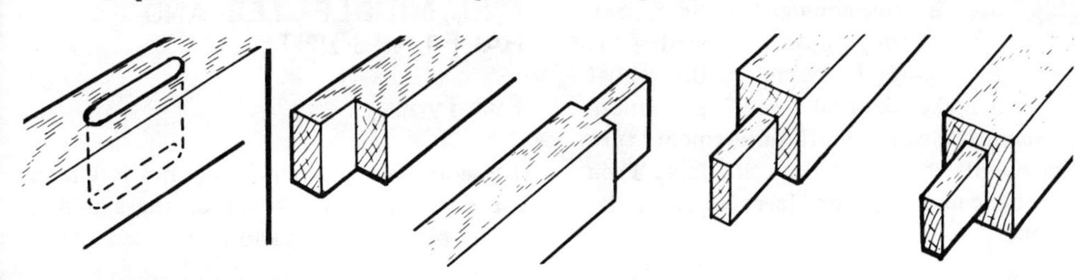

MORTISE **TENONS 1 to 4 FACES**

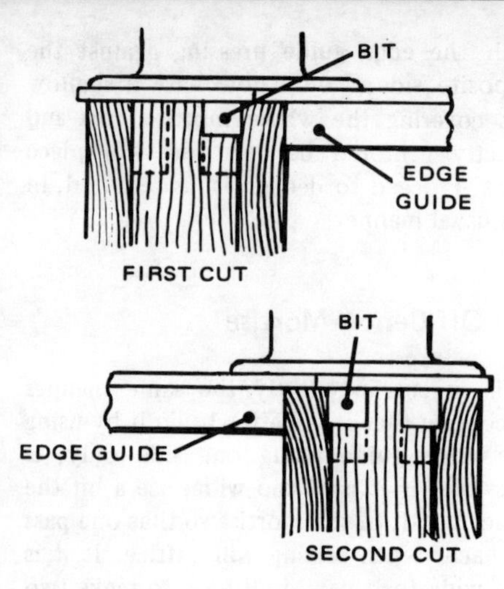

METHOD 1

NOTE: Sometimes the second two (on-edge) faces are made deeper or shallower than the first two (flat) faces. This, of course, would require a different edge guide setting . . . and choice of a different size bit.

If your bit isn't big enough to cut the full width of each face in one pass, preferably cut each face down to proper depth, placing your cuts right along the tenon outline (and leaving the uncut wood around the outer edges). The uncut wood can now be removed on a bench-, radial- or band-saw without touching the finished tenon at the center.

NOTE: Any reasonable number of workpieces can be simultaneously held in your fixture and cut, using this method.

For the second method, lay out your several workpieces as illustrated, clamping them securely to prevent wobble. Preferably use a straightedge guide . . . and simply make enough passes (relocating the guide each time) to complete the rabbet cut that makes the first face of each tenon. Keeping the same depth adjustment, turn the boards to do the opposite face. Then do the remaining two faces in a similar manner.

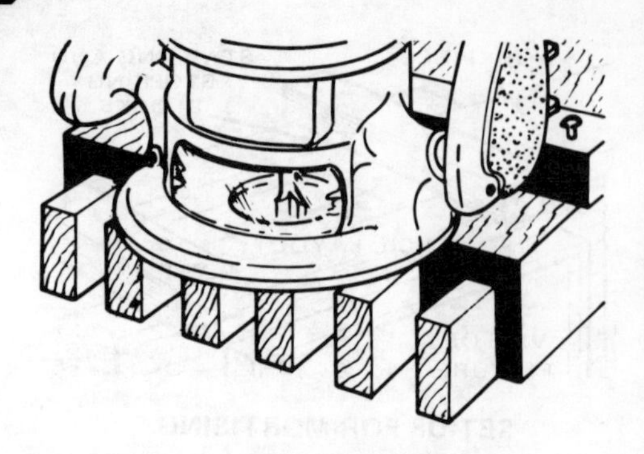

METHOD 2

This method has the advantage (as a rule) of not requiring very deep cuts, so that one depth setting (only) is sufficient. But it has these disadvantages: The workpieces must be *very securely* held . . . care must be taken not to let the router dip down and round off the end pieces (best use scrap boards at the ends) . . . and it is more difficult to accurately locate the straightedge for each pass.

Other Types of Tenons

Tenons also are made with only one, two or three faces — and with faces of varying widths, depending upon project requirements. The same two methods apply for making these variations.

NOTE: All routed mortises will have rounded corners (to the radius of the bit) . . . and all tenons (however cut) have square corners. It is easiest to round off the tenon corners to fit, using a file or rasp; but the mortise corners can be squared with a chisel, if preferred. Also, have a tenon about 1/64-in. short of mortise depth — to allow glue space.

END-, MIDDLE-, TEE- AND HALF-LAP JOINTS

Flat Types

These are convenience joints, not intended for great strength. In all of these joints, both pieces ("A" and "B") will have

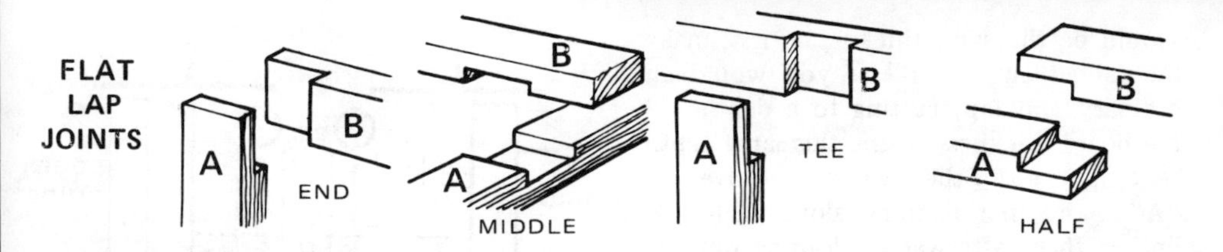

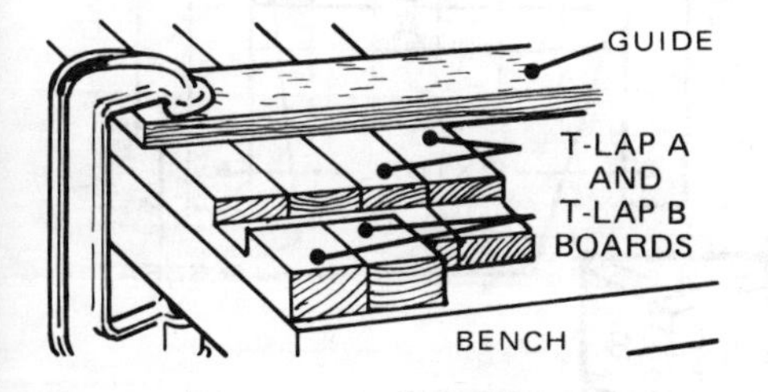

identical rabbet and/or dado cuts . . . providing both pieces are the same width. In this case, cut both pieces simultaneously by laying them side-by-side (as for Method 2 Tenon Cutting). If the pieces are of different widths you'll have to measure and cut the rabbets separately (except for the half-lap rabbets which are always equal).

On-Edge Types

These are similar to the above. They, also, can be cut simultaneously (with pieces stacked on their edges) if boards are of equal thickness. For all but the half lap, however, if boards are of unequal thicknesses each cut must be measured and made separately.

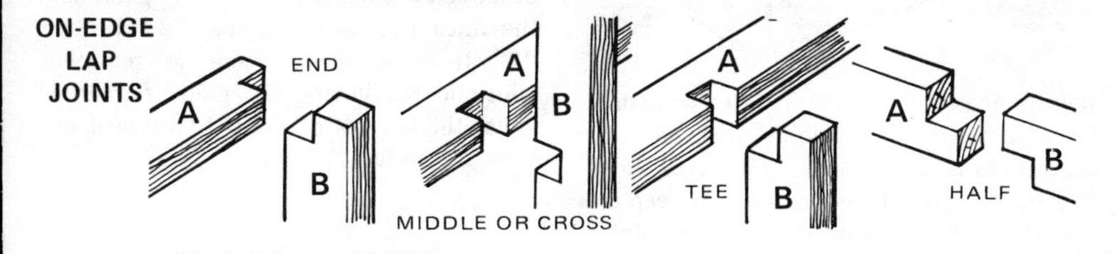

MIDDLE-LAP ON EDGE, WITH GROOVE

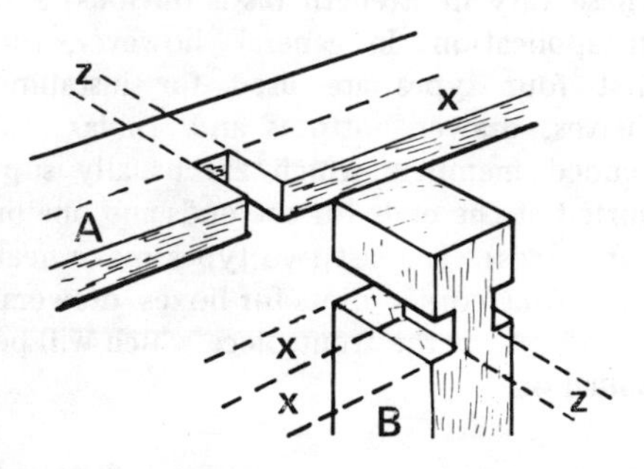

The cut in piece "A" must be made with the board on edge (to obtain a square bottom) . . . and so must the mating cut in "B". Make these to the same depth (x) equal to 1/2 the "B" piece width — and cut them simultaneously, using a bit having a diameter equal to width z. Afterwards, make a second pass through piece "B" (only) to widen its cut (x) to the thickness of piece "A". Last, cut the two side dados in piece "B", gauging the depth (equal at each side) so that the remaining width z will equal the width of the cut in "A".

DOVETAIL LAP

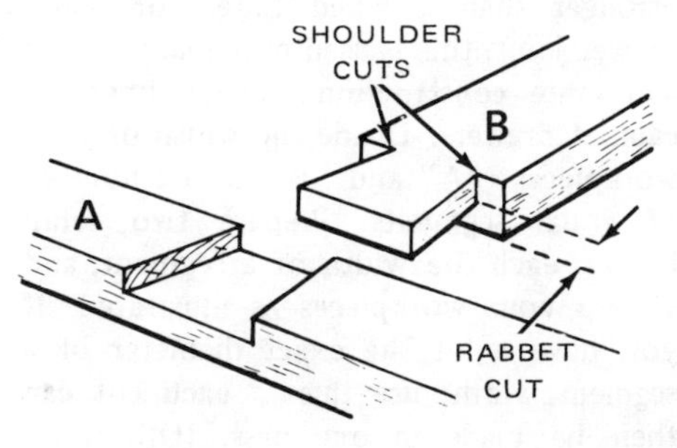

This is a strong "push or pull" joint; but requires careful layout. "A" and "B"

should be the same thickness. First, make the rabbet cut in "B" as you would an ordinary end lap, cutting to a depth 1/2 the board thickness. Using this same depth setting, cut the wedge groove in "A" . . . by first dadoing along each side line — then, afterwards, cleaning out the middle. Your straightedge guide must be repositioned at the correct angle for each side-line cut. Last, make the shoulder cuts in "B", preferably with a very thin saw followed by chiseling out the sharp angles.

COGGED JOINT

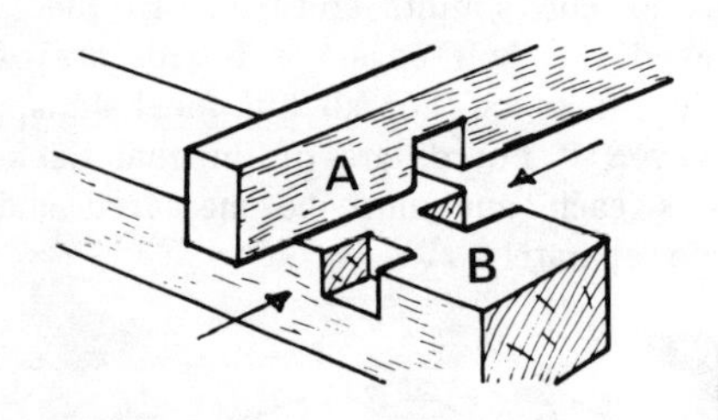

Reinforcing strips are often fitted to main-frame members by this joint. With "A" on edge, dado its slot — making it 1/3 as wide as the thickness of "B", and 1/2 as deep as the width of "A". Now, dado the two slots in "B" (cutting in the directions of the arrows), using the same depth adjustment and leaving the uncut center the same width as the slot in "A". Square the corners of these two cuts with a chisel.

BOX JOINT

Stronger than a glued miter- or plain-drawer joint, this is used principally in box and crate construction . . . sometimes for cabinet drawers. Divide the width of your workpieces ("A" and "B") into a number of equal segments. Prepare two scrap blocks, each the width of a segment, and set up your workpieces as illustrated. If you have a bit the exact diameter of a segment width, use this . . . each cut can then be made in one pass. (Otherwise, select a smaller bit and make two passes.) Adjust your edge guide for cut "1", and

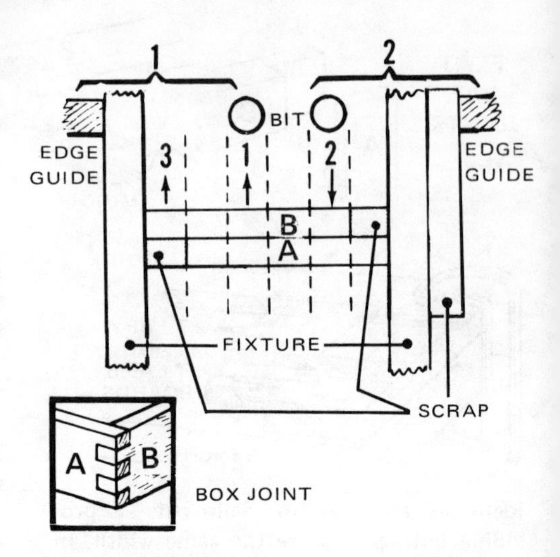

make it. Either readjust the edge guide or place a piece of scrap (same thickness as other scrap blocks) between the guide and the fixture . . . and make cut "2". For cut "3" (and as many more as required) continue readjusting the guide or adding equal thicknesses of scrap to space it out from the fixture.

THE VARIOUS DADO JOINTS

We list below six different dado joints. These vary in strength (as is obvious) and in application. In general, however, the first four types are used for installing shelves, drawer bottoms and similar suspended members which are usually supported at the ends (or the ends and one or both sides). The last two types make neat and strong corner joints for boxes, drawers, etc. if "A" is the front piece which will be pulled on.

The *plain dado* simply calls for a dado cut in "B" the thickness of "A", and to any depth desired (generally 1/3 to 1/2 through "B").

A *drawer dado* is the same, except that "B" is rabbet cut to a depth equal to the thickness of "A".

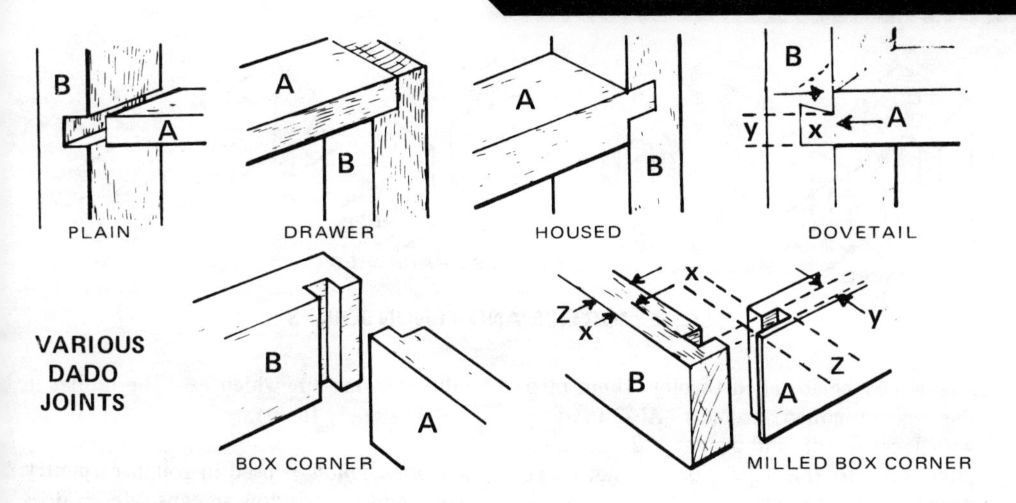

The *housed dado* calls for a rabbet cut in "A" (about 1/4 to 1/2 its thickness) with a correspondingly smaller width dado in "B". This joint will withstand swaying better than the first two.

Best of the shelf joints is the *dovetail dado* . . . it withstands swaying and pulling out of the side supports "B". Use a 1/2-inch or larger dado bit. Make the dovetail-bit cut *x* in "B". Next, set up "A" for an end cut. Use the same dovetail-bit and depth setting to make the cut in "A" . . . but allow only 1/2 (*exactly*) the diameter of the bit to be used in making this cut. Last, use a straight bit and the same depth setting to dado cut the bottom straight side of the slot in "B", widening this slot to the required thickness for "A".

The simple *box corner* is made in the same way as the housed dado, above.

A *milled box corner* is started by making the same two cuts as for a box corner. Dimension *y* should be about 1/3 the thickness of "A", and the lip at the end of "A" should be as thin as possible (to show very little end grain when assembled). Gauge the width and placement of the slot in "B" accordingly. The width of the rabbet *x* in "A" will be the thickness of "B" less the depth of the slot cut in "B" . . . and will be as deep as possible (per the above). Last, turn "A" on end to dado cut the slot *y* . . . to exactly mate with the lip left at the end of "B".

THE VARIOUS MORTISE AND TENON JOINTS

We show eight additional popular joints in this group. In most cases the mortise (or mortises) is (are) cut exactly as previously described. All the tenons also are shaped as previously described, with the following variations.

> *NOTE:* If you have learned to measure with extreme accuracy, much time can be saved in production work of centered mortises by selecting a bit 1/3 or slightly more the thickness of "B". The mortise is then cut with just one Edge Guide setting — at exact center . . . and the same bit will clean out all the wood at each side of the tenon, with one guide setting.

The *bare-faced tenon* is actually a two-faced one having one side and one shoulder face. These can be the same thickness to save time. This joint is often employed when setting chair rungs into the legs, the two faces being at bottom and inside where

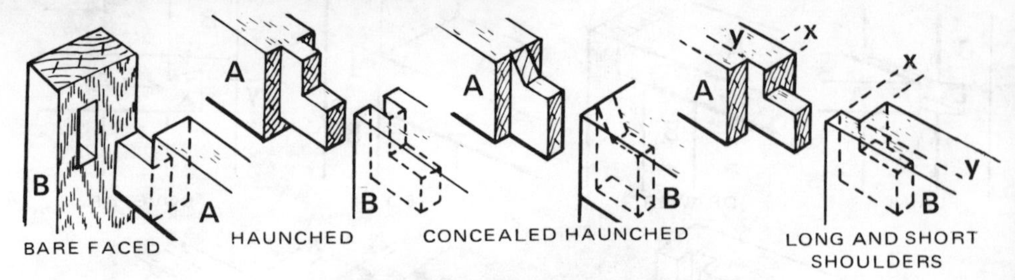

SOME MORTISE AND TENON JOINTS

screws can be installed through them into the leg for added strength. Also used — with faces at top and inside — for joining a table skirt to the leg . . . or any narrower board to a thicker one.

Haunched tenons are also used in joining table skirts to legs — since the top is hidden. Tongue and grooved members are also joined in this manner (in which case the shallow part of "B" mortise is already there). Notch the tenon of "A" (with a saw) to match the mortise in "B".

A *concealed haunched tenon* is like the above, except that the tenon is cut off so as not to show on top. Use this for more tenon strength when the width of "A" is too little to allow for a simple tenon of sufficient strength. To rout the slant portion of the mortise in "B", set "B" in your vise at an angle — after the square portion of the mortise has been cut.

The *long and short shoulders tenon* is made by first preparing "A" and "B" for a bare-faced tenon . . . then by rabbeting the uncut face of "A" and the opposite face of "B" to proper width and depth. This joint is used principally to join a piece (*A*) to a rabbeted one (in which case the rabbet in "B" is already there).

An *open tenon* — used in rough carpentry work and for window screens, etc. — does not have an actual mortise. The "mortise" is most easily made by setting "B" on end and ploughing a deep slot.

For a *through-wedged tenon* simply cut the mortise clear through "B", then flare it out to greater width at top by tilting the router as required. The flare at each side must equal the maximum thickness of one wedge minus the thickness of one of the saw cut slots in the tenon. Cut each wedge with a slight bow on one side and a straight taper on the other. This, also, is a rough carpentry joint — very strong. A neater appearing variation of it can be made by *not* cutting the mortise clear through "B" . . . in which case it is assembled by starting the wedges in their slots, then hammering "A" and "B" together.

The *mitered tenon* is useful for joining two parts (*A*) to one part (*B*) that is too small to offer strong support without this arrangement. The mortises in "B" meet (at a 90° angle) inside — and the tenon ends are

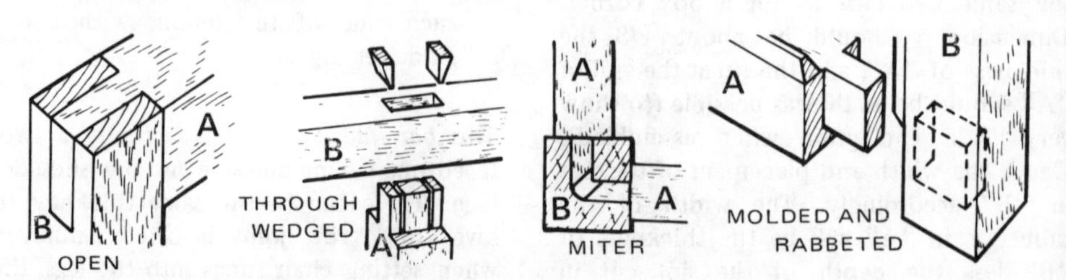

MORE MORTISE AND TENON JOINTS

mitered (by sawing) so that gluing will join them together inside of "B".

A *molded and rabbeted tenon* is merely a simple tenon used to join two members that have molded edges (as in picture framing). Whatever the shape of the molding, the treatment is the same. First make the mortise and the tenon. Afterwards, mark and miter saw each molding so that when "A" and "B" are joined their moldings will join in a simple mitered corner.

TONGUE-AND-GROOVE JOINT

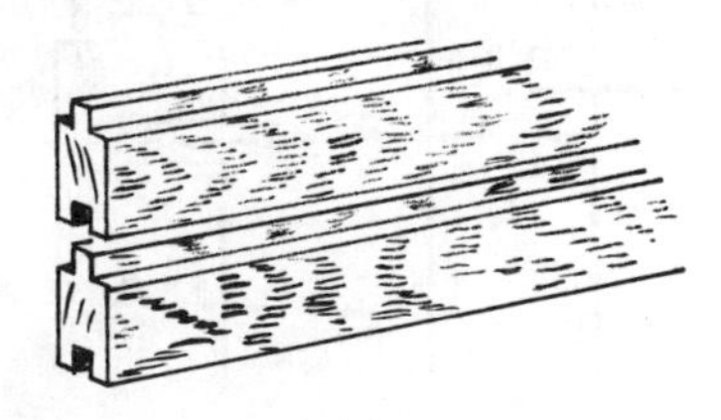

Commonly used for joining boards along their sides and ends to build up large areas (such as a floor), this is actually a tenon-type joint. The tongue is cut just as you'd cut a two-face centered tenon . . . the full length of the board. The mating groove is a plough cut (also the full board length) centered in the same manner used for a centered mortise.

THE MITERED JOINTS

We illustrate here four common variations of the simple miter used for added strength while preserving a neatness suitable for the finest cabinetwork. The "miter portion" of these joints must be saw cut (very accurately, if joint is to be neat); but the variations are best added by routing.

For a *slip-feather miter* first miter the two boards . . . then lock them together in your holding fixture so that you can rout the feather slot in both simultaneously. Use a bit about 1/3 the board thickness, and go as deep as you like (considering appearance and strength).

Saw cut the feather to proper thickness, but otherwise somewhat oversize. Its edges can be sanded down after the glue has set — will be barely visible.

The *splined miter* is also made by first mitering both boards. Afterwards, plough cut the grooves. Use the same technique as for a tongue-and-groove plough cut, but block your workpiece in the holding fixture at the correct angle to make the plough cut at a 90° angle to the mitered-edge face. Saw cut the spline piece to fit neatly, allowing about 1/64-inch slop for gluing space.

To make the *rabbeted miter* first rabbet-cut the end of each board (*A and B*). Rabbet *x* in "A" must be as deep as half the thickness of "A" and as wide as the thickness of "B". Rabbet *y* in "B" must be as deep as half the thickness of "B" and as wide as half the thickness of "A". Best lay out these cuts in pencil before making them — and allow extra at the board ends

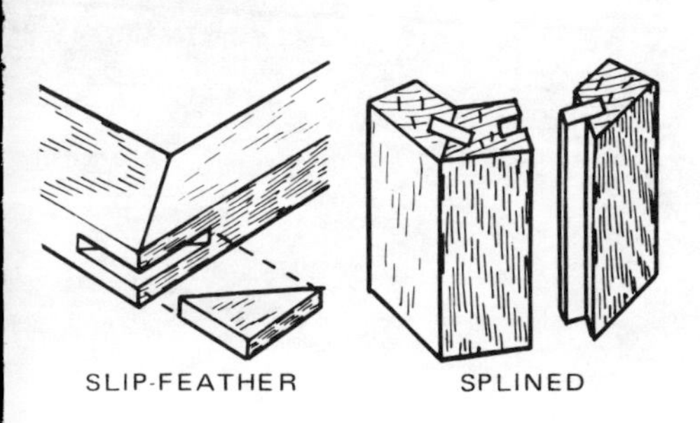

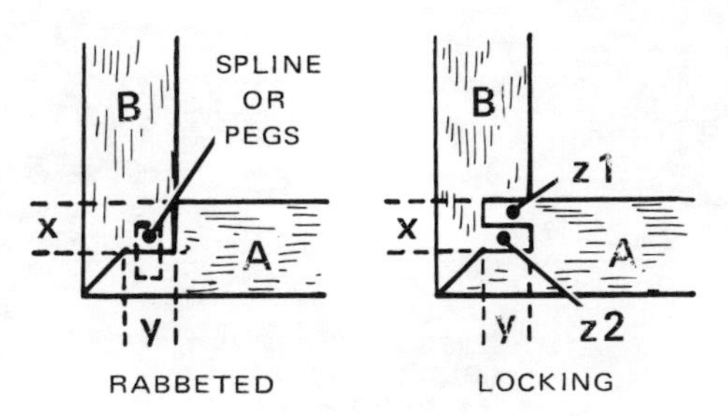

THE MITER JOINT

Rabbet *x* in "A" must be as deep as half the thickness of "A" and as wide as half the thickness of "B". Rabbet *y* in "B" must be as deep as half the thickness of "B" and as wide as half the thickness of "A". After the rabbets and miters are cut, plough cut the two grooves (*z1* in "B" and *z2* in "A"), making each as wide as one-fourth the thickness of "A" and as deep as half the thickness of "B".

The *locking miter* is much like the above. to be cut off when mitering. With the rabbets cut, saw cut the miters, staying on the outer sides of your pencil lines and taking care not to cut into the "hump" on "B". You can now either cut ploughs in "A" and "B" for a spline, or drill a series of holes to take small dowel pegs . . . either way you'll have a strong joint.

LOCK JOINT

This is one of the firmest of all cabinet-work joints, with strength in all directions. All of the cuts are simple dado or plough cuts, easily made if you first lay out the lines accurately in pencil, using careful measurements. With the layout marked, make the five cuts in the sequence and directions shown in the illustration. Slide the two pieces together for assembly.

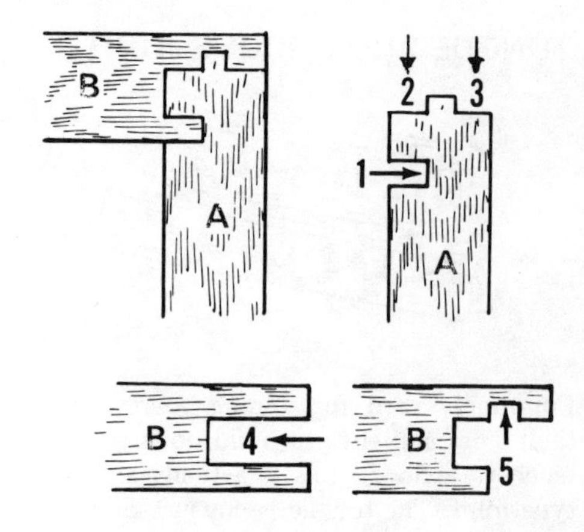

MILE/KILOMETER CONVERSIONS

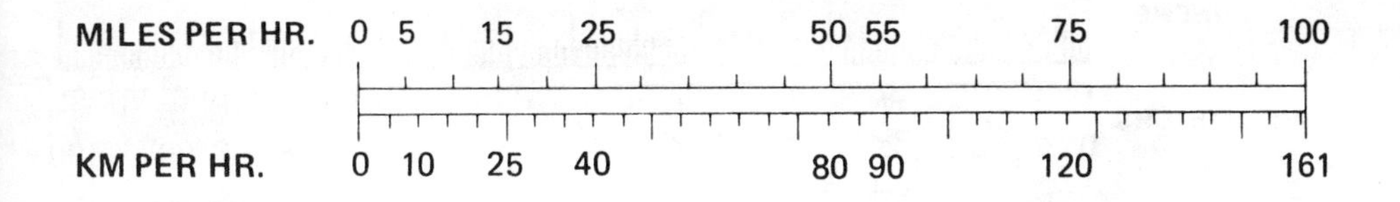

MILES TO KILOMETERS Multiply miles by 1.609344		KILOMETERS TO MILES Multiply Kilometers by 0.6213711	
MILES	KILOMETERS	KILOMETERS	MILES
1	1.609	1	0.621
2	3.219	2	1.243
3	4.828	3	1.864
4	6.437	4	2.486
5	8.047	5	3.107
6	9.656	6	3.728
7	11.265	7	4.500
8	12.875	8	4.971
9	14.484	9	5.592
10	16.093	10	6.214
20	32.187	20	12.427
30	48.280	30	18.641
40	64.374	40	24.855
50	80.467	50	31.069
60	96.561	60	37.282
70	112.654	70	43.496
80	128.748	80	49.710
.90	144.841	90	55.923
100	160.934	100	62.137
200	321.869	200	124.274
300	482.803	300	186.411
400	643.738	400	248.548
500	804.672	500	310.686
600	965.606	600	372.823
700	1126.541	700	434.960
800	1287.475	800	497.100
900	1448.410	900	559.234
1000	1609.344	1000	621.371

FARENHEIT/CELCIUS (CENTIGRADE) CONVERSIONS

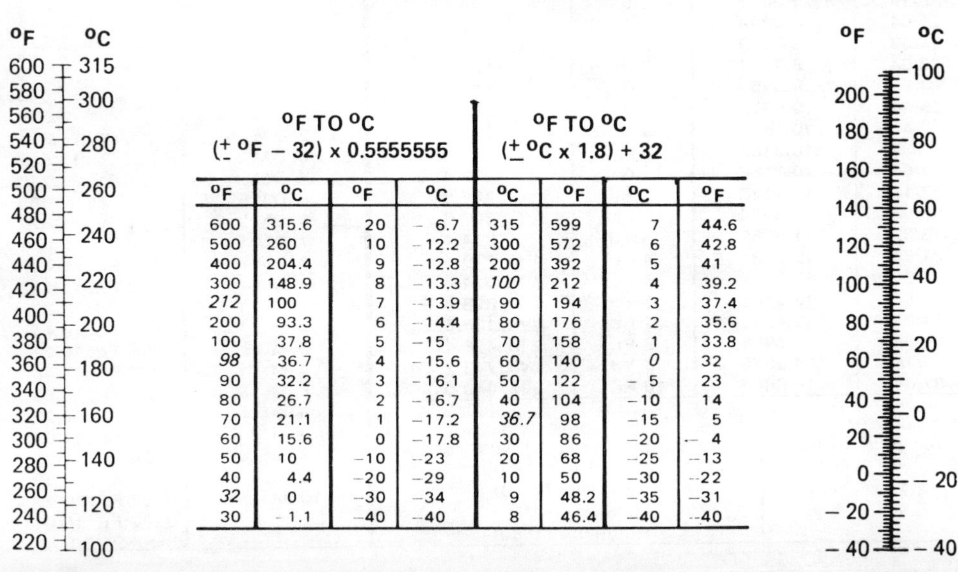

°F TO °C (± °F – 32) x 0.5555555				°F TO °C (± °C x 1.8) + 32			
°F	°C	°F	°C	°C	°F	°C	°F
600	315.6	20	– 6.7	315	599	7	44.6
500	260	10	–12.2	300	572	6	42.8
400	204.4	9	–12.8	200	392	5	41
300	148.9	8	–13.3	*100*	212	4	39.2
212	100	7	–13.9	90	194	3	37.4
200	93.3	6	–14.4	80	176	2	35.6
100	37.8	5	–15	70	158	1	33.8
98	36.7	4	–15.6	60	140	*0*	32
90	32.2	3	–16.1	50	122	– 5	23
80	26.7	2	–16.7	40	104	–10	14
70	21.1	1	–17.2	*36.7*	98	–15	5
60	15.6	0	–17.8	30	86	–20	– 4
50	10	–10	–23	20	68	–25	–13
40	4.4	–20	–29	10	50	–30	–22
32	0	–30	–34	9	48.2	–35	–31
30	– 1.1	–40	–40	8	46.4	–40	–40

INCH/MILLIMETER CONVERSIONS

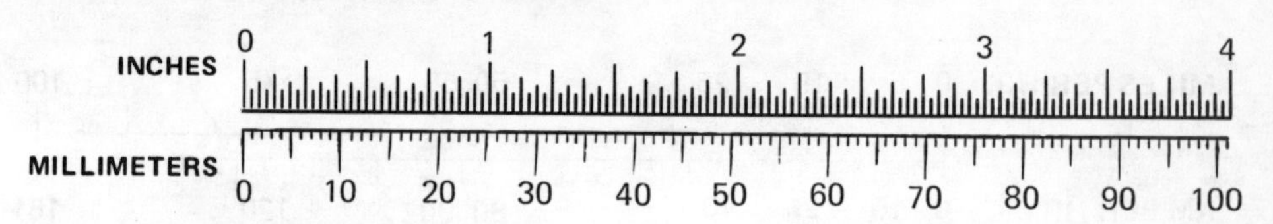

INCHES TO MILLIMETERS
Multiply inches by 25.4

INCHES	MILLIMETERS	INCHES	MILLIMETERS
.001	.025	19/32	15.0812
.01	.254	.6	15.24
1/64	.3969	39/64	15.4781
.02	.508	5/8	15.875
.03	.762	41/64	16.2719
1/32	.7938	21/32	16.6688
.04	1.016	43/64	17.0656
3/64	1.191	11/16	17.4625
.05	1.27	.7	17.78
.06	1.524	45/64	17.8594
1/16	1.5875	23/32	18.2562
.07	1.778	47/64	18.6531
5/64	1.9844	3/4	19.050
.08	2.032	49/64	19.4469
.09	2.286	25/32	19.8438
3/32	2.3812	51/64	20.2406
.1	2.54	.8	20.32
7/64	2.7781	13/16	20.6375
1/8	3.175	53/64	21.0344
9/64	3.5719	27/32	21.4312
5/32	3.9688	55/64	21.8281
11/64	4.3656	7/8	22.225
3/16	4.7625	57/64	22.6219
.2	5.08	.9	22.86
13/64	5.1594	29/32	23.0188
7/32	5.5562	59/64	23.4156
15/64	5.9531	15/16	23.8125
1/4	6.35	61/64	24.2094
17/64	6.7469	31/32	24.6062
9/32	7.1438	63/64	25.0031
19/64	7.5406	1.0	25.4
.3	7.62	2.0	50.8
5/16	7.9375	3.0	76.2
21/64	8.3344	4.0	101.6
11/32	8.7312	5.0	127.0
23/64	9.1281	6.0	152.4
3/8	9.525	7.0	177.8
25/64	9.9219	8.0	203.2
.4	10.16	9.0	228.6
13/32	10.3188	10.0	254.0
27/64	10.7156	11.0	279.4
7/16	11.1125	1 Ft.	304.8
29/64	11.5094	2 Ft.	609.6
15/32	11.9062	1 Yd.	914.4
31/64	12.3031	4 Ft.	1 M, 219.2
1/2	12.7	5 Ft.	1 M, 524.0
33/64	13.0969	2 Yd.	1 M, 828.8
17/32	13.4938	7 Ft.	2 M, 133.6
35/64	13.8906	8 Ft.	2 M, 438.4
9/16	14.2875	3 Yd.	2 M, 743.2
37/64	14.6844	10 Ft.	3 M, 048.0

ABBREVIATIONS

In. — Inch	MM — Millimeter (1/1000)
Ft. — Foot	CM — Centimeter (1/100)
Yd. — Yard	DM — Decimeter (1/10)
Mi. — Mile	M — Meter (1)
	KM — Kilometer (1000)

MILLIMETERS TO INCHES
Multiply millimeters by 0.03937

MILLIMETERS	INCHES
.001	.00004
.01	.00039
.02	.00079
.03	.00118
.04	.00157
.05	.00197
.06	.00236
.07	.00276
.08	.00315
.09	.00354
.1	.00394
.2	.00787
.3	.01181
.4	.01575
.5	.01969
.6	.02362
.7	.02756
.8	.0315
.9	.03543
1.0	.03937
2.0	.07874
3.0	.11811
4.0	.15748
5.0	.19685
6.0	.23622
7.0	.27559
8.0	.31496
9.0	.35433
1 CM	.3937
2 CM	.7874
3 CM	1.1811
4 CM	1.5748
5 CM	1.9685
6 CM	2.3622
7 CM	2.7559
8 CM	3.1496
9 CM	3.5433
1 DM	3.937
2 DM	7.874
3 DM	11.811
4 DM	1 Ft., 3.748
5 DM	1 Ft., 7.685
6 DM	1 Ft., 11.622
7 DM	2 Ft., 3.559
8 DM	2 Ft., 7.496
9 DM	2 Ft., 11.433
1 M	1 Yd., 3.37
2 M	2 Yd., 6.74
3 M	3 Yd., 10.11
4 M	13 Ft., 1.48
5 M	16 Ft., 4.85
6 M	19 Ft., 8.22
7 M	22 Ft., 11.59
8 M	26 Ft., 2.96
9 M	29 Ft., 6.33
10 M	32 Ft., 9.7
1 KM	3280 Ft., 10.0 (approx. 5/8 Mi.)

OTHER LINEAR MEASUREMENTS

FEET	METERS	METERS	FEET	YARDS	METERS	METERS	YARDS
1	0.3	1	3.3	1	0.9	1	1.1
2	0.6	2	6.6	2	1.8	2	2.2
3	0.9	3	9.8	3	2.7	3	3.3
4	1.2	4	13.1	4	3.7	4	4.4
5	1.5	5	16.4	5	4.6	5	5.5
6	1.8	6	19.7	6	5.5	6	6.6
7	2.1	7	23.0	7	6.4	7	7.7
8	2.4	8	26.3	8	7.3	8	8.8
9	2.7	9	29.5	9	8.2	9	9.8
10	3.0	10	32.8	10	9.1	10	10.9
20	6.1	20	65.6	20	18.3	20	21.9
30	9.1	30	98.4	30	27.4	30	32.8
40	12.2	40	131.2	40	36.6	40	43.7
50	15.2	50	164.0	50	45.7	50	54.7
60	18.3	60	196.9	60	54.9	60	65.6
70	21.3	70	229.7	70	64.0	70	76.6
80	24.4	80	262.5	80	73.2	80	87.5
90	27.4	90	295.3	90	82.3	90	98.4
100	30.5	100	328.1	100	91.4	100	109.4
1000	304.8	1000	3280.8	1000	914.4	1000	1093.6

AREA (SQUARE) MEASUREMENTS

SQ. IN.	SQ. CM	SQ. CM	SQ. IN.
1	6.45	1	0.16
2	12.90	2	0.31
3	19.36	3	0.47
4	25.81	4	0.62
5	32.26	5	0.78
6	38.71	6	0.93
7	45.16	7	1.09
8	51.61	8	1.24
9	58.07	9	1.40
10	64.52	10	1.55

SQ. FT.	SQ. M	SQ. M.	SQ. FT.
1	0.09	1	10.76
2	0.19	2	21.53
3	0.28	3	32.29
4	0.37	4	43.06
5	0.47	5	53.82
6	0.56	6	64.58
7	0.64	7	75.35
8	0.74	8	86.11
9	0.84	9	96.88
10	0.93	10	107.64
20	1.86	20	215.28
30	2.79	30	322.92
40	3.72	40	430.56
50	4.65	50	538.19
60	5.57	60	645.83
70	6.50	70	753.47
80	7.43	80	861.11
90	8.36	90	968.75
100	9.29	100	1076.39

1 Ft. = 0.3048 M; 1 M = 3.2808 Ft.
1 Yd. = 0.9144M; 1 M = 1.0936 Yd.

1 $In.^2$ = 6.4516CM^2; 1 CM^2 = 0.1550 $In.^2$
1 $Ft.^2$ = 0.0929M^2; 1 M^2 = 10.7639 $Ft.^2$

1 Acre = 0.405 ha; 1 ha = 2.471 Acre

1 Mi^2 = 2.5899 KM^2; 1 KM^2 = 0.3861 Mi^2

ACRE	HECTARE	HECTARE	ACRE
1	0.41	1	2.47
2	0.81	2	4.94
3	1.22	3	7.41
4	1.62	4	9.88
5	2.03	5	12.36
6	2.43	6	14.83
7	2.84	7	17.30
8	3.24	8	19.77
9	3.65	9	22.24
10	4.05	10	24.71
20	8.10	20	49.42
30	12.15	30	74.13
40	16.20	40	98.84
50	20.25	50	123.55
60	24.30	60	148.26
70	28.35	70	172.97
80	32.40	80	197.68
90	36.45	90	222.39
100	40.50	100	247.10

SQ. MILE	SQ. KM	SQ. KM	SQ. MILE
1	2.59	1	0.39
2	5.18	2	0.77
3	7.77	3	1.16
4	10.36	4	1.54
5	12.95	5	1.93
6	15.54	6	2.32
7	18.13	7	2.70
8	20.72	8	3.09
9	23.31	9	3.48
10	25.90	10	3.86
20	51.80	20	7.72
30	77.70	30	11.58
40	103.59	40	15.44
50	129.49	50	19.31
60	155.39	60	23.17
70	181.29	70	27.03
80	207.19	80	30.89
90	233.09	90	34.75
100	258.99	100	38.61

CUBIC (VOLUME) MEASUREMENTS

CU. IN.	CU. CM	CU. CM	CU. IN.
1	16.39	1	0.06
2	32.77	2	0.12
3	49.16	3	0.18
4	65.55	4	0.24
5	81.94	5	0.31
6	98.32	6	0.37
7	114.71	7	0.43
8	131.10	8	0.49
9	147.48	9	0.55
10	163.87	10	0.61

CU. FT.	CU. M	CU. M	CU. FT.
1	0.03	1	35.32
2	0.06	2	70.63
3	0.09	3	105.94
4	0.11	4	141.26
5	0.14	5	176.57
6	0.17	6	211.89
7	0.20	7	247.20
8	0.23	8	282.52
9	0.26	9	317.83
10	0.28	10	353.15

DRY MERCHANDISE

As Listed	LITER	LITER	As Listed
1 Pint	0.55	1/2	1 Pint
1 Quart	1.10	9/10	1 Quart
1 Peck	8.81	8-4/5	1 Peck
1 Bushel	35.24	35-1/4	1 Bushel

LIQUID MERCHANDISE

As Listed	METRIC	METRIC	As Listed
1 Dram	3.70 ml	3-3/4 ml	1 Dram
1 Teaspoon	4.93 ml	5 ml	1 Teaspoon
1 Tablespoon	14.79 ml	15 ml	1 Tablespoon
1 Ounce	29.57 ml	30 ml	1 Ounce
1 Cup	0.24 L	1/4 L	1 Cup
1 Pint	0.47 L	1/2 L	1 Pint
1 Quart	0.95 L	1 L	1 Quart
1 Gallon	3.79 L	3-3/4 L	1 Gallon

CU. YD.	CU. M	CU. M	CU. YD.
1	0.77	1	1.31
2	1.53	2	2.62
3	2.29	3	3.92
4	3.06	4	5.23
5	3.82	5	6.54
6	4.59	6	7.85
7	5.35	7	9.16
8	6.12	8	10.46
9	6.88	9	11.77
10	7.65	10	13.08

1 CU. M (cu. meter) = 1,000,000 CU. CM (cu. centimeter)
1 ml (milliliter) = 1/1000 L (liter) = 1 CU. CM

WEIGHT

AVOIRDUPOIS (EVERYDAY)

STANDARD	METRIC	METRIC	STANDARD
1 Grain	64.81 mg	1 mg	1/65 Grain
1 Dram	1.77 g	1-3/4 g	1 Dram
1 Ounce	28.35 g	28-1/3 g	1 Ounce
1 Pound	453.59 g	1/2 kg	1 Pound
1 Short Ton	907.18 kg	907 kg	1 Sh. Ton
1 Lg. Ton	1016.05 kg	1016 kg	1 Lg. Ton

TROY (JEWELERS')

STANDARD	METRIC	METRIC	STANDARD
1 Grain	64.81 mg	1 mg	1/65 Grain
1 Carat	200.00 mg	200 mg	1 Carat
1 Pennyw't.	1.56 g	1-1/2 g	1 Pennyw't.
1 Ounce	31.10 g	31 g	1 Ounce
1 Pound	373.24 g	373-1/4 g	1 Pound
		1 kg	2.68 Pound

1 mg (milligram) = 1/1000 g (gram)
1000 g (gram) = 1 kg (kilogram)
1000 kg (kilograms) = 1 metric ton

POPULAR MOLDINGS

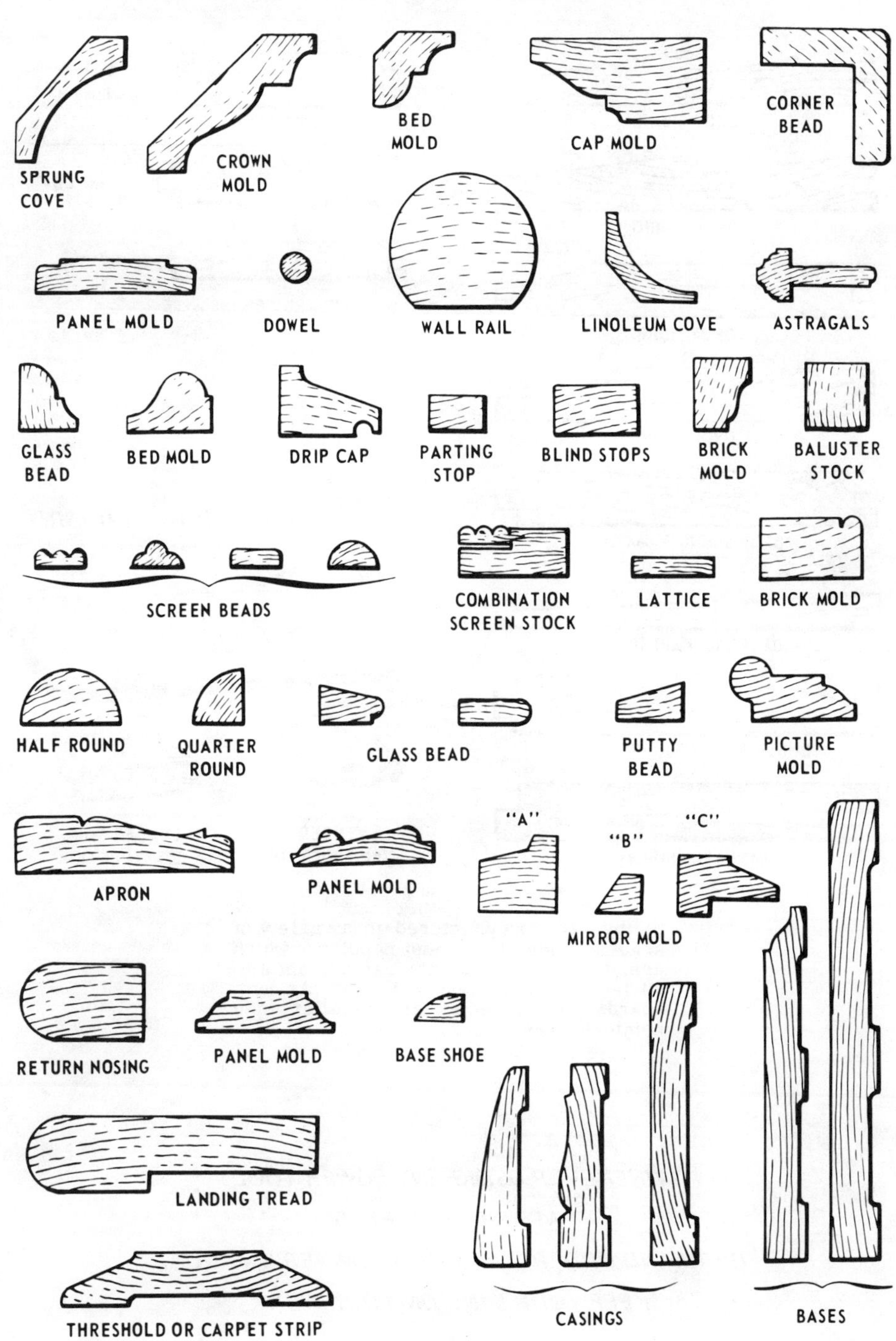

FOR SAFE OPERATION READ YOUR OWNER'S MANUAL

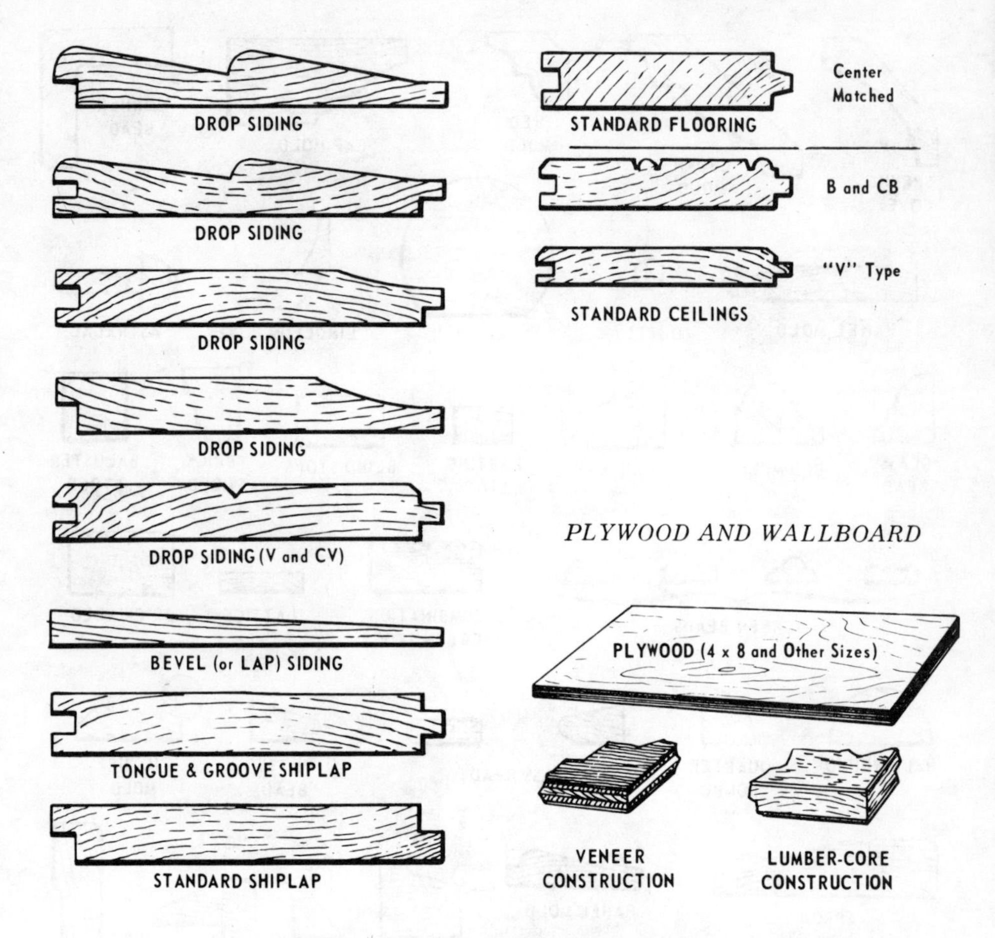

Sidings are manufactured in a variety of shapes, some of the most popular of which are shown here. Lengths range from 4 to 20 feet, in multiples of 2 feet. As with boards, actual sizes are smaller than nominal sizes.

WHENEVER USING ANY POWER TOOL

WEAR EYE SHIELDS

READ AND UNDERSTAND YOUR OWNER'S MANUAL

KEEP YOUR MIND ON YOUR WORK

AND

DO ALL OPERATIONS IN THE SAFEST MANNER